World History
4th edition
From Early Times to A D 2011

By the same author

History of Modern World (AD 1500-AD 2011)

History of Europe (1450-1815)

History of Modern Europe (1789-2002)

History of Asia

Concise History of the World

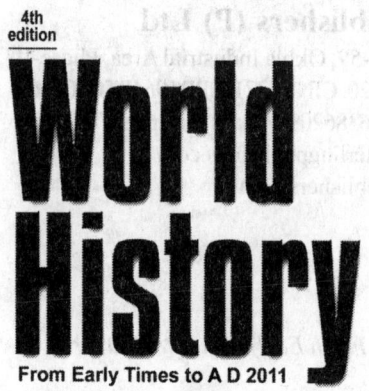

4th edition

World History

From Early Times to A D 2011

B.V. RAO

STERLING

Sterling Publishers (P) Ltd.
Regd. Office: A-59, Okhla Industrial Area, Phase-II,
New Delhi-110020. CIN: U22110PB1964PTC002569
Tel: 26387070, 26386209; Fax: 91-11-26383788
E-mail: mail@sterlingpublishers.com
www.sterlingpublishers.com

World History: From Early Times to A.D 2011
© 2014, B V Rao
ISBN 978 81 207 8841 1

First Edition	1984
Second Revised Edition	1991
Third Revised and Enlarged Edition	2006
Fourth Revised and Enlarged Edition	2014

All rights are reserved.
No part of this publication may be reproduced, stored in a retrieval system or transmitted, in any form or by any means, mechanical, photocopying, recording or otherwise, without prior written permission of the publisher.

Printed in India

Printed and Published by Sterling Publishers Pvt. Ltd.,
New Delhi-110020.

*Dedicated to
my father
Late Beldona Rama Rao*

PREFACE TO THE FOURTH REVISED EDITION

This revised edition has been brought out after making extensive changes in keeping with modern interpretation of events. It has also been expanded to cover major and momentous happenings of the recent past in the Middle East and various parts of Asia. Hope this version will enhance the knowledge of World History among the academic community.

B.V. RAO

Bengaluru
Email: vrbeld@gmail.com

PREFACE TO THE THIRD REVISED EDITION

A renewed interest in the study of world history is not out of place in this age of globalisation. Worldwide changes are in the making, with science and new technology playing its part. Peter F. Drucker predicts the evolution of 'knowledge society' which will largely manage our future. World disarmament and religious fundamentalism have become core issues to be dealt with by the world community in the new millennium. World leaders have great responsibility in averting 'clash of civilisation'.

The revised edition carry corrections, a few additions, a revised chapter on the U.N., and a new chapter on 'Towards the New Millennium'. The last one updates events and includes interesting topics such as the Cold War, the fall of the Soviet Union, reforms in China, relevance of the U.N., the U.S. after september 9/11 (2001), regional groups, globalisation, and science and new technology.

I sincerely hope the revised edition would evoke warm response by the academic community.

B.V. RAO

1234/680, 13th Cross,
Girinagar, Bangalore. 85.
E-mail. vrbeld@gmail.com

PREFACE

There are many good books available on world history but unfortunately a majority of them have been written by foreigners. So the selection of a good book on world history from among Indian writers is limited for students. Having taught world history to the undergraduate students for the last 31 years, I considered myself suited to undertake this arduous task. It took nearly ten months to complete the work and I am proud to say that I enjoyed every moment of it.

World history is a fascinating study for students and laymen alike. In this book I have organised the matter in chronological order. However, I have covered all the topics set by the University Board of Education, Karnataka State. Though the students may find more topics than what is necessary for them, the book, I am sure, would be highly useful to them.

I received assistance, suggestions and guidance from many in completing this book. I am obliged to Prof. Mustafa and Shri Jagtap of Shivaji University for rendering cartographic assistance. I am beholden to Dr. S. Settar of Karnataka University for his encouragement and assistance. I must thank my colleague, Dr. T.C. Sharma, for encouraging me to write this book. Our college typist, Shri Bhooi, shared some of my burden of typing the manuscript. My colleague in the department, Shri. Chougule, helped me in proof-reading work. My wife, Rakma, and my niece, Neeraja, also assisted me from time to time.

I am also thankful to the authorities of the National Book Trust for rendering financial assistance for the publication of this book.

In the end, I would like scholars and teachers to send me suggestions to improve the quality of the book.

B.V. RAO

R.P.D. College, Belgaum, Karnataka
1-3-1984

CONTENTS

1. **Importance of the Study of History** — 1
   Definition of History • Science or Art? • Values of History • Lessons of History • History and Archaeology • History and Geography • History and Other Social Sciences

2. **World History and Its Scope** — 7
   The Need for its Study • Periodisation of World History • Chronology of World History • Culture and Civilisation • Factors for the Rise and Development of Culture • Geographical Factors • Creative Minority • Economic Well-being and Leisure • Urban Bias of Culture • Trade • Culture Grows With New Knowledge and Ideas • Healthy Political and Social Climate

3. **Prehistoric Man** — 11
   The Origin and Life of the Earth • Old Stone Age

4. **Egypt : The Gift of the Nile** — 17
   Geographical Factors • Agriculture and Other Developments • Classification of Early Egyptian History • The Age of Pyramids or the Old Kingdom • The Age of Feudalism • The Imperial Age or the New Kingdom (1550 BC-1070 BC) Egyptian Religion • Monotheism • Art and Architecture • The Great Pyramid • Writing and Literature • Heiroglyphics or Sacred Writings • Other Contributions to Civilisation • Lunar and Solar Calendars • Advance in Science and Medicine

5. **Mesopotamia or the Fertile Crescent** — 27
   Geographical Factors • The Sumerians • Sumerian City-States • Decline and Fall of Sumerian Kingdoms • Babylonian Empire Under Hammurabi (1792 BC-1750 BC) Code of Hammurabi • Hittite Conquest • Assyrian Conquest • Their Military Glory • Assyrian Contributions • The Fall of Assyrians (612 BC) • The New Babylonian Empire • Persian Invasion (539 BC)

6. **Legacy of Babylonia** 33
Economic Life • Society • Religion • Architecture and Art • Learning and Literature • Sciences • Persian Empire • Cyrus the Great • Darius I • Zarathustra and Zoroastrianism in Persia

7. **The Hebrews (or Jews)** 38

8. **Phoenicians** 40
Cities Paid Tributes • Phoenician Alphabet • Their Colonies • Their Great Voyages

9. **Indus Valley Civilisation** 42
Date of Harappan Culture • Founders • Mohenjodaro • Drainage System • The Great Bath • Socio-Eccnomic Life • Amusements • Rural Economy • Urban Economy • Trade and Commerce • Seals • Religion • Funeral Customs • Defence • Secular Outlook • Contributions • Decline of Indus Civilisation

10. **Vedic Civilisation** 50
Aryan Wars and Settlements • The Vedic Literature • Area of Occupation • Political Organisation • Sabha and the Samiti • Other Forms of Government • Aryan Expansionism • Vedic Society • Beginnings of Class Distinctions • Food and Drinks • Dress and Ornaments • Amusements • Standards of Morality • Economic Conditions • Occupations • Industries • Professionals • Trade and Transport • Religion • Rigvedic Pantheon • Education

11. **Ancient China, Central and South America** 58
PART I: Geographical Factors • Unique Culture • Political History • Shange Rule in China • Chou Dynasty (1046 BC-256. BC) • The Shin Dynasty • Destruction of Old Literature

PART II: Han Dynasty (206 BC-220 AD) • Trade and Commerce • Buddhism in China • Educational Progress • Civil Service Examinations • State Patronage to Arts and Literature • Diplomatic Relations • Tang Dynasty

PART III: Political Organisation • Economic Conditions • Trade and Commerce • Early Chinese Society • Religion and Philosophy • Confucianism • Taosim • Mencious • Buddhism • Art and Architecture • Literature • Science • Mayan Civilisation • Religion • Art and Architecture • Intellectual Pursuits • Political Social and Economic Conditions • The Incas • Strings which Talk • Other Features of Their Civilisation

Contents

12. Ancient Greece — 70

Historical Background • Geographic Influence • Development of City-States • Forms of Government • Athenian Democracy • Cleisthenes • The Persian Threat • Revolt of Ionian Greeks • Persian Wars • Battle of Thermopylae (480 BC) • The Golden Age • Athens Rebuilt as the Most Beautiful City • Greek Philosophers Education • Greek Literature • Other Types of Literature • Science • Decline of the Greek City-States • King Philip of Macedonia • Alexander the Great • The Hellenistic Civilisation • Greek Language • Scientific Discoveries and Inventions • Art and Architecture • Philosophers • Decline

13. Jainism — 82

Parsvanatha (8th century BC) • Early Life of Vardhamana Mahavira • The Teachings of Mahavira • Religious Literature • Svetambara and Digambara Jains • Spread of Jainism • Its Contributions

14. Buddhism — 87

Early life of the Buddha • Great Renunciation • The Teachings of the Buddha • Buddhist Order of Monks (Sangha) Established • Spread of Buddhism • Rise of Mahayana Buddhism • Contributions of Buddhism to Indian Culture

15. Hindu Imperialism — 92

The Nanda Rule over Magadha • Alexander's Invasion • Chandragupta Maurya's Career of Conquest • Bindusara • Emperor Ashoka and the Kalinga War • Mauryan Administration • Social Conditions • Economic Conditions • Religious Conditions • Mauryan Art and Architecture • Learning and Literature • The Sungas • Kanva Rule • Satavahanas of the Deccan • Greek Rule in India • Parthians • Sakas or Scythians • Chashtana Rudradaman • Kushanas • Kanishka I (founder of Saka Era) • His Empire • Significance of Kanishka's Reign • The Gupta Age • Earliest Rulers • Religion • Gupta Age, the Gilded Age • Vardhana Dynasty • Early Chalukyas of Badami • The Pallavas of Kanchi • Their Contributions • The Cholas of Tanjavur • Raja Raja's Contributions • Rajendra Chola's Exploits • Chola Administration • Other Contributions

16. Roman Civilisation — 109

PART I: Geographical Factors • Latins • Extruscan Rule Overthrown • Expansion of Rome • Rome's Clash with Carthage • Punic Wars • Carthage Destroyed (146 BC) Rise of Dictatorship in Rome • Julius Caesar • 'Golden Age' Marked by Reforms • Birth of Jesus (4 BC) • Successors of Augustus • Fall of Rome

PART II: The Legacy of Rome • Pax Romana (Roman Peace) • Roman Law • Architecture and Engineering • Scienc • Religion • Philosophy • Conclusion

17. **Rise and Spread of Christianity**   **122**

Life of Jesus • His Crucifixion (33 AD) • Teachings of Jesus • Spread of Christianity

18. **Rise and Spread of Islam**   **126**

PART I: Arabia before the Birth of Mohammed the Prophet • Life of Prophet Mohammed (570-632) • Hejira (621-22) • Birth of Islam • Teachings of Mohammed the Prophet • Spread of Islam • Caliphs Othman and Ali • Sunnis and Shias • The Omayyads and the Abbasids

PART II: Enlightened Autocracy • Learning • Literature and History • Medicine Rhazes (865-925) • Exact Sciences • Their Manufactures • Travel and Trade • Art and Architecture

19. **The Crusades**   **135**

Causes of the First Crusade • First Crusade (1096-1099) • Second Crusade (1147-49) • Third Crusade (1189-1191) • Fourth Crusade • Children's and Other Crusades (1217, 1228 and 1270) • Results

20. **The Middle Ages in Europe**   **139**

Middle Ages Defined • The Early Middle Ages (476 AD-1000 AD) • The High or Central Middle Ages (1001 AD-1300 AD) • The Late Middle Ages (1301-1500) • The Holy Roman Empire • Carolingian Dynasty • Charlamagne and his Conquests • Learning • Laws

The Byzantine Empire—Diocletian and Constantine • An Estimate of Constantine • The Era of Justinian • Justinian Code • Decline of Byzantine Empire

Contributions of Byzantine Civilisation—Theocratic State • Architecture and Art • Law and Literature • Centres of Learning • Spread of Christianity • Trade and Commerce • Estimate

Medieval Cities and Guilds—Conditions in Europe After the Fall of Roman Empire • Crusades Caused the Growth of Towns • Role of European Cities • Hanseatic League • Political Role of the Cities • The Rise of the New Middle Class in Towns and Cities • Guilds and Crafts • Crafts Guilds

Medieval Universities—Learning in the Middle Ages • Early Universities of Europe • Student's life

Contents   xiii

21. **Feudalism in Europe**   154
    Definition • Evolution of Feudalism • Feudalism, A System of
    Land Tenure • Homage Ceremony • Age of Chivalry • Feudal
    Life • Decline of Feudalism

22. **The Christian Church in Medieval Europe**   159
    Monasticism • Medieval Church and Papacy • Church vs the
    State

23. **Medieval India, China and Japan**   162
    Zahiruddin Mohammed Babur • Humayun • Akbar
    • Establishment of Mughal Paramountcy in India • Akbar's
    Religious Policy • Administration • Estimate of Akbar • Jehangir
    • Shahjehan (1628-58) • Ming Dynasty (1368 to 1644) • Advent
    of the Europeans • Contribution of the Mings • Manchu Emperors
    (1644-1838)
    Early Chinese Influence on Japan • The Heian Period
    (794-1185) • Yoritomo Becomes the Shogun • Hojo's
    Administration • Tokugawa Shogunate (1603-1868)

24. **The Renaissance in Europe**   173
    Factors for the Growth of Renaissance • Renaissance Scholars
    • Renaissance Art • Venetian School : Titian (1488–1576)
    • Renaissance Sculpture • Renaissance Architecture
    • Renaissance Music • Renaissance in Northern Europe
    • England-France-Spain • Renaissance and Scientific Progress
    • Scientific Thought and Scientists

25. **Geographical Discoveries**   181
    Factors Aiding Geographical Discoveries • Explorations or
    Portuguese Navigators • Columbus Discovers the New Continent
    • Balboa Discovered Pacific Ocean in 1513 • Ferdinand Magellan
    • His Voyage Round the World (1519-22) • Hernando Cortez
    Conquers Mexico (1519) • Discoveries of English Explorers
    • French Explorations • Henry Hudson and the Dutch Claim
    • Conflicting Claims Lead to Wars • Results of Geographical
    Discoveries • Other Results

26. **The Reformation**   188
    Decline of the Papacy • State vs. the Church
    • Rise of Nationstates • Rise of Secular Attitude • Anti-Church
    Movements • Attack by Humanist Scholars • Sale of Indulgences
    • Protestant Reformation in Germany • Ulrich Zwingli (1484-
    1531) and John Calvin (1509-1564) • The Reformation Movement
    in England

The Counter Reformation • The Council of Trent (1545-63)
• The Society of Jesus Founded by Ignatius Loyola (1534)
• St. Francis Xavier (1506-1552)

27. **The Rise of the Nation-States in Europe** 196

England—the First Nation-state in Europe • Royal Absolutism • Limitations on Royal Power • Model Parliament (1295) • Tudor Rulers.
France—Bourbon Monarchy in France
Spain—Enlightened Despotism
Austria—The Habsburgs of Austria
Russia—Geographical Factors • Peter the Great (1682-1725) • Westernisation of Russia Under Peter • Foreign Policy • Catherine II (The Great) • Foreign Policy • War with the Turks

28. **American War of Independence** 209

Development of 13 English Colonies • British Mercantilist Policy • Enforcement of Mercantilist Regulations • The Stamp Act (1765) and its Repeal • Townshend Acts (1767) • Boston Tea Party • The First Continental Congress (1774) • Skirmishes at Lexington and Concord (April 19, 1775) • Declaration of Independence (4 July, 1776) • The War • Results of the War

29. **The French Revolution (1789)** 217

Political Causes • Social Causes • The First Estate (the Church) • The Second Estate (the nobles) • The Third Estate (the common people) • Economic Causes • Intellectual Awakening • The Role of the King • Course of the Revolution • The Constitution of 1795 • Results of the Revolution

30. **Napoleon Bonaparte** 224

Napoleonic Wars • His Lasting Achievements, Code Napoleon • Concordat • The Bank of France • Public Works • New Educational System • Legion of Honour • Overseas Empire for France • Centralisation of French Administration • Importance of Napoleonic Era

31. **Congress of Vienna (September 1814-June 1815)** 230

Role of Prince Metternich • The Principle of Legitimacy • The Principle of Compensation • Alliance Systems • The Spirit of Nationalism Suppressed • Metternich System Supported the Reactionary Rulers

32. Industrial Revolution 234
Origin of Industrial Revolution • Features of Industrial Revolution • Iron and Steel Industry • Coal Mining Industry • The Invention of Steam Engine by New Comen and James Watt • Factory System in Britain • Revolution in Transport • McAdam Improved Road Construction • Revolution in Communication System • Significance of Industrial Revolution • Spread of Industrial Revolution • Japan and the Industrial Revolution • Effects of Industrial Revolution

33. Revolutions in Latin America 241
Causes of Revolts in Latin America • Jose De San Martin • The Monroe Doctrine

34. Nationalism in Europe in the Nineteenth Century 244
Revolution in Spain 1820 • Greek War of Independence (1827) • Belgian Independence • July Revolution in France (1830) • Revolutions in Other Parts of Europe
The Unification of Italy • The Rise of Nationalism in Italy • Mazzini (1805-72), Role of Giuseppe Garibaldi (1807-1882) • "Young Italy" Movement • 1848 Revolution • Cavour 1810-61 • Venice United with the Rest of Italy (1866) • Rome Liberated in 1870 • The Unification of Germany • Rise of Nationalism • Zollverein (Customs Union) • The 1848 Revolution in France • Failure of 1848 Revolution • King William I of Prussia (1861-1888) and his Iron Chancellor, Bismarck (1871-1890) • 'Blood and Iron' Policy • War with Denmark (1864) Friction Over the Spoils of War • The Austro-Prussian War (1866) and Results • The Franco-Prussian Relations • Bismarck's Diplomacy • Events Leading to Franco Prussian War, Sedan • French Defeat at Metz and Sedan • The Treaty of Frankfurt 1871
Nationalism in the Austrian Empire • Quarrel Between Hungary and Austria • The 1867 Compromise Between Austria and Hungary • Irish Nationalism • Agitations and Redressal of Grievances • Land Reforms • Home Rule Bill • The 'Easter Rising' and Division of Ireland • The Irish Free State (Eire) Under Eamon De Valera

35. The Eastern Question and Balkan Nationalism 263
Meaning of the Eastern Question • Balkan Nationalism on the Rise • The Crimean War • "Pan Slavism" • Russo-Turkish War (1877-78) • Congress of Berlin • Political Turmoil • Young Turk Revolution (1908) • Bulgaria Declares Independence (1908) • Austria Annexes Bosnia and Herzegovina Break-up • The Italo-Turkish War (1911-12) • The First Balkan War • The Results

• The Second Balkan War (1913) • The Balkan Crisis as Prelude to World War I

36. **Modern Imperialism** 269
British East India Company's Wars • Wars in the South • Expansion of British Empire • William Bentinck • Bentinck's Radical Reforms • Lord Dalhousie (1848-56) • China • Opium Wars • Sino-Japanese War (1894-1895) • U.S.A. Advocates 'Open Door Policy' with Regard to China • Japan • Meiji Revolution

37. **Western Imperialism in Africa** 277
Partition of Africa

38. **Nationalism in the Far East** 280
China: Boxer Uprising (1899-1900) and Results • Dr Sun Yat-sen • Sun Receives Help from Russia • Undeclared War Between China and Japan • Chinese Revolution (1949) • Japan: Economic Reforms • Educational System • Re-organisation of the Japanese Forces • Japanese Imperialism

39. **Nationalism in South and Southeast Asia** 286
Persia (Iran) • Afghanistan • British Conquest of Burma • Burmese Nationalism • Ceylon • South East Asia, Philippines • French Indo-China (1893) • World War II and LiberationMovement • Thailand • Indonesia • Nepal Ruled by King Mahendra • Indian Nationalism • The Legacy of the British Rule • Factors Responsible for the Rise of Nationalism • Lord Curzon's Regime (1899-1905) • Rise of Extremism • Further Developments Jallianwala Bagh Tragedy • Gandhian Era • All-white Simon Commission Boycotted • Gandhiji's Dandi March • The Gandhi-Irwin Pact (1931) and the Communal Award • The Act of 1935 and the Origins of Pakistan Movement • Mohammed Ali Jinnah • Muslim Poet, Mohammed Iqbal • Failure of Cripps' Mission • 'Quit india' Movement (May, 1942) • Wavell Plan and Simla Conference (1945) • Subhas Chandra Bose and the I.N.A. Cabinet Mission (1946)

40. **Emergence of the U.S As a World Power** 305
Early years of the New Republic and President Washington • (1789-97) Expansion of U.S Territory • The War of 1812 and Its Results • Monroe Doctrine • Controversial Issues Which Divided the Nation • The North-South Differences • Abraham Lincoln and the Civil War • Further Expansion of U.S.A

Contents xvii

41. **World War I** 309
    Bismarck's Plan to Keep France Isolated • Colonial Rivalry Heightens Jealousies • Economic Imperialism of Britain and Germany • Armament Race • International Crises • Balkan Wars Created Tension • Murder of Crown Prince of Austria • Course of the War • Results • Treaty of Versailes—Its Humiliating Terms of Germany • Beneficial Results of World War I

42. **Russian Revolution (1917)** 314
    The Czarist Autocrats • Czar Alexander II (1855-1881) • Reactionary Rule of Alexander III (1881-1894) • Industrialisation • Reign of Czar Nicholas II (1894-1917) • 1905 Russian Revolution • Downfall of Czar Nicholas (March 1917) Karensky's Menshevik Government Not Popular • Vladimir Lenin (1870-1924) and Bolshevik Revolution (Nov 7, 1917) • Lenin's Early Measures • Lenin's New Economic Policy (1921-24) • Joseph Stalin (1879-1953). Russia's Five Year Plans

43. **Post-War Europe** 322
    League of Nations • Aims of the League • Organs of the League • I.L.O. W.H.O • The International Boundaries Commission • Achievements of the League • Causes of its Failure

44. **Peace Movement in Europe (1919-1939)** 326
    Washington Conference (1921-22) • Efforts of the League • Locarno Pact

45. **Europe Between the Two World Wars** 328
    Fascism in Italy • Post-War Conditions in Italy • Benito Mussolini (1883-1945) and the Rise of Fascism • Mussolini's Dictatorship • The Lateran Treaty (1929) with the Pope Measures to Improve Italian Economy • Mussolini's Foreign Policy and Its Failure • Spanish Civil War (1936-39)

46. **Germany and World War II** 334
    Weimar Republic • Difficulties of Germany and the Rise of Adolf Hitler Nazi Party • Foreign Policy of Nazi Germany • The Course of World War II • America's Entry into World War II • Japan and German Offensives (1942) • Germany Surrenders • Pacific Theatre

47. **The United Nations** 341
    The General Assembly • The Security Council • The Economic and Social Council • The International Court • The Secretariat

• Specialised Agencies • Achievements of the UN • The UN Failures • Cold War

48. **Turkish and Arab Nationalism** 350
   Nationalism in Egypt • President Nasser • Syria and Lebanon • Iraq • Trans Jordan • Saudi Arabia

49. **Decolonisation of Africa (1956-62)** 354
   North Africa • Sudan• Independence of Tunisia • Morocco • Algeria • West Africa • Ghana • Nigeria and Other Colonies • French West Africa • French (Central) Equatorial Africa • Central Africa • Belgian Congo •Southern Africa • Republic of South Africa • East Africa • Kenya, Uganda • Tanzania • Somalia • Madagascar

50. **Science and Technology in the Modern World** 362
   Terms of Science and Technology Defined • Geology • Astronomy—Halley's Discoveries • Development of the Science of Physics • Modern Physics • Developments in Chemistry • Progress in Biology • Progress in Medical field • Technological Innovations • Motion Picture • Technological Innovations in the Means of Transport • Motor Vehicles • Revolution in Communication System

51. **Towards the New Millennium** 370
   The Fall of the Soviet Empire • Rise of Communist China • China's Foreign Relation • The Role of the UN • US after 9/11 (2001) • Regional Groups • Globalisation • Human Sufferings • Terrorism • Violation of Human Rights • Expanding Frontiers of knowledge • Medical Science • Information Technology

52. **From the Afghan Civil War to Arab Spring** 382
   • Afghan Civil War and the Rise of Taliban • Iran-Iraq War (1980-88) • Gulf War (1991): Cease-Fire Agreement, Plight of Iraq, Oil for Food Programme, The Threat of War • The Second Gulf War: Financial Aspects of the War, Iraq Today, Report of the Commission, Iraq's Economy • Dawn of the 21st Century • Sri Lanka • Japan • The Chinese Dragon • Thailand • Nepal • North and South Korea • The Arab Spring: Tunisia, Egypt, Algeria, Bahrain, Libya, Jordan, Syria.

Bibliography 402
Index 404

1
IMPORTANCE OF THE STUDY OF HISTORY

The ancient Greeks were seekers of knowledge and wisdom. One of the subjects which added to their knowledge and wisdom was history. The English word 'history' is derived from their Greek noun *historia*. 'History' or *Historia* simply means enquiry or research. Learning by enquiry about the past of mankind was later developed into a discipline by the ancient Greek historians, Herodotus and Thucydides. Herodotus, known popularly as the 'Father of History', wrote about the Graeco-Persian wars which contained a mine of information, including those relating to the ancient Egyptians and Persians. Thucydides developed this subject on scientific lines. He wrote the *Pelopenesian Wars* purely on the basis of evidence and showed the relation between causes and effects.

Definition of History
Since then historical writings became varied in form and theme reflecting the dominant interests of historians. As such even the definitions of history reflect what history ought to be according to each historian. A few interesting definitions would not be out of place for students who are eager to know what the subject is about.

Thomas Carlyle, a famous historian of 'French Revolution' viewed world history as "biography of great men". E.H. Carr, among other things, defined history as an "unending dialogue between the present and the past". Prof. Renier laid stress on the social role of history and so defined it as "the memories of societies". Will Durant, world renowned historian, gave a sweeping definition by saying that it is "a narrative of what civilised men have thought or done in past time". From the above definitions one can easily assume the nature and purpose of history. It is a narrative of past events which have moulded the destiny of mankind.

Science or Art?

Does history belong to science or art? This is a much debated question defying satisfactory answer. The role of history is to record and explain the past events as accurately as possible. But all the events of the past are beyond one's recollection and hence it falls short of the standard achieved by science. Nevertheless, R.G. Collingwood conceives the role of history similar to science by saying, "Science is finding things out; and in that sense history is science". Both make relentless search for truth. Both have evolved their *own* methods and arrive at some conclusions or laws. While science applies methods like observation, hypothesis and experiment to derive scientific laws, writing of history involves collection of sources, verification of the authenticity of sources, classification of sources, synthesis, exposition of results and lastly criticism. Scientific laws are exact but historical knowledge is imperfect for the fact that it deals with the actions of human beings in the past. Where such knowledge is not forthcoming, it derives by *inference*. Therefore the question arises whether history can be classified under arts.

As already mentioned, a historian will have to make use of his talents to present his matter in a creative manner. Unlike a scientist who deals mostly with dead matter, a historian deals with interesting human situations of the past. If he cannot add flesh, blood and soul to the dry bone of facts of history, his narrative of the past appears so unreal. Therefore, he has to use his imagination to make the past real and credible to his readers. This manner of presentation—a process known as historiography—is more likely to come under art than science. Therefore history can be considered as a science insofar as it uses scientific method and an art for the manner of its treatment and composition. Many historians have considered history as the oldest humanistic science.

Values of History

Each subject of study taught in schools or universities is supposed to help students to imbibe certain values. What values do we derive from the study of history?

Long time ago, Herodotus wrote his history with the avowed purpose that the deeds of the ancient Greeks "shall not be forgotten by posterity". History refers to the deeds of kings and great men at different times and thereby adds to man's knowledge of man. Again, history does not simply catalogue the deeds of men but explains motives behind those deeds in an interesting or humanistic manner. To cite an example, Carlyle's *French Revolution* depicts not only the deeds of historical figures but the *rationale* behind their actions.

Importance of the Study of History

History can be our personal experience too. Many of our struggles for either independence or against exploitation or against oppression may well have been experienced by those in the past. Historical parallels abound. Mahatma Gandhi always derived inspiration during the time of our struggle for freedom from reading the exploits of freedom fighters of Italy a century earlier. Again, at the time of freedom struggle, many compared Gandhiji with Italy's Mazzini, Cavour with Nehru, and Subhas Chandra Bose with Garibaldi. Their personal experiences at the time of freedom struggle appeared more or less similar.

One of the important values derived from the study of history is that it enables us to grasp relationship with our past. Our culture and civilisation have had their beginning in the past. Our links with the past are so deep-rooted that even if we want to sever them, it is not possible. To cite an example, take the case of any one of the social evils such as untouchability or ill-treatment of *Harijans*. They have their origins in the past.

A study of history can be of immense value particularly to social scientists who are engaged in research. It may give them an insight into the problem they are studying. It may also provide the necessary data for enquiring into any sociological or economic phenomenon. A sociologist doing research work on the prevailing *Devadasi system* or a political scientist doing work on parliamentary form of democracy, or a psychologist on mob violence, or an economist engaged in deep study on the effects of energy crisis, may all have to draw his source materials liberally from the treasure-house of history. No wonder history has been called as the laboratory of social sciences.

Its study can be quite rewarding to many of our intellectuals, politicians and statesmen, army generals, scientists, and administrators. Napoleon could achieve so much in his brief career on account of his historical mindedness. A study of history increased the perspicacity of great men of our own times —late Jawaharlal Nehru and late President John F. Kennedy. Historical Knowledge influenced their sensitive minds. They discharged their debt to history by their invaluable contributions—Nehru wrote *Glimpses of World History* and Kennedy *Profiles in Courage*.

In the history of a nation, its society continues to confront many crises. Its leaders fervently hope to steer through the crises and reach the end of the tunnel. In their hour of trial, history serves as a guide or a beacon of light. It guides a society to reach its destination safely. In the middle of nineteenth century, many Americans believed in what was then called "manifest destiny". They believed that their nation was ordained by destiny to expand up to the Pacific coast. Allen Nevins, therefore perceives, history as not merely a narrative of the past but "a bridge connecting the past with the present and pointing the road to the future".

A sound knowledge of history may enable students to understand current events better. Some of them may have been prophesied by great men in the past. For example, Leonardo Da Vinci visualised the invention of flying machines as early as the sixteenth century. Modern space travel was more or less prophesied by historians like H.G. Wells and Jules Verne. Again, current space travels or voyages may be compared to those of the voyages of early explorers like Columbus, Vasco Da Gama or Magellan. With the hindsight of history it should not be difficult for a student to get a bearing on most of the current events taking place in his own country or abroad.

It is necessary to mention that history protects and preserves traditional and cultural values of a nation. Historians have played an important role in constantly reminding their compatriots as to how their nation played a key role in the history of the world. German historians fanned the flames of nationalism against the oppressor, Napoleon, in the early nineteenth century. Hitler, misguided by the ideas of early historians, thought Germans as pure Aryans and therefore fit to rule the whole of mankind.

Other values, although implicit, which history inculcates among students are feelings of love and compassion, and spirit of tolerance. While going through the pages of history, one comes across untold sufferings of the slaves and the Christians in the Roman Empire. In modern times, the sufferings of the Jews at the hands of Nazi Germans and the plight of the Palestinian and Bangladesh refugees, evoke in us feeling of compassion.

Lessons of History

A few historians like Carlyle and Bolingbroke laid too much emphasis on the didactic nature of history. Writing about the instructive role of history, the former said, "all learners, all inquiring minds of every order are gathered round her footstool, and reverently pondering her lessons as the time basis of wisdom". Lord Bolingbroke regarded history as "philosophy teaching by examples". However, modern historians do not accept the above role assigned to history and emphatically state that history does not repeat itself. Only common people seem to think so.

Finally, history acts as a great source of inspiration. Under its influence, man achieved things which were beyond his reach. History influenced great men like Julius Caesar and Napoleon. History offers solace and hope to the oppressed millions. German philosopher Hegel says that men do not learn very much from the lessons of History is the most important of all the lessons that History has to teach.

History and Archaeology
If there is any science which has enabled historians to grasp the unrecorded past (pre-history), it is undoubtedly archaeology. It is a scientific study of the remnants of the past. Ancient sites, relics, monuments, coins, inscriptions and other artefacts all enable an archaeologist to reconstruct history in a most plausible manner. It is a common knowledge that the Indus valley civilisation was uncovered by the spade of Indian archaeologists (1921-22).

History and Geography
While discussing which came first, geography or history, German philosopher Kant said, "geography lies at the basis of history", and Herder said that "history is geography set in motion". There are others like Ellsworth Huntington and Allen Semple who emphasize the importance of climate as having crucial influence on the course of history as well as on race temperament. It is a fact that many geographical factors, such as climate, soil, rivers, mountains, sea, coastline, and mineral resources aided the development of riverine-valley cultures as in early Egypt, Mesopotamia, India and China. Herodotus, the early Greek historian, described that "Egypt is the gift of the Nile". The ancient Greeks took to outdoor as well sea-faring life on account of many geographical factors, such as infertile soil, nearness to sea, and broken coastline.

Whatever may have been the influence of geographical factors in moulding the life and history of peoples, one should be cautious enough *not to overemphasise* the same. With the passage of time, man acquired the knowledge to harness nature to suit his needs. Instances of people like the modern Israelis turning their desert region into inhabitable condition are there to disprove influence of geography. So it would be wise to accept limited interpretation of geographical influence on man's conduct or on his history.

History and Other Social Sciences
The scope of history has been so much widened in modern times so as to include the whole gamut of human activities of the past. In the past, history was regarded as a humanistic science only. But a new Social Science Research Council set up in the U.S.A. in 1924 included history in its social science disciplines. This was done in order to promote inter-disciplinary approach in research and teaching. A collaboration between historians and social scientists would go a long way in the understanding and teaching of social science disciplines better.

Anthropology and history are closely related. The former enables a historian to understand the cultural pattern and behaviour of primitive peoples belonging to different races. Thus knowledge gained by a historian about this subject would go a long way in explaining the many behavioural patterns, customs, and institutions of previous and present generations. A true historian should be able to trace the course of social and cultural revolutions of prehistoric and pro-historic men. He would be able to do justice to this subject only through his knowledge of anthropology.

History helps in the understanding of other social science disciplines such as political science, economics and psychology. Man's eternal quest for power and orderly government suited to his needs constitutes the theme of political history. Again, man's eternal quest for better livelihood and material goods constitutes the main theme of economic history. History deals with group behavioural also and gives its interpretation or analysis of such important events as revolutions, popular movements, and mob violence or reactions. Historical characters are analysed.

Thus history and other developed social sciences have a role to play in explaining multifaceted human behaviour and conditions. The knowledge of both may enable the ruling elite everywhere to plan and work for a better future. History has studied human nature for centuries, and therefore is in a position to promote peace and happiness of mankind.

Lesson Review
1. What do you mean by 'History'? Explain its values.
2. Discuss the relation between history and other social science subjects.

2
WORLD HISTORY AND ITS SCOPE

The purpose of world history is to focus the attention of the students on the many sided achievements of the human race as a whole from the dawn of history to the present. Therefore, this general treatment includes in its purview the progress made by each individual society and consequently its contribution to world civilisation.

To be more explicit, the world history takes into account the genesis and evolution of early man as a human species, his interaction with his environment, his early settlements in the river valleys, his advance in religion, art and architecture, literature, industry, agriculture, trade and commerce.

Western nations entered a new era marked by enlightened royal despotism, renaissance, geographical discoveries, and scientific discoveries and inventions. The industrial revolution in the west set many of its nations on the quest for colonies in America, Africa and Asia. It took a long time for the peoples of the colonies to break the shackles of western imperialism and emerge independent. Thus world history not only renders account of the progress of mankind, but man's struggle against many forms of oppression. The birth of the United Nations Organization to save the world from nuclear wars and anarchy truly symbolises the aspirations of the present mankind.

The Need for Its Study

Why should we study world history? This question has several answers. Firstly, the world has become a small place thanks to the scientific and technological revolutions. Big and small nations will have to coexist in peace. Peaceful coexistence can be achieved through mutual goodwill and understanding among nations. Therefore, there is a common desire among people to know each other better. In this respect the study of world history fulfils their need.

Secondly world history performs the role of a teacher by explaining the problems and dangers facing mankind. If these challenges are not met effectively, the outbreak of World War III may take place.

Thirdly, the study of world history broadens one's mind and outlook. It enables them to view problems in a dispassionate manner—a key to success in life.

Lastly, the study of world history enables students to acquire qualities of wisdom, spirit of tolerance, civic sense and duties.

Periodisation of World History

The history of mankind has been broadly classified into two parts, namely, prehistoric (from 1,000,000 BC to 5000 BC) and historic (from 5000 BC to the present). Archaeologists divided the history of man into different ages taking into consideration the different implements he used. For example, we hear of the Palaeolithic Age, Mesolithic Age, Neolithic Age, Chalcolithic Age, Bronze Age, Iron Age and Modern Age.

As most of our study is devoted to the historic age, historians further classified this age into: Ancient world (5000 BC-500 AD), Medieval World (500 AD-1500 AD) and the Modern World (1500 AD to the present).

The reason for making the above classification is to emphasise the mode of living of people in different times. A world history text which does not bring to the notice of students the variations in the mode of living of people creates a big void in their knowledge. Hence the emphasis on periodisation in world history.

Chronology of World History

A number of important events are naturally dated as per Christian calendar. The birth of Jesus Christ heralded an important era to the Christians. So they started counting the years as either BC i.e., before Christ or AD, (*Anno Domini,* meaning in the year of our Lord). In recent decades, historians are also using abbreviations BCE (Before Christian Era) and CE (Christian Era). The Christian era is dated four years after the birth of Jesus. One should know that Jesus Christ was born on 25th of December, 4 BC.

Culture and Civilisation

A student of history should ordinarily be familiar with the meanings of many words, particularly words such as culture and civilisation. The word 'culture' simply means a way of living of a human group. It includes daily needs of man such as food, clothing and shelter; and also his customs, habits, manners, attitudes, ideas and perceptions. In other words, a man's entire range of activities in a society to better his lot in many fields comes under the purview of culture. His interest in art, architecture, literature, learning, music, philosophy and all other things he does to make his life happy are included in culture.

Civilisation denotes an advanced state of culture. A large community acquires this status by revolutions in each sphere or aspect of culture. It is said that when a society invented tools, writing, and a calendar, it took a giant step in its march towards civilisation. MacIver said, "our culture is what we are, our civilisation is what we use".

Factors for the Rise and Development of Culture

Geographical Factors

It is necessary to discuss the factors which contributed to the rise of culture. The most important factor, according to Elsworth Huntington, is the geographical elements such as climate and soil. No culture worth the name would rise in a hostile environment. Life-sustaining sources of a group are water, soil, climate, natural barriers and instinct of self-preservation. All these geographical factors gave rise to the early civilisations in Egypt, Mesopotamia, India and China.

Creative Minority

In his epic work, *Study of History,* the famous historian Arnold J. Toynbee, traced other factors besides the geographical causes. He made reference to the dynamic role of the creative minority in each society. In each culture, the *intelligentsia* created conditions favourable for the growth. They occupied places of importance in the civil and military administration of the state. Another factor, which he mentioned as of crucial importance for the self-preservation of culture, was the series of challenges. A newly born culture is exposed to a series of challenges and its survival depends upon effective responses. It may mostly come in the form of war, or a civil war, or a rebellion, or an earthquake or a famine. If this type of hostile environment is not surmounted by effective responses, a culture becomes extinct, or succumbs to the influence of alien culture. In his *World and the West,* (BBC Reith lectures) Toynbee referred to the impact of one superior culture on another inferior culture.

Economic Well-being and Leisure

A culture may die if not nourished properly by creative activity. In a society, poverty may act as an enemy of creative activity. Its individuals would be bothered for want of daily necessities of life. Therefore, there may not be leisure for people to involve themselves in creative activities. So, a certain level of economic well-being may prove conducive to the rise and development of culture. Alfred L. Krober in his *Configurations of Culture* and C.E.M. Joad in his *What is Civilisation?* have emphasised the importance of creative activity.

Urban Bias of Culture
Culture normally flourished in cities. It is there that people exchanged their ideas and thoughts. In cities, educational centres are patronised. They act as agents for the spread of culture. In ancient Greece, Athens served as a great cultural centre and attracted students from neighbouring countries to its educational centres. So culture gets its nourishment in cities.

Trade
Economic well-being and growth of cities depends upon extensive trade. A large number of towns and cities sprang upon the trade routes during the Middle Ages. It was after the crusades that Italy enjoyed a monopoly of Mediterranean trade. Her cities became very prosperous. Her wealthy merchants provided enough impetus for the rebirth of new culture—renaissance in the fifteenth century.

Culture Grows with New Knowledge and Ideas
A culture should be able to adapt itself not only to a new environment but welcome new knowledge and ideas. After Commodore Perry's visit and warning, Japan could no longer keep her doors closed to the entry of an alien culture. Her reaction was not one of resistance but submission. The new government under the Japanese Emperor encouraged the process of westernisation. The West's greatness lay in its superior knowledge—i.e., science and technology. Japan too acquired it and became a great power.

Healthy Political and Social Climate
In the previous paragraph a reference has been made to state-patronage. It is therefore necessary to know that a culture grows in a healthy political and social climate. A state and society should allow individuals to "think freely and newly" so as to develop their personalities. Many a time great men and women like Socrates, Jesus Christ, Joan of Arc, and Mahatma Gandhi became martyrs to the causes they dearly upheld.

To sum up, a culture's rise and growth depends upon such factors like geographical and social milieu, creative minority, effective responses to challenges, economic well-being and its consequent leisure, trade, knowledge and ideas and healthy political and social climate.

Lesson Review
1. What useful purpose does the study of world history serve?
2. Discuss briefly the importance of periodisation of world history.
3. What elements constitute culture?
4. What were the geographical factors which influenced evolution of early history?

3
PREHISTORIC MAN

It is interesting to know how man came to dominate the earth and its millions of living creatures since aeons. As a first step it is necessary to know how and when our planet, the earth, appeared and gave birth to billions of creatures.

The Origin and Life of the Earth

Geologists say that the earth was formed nearly 4600 millions of years ago. A popular theory among the scientists goes to say that the earth first appeared like a red hot ball full of clouds of hot gases. It began to cool down after hundreds of millions of years so as to make it possible for life to appear. Seas, land and mountains began to make their appearance. But how life began remains even now a mystery to scientists. Anyway, life appeared suddenly as if by accident in water a billion years ago. This tiny one cell creature (Algae) began to multiply, develop and appear in varied forms for countless ages. Some plants and animals took shelter in shallow waters. They began to adjust to the environment of the land.

In the history of the earth, the Middle Age (Mesozoic age) is known for huge reptiles like dinosaurs which walked on land. The mammals too appeared who suckled their young. When the earth became too cold on account of the advent of the Ice Ages, millions of creatures became totally extinct which included the dinosaurs and others. Only the mammals survived. New species began to make their appearance. The earth has experienced four Ice Ages so far according to the geologists.

Our Earliest Man

We do not have adequate knowledge about the earliest man who appeared on this planet. Darwin traced the origin of the earliest man to the ape for which he was very much criticised. Eighty years ago a Dutch doctor, named Dubois, discovered the remnants of the earliest known man on the earth— the Java man. Skeletal remains of the earliest men were also found in Peking and Heidelberg. The Java and Peking men must have inhabited our planet about a million years ago. They looked better than the apes and walked erect.

In Neanderthal valley in Germany, traces of a different race of men and women of prehistoric times were found. They might have lived any time between 100,000 and 50,000 years BC. The Neanderthal men were primitive in appearance with their thick bodies, small foreheads and receding lower jaws. But they appeared to be more advanced than their predecessors. The latest in the series of these of prehistoric men were the Cro-Magnons who lived in caves of France about 20,000 years ago. They were taller, decent in appearance, and more civilised.

Old Stone Age
Modern anthropologists and archaeologists have been studying about the life and tools used by men in the prehistoric times since long. The long history of prehistoric man is conveniently divided into the Paleolithic Age and the Neolithic Age. The former seemed to have commenced from the very time when men began to make crude tools, weapons and implements from stones for hunting and living. Probably, his greatest achievements could be traced to his learning as to how to make a fist hatchet the spear, and the fire. All these things enabled him to survive the ordeals of his dangerous existence amidst ferocious animals. Men during this period had no fixed abode. They wandered from place to place in search of food in the jungles. They hunted and killed animals with ease and ate their flesh. He began to use the skin of the animals for wrapping his body. The Neanderthal man also used the caves for protecting themselves from cold during the winter seasons. He knew how to make fire and frighten the animals with the flaming torch. He spoke to his men in grunts and growls. When his men died, they were buried.

The Neanderthal men began to disappear by the time the Cro-Magnon men moved to the north. This must have happened about thirty thousand years ago. The Cro-Magnon men used better tools and weapons for hunting such as a spear thrower, bow and arrow, and harpoons (for fishing). Their women made clothes out of animals skins. Also the Cro-Magnon men showed their artistic ability by painting coloured pictures on the walls of the caves which were found in France and Spain. The Cro-magnon men could be described as belonging to our own species—The Homo Sapiens.

Migration of Human Race
As mentioned earlier, the earth experienced four Ice Ages or glacial epochs. The last one probably ended 11,000 years ago. Extensive parts of northern Europe, Asia and Canada were enveloped in ice. So men in the old stone

age had taken shelter in warmer climates. So they got scattered. Mankind has been classified into several human races like Caucausoid, Mongoloid, Mediterranean and Negroid.

New Stone Age

The New Stone Age must have begun about 10,000 BC heralding a new era in the life of man. Man's nomadic life in search of food came to an end. Instead, he learnt the art of producing food. Naturally it led to a more settled way of life. Archaeologists discovered lake-dwellings in countries like Switzerland, Italy, France, Russia, Scotland and North America. Neolithic men left the jungles and began to live on the plains, especially on the banks of the rivers.

To help him in agriculture, animals were domesticated, bullocks assisted him in agriculture. Cows and goats gave him milk. Dog and horse became useful animals in many ways. With sheep's skin, he made woollen garments. Sometimes men hunted and women looked after their fields which produced flax, barley and wheat.

Neolithic Crafts

Neolithic man produced clothes out of fibre and cotton. He learnt the art of spinning and weaving and also sewing of garments. He made use of polished stone tools, implements and weapons. This makes his age known as the New Stone Age. He also developed numerous crafts such as pottery, making of baskets, mats, boats, wooden or wattled huts, and crude wooden tables and benches. In the course of time Neolithic men made many tools out of wood, stone and ivory. Their life became comfortable when they made pulleys, axes, needles, ladders, fish-hooks, grindstones, spindles etc. Probably the most historic invention of that time was the wheel which heralded his progress.

Neolithic men could hardly find time to produce paintings like their predecessors, the Cro-Magnon men. However, they decorated their pots with some designs, made figurines of clay or wood and wove bright designs on their cloth. Their languages developed. Singing and dancing during festival time were in vogue.

Barter System

As Neolithic society developed, the needs of common man also multiplied. People began to produce a variety of goods which were in demand. The barter system came to be used. Practice of primitive religion also began.

The Age of Metals

Men in West Asia found copper around 4000 BC and made tools and weapons such as daggers, knives, axes and hammers. As the metal was soft, the edges of these tools and weapons often became dull. Some one found tin, melted it and mixed it with melted copper. This combination produced a harder metal now known as bronze (3000 BC). But copper and bronze periods in history first began in West Asia and the Near East. Their discovery and uses spread to the other parts of the world slowly. It was around 2000 BC that the use of a stronger metal, iron, came to be known to the West Asians. It is believed that the Mesopotamians were the earliest to use this metal. The age of metals constitutes an important milestone in mankind's long march towards progress.

Races of Mankind

Before we proceed to study the Historic Age, it is necessary to know how mankind is classified according to well-defined races. In the world today many people belong to a mixture of human races. In India we have the mixture of Aryans and Dravidians. Similarly, we find mixture of races in the American continent. Taking the colour and physical features into consideration, the present mankind is broadly divided into three races: (a) The black or *Negroid,* (b) the yellow or *Mongolid,* and (c) the white or the *Caucasian.*

(a) Those who belong to the Negroid race have black skin, woolly hair, broad nose and thick lips. Among the Negroid, there are two main types namely, the short statured Negroes who are found in Malaya, the Philippines, and some parts of Australia, and the normal statured Negroes who are found in central and western Africa.

(b) The people of Tibet, Nepal, Indo-china, Japan, Formosa belong to the Mongoloid race. They have yellow skin, flat face with high cheek bones and slanting eyes. Even the American Indians belong to a branch of Mongoloid race. So also the Eskimos of the Northern American Arctic and Indians of South America.

(c) The majority of the people who live in Europe, Northern Africa, Arabia, some Pacific islands, New Zealand, South India and Ceylon belong to the Caucasoid race. There are many types of caucasoids, like the Nordics, East Baltics, Alpines and Mediterraneans. The Nordics are tall, long-headed, blond and with blue eyes. The east Baltics are short with a round head and round face. The Mediterraneans have dark skin, dark eyes, wavy hair, and a long head. Most of the slavs in Russia belong to the Alpines sub-race.

It is better to note that we hardly come across any ethnically pure race or races in view of constant migration of people from one region to the other. Further, it is to be mentioned here that no single culture at present could be associated to any particular race.

Lesson Review

1. Write a note on
   - (a) Palaeolithic Age;
   - (b) Neolithic culture;
   - (c) Neanderthal Man;
   - (d) Cro-Magnon man;
   - (e) Migration of human race.

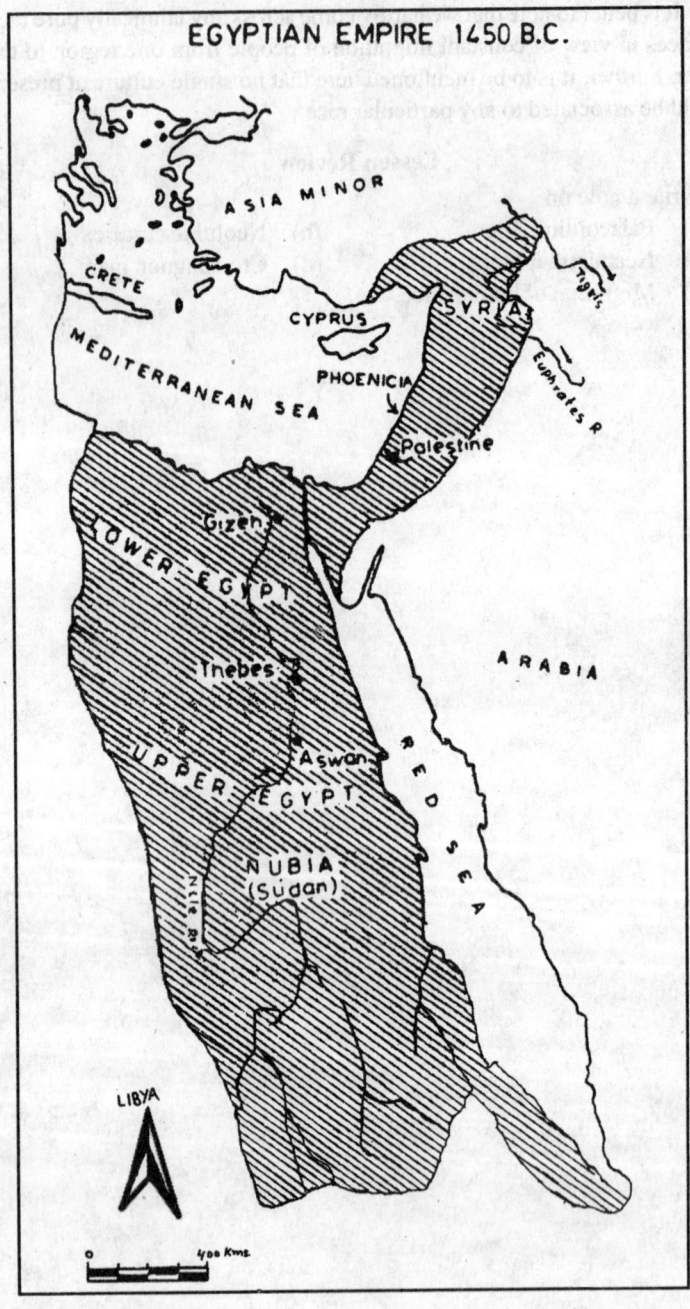

4
EGYPT : THE GIFT OF THE NILE

In the north-east side of Africa lies Egypt. Like the rest of North Africa it would have become a desert but for the Nile river valley. Long ago, this Nile valley cradled and nourished one of the oldest and finest civilisations in world history. The longest history of Ancient Egyptian Civilisation exercised its profound influence on the rest of mankind. As a first step, let us examine how geographical factors influenced to bring about the birth of this mighty civilisation.

Geographical Factors

To begin with, the river Nile played its role as source of livelihood to the people around it. Herodotus, the ancient Greek historian, called Egypt the 'gift of the Nile' particularly after realising its importance. The Nile river takes its birth in the central African mountains and flows hundreds of miles to the north to reach the Mediterranean Sea. The soil on its bans, and near the mouth where a fan-shaped delta is formed, became fertile due to annual flooding of the river. When the climate changed in North Africa, the grassy Sahara region received no rainfall, many tribes of hunters left their abodes and settled on the banks of the river Nile. The climate was hot and dry and the river became navigable soon after it reached the plains. The natural frontiers of Egypt such as the Mediterranean Sea in the north, the desert on the west, the Red sea on the east, and the cataracts in the south furnished protection from foreign invasions. Furthermore, building materials such as stones, and minerals like copper, were available to meet the needs of the builders and craftsmen. Hence these factors encouraged the rise and growth of a great culture and civilisation.

Agriculture and other Developments

As already mentioned, tribes of hunters from the plateaus migrated to the Nile valley. Many of them gave up hunting and started cultivating the top rich soil of the Nile. As the river receded after the rainy season, these men built tanks, dykes, and canals for the purpose of storing water and irrigating the land. They invented the *shadoof* to lift the water from the tanks and also used many new implements for smooth agricultural operations. For example, they used wooden plough, sickle, and other implements and also harnessed oxen in their agricultural operations. They raised three crops in a year. They grew flax, vegetables and wheat. In the course of time they produced a variety of fruits like watermelons, lemons, dates and figs.

Villages grew in large numbers on both the banks of the Nile river. Each village was inhabited by a particular tribe and all the tribes belonged to the Hamitic race, a branch of the Caucasian race. Each tribe had a badge or a totem usually of an animal, which was considered sacred.

Each tribe was led by a chieftain who created favourable conditions for his men to improve agriculture and crafts like metal working, carpentry, stonemasonry, pottery and weaving. Sometimes he led them in battles and conquered the neighbouring tribes. Thus, over a span of centuries the small tribal kingdoms merged to form two large kingdoms (4000 BC), lower Egypt (around the delta) and upper Egypt. It was around 3400 BC that these two kingdoms were united by a strong king called Menes. Probably he was the first to establish dynastic rule over what we now call the old kingdom. One may as well remember that ancient Egypt was ruled by nearly 31 dynasties of Pharaohs over a period of three thousand years. King Menes built the first known capital city called Memphis.

Classification of Early Egyptian history

The long history of ancient Egypt is divided into (a) early dynastic period (3000-2700 BC), (b) the Old Kingdom 2700-2150 BC, (c) the Middle Kingdom (2040-1640 BC), and the New Kingdom (1550-1070 BC). One may also note that chaotic conditions or foreign invasions prevailed between the end of one period and the beginning of another.

Early Dynastic Period

It was around 3000 BC that an Egyptian King by name Menes united lower and upper Egypt and built Memphis to serve as his new capital. His successors ruled for nearly three and half centuries and left behind their tombs at Abydos and Saqqara.

The Old Kingdom (better known as the Age of the Pyramids)

Regarding construction of pyramids by Pharaohs of Egypt, the first built by King Zoser (called step-pyramid) marked the beginning of the age. The age is also known for the undisputed power enjoyed by the Pharaohs who set up strong central government which was run by a large number of officials and priests. The Pharaohs made laws, levied taxes and governed the land wisely. People of the villages, towns and cities felt the authority

Egypt: The Gift of the Nile

of the Pharaohs, whom they worshipped as divine representatives of God and faithfully carried out his orders.

The old kingdom was ruled by four dynasties of Pharaohs with Memphis as the seat of their capital. Sneferu, the first Pharaoh of the fourth dynasty conquered a few neighbouring kingdoms. Three Pharaohs of the same dynasty, namely, Khufu (Herodotus called him Cheops), his son Khafra, and Men Kau-re became famous for constructing pyramids which served as royal tombs. The ancient Egyptians believed that their dead Pharaohs would come back alive. Hence they preserved the dead body of the Pharaoh by embalming it and keeping it in the secret chamber of the pyramid.

The Middle Kingdom (2040-1640 BC)

Before the advent of the Middle Kingdom, there was the Age of Feudalism (2150-1550 BC). During this age the power of the Pharaohs gradually declined, and the nobles gained power and importance. Each one of them ruled his province like a king without paying any respect to the Pharaoh. Rival groups of nobles tried to influence the Pharaoh to toe their line and caused great political chaos in the country.

Unsettled conditions ended around 2000 BC, when an Egyptian prince of Thebes reunited Egypt and restored law and order. Thebes became the seat of the capital of the Middle Kingdom. The kings stopped building pyramids but "carved tombs out of the sides of the cliffs along the desert bordering the Nile Valley". Under their leadership, mining of copper, repairs to irrigational system, and the construction of dams were undertaken. During this period, the rulers developed the cult of Osiris (Egyptian God) and sculpture. The Middle Kingdom expanded into an empire after the conquest of Nubia.

The prosperity of Ancient Egypt attracted the attention of foreigners. Hyksos, a war like people from Syria, came in horse-drawn chariots and conquered Egypt. They ruled Egypt for nearly a century. However, in the end the Egyptians led by Ahmos were able to drive out the foreigners and revive the imperial rule of the Pharaohs.

The Imperial Age or the New Kingdom (1550-1070 BC)

Ancient Egypt reached the heights of great power and glory under the leadership of the great Pharaohs of the 18th dynasty. After Ahmose, his son Amenhotep-I transformed the Egyptian kingdom into an empire by his conquests which included Nubia in the south and Babylonia in east. The next great ruler was Thutmose I who also extended his authority to some parts of Asia. As he had no son, his daughter (later married to

Thutmose II) ascended the throne as Queen Hatshepsut (1472-1458). She was the first woman ruler who governed over an extensive empire in the history of the world. Her rule was marked by flourishing overseas trade with distant countries like the 'Punt' (Eastern Somaliland) and liberal patronage to art and architecture. The great temple at Karnak near Thebes stands in her name, and a tall obelisk (97½ft) near it contains engraving of her glorious achievements. Her stepson, Thutmose III (1458-1426 BC) proved to be the greatest conqueror of Ancient Egypt. He led his army into Syria, Palestine and the 'Fertile Crescent' and compelled them to pay tributes to Egypt. He conquered Nubia and forced the captives to work in the gold mines there. He carried out improvements to the temple of Amon at Karnak. He gave Egypt a powerful army, an efficient administration and prosperity and glory. No doubt he has been nicknamed as 'Napoleon of Ancient Egypt'. The next great Pharaohs was Akhenaten (1353-1336 BC). He was a great reformer who introduced monotheism and granted women certain rights in his country. The last great Pharaoh who ruled Ancient Egypt was Rameses II whose reign was the longest (1279-1213 BC). He made a sincere attempt to revive the glory of ancient Egypt which had declined after the death of Akhenaten. He attacked the Hittites of Asia Minor at Khadesh but later made peace with them in 1258 BC. He patronised art and architecture. He completed the construction of the temple of Osiris begun by his father.

The massive Abu Simbel temple (shifted from its original venue to a nearby hill and the colossal statues of Rameses II and his wife, the Colossi, always remind the visitors about his glory. The Jews, who were kept in bondage in Egypt during his time, fled his country and Moses led them to the 'promised land'. After the death of Rameses II, Ancient Egypt lost her empire and glory. Later she came to be ruled by the Assyrians, the Persians, and the Greeks under Alexander. After Alexander's death, his general, Ptolemy, established his dynasty which ruled Egypt till the Romans conquered it. The last Ptolemaic ruler of Egypt was Cleopatra, the most beautiful queen of the ancient world. Let us now turn our attention to the culture in Ancient Egypt.

Early Egyptian Society

The early Egyptian society was composed mainly of three classes, namely, the aristocratic, the middle class and the slaves. The aristocratic class included the Pharaoh, the nobles and the priests who enjoyed much power and wealth in the country. They owned large estates, beautiful houses, fine jewellery, linen clothes and large number of slaves and servants. Their decorated homes and beautiful furniture caused much envy among the lower classes. Moreover, they enjoyed status, Privileges, and power. They sent their children to schools.

The rise of the middle class in Ancient Egypt was the direct result of the growth of towns and cities. The middle class included the merchants, scribes, artisans and other professional men like physicians. All these professionals enjoyed modest comforts. The peasants who constituted the bulk of Egyptian population, found it difficult to make both ends meet. They worked for long hours and a major part of their income went to meet the cost of paying taxes (in kind) to the state.

The conditions of slaves were no better. They were mostly taken as captives after the war and brought to Egypt. They were sold in the market, and their life became miserable when they were put to hard work like building the pyramids. Some of them worked in copper mines, stone quarries and the big estates of the nobles.

Egyptian women enjoyed a great deal of freedom and a high position in society. They owned property and transferred the same to their children in their old age. Akhnaton believed in raising the status of women in society. He granted them certain rights.

From our point of view, Egyptian morals as followed by Pharaohs lacked decency. An Egyptian Pharaoh married his own sister or daughter in order to retain the purity of royal blood. This practice was followed by others in society.

Economic Life

The majority of the ancient Egyptians were engaged in agriculture. They raised crops of wheat, flax, fruits and vegetables. From flax they produced textile goods. They produced papyrus from the papyrus reeds which were grown on the banks of the Nile. Papyrus rolls were used for writing. The early Egyptians learnt to make several articles of metal from bronze. They also learnt the art of making beautiful jewellery, glassware and furniture. The world was amazed at the beautiful things the early Egyptians had produced soon after the discovery of the tomb of Tutankhamen. The early Egyptians excelled in crafts like leatherwork and pottery. They built boats with sails for the first time in the world and sent their manufactured goods to far off countries.

They adopted a crude system of barter, that is exchanging one type of goods for another in the early stages of their history. It was, however, replaced by metal currency. Several types of boats carried goods on the Nile, and a few of them carried Egyptian grain, linen, textile, beautiful jewellery, furniture, glassware and pottery to countries like Nubia, Syria

Phoenicia and Lebanon. The Egyptian merchants exchanged them for ivory, gold, ostrich feathers, silver, tin and spices.

Egyptian Religion

The early Egyptians were very religious as can be observed from their literature, art and monuments. In the early stages of their civilizations, they worshipped the forces of nature and also some birds and animals. However, in due course of time, each village, town or city had a patron God. The most important who was worshipped by all was the Sun God, Ra, who was supposed to sail across the sky in a golden boat daily. He destroyed darkness and injustice and made life enjoyable on the earth. During the period of the Middle Kingdom, God Osiris, the great grandson of Ra, assumed importance. A legend mentions that he was killed by his bad brother, Seth, but his devoted wife, Isis, with the assistance of her sister Nephthys, brought him (Osiris) back to life. Osiris became the God 'after life' and judged the souls of the departed. He caused the Nile River to overflow so as to make the soil fertile. Equally popular was his son, Horus, the God of the Universe. The other gods who were popular were Ptah, Isis, and Amon.

The Egyptians offered prayers and sacrifices to these Gods in order to receive their blessings. They believed in life after death. The Pharaohs believed in immortality and hoped to be reborn after death. Hence the pyramids.

The temples built by Pharaohs like Thutmose III, Ramses I and II of ancient Egypt are of two types, namely, temples for worship and temples for mortuary purpose. The ruins of many temples are seen in and around Thebes (Luxor and Karnak). Priests conducted ceremonies and prayers. *The Book of the Dead* was produced in order to give knowledge to the dying man whose soul would appear before God and answer questions. If the soul did not pass the test, it would go to hell.

Monotheism

Pharaoh Akhnaten (originally known as Amenhotep IV, 1353-1336 BC) rejected the idea of worshipping many Gods and advocated the worship of God Aton (Sun God). He got all the temples, other that the Sun God, closed. He asserted his authority inspite of priestly opposition, and shifted the seat of his capital from Thebes to the new capital Akhetaton (Tell-el-Amarna). His queen Nefertiti supported him in all his efforts to bring monotheism in the country. After his death, monotheism was given up with boy-king Tutankhamen (1332–1323 BC) ascending the throne. The priests influenced this very young Pharaoh to go back to Memphis.

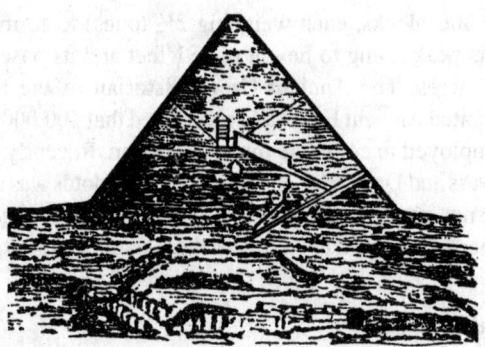
The pyramid of Giza indicating inner Chamber

Art and Architecture

As mentioned earlier, the early Egyptians were deeply religious. Their rulers and nobles built temples, pyramids and tombs. Among the temples known for their beautiful construction are those at Karnak, Luxor, Philae and Abu Simbel. Most of these temples have spacious halls with their high roofs supported by columns of pillars reaching some times to great heights. The walls of the temples have paintings depicting the religious or daily life of the people. The pillars are engraved.

Among the tombs, the most celebrated is the one which belongs to Pharaoh Tutankhamen (discovered by Howard Carter in 1922) who died in his teens. Recently, radiologists have concluded that he might have died due to a broken and infected leg, and not due to injury caused by a blow to his head as believed earlier. Fortunately, this secret tomb was discovered intact and gave a true glimpse of early Egypt's artistic splendour. Besides, his mummy found in the coffin, which is made of a quarter-inch thick gold, contained jeweled portraits. The other tombs near Thebes have brilliant paintings which give a glimpse of the life of early Egyptians belonging to all classes.

Many sculptors of Ancient Egypt depicted various scenes on the walls of the temples, tombs and on the obelisks. The sculptors carved small as well as massive stone statues of Pharaohs which are well-known for their "dignity and simplicity". One of the massive stone-statues of ancient Egypt is the great Sphinx at Giza (2500 BC), the figure of a recumbent lion with the head of a man. It is situated near the Great Pyramid.

The Great Pyramid

Pyramids of Ancient Egypt are great architectural wonders. They are huge structures built to serve as royal tombs. The first pyramid was built by King Zoser at Saqqara which was designed by his Vizier, Imotep. The Great Pyramid at Giza was built by Pharaoh Khufu. It is built of limestone blocks (2,70,000 blocks, each weighing 2½ tones) to form a triangular shape with its peak rising to height of 481 feet and its base covering an area of 13.1 acres. The Ancient Greek historian of the fifth century, Herodotus, visited Ancient Egypt and mentioned that 100,000 slaves might have been employed to complete the construction. Recently scholars like Dr. Zahi Hawass and Dr. Mark Lehner say that Herodotus was misinformed. Slaves were not employed and only 20,000 conscripts and volunteers might have been employed to complete the task of constructing the Great Pyramid.

Writings and Literature
Hieroglyphs or sacred writings:
Much of what we know about ancient Egypt has come from their writings. The ancient Egyptians developed picture-writing which is known as hieroglyphs. Priests and scribes knew this art of writing since the advent of the first dynasty. Sacred documents contain this script. It was not until the discovery of Rosetta Stone in 1799 by Napoleon's army in Egypt, that hieroglyph remained undeciphered. Rosetta Stone contained three scripts – hieroglyphs, demotic-Egyptian, and Greek. In 1802, Rev. Stephen Weston translated the Greek script. Thomas young made a beginning of decipherment of this script and it was completed by Jean Champollion, a French scholar in 1822.

A faster means of writing non-sacred documents was developed in ancient ages, which was subsequently called Hieratic with the advent of the New Kingdom, the scribes used this scripts for sacred documents also. In course of time hieratic script yielded place to Demotic language. Egyptologists like J.H. Breasted (1865-1935) and Sir W.M. Flinders Petrie (1853-1942) have added their contributions to the understanding of the history of ancient Egypt. In recent decades a large number of scholars and archaeologists have contributed a lot. Egypt's supreme council of antiquities led by its scholar Dr. Zahi Hawass and other American scholars are doing good work in the preservation and dissemination of knowledge on ancient Egypt.

A good deal of ancient Egyptian writings relate to the religion as proved by papyrus scripts. Their most important works are *The Book of the Dead* and *the Coffin Texts*. Both works contain charms and prayers a soul should recite to get easy passage to the after-world. Papyrus rolls also contain stories, poems, and dramas.

Other Contributions to Civilisation
The early Egyptians not only gave the world their first form of writing but also the writing materials such as paper, pen and ink. They produced

paper out of the papyrus plants, used pointed reeds, and made ink with vegetable gum and soot. Archaeologists have recently discovered 3000 thousand year old glass furnace at a site in Amarna (probably belonging to Akhnaton's time). Perfume used by Queen Hatshepsut is being recreated.

Lunar and Solar Calendars

The early Egyptians were the first to devise a calendar on the basis of the moon-cycle. However they found it inadequate to measure time correctly and so evolved a new calendar based on the solar system. The year was divided into three seasons (Inundation, Coming Forth and the Harvest), each having four months, and each month having 30 days. The last five days were enjoyed as holidays. Thus in their *solar* calendar they had 365 days. Their calendar's fist recorded year was 4241 BC. The early Egyptians were also conscious of the time factor in daily life. For this purpose, they invented the sundial, waterclock, and the hour-glass.

Their Advance in Science and Medicine

The early Egyptians made significant progress in mathematics. They were familiar with the elementary mathematics like addition, subtraction, multiplication, division and fraction. All these helped them in maintaining their accounts. They knew how to calculate the area of triangles and rectangles. All this knowledge enabled them to measure their lands accurately.

They gained considerable knowledge in fields like architecture and engineering and without these they would not have been able to build pyramids, temples and tombs.

It is surprising to note that they made conspicuous progress in the field of medicine and surgery. The early Egyptian Physicians gained a fair knowledge about various diseases by studying their symptoms, and prescribed remedies for each. The *Ebers Payrus* refers to 700 remedies in all including prescription of castor oil and other drugs. Imhotep, adviser to King Zoser (and also the architect of the first pyramid) became quite popular as a great physician of his times.

The early Egyptians went a step further and performed setting of bone-fractures and surgery. The 'Edwin Smith Papyrus' clearly shows the progress made in the science of surgery (48 surgical operations) by Egyptian doctors.

When their medicines failed to cure, the patients turned to the witch-doctor for help, or magical remedies. The early Egyptians knew the secret of embalming dead persons. One can see the Egyptian mummies even to this day.

The world is deeply indebted to them not only for their contribution to civilisation but also for their excellent arts and crafts. Their paintings, beautiful jewellery, pottery, musical instruments, fine linen-cloth, weapons and tools, enchanting glassware and excellent sea-going vessels have evoked our great admiration. Much of what they did influenced others like the Hebrews, Greeks and Phoenicians.

Lesson Review

1. Explain the progress made by early Egyptians in the following:
   (a) Administration (b) Art and Architecture
   (c) Literature (d) Science
   (e) Society (f) Economic life
   (g) Religion.
2. Write a note on the following in not more than *five* sentences:
   (a) Queen Hatshepsut (b) King Thutmose III
   (c) Akhnaton (d) The Great Pyramid
   (e) Sphinx (f) Rosetta stone.
3. Draw a map of Egypt with the river Nile on it and locate the following places:
   (a) Memphis (b) Gizeh
   (c) Thebes.

5
MESOPOTAMIA OR THE FERTILE CRESCENT

Geographical Factors
From the mountains of Asia Minor flow great rivers, the Tigris and Euphrates, in southerly direction and finally join the Persian Gulf. Long time ago, this Tigris-Euphrates valley was called Mesopotamia by the ancient Greeks, and by others as the Land of the Shinar and the Fertile Crescent. It was here that a great civilisation was born around 3500 BC. The flood waters of these two great rivers deposited a layer of fertile soil each year thus making it fit for large-scale agriculture. The availability of fine clay enabled many craftsmen to make beautiful pots. The soil was suited for making building materials like sun-dried bricks with which the immigrants began to build houses. Unlike Egypt, this valley did not have natural barriers, which could afford protection to the inhabitants from the invasions of foreigners. However, in its long history, this fertile valley attracted hordes of immigrants and invaders.

The Sumerians
The Sumerians belonged probably to the Indo-European group. They were the first settlers who occupied the land very near to the Persian Gulf which they called Sumer. The Sumerians (meaning blackheaded people) reclaimed the lands in their region after draining the marshes and brought it under cultivation. They cultivated wheat and barley and reared cattle, oxen, and donkeys to help them. The Sumerians were also known for their craftsmanship. They made beautiful pots and vessels of alabaster. They also made exquisite ornaments of silver and gold. They excelled in painting and sculpture.

They invented the metal plough which helped farmers in ploughing the land easily. They invented a system of writing called cuneiform (wedge-shaped writing). As they had no paper to write on, they used clay tablets on which wedge-shaped marks were made with a sharp reed. Thousands of these clay tablets have been discovered which reveal the history of the people. The cuneiform writing consisted of 400 symbols.

The Sumerians knew how to reckon time. They introduced the system of counting in sixties. They used it for measuring the time, a thing (like sixty seconds make a minute and sixty minutes make an hour) which has come down to us. Another popular unit was the number 12. They maintained regular account of their transactions of business and kept records of tax receipts. They also made progress in engineering science and architecture. The Sumerian builders were the first to use the arch in construction after working out the principle of the keystone. They used the wheel for making pots and for running their carts and chariots.

Like the early Egyptians, the Sumerians worshipped many nature gods and built temples on mounds and hills in their honour. These temples called Ziggurats look like very small pyramids with an ascending staircase in the middle leading to a tower where the idol of God was located. Each city had a patron God. People brought food and animals to the temples to offer them as sacrifice. The priests helped them in conducting prayers and rituals. The priests commanded great respect for they were thought to be representatives of God.

Sumerian City-States
Unlike ancient Egyptians who were united under a strong monarchy, the Sumerians developed independent city-states which were governed by *patesis*, i.e., priest-kings. The most prominent among their city-states were Ur, Kish, Karsa, Lagash and Erech. According to the Holy Bible, Ur was the native city of the Hebrew prophet, Abraham.

A Ziggurat reconstructed

Besides their religious functions, the priest-kings supervised revenue collection, irrigation, construction of public buildings and tower-temples (*Ziggurat*) with the assistance of the nobles. The main temple with its tier-terraces was full of markets, banks, factories, and store-houses of food-grains. Thus, the whole economic life of the people was centred in the tower temple. Standard weights and measurements and money economy were in vogue.

Decline and Fall of Sumerian Kingdoms

The Sumerian city-states were constantly waging wars with one another. Floods often caused heavy damage to these city-states. Added to these two, their country had no physical barriers to prevent the onrush of foreign hordes. So their kingdoms were easily conquered by the most powerful semitic king of the Akkad, Sargon I. The whole of Mesopotamia was unified around 2600 BC by this ruler whose subjects adopted the Sumerian culture. After Sargon's death, his empire did not last long. It witnessed frequent attacks by barbarians coming from the desert regions. It was also weakened due to frequent internal rebellions.

Babylonian Empire Under Hammurabi (1792 BC-1750 BC)

About 2000 BC, Mesopotamia witnessed the rise of another Semitic tribe called the Amorites which had settled in Babylon, a city on the banks of the Euphrates river. Babylon became the most famous capital city under the sixth Amorite ruler, King Hammurabi. So the Amorites were called as the Babylonians. Under Hammurabi's leadership, the Babylonians conquered the whole of Mesopotamia and enjoyed a long spell of peace and prosperity. Historians have considered his age as the "Golden Age" in the history of Mesopotamia.

Code of Hammurabi

Hammurabi is chiefly remembered by us for two things, namely, his code of laws and its just and humane administration. A legend says that he received the code of laws from the Sun God Shamash. The Hammurabian code included some of the wise laws of the Sumerians, Akkadians and the Amorites. It contains 285 sections pertaining to civil and criminal laws, all expressed in a simple language covering subjects like marriage, property, debts, thefts, wages, contracts, banking, public morality and murder. From our point of view, his laws are known for their extreme harshness and iniquity. His laws also gave due recognition to women's rights. His code, which is considered as a crowning achievement has earned him the title, "the world's first great legal genius".

His earnestness to gear up the administrative machinery in order to achieve the welfare of his subjects has earned him encomiums from the historians. His fifty-five letters (in the form of clay tablets) addressed to the governors of the provinces reveal his curiosity to know administrative details as well as his interest in the welfare of his subjects.

After the death of Hammurabi, his Babylonian empire fell after the attacks of the barbarians called the Kassites. The Kassites held Mesopotamia under their control for nearly six centuries.

Hittite Conquest

After the Kassite conquest of Mesopotamia, there followed the attack on Babylon by another most powerful and civilised group, namely, the Hittites of the Asia Minor. The Hittites were the first to know how to make use of iron. Their army was equipped with sharp and strong weapons like swords and spears made of iron which enabled them to easily overpower their enemies. They conquered the middle part of Mesopotamia but did not rule it for long. Their long conflict with the early Egyptians exhausted all their energies.

Assyrian Conquest

Near the homeland of the Hittites lived another highly war-like community called the Assyrians. As their country was exposed to constant attack by the enemies, they learnt the art of self-defence and developed a new method of warfare. The Assyrians were extremely cruel by nature and believed in terror tactics. They learnt the use of iron to make superior weapons, and their commanders planned carefully the conduct of war before the actual attack on the enemies. They invented a battering ram tipped with iron to destroy the enemy's outer city fort wall. The chief centers of Assyrian power were Assur and Nineveh which lay on the banks of the River Tigris.

Their Military Glory

The Assyrians rose to great heights of power under the leadership of their powerful kings like Tiglethpileser III, Sargon II, and Sennacherib. The first king conquered Babylon around the middle of the eighth century BC, and further extended his authority over Syria after the fall of its capital, Damascus. The second king captured Israel's capital Samaria where many citizens were taken as captives and whose (The lost Ten Tribes) fate nobody ever knew. The third ruler, Sennacherib, reconquered Israel, captured the coastal cities of Asia Minor, and attacked Jerusalem, the capital of the kingdom of Judah. He failed to capture it because plague broke out in his military camp and the Jews believed that it was an act of God. When a revolt broke out in Babylon Sennacherib destroyed that city and shifted the seat of his capital to Nineveh.

The glories of Assyrian culture might have been totally forgotten but for the effort made by the scholar-king, Assurbanipal, who carefully preserved the records in his famous library. His reign is described as the golden age.

Assyrian Contributions
The Assyrians built and ruled over a large empire which extended from the Persian Gulf to Egypt along the Fertile Crescent. Their love of war and capacity to organise the administration on sound lines have earned them the nickname, "Romans of Asia". Their capital, Nineveh, became a truly cosmopolitan city attracting a large number of merchants from all over the world. Its markets, banks and trade brought prosperity to the people. The Assyrian Emperors established a postal system which enabled them to receive reports of their governors from newly conquered countries. Their emperors encouraged agriculture and industries. Cotton plants were imported from India to start cotton growing as an industry. With the exception of Assurbanipal, the others paid hardly any attention to learning. He was highly educated in subjects like science and literature. His love of learning made him open a library in the capital with books (clay tablets) on contemporary religions and science.

The Fall of Assyrians (612 BC)
The last days of Assurbanipal's reign witnessed continuous trouble and disturbances. The revolt of Babylonia was suppressed with difficulty. After his death, the Assyrian power collapsed because the Medes and the Persians attacked it from the north and the Chaldeans from the south. Later the Chaldeans and the Medes attacked and destroyed Nineveh in 612 BC.

The New Babylonian Empire
The Assyrian Empire was divided into two parts, and Nobopolassar, the Chaldean victor, received his share, which included Mesopotamia, Syria, and Cyaxares. He began to rule from Babylon, the seat of his new capital. It was rebuilt and the Chaldeans came to be known as the new Babylonians. Nobopolassar's son, Nebuchadnezzar, was undoubtedly the greatest among the Chaldean rulers. His glorious reign was full of wars. The first was directed against the small kingdoms in the west, which were backed by Egypt. After defeating them, he turned his wrath against the Egyptians and defeated them in Carchemish. He later conquered the Phoenician cities (excluding Tyre). Then the Jews caused trouble for him. He attacked and destroyed Jerusalem and took thousands of Jews as captives to his capital.

Under Nebuchadnezzar, Babylon became the most beautiful city in the world. With its Hanging Garden, the newly built Marduk temple, and the strong outer wall surrounding the city, it truly became great cultural and commercial capital of the world. Nebuchadnezzar also built a bridge, probably the first in history, across the river Euphrates. Under this great ruler, art and science made a high degree of progress. Astrology and Astronomy received much attention. The people believed in the influence of stars on human life. The Chaldean astronomers prepared a number of astronomical charts and predicted eclipses. Again, they made rapid advance in the study of medicine. Their doctors prescribed "five hundred and fifty different kinds of drugs" for general use.

Persian Invasion (539 BC)

The successors of Nebuchadnezzar lacked ability and capacity to rule over a large empire. The wealth of Babylon, and the weakness of the new rulers, tempted the Persians to attack Babylon. In 539 BC the Persians captured and destroyed Babylon, and all its wealth was carried away.

Lesson Review

1. Write a note on the contribution of Sumerians in Mesopotamian civilisation.
2. On the outline map, show the boundaries of the empire of King Hammurabi.
3. Locate the following towns on the map of Mesopotamia:
   (a) Babylon   (b) Assur
   (c) Nippur   (d) Susa
   (e) Akkad   (f) The rivers Tigris and Euphrates.
   (g) Nineveh.

6
LEGACY OF BABYLONIA

The Babylonian civilisation blossomed during the time of Hammurabi. He was the first to build an empire in Mesopotamia and govern it efficiently with his code of laws, a sign of civilised state. From modern point of view, his laws were severe and harsh, for it prescribed heavy penalties for the guilty even for petty offences. However, more benign aspects of the code included certain rights for women, contractual obligations, and safeguards of public morality. One salient principle included in the criminal code was the distinction made between the premeditated crime and accidental crime and it is no surprise that we have adopted this principle in our modern code. The code provided for the dispensation of justice to the poor.

The Babylonians, like their contemporaries, had full faith in the efficacy of a strong monarchy. The divine origin of their kings was hardly challenged. A shaft of stone rising to eight feet in height discovered at Susa in 1901 contains the picture of Hammurabi receiving the code of laws from the Sun God.

Hammurabi divided his empire into number of provinces and appointed able governors to administer them efficiently. He always kept himself in touch with these governors through his letters—fifty-five of these in the form of clay tablets were discovered. Some of these letters show his keen interest in the welfare of the governed. He built a big canal and improved the irrigation system in order to help the farmers to grow more food and vegetables. Date-palm was cultivated. The people reared flocks of sheep and goats. They used oxen and camels for transport purpose.

Economic Life

The code of Hammurabi gives an insight into the high state of commerce that had existed in Babylon, the seat of Hammurabi's capital. In the early days a kind of barter system developed. Later, it was replaced by the use of fixed weights and measures. The only coinage was silver lumps of fixed weights and in standard shapes. The city temples became centers of business with a number of banks, shops and markets located in its premises. A loan normally carried 20 per cent rate of interest. Taxes to the government were paid in kind and the temples contained warehouses to store foodgrains. Merchants came from neighbouring countries to Babylon to sell their products in its street markets. Thus, it became a centre of international commerce. The steadily growing commerce required a system of keeping accounts. Professional accountants were appointed by traders and businessmen who were well-versed in the cuneiform writing. The discovery of private-letters, royal edicts and business contracts show a glimpse of the economic life of that great city.

Society

The Babylonian society could be broadly divided into three classes. The first was composed of the ruling class like the king and his family, priests, nobles, officers and rich merchants. The middle class included artisans, peasants, shopkeepers and other freemen. The lowest class was that of slaves. They were mostly prisoners of war and brought from conquered countries. Slaves were better off in Babylonia because they enjoyed certain rights such as owning of property, marrying with freemen, and right to buy their freedom with their savings. The Code of Hammurabi favoured the upper classes, for it imposed harsh penalties if crimes were committed against them. Correspondingly similar crimes committed against the slaves were let off with light punishment. During the age of Hammurabi women enjoyed rights such as owning and disposing of property and freedom to pursue the profession of their choice. They were also given the right to divorce. Widows were protected. But the code prescribed desertion if a woman happened to neglect her house and husband.

Religion

Religion played an important role in the lives of the people. The priestly class enjoyed a position of status for they considered themselves as agents of gods. The principal God of the Sumerians, *Enlil,* was relegated to the background, and the Babylonians worshipped *Marduk* as their supreme God besides others like *Ishtar* (mother of gods and also goddess of love) and *Tammuz* (God of Vegetation). At the time of the Chaldeans or the new Babylonians, seven main gods (the sun, the moon and five other planets) came to be worshipped in rotation based on the principle of each god a day—like the Sun God on the first day (called Sunday), and the Moon God on the second day (Monday) etc.

Babylonian cities were full of temples, and the capital itself had at one time 53 temples, 55 shrines and 180 altars for different Gods and minor deities. The priests offered prayers and sacrifices on behalf of their clientele and predicted the future after looking at the livers of sacrificed animals and at the stars. They gave talismans (metallic image of gods) to ward off evil spirits. The people were superstitious and developed faith in magical remedies.

Architecture and Art

The most imposing buildings in the Babylonian cities were the Ziggurats and the palaces. The construction of Ziggurats began during the days of Sumerians. The Ziggurats were tower temples built in the form of small pyramids but divided by tower-terraces at each stage. On the top of this structure stood the main shrine. One of their famous Ziggurats rose to a height of 650 ft. It was built in seven stages. A large number of seals, a few sculptures, and their decorations on the brick walls reveal their artistic achievements.

Learning and Literature

The Babylonians took pride in learning and one of their tablets says that "he who shall excel in tablet writing shall shine like the sun". Most of the schools were attached to the temples where the students learnt cuneiform reading, 350 signs writing, arithmetic, keeping of accounts and religious literature.

The literature that has survived relating to the Babylonians is historical and mythological. The most famous is *The Story of Gilgamesh,* an epic which mentions, among other things, about the creation of this world and the great flood. There are other copy books which contain moral sayings.

Sciences

As mentioned earlier, the Sumerians had left behind them their legacy in science. Their interest in astronomy resulted in the making of a lunar-calendar. Their invention of writing, and the division of hour into sixty minutes and each minute into sixty seconds, enabled the Babylonians to make considerable progress in astronomy. Along with astronomy, astrology also developed. The Chaldeans or the new Babylonians made rapid progress in astronomy. The Chaldean kings encouraged the development of science by building observatories for astronomers. All astronomical observations including the eclipses were duly recorded. The two great astronomers who lived during the days of Chaldeans were Naburimannu and Kidinnu. The Chalean engineers created a wonder when they built a hanging garden on the terraced roof of the royal palace and supplied water through hydraulic pumps.

Recently discovered ancient tablets belonging to Babylonian period indicate advanced state of mathematics in this region.

The Babylonian civilisation, in spite of numerous wars, flourished for centuries till it was overthrown by Medes and, the Persians about the middle of sixth century BC.

PERSIAN EMPIRE

One of the earliest empires to reach great heights in the ancient world belonged to the Persians. Today Persia is called Iran, a name given to it by the ancient Aryans. Persia's earliest inhabitants in history were Armenoid mountain people. It was around 1000 BC that their culture was influenced by the new conquerors, the Indo-Aryans.

Cyrus the Great (550 BC-529 BC)

It was during the sixth century BC the Persians reached great heights of power. One of her earliest kings, Cyaxares united the Medes (descendants of the Aryans) of the north and the Persians of the south. It was Cyrus the Great who welded the people into a nation. It was due to his untiring efforts that a large empire could be built and wisely governed. After coming to power in 550 BC he conquered Lydia and set the Jews free in Babylonia. Cyrus was known for his religious tolerance and the temple of Jerusalem was rebuilt at his orders. At the time of his death his archaemenid empire was largely composed of territories of not only Persia but also the former kingdom of Assyria, Lydia and the Asia Minor. The borders touched the Mediterranean in the west and the Hindukush mountains in the east. Cyrus's greatness not only rests on his military exploits but also on his great generosity to the conquered subjects. Religious and cultural tolerance became the basic tenets of his public policy.

Darius I (521 BC-486 BC)

Cambyses II, successor of Cyrus, was noted for his wild temper, extreme cruelty and religious intolerance. He succeeded in conquering Egypt but failed to retain it for long. His death followed this event. The next ruler was Darius I who succeeded to the throne after eliminating his rivals. He was undoubtedly the greatest among the Persian rulers. During the early years of his rule the empire witnessed numerous revolts in the conquered states. With a firm hand he quelled these revolts. After some thought he wisely decided not to embitter the feelings of his conquered subjects by ruthless persecutions but to govern them efficiently. He divided the empire into 20 satrapies and appointed able and wise rulers to govern them. To maintain the integrity and solidarity of the empire his subjects were given religious and cultural freedom. Soon he knit the empire with a network of

Legacy of Babylonia

roads and numerous staging posts for transport and communication respectively. His long reign witnessed the introduction of coinage, postage, communication and irrigation systems. He succeeded in all his projects the only exception being the defeat of his soldiers by the ancient Greeks at Marathon (490 BC). His son Xerxes continued the war with Greeks and defeated them at Thermopylae. In the long run the war with the Greeks resulted in a series of defeats for the Persians. The Empire began to decline under Darius II and Darius III. The latter was assassinated soon after his defeat at the hands of Alexander the Great. The revival of the Persian empire was seen when the Parthians and Sassanids came to power one after the other.

Zarathustra and Zoroastrianism in Persia

During the sixth century BC Persia witnessed the birth of a great religion called Zoroastrianism. Its founder Zarathustra advocated monotheism and urged his followers to worship the almighty God Ahura Mazda who is omnipresent and omnipotent.

Lesson Review

1. Sketch briefly the legacy of Babylonia under the following headings:
   (a) Administration (b) Art and Architecture
   (c) Learning and literature (d) Science.
2. Write a note on the achievements of Persian Emperor Darius I.

7
THE HEBREWS (OR JEWS)

The history of ancient Hebrews or Jews comes to us from their most important work, the Bible. The Hebrews belonged to one of the semitic tribes living in Mesopotamia around 2000 BC. Their great patriarch, Abraham, led his tribe from Ur to the Mediterranean coat-region called Palestine around 1400 BC. They considered this region as their "Promised Land" by God Jehovah. When their land was affected by a severe drought during the 13th century BC, the Hebrews were forced to leave and settle in northern Egypt. The new Pharaohs of ancient Egypt enslaved the Hebrews till Moses came to their rescue. It is not clearly known whether Moses an official in Egypt was a Hebrew or not. He told the suffering Hebrews that God had told him in a vision to deliver the children of Israel (namely Hebrews) from their captivity in Egypt and lead them to the "Promised Land".

Led by Moses, the Hebrews escaped from Egypt and reached Mount Sinai. It was there that Moses received that Ten Commandments from God. The people reached the "Promised Land" and settled. Around 1000 BC, their king, Saul, built a kingdom after many wars and united his people. After his death, his son-in law David succeeded in uniting all the Hebrew tribes. He captured Jerusalem and made it his capital. He encouraged commerce with the neighbouring countries. King David was a poet and many of the Psalms in the Old Testament were composed by him. David's son was Solomon who gave up simple living and liked luxury. He taxed the people heavily to collect funds for building his palace and a big temple in Jerusalem. After his death, the Hebrew kingdom got split into two parts, the northern part called Israel and the southern part Judah. During the next few centuries, these kingdoms did not live in peace. However, Israel grew prosperous with more people living in big towns and cities. In the southern kingdom of Judah, the people lived in villages and led a simple life. A great Hebrew prophet, Amos, went to the Kingdom of Israel and appealed to its subjects to return to simple ways of living and

The Hebrews (Or Jews)

belief in one God. *Yahweh*. He predicted a catastrophe for Israel which may come from outside. His prediction came true for Israel was attacked and conquered by the Assyrians in 722 BC and many of the inhabitants were taken away as captives. The kingdom of Judah was spared. However, this kingdom was also attacked and conquered by the Chaldean king, Nebuchadnezzar, in 586 BC. The city of Jerusalem was destroyed and many of its inhabitants were taken as captives to Babylonia.

Ethical Monotheism

Unlike their contemporaries, the Hebrews believed very firmly in the existence of one God, whom they called *Yahweh*. Their great prophets, Samuel, Amos Hosea, Micah and Isaiah preached the unity of God, which is sometimes known as "Ethical Monotheism." They believed that God made universal moral laws for all people to obey. The Ten Commandments did much to infuse in them standards of individual morality. They gave the world their greatest literary works, the Bible, and the code of laws, the Talmud.

Lesson Review

Write a note on the Hebrews in not more than 10 sentences under the following headings:

(a) Early settlements
(b) Moses
(c) Saul and David
(d) Solomon
(e) Hebrew religion

8
PHOENICIANS

On the eastern shores of the Mediterranean sea and just above Palestine, lies a strip of land which was once known as Phoenicia. As their land was infertile and their expansion to the east blocked by the Lebanese mountains, the early Phoenicians took up trading on both land and by sea. They built city states on the coast like Tyre, Sidon, Byblos, Ugarit and Beirut around 1500 BC. Early in their history, the Phoenicians learnt to build ships from the wood of the cedar trees. They also set sail on the Mediterranean and travelled to the other side. In the course of time, they set up colonies and exchanged goods with other countries. They sold timber, metals, ships, glass and cloth and bought gold, ivory, corn and livestock. They carried the goods of other people from Asia to Egypt, Greece, and other islands in the Mediterranean.

Cities Paid Tributes
As they did not have a unified kingdom, they could not resist the demands of powerful neighbours like the Egyptians and the Assyrians. The pharaohs of ancient Egypt and the Assyrian emperors exacted tributes from the Phoenician cities. The Persian Emperor, Cyrus the Great, annexed Phoenicia into his growing empire. After the defeat of the Persians by Alexander, Phoenicia became a part of his empire (333 BC).

Phoenicians built a chain of trading stations and colonies along the coast of the Mediterranean from the 12th century BC, and subsequently became prosperous on account of their flourishing trade. As they moved from one country to the other to exchange goods, they became familiar with the culture of each country. Eventually, they spread ideas and cultures for which they were described as "carriers and missionaries of culture".

Phoenician Alphabet
They spoke a semitic language. They evolved their writing which had an alphabet of 22 consonants. Their script influenced the ancient Greeks and the Romans.

Their Colonies
The Phoenicians built colonies among which Palermo in Sicily, Gades in Spain, Utica and Carthage in North Africa became important.

Their Great Voyages
Of their great expeditions on the uncharted seas, mention must be made of the adventures of Hanno and his men as given in a carthagian work, *The Periplus of Hanno*. Hanno and his men sailed in sixty ships around 520 BC from the Straits of Gibraltar towards the south along the coast of Western Africa and reached the shores of Liberia. Another Phoenician sea voyage round Africa which took nearly three years to complete is described by the Greek historian, Herodotus. Phoenicians were also known to have sailed upto Cornwall (Britain).

Lesson Review
1. Who were the Phoenicians? What were their important contributions to world culture?
2. On the outline maps supplied to you locate the important colonies of the Phoenicians. And locate the following centers:
   (a) Byblus   (b) Sidon
   (c) Tyre   (d) Mark the trade routes.

9
INDUS VALLEY CIVILISATION

The discovery of Indus Valley Civilisation in 1922 was of great significance to the world in general and India in particular. To India it added a new chapter to her history. As a result she could rightly be proud of having produced a civilisation which is as old as that of ancient Egypt or Mesopotamia.

Excavation work mostly carried on in the Punjab, Sind and Baluchistan has revealed that the Indus culture—always known as Harappan culture—has spread over an area of 1200×700 miles. Of more than 140 sites discovered so far, three are of great importance. They are Mohenjodaro on the banks of the Indus, Harappa on the banks of Ravi and Lothal on the Kathiawar coast. The discoveries in these three important sites revealed the extent of urbanity achieved by its inhabitants. In the absence of written records (the script on the seals is yet to be deciphered) it would be premature to draw inferences or conclusions. Even then the noted archaeologists and historians have been giving accounts of the culture of the people.

Date of Harappan Culture
The antiquity of this civilisation has been engaging the attention of great archaeologists and scholars for quite some time. A few have ventured to suggest tentative dates as to when this civilisation must have flourished. A few Harappan seals found in Mesopotamian sites, dating back to King Sargon of Agade (Akkad) made scholars like Dr. Wheelers fix the chronology of this civilisation to about 2500-1500 B.C. Sir Johan Marshall has given a much earlier date, that is 3250-2750 B.C., taking into consideration the striking similarities between Indus and Sumerian cultures. The radio-carbon dating test conducted at the Tata Institute on Harappan culture revealed that the civilisation was flourishing around 3000 BC.

Founders
Probably the most important issue that comes up every time in our study is regarding the founders. Were they foreigners or Aryans or Dravidians?

After examining a few skulls at the sites, scholars are of the opinion that the Indus people belonged to a mixed stock—proto-Austroloid, Mediterranean, Alpine, and Mongoliod. The present South-Indian population belong to the first two elements generally. Similarities have been found between Harappan religion and Dravidian religion. So all these indications have made some scholars believe that Dravidians founded the Harappan culture. There are strong indications to show that the Harappan culture was essentially native in character.

To have a glimpse of their achievements, one should observe their ruined cities and other relics.

A few scholars believe that Harappa and Mohenjodaro were once the twin capitals of the Indus civilisation. These two, cities, located 400 miles from each other, show similar features. While Mohenjodaro appears to be well preserved, Harappa is in a state of utter ruin, and sometimes the features are beyond recognition.

Mohenjodaro
One of the conspicuous features of the city of Mohenjodaro is its town-planning. Systematic town-planning must have preceded before the construction of the city. The city could boast of straight streets running due north and south and east and west with each other bisecting at right angles. Some of the broad streets (34 feet in width) run for nearly half a mile. The roads are paved. The houses are of varying sizes and built of burnt bricks with mud and mortar as binding materials. Stones have not been used for construction purpose. In each house there were rooms, a kitchen and a bathroom. The bathroom was constructed nearest to the street so that the waste water drain is directly connected to the main drainage-system of the city. Each house was well-supplied with water from a bricklined well. Most of the houses had an upper storey connected by a narrow staircase.

Drainage System
One of the unique features of Mohenjodaro city is found in its elaborate drainage system. It is a fact that no other city in the world at that time had such an excellent drainage system. Each street and bylane had well-paved drains on either side which collected waste water from each house. The drains were laid well below the street level and the waste water of the big city was flushed into the Indus river.

The Great Bath

Towards the west of this city lay the citadelmound and a few public buildings. One of the most prominent of these is the Great Bath (180'×108') which contains a swimming pool (39'×23'×8'). This swimming pool is surrounded by thick walls, wide verandahs and small bathrooms. On all sides of the pool there were steps. Provisions were made to drain all the dirty water from the pool regularly and fresh water brought in.

The other structures are the granary and a college. The former served as a warehouse for storing foodgrains and the latter was probably used as a meeting place of public officials. One may say that the whole city was well-maintained by the municipal authorities by supplying water, constructing public-wells, dustbins to throw garbage, providing street-lights and excellent drainage system.

Socio-Economic Life

In many respects the people living in the cities must have enjoyed quite a luxurious life as can be surmised through some of their relics. Their daily food consisted of beef, mutton, pork, fish, corn-products, vegetables, fruits and milk. The discovery of a large number of spindle-whorls testifies to the fact that they generally wore stitched cotton garments. Men used a *shawl* or *chadar* which was drawn over the left shoulder, and a *dhoti* to cover the lower part of the body. They kept short beards and whiskers and sometimes shaved the hair on the upper lip. They kept long hair and combed it backwards regularly. Sometimes they coiled it into a knot on the top of the head.

Women seemed to have enjoyed freedom and status in the society. Many of them were fond of fashions and luxuries as can be seen from the articles they used. They kept themselves beautiful by using a wide variety of toilet and cosmetic articles. Their toilet table contained bronze-mirrors, ivory combs of different shapes, lipsticks (Chanhu-daro finds), collyrium, face-paint, powder, hair-wash. They were familiar with different hair-styles.

Along with cosmetic articles, the women of Indus adorned themselves with a wide variety of ornaments. Wealthy women wore ornaments of gold silver, ivory, faience and precious stones. Their ornaments consisted of necklaces, girdles, finger-rings, girdles, nose-studs, earrings, bangles and anklets. The poor were happy with ornaments which were made of shell, bone, copper and terracotta. Ornaments, like necklaces, were made of different types of beads and they were in great demand. The wearing of ornaments was not confined to womenfolk only but the male members of the family also wore them. The toilet articles of male members such as

Indus Valley Civilisation

The Great Bath

ivory combs and razors were also discovered. Even dressing tables with bronze mirrors were found.

Amusement

A number of playthings such as a game-board with dice pieces, marbles balls and other things belonging to the children like the toys were discovered at the sites. So one can say that a crude game of chess was probably the most popular form of pastime. We may also say that the children were not neglected as can be surmised from a number of playthings and toys of children. Other forms of pastime of the elders were the bull-fighting and hunting of wild animals.

Rural Economy

To feed the vast population residing in a number of cities, large-scale cultivation of food grains must have been undertaken. While the Indus population showed urban characteristics and bias, considerable size of rural population lived in the surrounding villages with agriculture as their main occupation. Besides, they kept livestock, raised poultry and looked after the dairy. They sent cartloads of wheat, barley, cotton and datepalm to the cities for sale.

Urban Economy

In the cities like Mohenjodaro and Harappa several industries including the home-spun cloth developed. There were professional classes like the potters, carpenters, masons, jewellers, ivory-workers, goldsmiths, weavers, blacksmiths and dyers. Among these the potters no doubt take much credit for producing beautifully decorated pots. Most of the pots were wheel-turned. Polychrome pottery (painted in several colours) was also discovered at Amti, 70 miles south of Mohenjodaro. The potters also made big jars for storage of foodgrains and other things. Chanhu-daro must have also become a great centre of pottery and terracotta toys for children.

The Indus craftsmen showed their great skill by producing beautiful copper and bronze vessels, household utensils, objects and ornaments, and bronze figurines. A little bronze-figure of a dancing girl exhibits their remarkable craftsmanship. Indus craftsmen achieved remarkable success in lapidary work. They produced artistically made stone-beads, especially of agate and carnelian.

Trade and Commerce

There is undoubtedly some evidence to prove that many people in the cities were engaged in trade and commerce. They used bullock-driven cart as a means of transport to carry goods from one city to another. Inland

Indus Valley Civilisation

trade was flourishing. Besides, the Indus traders had developed commerce with many countries of West Asia, Crete, and Egypt. There is good deal of evidence to show that the Indus people maintained commercial relations with the Sumerians. Lothal must have served as the most important port of Indus people to carry on maritime trade. It had also a dockyard where ships were built for overseas trade. Some Indus seals were discovered in the ruined cities of Sumeria.

Seals

In what connection seals were used for trade purpose is not yet known. The Indus seals are square in shape and made of steatite. More than 2000 seals have been found. They must have been used by the consignors to seal the packed goods before sending them to the proper destination. They might have been used by the customs authorities also.

The carvings on the seals include human beings, divinities, animals, composite figures, and mythological figures. Some seals contain secular scenes such as a man attacking a buffalo.

Religion

In the absence of any temple found as such, our ideas about their religion are mostly derived from the seals stone-statuaries and some terracotta figurines. A large number of terracotta figurines of a female elaborately decorated with a crescent-shaped head-dress have been found in many Indus cities. So, it is assumed that these figurines represent the Mother Goddess. To substantiate further, another seal from Harappa contains a scene depicting a human sacrifice being offered to the Goddess Earth. Many historians believe that the Shakti cult was then very popular, particularly during the pre-Aryan age. Numerous seals from Harappa and Mohenjodaro contain the representation of the Male God. The most common among them was that of a God with three faces seated on a platform in a yogic pose with a trident and surrounded by a few animals. Scholars believe that he is the prototype of the later Indian Lord Shiva. Again, the discovery of many cylindrical and conical stone pieces which look like *Shivalinga*, has confirmed the view that Shiva-worship was common. The Indus people must have worshipped a number of semi-human and semi-bovine Gods. The worship of a number of mythical animals, snakes, and sacred trees like the papal and neem, was in vogue. The representation of *Swastik* and the wheel also suggest the worship of the Sun God. The people offered animal sacrifices. The discovery of sacrificial altars of a square shape suggest offerings to Fire God.

Funereal Customs
The disposal of their dead was done in three forms, namely, complete burial, fractional burial and post-cremation burial. The first involved the burial of the whole body with other articles such as pots and offerings in a pit. The second involved the burial of the bones and skull of the dead person, all placed in a big urn with other objects. The third refers to the collection of the ashes and bones of the dead and placing it in an urn along with other articles and burying it underneath the floor of a house. A few cemeteries were found in Harappa and Lothal.

Defence
Harappa which lies on the bed of river Ravi is known for its fortification and a citadel. It appears that the city was well-fortified to prevent the invasions of foreigners. Mortimer Wheeler, after seeing the granaries, barracks and working platforms of Harappa, observed that they constitute "an example of cantonment-planning significantly within the shadow of the citadel". A large number of weapons such as axes, spears, daggers, stone-maces, slings, swords, bows and arrows indicate that they were acquainted with the art of warfare. It should be noted that the weapons of war were made of copper and bronze. Looking at the kinds of weapons used and the metals of which they were made, it is observed that the Indus people were unwarlike in character.

Secular Outlook
A noted archaeologist, S.R. Rao, is of the opinion that the Indus people "were pioneers in founding an empire even before the establishment of the Sargonid Empire in Mesopotamia," and in all probability it was "administered by a benevolent ruler with a secular outlook."

Due credit should be given to the rulers for introducing a uniform system of civic administration, town-planning, public sanitation, enforcement of regulation of trade, introduction of weights and measures and standardisation of all products suitable for internal and international trade.

Contributions
Among the notable contributions they made were the Indus script, tolerance towards religious practices in their empire, their art and craft as seen on the seals, clay models and ornaments, and finally to the science of yoga.

Decline of Indus Civilisation
Much speculation has been made on the decline and fall of this great civilisation. Of the many popular theories concerning this, one many accept

Indus Valley Civilisation

that natural calamities such as widespread flood, shifting of the monsoons and soil-erosion as contributing factors for its decline.

Lesson Review

1. Discuss the principal features of the Indus Valley Civilisation.
2. Describe the Socio-economic life of the Indus people.
3. After demarcating the boundaries of the Indus Valley Civilisation, locate at least five centres discovered showing Harappan civilisation.
4. Write a short note on the following:
   (a) Seals; (b) Indus Pottery;
   (c) Trade and Commerce.

10

VEDIC CIVILISATION

The founders of the Vedic Civilisation were the Indo-Aryans. It is generally agreed that the early Aryan tribes had originally lived somewhere in western part of Asia. Aryan 'invasion' of India has taken a controversial twist in recent years. They left their original homeland due to many causes such as the dearth of grassy lands for feeding their cattle, increase in their population, climatic changes and curiosity to visit new lands. Thus, large-scale migrations of Indo-Europeans (Aryans) took place around 2500 BC. One of their branches moved towards Europe and the other towards Iran. Those Aryans who lived in Iran were called as Indo-Iranians. However, another big batch of Aryans moved farther east and reached India. They are called as the Indo-Aryans. The fact that the Indo-Aryans were in some way related to the other branch of Aryan family ruling over some parts of Mesopotamia (Mittanis and Kassites) is revealed after an inscription was discovered in Boghozkoi (Asia-Minor). The Mittanis of Upper Euphrates and the Kassites of Babylonia worshipped Aryan Gods such as *Indra, Varuna, Mitra and Nasatyas.*

Aryan Wars and Settlements
Their early entry into India (around 2000 BC) was opposed by the native inhabitants (most probably Dravidians) resulting in wars. The Rigveda mentions numerous battles fought between the early Aryans and the *Dasyus*. Furthermore, the Rigveda describes how the Aryans destroyed the numerous towns and forts belonging to the *Dasyus* before making their settlements in the *Sapta-Sindhu* region (the Punjab). The process of Aryanisation of the sapta-sindhu region was gradual because the wars with the local inhabitants were continuing for a long time. However, those who were defeated got absorbed into the Aryan population.

The Vedic Literature
Much of our knowledge about the Aryans is derived from the four Vedas. The earliest and most important among them was the Rigveda. The

Vedic Civilisation 51

language in which it is written is commonly known as Sanskrit. According to a few reputed scholars, its composition must have been completed about 1500-1200 BC. The Rigveda is considered by many scholars as a great "source-book" for the study and appreciation of the development of Hindu culture. The *Rigveda Samhita* was followed by *Yajur Veda Samhita, Sama* and *Atharva Vedas*. While *Rig Veda Samhita* is a collection of 1017 hymns divided into ten *mandalas,* Sama Veda happens to be a collection of melodies. The Yajur Veda is something like a 'guidebook' for the rituals. The major part of this work contains a collection of magic spells which were chanted by priests at the time of sacrifices. From the point of view of a historian, Atharva Veda is important in the sense that it describes the beliefs and superstitions of the early Aryans.

The *Brahmanas* are prose commentaries on the Vedas. The *Aranyakas* (forest-texts) were probably composed in seclusion at the hermitages and include philosophical doctrines and mystic meanings of the text of the Vedas. The *Upanishads* deal with speculative thinking on the part of our sages. They contain spiritual thinking on such topics like the universal soul, the absolute, the individual self, the mysteries of nature and other things. To put it briefly, they contain the wisdom of our ancestors.

The next class of literature is known as the *Vedangas*. They are six in number, namely, *Siksha* (phonetics), *Kalpa* (ritual), *Vyakarana* (grammar), *Nirukta* (etymology), *Chhandas* (metrics), and *Jyotish* (astronomy). These six *Vedangas* are meant to help one in the proper understanding, recitation, and the sacrificial use of the Vedas.

The second Vedanga deals with the ritual part of the study. If one desires to acquaint himself with this, he should begin with the oldest Sutra works known as *Kalpa Sutras*. The Kalpa Sutras are again classified into two categories—the *Srauta Sutras* (great rites performed by a number of priests) and *Grihya Sutras* (a house-holder's domestic rites and sacrifices). The two other Sutra works are *Dharma Sutras* (Customary Law and practice), and the *Sulva Sutras* (rules laid down for constructing the Fire-altars). Kalpa sutras are of importance to us in "the correct understanding of the Vedic passages".

Area of Occupation

As mentioned earlier, the early Aryans occupied the land of the seven rivers (the Sapta-sindhu) which extended from the Kabul valley in the north to the River Ravi in the south. The Rigvedic people were tribal in character and each tribe occupied a particular region. Sometimes they fought among themselves. The Rigveda mentions the *Dasarajna,* that is the battle of Ten Kings which resulted in the victory of the Bharatas who gave their name to this country.

Political Organisation

To begin with, the early Aryans were led by their tribal leader both in times of war and peace. The dictates of the tribal leader were obeyed by all. However, after their settlements in the Sapta-sindhu, they evolved monarchy as their form of government. The tribal leader came to be called as *Rajan*. Kingship became hereditary in the course of time. Thus the Saptha-sindhu area was divided into a number of small kingdoms, each ruled by a king. His main function was to lead the people in times of war; and during peace-time he was to protect his subjects from the attack of his enemies. Other kingly duties included punishing the wicked and upholding of the *Dharma*. The Aryan king lived in a royal palace in the capital with all pomp and majesty and received taxes from his subjects.

Next to the king in importance was the *Purohita* (the Chaplain) who invoked the blessing of Gods through his hymns to confer favours upon the king. The Rigveda mentions great Purohitas like Visvamitra and Vasishta and their great services to the state. Sometimes they acted as a check on the growing powers of the king. They commanded great respect from the ruler and the subjects alike.

The *Senani* was appointed by the king to be in charge of armed forces of the kingdom. He recruited able bodied men and gave them training in the art of warfare. His other duties included providing the soldiers with necessary weapons and keeping the army alert and well-trained during peacetime.

The *Gramani* was the leader of the village. He was entrusted with the task of collecting revenue of his village on behalf of the king. The village was generally looked after by him.

Sabha and Samiti

The most popular representative bodies of the Rigvedic age were the *Sabha* and the *Samiti*. A few lines in the Rigveda indicate that the former was associated with men known for their wealth and position. When they assembled in a big hall they discussed not only social matters but also important political issues, if any. Collectively, the Sabha wielded great influence over the king and the administration. It might have also acted as a check on the arbitrary powers of the king. The samiti was more political in its character than the sabha. It included the representatives of the common people and a few influential brahmans and heads of aristocratic families.

Vedic Civilisation

It was in the samiti that the political affairs of the kingdom were freely discussed. The debates in the samiti must have been of a high order; and the decisions arrived at by the king in his individual capacity must have been influenced by their wisdom.

Other Forms of Government

Non-monarchical forms of government also existed among a few states. Oligarchy was in vogue in a few states where several members of the royal family exercised power jointly. References are also made in Rig Veda, to *Jana* (republics) where a *Jyeshtha* (elder) exercised his authority.

The idea of one world government under an enlightened ruler was also not unknown to the early Aryans for the Rig Veda mentions it in the phrase *Visvasya bhuvanasya raja*. So it was natural that the early Aryan rulers strived hard to rise from a position of tribal chieftaincy to that of the status of an emperor by a continuous process of expansionism through wars. They received tributes and oaths of loyalty from the defeated rulers.

Vedic Society

The main prop of the Vedic society was the family. A healthy family life based on love and affection among the family members was an important feature. Father was the head of the family and therefore commanded respect and obedience from the other members. All the members of the family or joint family lived in the same house made of wood and bamboos. Next to him in importance was the mother. She looked after the management of household affairs and helped her husband in performing religious ceremonies and sacrifices. Marriage was considered sacred and binding. The marriage tie bound husband and wife for life till death separated them.

Children were educated. The education of girls was not neglected and is proved by the fact that Visvavara, Apala and Ghosha composed hymns and rose to the position of rishis. It was the duty of the parents to get their daughters married when they attained the age of puberty. Girls and boys enjoyed the liberty of choosing their life-partners.

Monogamy was common and polygamy was not altogether unknown. Only kings and nobles practised the latter. No reference to polyandry is made. So also there is no reference to child-marriages. The birth of a son was always preferred to the birth of a daughter. A number of families bound by kinship and living in a village formed a clan. A number of clans living in an area constituted a district. A number of these districts formed the tribe.

Beginnings of Class Distinctions

When the Aryans entered India and settled in the Sapthasindhu region, their *varna* (colour) and *Sajatya* (kinship) tightly knit them into a Aryans were taken into the fold of the society as free men. The class distinctions must have begun at the fag end of the Rigvedic period. The *Purusha sukta* appears in the tenth *mandala* (chapter) of the Rigveda saying that the Brahmans, Kshatriyas, Vaisyas and Sudras appeared from the Purusha (the primeval Creator) through His mouth, from His arms, from the thighs and from His feet respectively. None of the ugly features of the present caste-system seemed to have been present as inter-marriages, inter-dining and change of occupation were quite common. Untouchability was almost unknown. Then when did the caste system develop? The answer to this question should be traced to the new environment the Aryans had to adjust with when their tribes migrated farther east. The genesis of the warrior class (Kshatriyas) was the result of systematic conquests undertaken by the Aryan rulers. They needed a permanent class of fighting men. Those who specialised in the Vedic studies and rituals constituted the priestly class (Brahmans). Many others who settled down and engaged in the pursuit of agriculture and trade and commerce were known as Vaisyas. Many aborigines living in the villages as well as those who belonged to the wild tribes came to be known as Sudras. The caste system in its rigid form must have taken place when the Aryans conquered the Middle country (Madhyadesa).

Food and Drinks

Their food was mainly composed of animal flesh, vegetables, rice, barley, bean and sesame. They made bread and cakes out of flour. They liberally consumed milk and milk products such as ghee, butter and curds. They ate fruits. They were addicted to drinking of *surea,* a liquor made from barley and corn. Soma, a plant juice, was also a popular alcoholic drink which they even offered to the Gods.

Dress and Ornaments

The dress (*vastra*) consisted mainly of *vasas* (lower garment) and the *adhivasa* (an over-garment). The wearing of an under-garment (*nivi*) came into vogue during the later Vedic age. References are made to special type of garments, some embroidered, worn by dancers, brides and others. People living in the hermitages made good use of the skin of animals (especially deer) for making garments.

Names of several ornaments worn by men and women are mentioned in the Rigveda. The *Karnasobhana* was an ornament attached to the ear

Vedic Civilisation

and mostly worn by men. The brides wore *Kurira,* a kind of head ornament. *Khadi* was something like a ring worn as an armlet. *Nishka* was an ornament of gold gracing the neck. There were other ornaments like the *Mani* and *Rakma.*

Amusements

Some of their amusements included gambling, chariot-racing, dancing with females to tunes of *dundubhi,* playing dice and wrestling. Music was both vocal and instrumental. The Aryans were very fond of material pleasures of life and did not worry about disease or death.

Standards of Morality

They maintained high standard of morality. People lived in contentment and did not take to crimes such as stealing, robbery and murder. Morality among women was also very high.

Economic Conditions

Occupations

A large majority of the early Aryans were cattle-breeders. They loved pastoral life. They lived in villages. They owned land, houses, horses and cattle. They cultivated the lands and

Vishnu

Brahma

Shiva as Nataraja

grew crops of wheat and barley. They considered cow as a sacred animal (*aghnya*). A man's wealth was known by the size of his cattle.

Industries

Weaving in cotton and wool flourished as an industry. Textile and woollen garments were produced in various colours. Dyeing and embroidery were known. The services of a carpenter were found necessary for constructing houses, for household utensils and also household furniture. Carpenters supplied chariots, carts, boats and ships. The village blacksmiths supplied articles made of iron such as sickles, razors, and plough shares. They also produced weapons such as spears and swords.

Professionals

Goldsmiths produced excellent ornaments in gold and catered to the fanciful rich. The leather workers supplied a number of articles such as shoes, bow-strings, reins, water-casks, thongs and hand-guards. There were number of other professionals like the butchers, potters, barbers, boat men, moneylenders and hunters. There were physicians and priests whose services were found to be invaluable.

Trade and Transport

Inland and river-trade seemed to have flourished most. A few hymns of the Rigveda refer to trading with distant lands for profit. The chief means of transport of goods was the cart driven by oxen. Boatmen helped traders to transport the goods across the river. Most of the trade was carried on by barter. A few traders accepted *nishka,* a small gold piece. The Aryan traders may have been engaged in sea-borne trade.

Religion

The early Aryans were religious. They offered prayers and sacrifices to their beloved Gods. They were known for "the punctilious observance of religious rituals." They did this in order to please the Gods and expected many things in return such as birth of male children, good harvest and prosperity.

Rigvedic Pantheon

All the Vedic gods are manifestation of the forces of nature. They can be classified into three categories, namely, (1) the *terrestrial gods* like Prithvi, Agni, Soma and Brihaspathi; (2) the *atmospheric gods* like Indra, Marut, Vayu, Parjanya and Rudra; and (3) the *celestial gods* such as Varuna, Dyaus (the Sky god), Ushas (dawn), Asvins and all the gods associated with the Sun God like Mitra, Savitri and Vishnu. Almost all the gods are male gods. Temple and image-worship seemed to have been absent. Many early Aryans appear to have been fond of Indra (Thunder-god associated with war) and Varuna (god of Rain), Agni personified as fire-god was the beloved of all and through him the other gods received sacrifices of their devotees. The early Aryans believed that the gods "subdue the forces of evil", reward the righteous and punish the sinners. They were not particularly concerned about death or life after death. As a matter of fact they were more interested in earthly existence and therefore offered sacrifices to various gods asking them to bestow boons such as prosperity, longevity of life, health, male-children, power, and defeat of their rivals.

Education

The art of writing was most probably not known. A teacher used to recite the hymns of the vedas and his pupils recited the same in chorus.

Lesson Review

1. Sketch the life of Vedic Aryans under the following headings:
   (a) Political organisation;   (b) Society;
   (c) Economic conditions; and   (d) Religion.
2. Write a short note on : Education in the Later Vedic Age.

11
ANCIENT CHINA, CENTRAL AND SOUTH AMERICA

PART I

Geographical Factors

The mainland of China is watered by the three great rivers, namely, the Sinkiang, the Yangtze and the Hwango Ho (Yellow), and all of them flow from the west to the east and join the Pacific ocean. It is along the bank of the Hwang Ho river valley that the ancient civilisation of China had its origin. The Hwang Ho flows for nearly 3000 miles from the mountainous Tibet and deposits a rich top soil along its banks which is suitable for extensive cultivation. The Hwang Ho is also known as the Yellow River and also 'the river of sorrow' for it has changed its course many a time causing heavy damage to life and property.

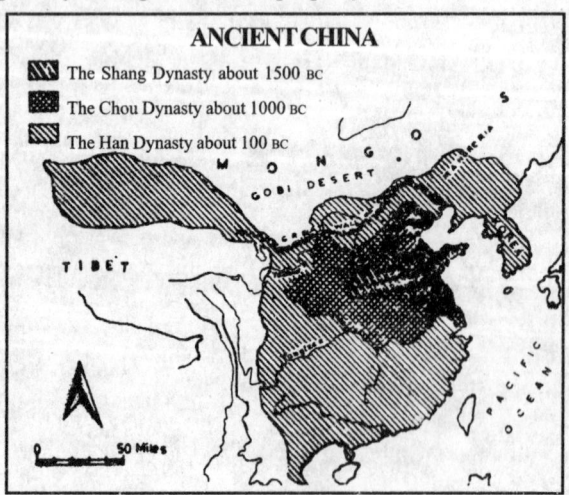

Ancient China

Unique Culture

The early Chinese did not have contact with the rest of the world for a long time because of the natural barriers. Therefore they built a civilisation of their own and now claim it to be the oldest. Traces of human habitation have been known from the Palaeolithic Age as testified by the remains of the 'Peking Man'. The Chinese belong to the Mongoloid race. In the course of time, however, they absorbed many Turks and Tibetans into their culture.

The ancient history of China is in the form of legends and stories. It is only from the twelfth century BC that history, in the real sense of the term, begins. Before that the Chinese had made progress in agriculture and other crafts like silk-weaving, basket-making, utensil-making and ornaments. They reared cattle and domesticated animals including horses. They also excelled in making metalwares and porcelain products. It was about this time that many Chinese drifted towards far off lands like Tibet, Burma and Indo-China.

Political History

Shang Rule

The history of China from historians' point of view commences from the rule of the Shangs. They reigned for nearly six centuries (1600 BC to 1046 BC). The rulers paid attention to agriculture. The people domesticated animals which included the horses. Bronze castings, among other things, of this period have been discovered in Anyang recently. The Shang rulers brought about the unification of all the city-states near the Yellow River. Unfortunately, they did not develop it into a well-knit kingdom. The people developed many crafts, among which the most prominent were glazed pottery, silk-weaving, and making the bronze vessels. The Shangs ruled their kingdom from their capital, Anyang. The Chinese started worshipping their great God Shang Ti and other nature gods. They offered prayers and sacrifices to gods in the temples.

It was around 1046 BC, that the Shang capital, Anyang, fell into the hands of the Chou, who lived on the western borders. The Chou set up their own dynasty and proclaimed their king as the "Son of Heaven".

Chou or Zhou Dynasty (1046 BC–256 BC)

The Chou rulers ruled China for nearly eight centuries. One of their greatest rulers was Wu Wang. He led a number of campaigns and established an empire stretching its southern borders up to the river valley of Yangtse. As long as he lived he controlled a number of feudatory rulers and maintained the integrity of his empire. But loyalty to the Chou emperors continued as long as they remained strong. Therefore, when weak emperors succeeded, the feudatory chieftains frequently asserted their independence. Sometimes they threatened the very existence of the central government. Like in Ancient Egypt, China witnessed the rule of the feudal lords from the middle of the eighth century BC. The Chou emperors became mere figure-heads. Whatever may have been the political conditions, China continued to register progress not only in agriculture, industry and commerce, but also in education and philosophy. The Chou age came to be called as the classical age for its contribution to learning and philosophy. It produced great moral teachers—Lao-Tze, Confucius and Mencius. The art of writing was probably known to the Chinese as early as the commencement of the Shang rule. It fully developed into a combination of pictures and sounds. An average Chinese student learnt about 3000 signs. They did not produce alphabet like the Phoenicians or the Greeks.

Qin Dynasty (221 BC–207 BC)

It was around 256 BC that the Chou emperor yielded place to a powerful feudal lord of the Ch'in. About 221 BC the Qins produced their greatest warrior and statesman, Qin Shihuangdi. He reduced all the rebellious feudal lords to subjection and carried wars of conquest. He ended feudalism which had proved to be a great curse to his country. He built a well knit empire having 36 provinces. He encouraged feudal lords to live in the Chinese capital and appointed trusted and loyal governors to administer those 36 provinces. To protect his subjects living near the north-western borders of his empire from frequent attacks of the barbarians like the Huns, he erected the Great Wall of China. Successive rulers continued this work, and the present wall is 1500 miles long, 22 feet high, and 20 feet thick. It has watch-towers at regular intervals.

Destruction of Old Literature

Qin Shihuangdi styled himself as the first Universal Emperor and set about the task of destroying the works of Confucius and others by saying they were feudal in outlook. Only books on medicine and other technical subjects were spared. Qin Shihuangdi also encouraged a new kind of literature and rendered help to reform the Chinese language and script. He introduced a uniform code of laws throughout the country. The central government also forced merchants to use standard weights and measures. With the death of Qin Shihuangdi in 210 BC, the Qin empire began to decline rapidly and was replaced by the rulers of the Han dynasty.

PART II

HAN AGE DESCRIBED AS THE "GOLDEN AGE"

Han Dynasty (206 BC-220 AD)
During the next four hundred and odd years, China came under the control of Han rulers, among whom Wu-Ti (140 BC-87 BC) was undoubtedly the greatest. The Huns who invaded the country in spite of the Great Wall, were driven out. He embarked upon a career of conquest and in the end annexed territories to expand the borders of his empire. These territories included Korea and Manchuria in the north and the Pamirs and Khokand in Central Asia.

Trade and Commerce
It was he who gave encouragement to international commerce. The Chinese merchants for the first time carried their goods along the routes discovered earlier by the Chinese army and reached India, Persia, Syria and the Roman Empire. The Chinese silk became extremely popular in the Roman Empire. The trade route which connected the mainland of China and the Roman Empire came to be called the silkroute. The Chinese exported silk and iron and imported glass, amber and precious stones.

Buddhism in China
The Age of the Hans witnessed not only the growing prosperity on account of the brisk trade but also the spread of Buddhism. Buddhism gained entry into China during the last quarter of the first century BC.

Educational Progress
The study of the Confucian classics was revived with the opening of an Imperial University in 124 BC. This university trained students for the civil service. The development of education was greatly facilitated by the invention of paper and other writing materials like the camel-brush and ink.

Civil Service Examinations
The Han emperors and the local governors felt the need of a team of civil servants for the efficient running of the administration. So they recruited civil servants after conducting civil service examinations.

State Patronage to Arts and Literature
The Han emperors revived the practice of patronising the arts. Singing and dancing to the tunes of musical instruments became extremely popular. The Chinese paintings and sculptural works received support from the aristocratic class. As learning came to be highly respected in the Chinese

society, this age witnessed sudden outburst of literary activities. Copious works were produced on history and poetry.

Diplomatic Relations
It was during this age that China broke its traditional attitude of self-imposed isolation. Her merchants were found frequently visiting other countries. So it became necessary to maintain diplomatic contact with foreign countries. Ambassadors from Rome and West-Asian countries visited the Chinese imperial court.

Due credit should be given to the Chinese Emperor Wu-Ti for taking steps to guard the public from the exploitation of monopolist merchants. He put an end to private monopolies, regulated market-prices, and levied income tax on the excess wealth. He established state monopoly on such items like iron, salt and fermented drinks.

Tang Dynasty
After the fall of Han dynasty China lapsed into political chaos marked by civil war and political rivalries. It was only in the early seventh century A.D. that order was restored by the Tang rulers. There was the revival of the golden age, particularly after the accession of Tai Sung in 627 AD. He built the largest empire and encouraged trade and commerce with the outside world. Although he was a Taoist, he tolerated other religions such as Buddhism, Zoroastrianism and Christianity. The Tang dynasty ruled Chian till the early tenth century AD.

PART III

FEATURES OF ANCIENT CHINESE CULTURE AND CIVILISATION

Political Organisation
Political conditions from the earliest times favoured the growth of benevolent monarchy. However, it is also a fact that China was frequently convulsed by political disturbances. Between the end of one dynasty and beginning of the other, political disorders followed. In spite of this recurring phenomenon, it should be said to the credit of China for having produced great rulers in times of crisis. Shi-Huang-Ti had united China as had never been seen before. His political genius lay in abolishing feudalism and establishment of a strong central government. Through his uniform code of laws, standard weights and measures, reforms in language and script, and protection of outlying provinces, he welded the people into a nation. Following in his footsteps were others, like emperors Wu-Ti and Tai Sung.

The main prop to the Chinese political system, based on benevolent monarchy, came from the bureaucracy. From the early days the Chinese emperors introduced a civil service whose personnel came to be selected. The Han emperors introduced a competitive examination to recruit civil servants.

For the purpose of efficient administration, the empire was divided into provinces and each province subdivided into a number of districts. The emperors appointed trusted civil servants (mandarins) to govern over them. The border provinces came under special care for they witnessed the inroads of barbarians. The Han emperors provided for the border security force to guard vulnerable places near the border.

Economic Conditions

The bulk of Chinese population was engaged in agriculture. Through proper irrigation system they developed intensive farming and practised rotation of crops. They used good seeds and better manures for getting yield. Their food crops consisted of millet, wheat, barley, better rice, soya-beans and sweet potatoes. About the 2nd century BC drinking tea became a habit among the Chinese. The peasants also maintained livestock. Floods and famines always ravaged the Chinese throughout their history.

Since the early days of Shangs, the Chinese came to be known for their metal products like excellent bronze vessels and glazed pottery or porcelain ware. They used wood and bamboos for making furniture. They are known for producing beautiful lacquer-ware.

Raising silk worms and silk weaving became a popular industry in China. The Chinese silk commanded world market and the Roman craze for silk and other Chinese products resulted in commercial ties between these two empires. The other famous industries in China included the manufacture of paper, black ink, dyes, varnished tiles, attractively designed fans, articles of jade.

Trade and Commerce

China's internal trade developed to a great extent after the construction of canals and waterways. Manufactured goods coming from the lower valleys were exchanged for the raw materials produced in the upper valleys. Commercial contacts with various countries in South Asia, Asia Minor, and the Mediterranean region were established during the time of Han emperors. The Chinese exports included silk, salt, iron, rhubarb, spices, jade, lacquer and fruits and imports included precious stones, amber, coral and glass.

Coin currency appeared sometime during the late second century BC. Banking and money-lending came into vogue. The merchants of China formed guilds to protect their interests.

Early Chinese Society

The early Chinese society was composed of varied classes whose obligations and duties to the state were duly recognised in a particular order. The social hierarchy consisted of Mandarins (literary class), the peasants and workers, and the merchants. There was stigma attached to the warrior class because they were recruited from the lowest class which included criminals and men of doubtful reputation. Slavery existed in China.

After the spread of Confucianism, there was marked change in the society. Family life became more secure and stable on account of attachment between children and parents. It was a social custom to divide the ancestral land equally among all the sons.

Women did not enjoy high social status or any special privileges in the society. Confucius preferred giving rights to women. Instances of women occupying high posts during the reign of two empresses after the death of Tai Sung are recorded.

Religion and Philosophy

The earliest religion which flourished in China was worship of gods of nature which was followed by ancestor-worship. In each Chinese house, the family members practised ancestor worship. However, in the course of time, three religions found favour among the Chinese. They were Confucianism, Taoism and Buddhism.

Confucianism

It is no exaggeration to say that Confucius dominated the minds of the learned for centuries and he was finally deified. He was born in the state of Lu (now in Shantung province). He rose from the post of the director of public lands to the chief ministership of the Lu state. He finally resigned his post when the ruler did not like his reforming zeal. After that he wandered for nearly 13 years attracting a large number of disciples. He died in 479 BC.

It must be said of Confucius that he was a great student of human nature. His country was in deep trouble and he felt that it was due to lack of moral principles and social ethics on the part of the individuals in the society. Therefore, he started building a society by reviving the old norms like ancestor worship and filial piety and obedience to authority. He tried to bring about harmonious human relations between the rulers and the ruled, between parents and children, elder and younger brothers, husband and wife, and among friends. He prescribed a code of conduct for almost every class of human beings. He taught good manners, humility, devotion to duty and trust and faith in others. His golden rule on etiquette was, "what you do not like when done to yourself, do not do to others". His teachings had great effect on moulding the character of the Chinese for many centuries. Confucius is also given credit for having written or edited five works (classics), viz., the *Book of History, Spring and Autumn Annals, Book of Odes, Book of Changes* and *Book of Rites*.

Confucius

Taoism
Taoism was founded on the basis of the writings of Lao Tze (604 BC-517 BC). He worked as an archivist during the Chou rule and soon became disappointed at seeing people turning selfish and wicked. He became a mystic thinker and writer. His work, *Tao Te'Ching,* contains his maxims and principles. He insisted on leading a very simple life in harmony with nature. He said that people can know better of Tao (eternal spirit) not by study or reason but by deep contemplation and prayer. Among other things, he mentioned that the root cause of unhappiness lay in greed and desires. He said that moral virtues should be developed and good conduct should govern individual life. His teachings attracted thousands of adherents. But when Buddhism spread all over China from the first century AD, Taoism began to decline rapidly.

Mencius
Meng Tzu or Mencius (372 BC-289 BC) was another great philosopher who tried to bring about moral regeneration of the Chinese society. He was a great follower of Confucianism. He attacked the prevailing corruption in the Chinese administration and society and expressed that the State exists for the welfare of the people. He criticised forced labour and forced taxes. He believed that the people had the right to overthrow tyrants.

Buddhism
Buddhist missionaries preaching principles of Mahayana Buddhism were received warmly in China during the first century AD. Among the Indian Buddhist monks who assisted in setting up a Mission in Central China,

two are noteworthy. They were Kasyapa Matanga and Dharmaraksha. They went there with the sacred texts and relics of the Buddha. Buddhism became popular in China from the third century AD. Many Buddhist schools were set up in China, the most popular being Ch'an. The spread of Buddhism had its impact on Chinese art like painting and sculpture.

Art and Architecture

The early Chinese painters used the camel's hairbrush and water colour to paint scenes of daily life on their canvas. Sometimes the canvas happened to be a woven silk. The subject matter of painting differed as per the varying interests of the period (like historical, religious, landscape, and portrait). In the field of sculpture, we came across several bronze works with decorated figures belonging to the Shang, Chou, Han and Tang dynasties. The figures of a celestial flying horse or other animals like the dragon are commonly observed on a variety of bronze vessels. We also come across the Buddhist school of sculptors producing the statues of the Buddha.

The Great Wall of China may be counted as one of the Great architectural achievements of the Chinese. Its vaulted gates and impressive square-towers are quite remarkable. The palace of Qin Shihuangdi must have been the most beautiful in those days. The Chinese architecture is always associated with their pagodas. The number of storeys and its peculiar shaped roofs arrest the attention of onlookers.

Literature

Pictograms are the earliest form of Chinese writing. They had about 40,000 of these of which about 600 were commonly used. The Chinese wrote on chips of wood or on linen paper. The Chinese imperil court had number of poets. Tu Fu's poems became popular. Ssu-m Chien began writing bout the first dynastic history of China. His *Historical Record* is noted for its objectivity. Lyrical poetry flourished during the Tang dynasty. Besides Tu Fu's poems, we come across 30 volumes of Chinese verse composed by China's great poet, Tai Li Po. The works of Confucius and Lao Tze also constituted an important part in the early Chinese literature.

Science

The early Chinese evinced keen interest in scientific development. The elementary mathematics included ordinary arithmetic and a form of algebra. Along with algebra they developed theories of geometry. They knew the value of $n(22/7)$. Their early astronomers were able to evolve a new lunar calendar and predict eclipses correctly. Astrology developed and became popular with the priests. They also developed interest in chemistry and became familiar with the basic elements of matter.

In the field of medicine, the Chinese made remarkable progress. During the Chou dynasty a Canon of Medicine was compiled which described the functions of several organs. The Chinese physicians gave herbal drugs for curing many diseases including malaria and bronchial disorders. They performed minor operations and used anesthetics. In the later years they developed the technique of acupuncture, which has been recognised now by the modern medical practitioners.

The ancient Chinese were known for their many inventions which include paper, a lunar calendar, sun-dial, and a waterclock. I-Hsing produced the first mechanical clock. Blockprinting was also invented. They were the first to use gun powder for making crackers. Chang-Heng, a famous astronomer, mathematician, and writer of the Han period, invented the first seismograph to record earthquakes. Subsequently, they invented the mariner's compass.

Thus, the Chinese contributed to the enrichment of world culture and civilisation.

MAYAN CIVILISATION (CENTRAL AMERICA)

Before the arrival of Europeans in Central America, the American Indians living there had developed a high degree of culture and civilisation. This credit goes to the Mayas who lived in the Yucatan peninsula of Mexico, British Honduras and parts of Guatemala. It is believed that their ancestors might have been the prehistoric immigrants who came over from Asia to North America through the then Bering Straits. The Maya's march towards high degree of civilisation began from 325 AD to 900 AD—sometimes described as the classic period. In the early stages of their development, they knew how to cultivate maize, make pots and weave cloth. In the course of time they built magnificent and highly decorated temples for their Gods. Their priests developed a large number of ceremonial centres among which four, namely, Tikal, Calakmul, Capon and Palenque, grew into Maya capitals.

Religion

The Mayas worshipped Gods of nature such as the Sun, Moon, Fire and Wind. Their priests were highly respected and some of them became rulers. They not only helped the people in ritualistic worship but rendered advice as to when they should commence planting of seeds and other agricultural operations. As religion influenced their life so much they built ceremonial centres which developed into cities. They include Uaxactun, Copan, Quirigua and Chichen Itza.

Art and Architecture

The superb craftsmanship of the Mayas could be seen all around their ruined cities now. They produced excellent and beautiful pottery. Their sculptors carved huge monolithic stones called *stelae* on which their calendrical records are inscribed. Their stone temples and other sacred buildings speak highly of their architectural ability. Besides temples and sacred buildings, they constructed palaces, pyramids, observatories and dancing platforms. They built stone causeways to connect their religious centres, some of which run a length of more than 60 miles.

Intellectual Pursuits

The Mayas were the first natives of America to invent a good system of writing. Their writings consisted of many picture symbols. Their writings are found on papers made from the inner bark of the fig tree. At a time when most of the Europeans hardly knew much about mathematics, the Maya-Mathematicians developed a workable system using the concept of zero. The Mayas were great star-gazers and some of them made important astronomical discoveries in their primitive observatories. Their astronomers produced a calendar consisting of 365 days. The Mayan calendar is 5000 years old and its last year and month are shown as 2012 December (an Omen suggesting an apocalypse!).

Political, Social and Economic Conditions

It appears that the Mayas lived in independent city-states, each under the control of a governor or a priest king. They and their agents looked after civil and judicial matters. The priestly class was highly venerated. Maya merchants travelled far and wide selling their hand-made articles. Their farmers worked very hard as they had to clear the rain-forest jungles for making lands cultivable.

The decline of Maya civilisation must have taken place around 900 AD. It might have been caused by volcanic eruptions or any other natural calamity. The warriors from the north called Toltecs conquered the Maya country around 1000 AD. The revival of Maya culture began with the Toltecs but the Spaniards invaded their lands and put an end to it.

THE INCAS (SOUTH AMERICA)

In the western highlands of South America there flourished a great civilisation from the eleventh century to the middle of sixteenth century.

Ancient China

The architects of this civilisation were the Incas, originally a small 'red' Indian tribe. It was during the last hundred years that (1438-1525) build a vast empire whose borders stretched from the western coast to the Andes mountains and from Columbia to Chile. The seat of their capital was Cuzco. The last three rulers who governed them were Pachacuti, Tupa Inca and Huayna Capac.

Strings which Talk

The language of the Incas was *Quechua* which is still spoken in Peru. Although they did not develop a writing system, they used *quipu,* a multi-coloured knotted-string device to record and calculate numbers. Only the man who used the knotted string device could remember what he recorded.

Other Features of their Civilisation

They developed efficient system of irrigation for agriculture. As they lived on the highlands and mountain sides, they used the terraced mountain sides for agriculture. It is said that the Incas gave the world different kinds of potato and cocoa. They used cinchona bark (quinine) for medicinal purpose. They used pack animals.

The remains at Machu Picchu show evidence of their great progress achieved in the fields of transport and communication, painting, pottery, architecture and weaving. They showed superb skill in masonry work in building temples for their Sun God, forts and palaces. They made ornaments, tools and weapons with metals like copper, silver, gold and bronze. It was their hoarded gold which attracted the Spanish adventurers in 1532 AD. The great grandson of Emperor Pachacuti, Atahualpa, was captured and killed and all the gold ornaments were melted by the Spanish conquistadors, to enable them to carry it home. Some of the brave Incas established a jungle state of Machu Picchu, high in the Andes perches. After some time the Incas abandoned even this fortress city. Some of the lost cities of Incas have not yet been discovered, and when it happens they may tell the story of the Incas completely.

Lesson Review

1. Write a note on Shi-Wang-Ti in not more than 10 sentences.
2. Why is the age of Han Emperors described as the 'Golden Age'?
3. On the outline map of China show the extent of Han Emperor silk route.
4. Give a brief account of Maya civilisation.
5. Write a note on The Incas of Peru.

12
ANCIENT GREECE

Historical Background
The contributions of Ancient Greece had been quite substantial to the making of what we now call as modern European civilisation. She is situated in the south eastern part of Europe and separated from the Asia Minor by the Aegean Sea. A number of islands appear on all the three sides of the main peninsula. One of the largest islands which appears directly below the peninsula is Crete. It was here that the predecessors of ancient Greeks pioneered a great civilisation called the Aegean Civilisation. The Aegean Civilisation is also known by other names such as the Cretan or Minoan. Even before the advent of the Phoenicians as traders and sailors in this region, the Aegeans or Cretans flourished as trading people and built an empire. They built cities on the mainland of Greece, on Aegean islands and in the Asia Minor. Their main outpost in Asia Minor was the city of Troy. The Aegean empire flourished between 2500 and 1400 BC, probably with its capital, Cnossus. It was at Cnossus that the splendid palace of King Minos was found. The Aegean Civilisation on the island of Crete was probably destroyed due to the disastrous eruption of the volcanic island of There. Years later the Mycenaeans from the mainland conquered Crete and seized power from the Minoans. In all probability the Mycenaeans might have been Greek-speaking.

About 2000 BC, the mainland of Greece was invaded by Achaeans, a branch of Indo-Europeans. Several migrations of this semi-barbaric tribesmen into the mainland of Greece took place. These invaders settled on the mainland and some of them even occupied the islands nearby (including Crete). About 1200 BC they attacked the city of Troy—a ten years siege and final destruction of this city are described by Homer in one of his epic poems, *Iliad*. Other Greek-speaking tribes who invaded the mainland of Greece include the Dorians, Ionians and Aetolians. The conquerors through inter-marriages with the locals became a mixed race.

Geographic Influence

The mainland of Greece is full of rugged mountains. Its criss-cross ranges cut up the mainland into hundreds of valleys. The Greek tribes migrated into these valleys. A vast majority of people cultivated on the limited farms and the rest tended their herds. They imbibed much of the culture of the Minoans and built new cities in the place of the ruined ones. The geographical barriers came in the way of welding all the Greek tribes into a nation. Therefore, there developed a number of small Greek city-states. Scarcity of cultivable land in their country and nearness to the sea forced many Greeks to seafaring and trade. They set up numerous colonies on the coast of the Mediterranean. They came into contact with the Phoenicians who supplied them with necessary goods. The early Greeks learnt Phoenician alphabet, and with necessary modifications adopted it for their script.

Development of City-states

Geographical factors and the tribal character of the early Greeks were mainly responsible for or conducive to the growth of city-states. Each tribe occupied a valley which was separated from the other by mountains and rivers. In addition to this, tribal loyalty was strong enough to keep them separate. In such circumstances the unity of all the Greeks was hardly possible. Furthermore, each city-state guarded zealously its independent status and often was jealous of her neighbours. Each city-state with its countryside formed its own government with a king and a council. The most prominent among several city-states were Athens, Sparta, Corinth and Thebes. All these four city-states were comparatively larger in size and population than many others. Though the Greek city-states were jealous, independent and quarrelsome, all the Greeks strongly believed they were all hellenes (descendants of a common ancestor, Hellen). Another bond which united them was the common language and literature. Every Greek citizen read Homer's poems, *Iliad* and *Odyssey* and considered these as a part of his heritage. One more factor which united all the Greeks was religion. Besides worshipping the patron-god or goddess, they worshipped common and popular gods like Zeus (Sky God), his son Apollo (the Sun God), Poseidon (God of the Sea), Athena (goddess and protectress of cities) etc. They believed that these gods and goddesses often played a considerable role in their daily affairs and so treated them with great respect. All the Greeks consulted the oracles to know about their future and often visited famous shrines such as the Shrine of Apollo at Delphi. Festivals were organised in honour of their gods to which all were welcomed to attend. Last but not the least, was the conducting of Olympic games once in four years, held at Olympia in honour of the God Zeus. Participants from almost all the states came to compete in athletic events and poetry and music compositions. The winners were given garlands of sacred olive leaves. It was not prize-winning that mattered most but the spirit of excellence.

Forms of Government

To begin with, all the states had monarchy. Each monarch began to govern his city-state with the assistance of a council consisting of nobles. But due to several reasons monarchy did not remain as a popular form of government. There were changes and particularly with regard to Sparta and Athens. Sparta was probably the largest city-state. There were three classes in society namely, peers, freemen, and helots. Only the peers got full citizenship and the rest remained without privileges. The helots were always revolting and, therefore, the peers received military training and kept themselves in readiness to suppress their revolts. Thus, Sparta turned into a military state. Her government was ruled by a few nobles. Two of these nobles became kings. So Sparta was led by two kings and other nobles. According to tradition, Sparta received her laws from a wise nobleman, Lycurgus. His laws helped the peers (nobles) in not only setting up of military state but also enabled them to keep the helots under subjection. Sparta did not make much progress in fields other than military training.

Athenian Democracy

In contrast to Sparta, Athens registered remarkable progress in politics, laws, literature, art, science and philosophy. Athenians were fond of trying political experiments. Monarchy and oligarchy were not suited to their temperament, so they discarded them. Finally, democracy was ushered in. It was a product of the labours of three wise law-givers. viz., Draco, Solon and Cleisthenes. The first step towards democracy was taken by a wise nobleman, Draco (621 BC), who gave the Athenians a written code of laws. Although the laws were harsh, the citizens felt pleased for they at least knew positively what the laws were. They also felt safe from the tyranny of dishonest and corrupt judges. But Draco's code did little to help the poor farmers who were at the mercy of rich nobles. Due to highly profitable trade and colonisation, there developed a new class of landed-aristocrats. The poor farmers borrowed money from them during lean years with themselves or their children standing as security. When they could not repay they were turned into slaves. As the common people were on the verge of revolt, the nobles of Athens chose a liberal statesman, Solon, to prevent chaos. Solon's laws or reforms liberated the enslaved farmers, made debt-slavery illegal and cancelled all mortgages on land. He helped Athenian merchants by introducing coin-currency and encouraged foreign artisans to settle in Athens. Henceforth an Athenian father had to "teach his son a trade by which he could support himself". His other reforms included permission to all the citizens to take part in the Assembly (law-making body), appointment of common citizens as jurors in courts, and a provision for appeal to a common man in common law-courts against the decisions of the aristocratic judges.

Cleisthenes

But the lot of the common man remained worse because he was denied voting rights and public offices. Taking advantage of this situation, the tyrants ruled Athens for about half a century. In spite of their reforms they became unpopular and had to leave. Cleisthenes, a member of the influential family of Alcmaeonidae, broke the power of the ruling clans belonging to the four old tribes by granting citizenship rights to male adults on the basis of residence in a particular locality. In other words, the power of the four old tribes was equally distributed among the newly organised ten tribes, and each tribe sending fifty members to the Council of Five Hundred. Thus, poor people also got the right to vote. Again, no member could continue in office for more than two terms and therefore a large number of citizens got the chance to work in the Council of Five Hundred—a body which administered laws and controlled the magistrates. In this way the early Athenians came to have a democracy. Women and slaves could not exercise voting rights. So, after a century of hard struggle, the common people of Athens got a democratic government worth the name.

The Persian Threat

Under the leadership of Emperor Cyrus, the Persians built a large empire whose border stretched from the Aegean seashore in the west to the border of Afghanistan in the east. Croesus, the world's richest king of Lydia was defeated in 546 BC by the Persians under Cyrus thus paving way for further expansion. The Greek cities of Asia Minor came under the rule of the Persian emperors.

Revolt of Ionian Greeks

The Ionian Greeks of the cities of Asia minor resented the loss of their freedom and so revolted against the Persian masters (499 BC-494 BC) and sought assistance from the Greek cities on the mainland. Athens and a few other states sent aid. But the new Persian Emperor, Darius the Great, crushed these revolts and turned his attention to Greece. He desired to teach a lesson to Athens for sending help to his rebellious Greek subjects.

A boxer athlete throwing a discus

Ancient Greece

Persian Wars

The Persian emperor sent a large army (which outnumbered the Athenian soldiers) to attack Athens. The valiant Athenians engaged the Persians in a battle at Marathon (490 BC) and fought so bravely that the Persians had to flee. The Persians suffered heavy casualties (6400 dead) while the Athenians lost 200 of their brave soldiers. Soon after the victory the joyous Athenian leader sent a runner to inform the people at home about the glorious victory. The runner covered the distance of 26 miles and 385 yards at a stretch, relayed the happy news and fell dead. In modern Olympics this sport items is included as the last event.

Battle of Thermopylae and Others (480 BC)

The Persian war did not end with the Marathon battle. Ten years later Xerxes, the successor of Darius, decided to avenge the Persian defeat. Himself assuming the lead he organised land and sea expeditions to bring about the defeat of the Greeks. He encouraged the Phoenicians to attack Greek colonies in Italy and Sicily. The Spartans realised the danger threatening their existence. Her king, Leonidas, with 300 brave soldiers held the narrow pass at Thermopylae for nearly three days till he was betrayed. They fell to the last man fighting heroically. After overcoming this obstacle the Persian army entered the Athenian plains. They marched towards Athens and burnt the city. But the Athenians had their revenge soon when they defeated and destroyed the Persian fleet in the naval battle of Salamis (480 BC). The architect of this glorious victory was the shrewd Athenian statesman, Themistocles. The Persian emperor suddenly made a hasty retreat to Asia Minor leaving his army on the Greek soil. The Athenian fleet gained another victory over the Persians at Mycale on the Ionian sea-coast. The Persian army led by Mardonius suffered convincing defeat at Plataea (479 BC) at the hands of the combined Athenian-Spartan forces. The Phoenicians attacking the Greek colonies also could not make much progress. Thus, Greek cities were saved due to the valour of the Greek soldiers. Her great statesmen gave a good lead which resulted in their victories. The Persian emperor gave up all hopes of conquering the Greek city-states. Even the Greek cities of Asia Minor gained freedom. By championing the cause of Greek freedom, Athens stood foremost among the Greek states. Free from fear, the Greek city-states grew prosperous. Their success in the naval battles paved way for prosperous sea-trade with the neighbouring countries. The Delean League was formed by many Greek city-states in alliance with Athens for self-protection. Athens was to achieve the climax of her glory during the time of Pericles (462-429 BC).

The Golden Age

Pericles was the great grandson of Clesisthenes. He led his soldiers to victory at the battles of Salamis and Mycale. Being a nobleman by birth he was taught by the best teachers of his time. The Athenians had so much trust and confidence in him that they elected him to the highest office (Strategos) for the next thirty consecutive years. It was he who completed the work of laying foundation for democracy. Being a radical politician, he believed in reforms. He deprived the Areopagus of its political powers and transferred the same to the Council of Five Hundred. This body suggested measures to the Assembly (Ecclesia) where it was freely discussed by all the citizens of Athens and passed into laws. Another important feature of the Periclean age was the Jury system. Every year about 5000 jurors were elected for a term of one year to act as judges. There were no lawyers or judges and so the plaintiff and the defendant had to argue their own cases before the jurors. The jurors decided the guilt and accordingly passed sentences. The Assembly consisting of all the Athenian citizens elected ten executive officers (Strategos) to command the army, navy and conduct foreign policy. Pericles was one among those ten, but he dominated the rest. Being a great lover of democracy he wanted even the poorest citizens to take interest in public affairs. For this purpose he introduced the system of payment of salary to the archons (magistrates), members of the Council of Five Hundred and the jurors in his state.

Athens Rebuilt as the Most Beautiful City

During the Persian war, Athens had been destroyed. Pericles undertook the task of rebuilding the city. Hundreds of artists and architects worked to construct large public buildings. The most attractive feature of the new city was the Parthenon on the Acropolis. The Parthenon was the most beautiful temple ever built out of coloured marble stones. Inside the temple stood the tall marble statue of the patron Goddess of the city, Athena. Besides this marble statue, Phidias (the most famous sculptor of his times), also made the statues of Goddess of Athena in ivory and gold. Ictinus, the famous architect of this temple, blended the three styles—Doric, Ionian Corinthian—to make this temple a wonder of the world. The Acropolis (a small hill in the centre of the city of Athens) with a collection of temples including the famous Parthenon became the main religious centre of Athens. Polygnotus was employed by Pericles to decorate the temples and buildings with his beautiful paintings. Pericles patronised music. No doubt the Athenians were rightly called the lovers of beauty and music.

To protect his beautiful city from foreign invaders, Pericles got the "long walls" built which ran for nearly five miles connecting the city with the port, Piraeus. A big gymnasium was also built for the youth of Athens. Another important place in Athens was the market place, the Agora.

Greek Philosophers

The Age of Pericles was also 'the age of reason'. Great Greek philosophers wanted to learn or seek true knowledge "about man and the universe". They were not prepared to accept anything which did not withstand the test of reason. The greatest among them was Socrates (469-399 BC), an Athenian, who taught his pupils not to accept any principle or dogma without putting it to a severe test of reasoning. He tried to break down many prejudices of his pupils by his searching questions and discussions. The Athenian government considered his ideas about Greek religion as dangerous and corrupting the youth, found him guilty, and sentenced him to death. One of the pupils of Socrates was Plato who became a great philosopher (427-347 BC). His *Dialogues* contain the teachings of his master. Plato's greatest work is the *Republic* where he describes an ideal state governed by a philosopher-king. Plato opened an academy to train students and one of them was Aristotle. The latter is considered by many as one of the world's greatest philosophers.

Educations

There were Sophists (wise men or Teachers) who became very popular among the educated youths. They taught oratory, mathematics, astronomy, grammar and literature. Military training was made compulsory in all the schools.

Greek Literature

The Periclean age was the golden age of Greek plays. The ancient Greeks loved to see the tragic plays of Aeschylus, Sophocles and Euripides enacted on the stage. The Athenian government awarded an annual prize to the best playwright after an open contest. Among the most successful were the three above named whose plays attracted all the citizens of Athens. Aristophanes was known for writing comic drama. The epic poems of Homer always inspired the Greeks.

Knowledge of the past was popularised through myths, legends and folklores. But its authenticity was always questioned. Herodotus (484-425 BC) raised the status of history and is now regarded as "the Father of History". He is known for providing an interesting account of the Persian wars and also of his travels to the near east. It was Thucydides (471-400

BC) another Athenian, who gave the world the first scientific history. His most important work was on the Peloponesian war i.e., the great war between Athens and Sparta.

Other Types of Literature

Lyrical poetry set to music became a popular form of expression of love or sadness or gaiety. The first poetess who composed this type of lyrical poems (odes) was Sappho. Another great poet who produced this kind was Pindar.

An important branch of Greek literature, if one may call it so, is the oratory i.e., the art of making public speeches. The learned students were trained in this field. The most prominent orator of the Periclean age was Demosthenes whose famous speeches have earned him a niche in the temple of genius. Among the lighter type of literature, the Ancient Greeks produced, is the most popular Aesop's fables.

Philosophy and Science

Thales of Miletus, a pre-Socratic philosopher and mathematician, is considered by many as the founder of western philosophy. The Classical Period (500 BC-323 BC) produced great philosophers and mathematicians like Pythagoras, Hippocrates and Anaxagoras. Pythagoras (570 BC- 495 BC) is credited with discovering the Pythagoras theorem in geometry that states that in a right-angled triangle, the square of the hypotenuse is equal to the sum of the squares of the other two sides. Hippocrates (460-377BC) laid the foundation of scientific practice of medicine. He "taught that diseases are of natural origin", and not caused by evil spirits as many believed in those days. He became an inspiring figure to other physicians of his time. He prescribed an oath binding fresh medical practitioners to follow an ethical code in their profession (even now administered at the graduation ceremony). Anaxagoras (503-428 BC) was a great philosopher and cosmologist who taught in Athens. Democritus (460 BC-370 BC) set forth his theory of atoms. The Greek scientists made important contributions to the scientific knowledge for which the world is greatly indebted. Therefore it is no surprise if historians have regarded Athens as 'the School of Hellas'.

Decline of the Greek City-States

Athens which was the architect of the Delian League built an empire at the expense of the other members. When the Persian threat seemed to be over, a few members of the Delian league desired to withdraw. But they were not permitted to withdraw and were asked by Athens to continue to pay tributes to her. This caused great resentment. Members began to quarrel with one another. Sparta became extremely jealous of the growing powers of Athens and so the war between them—called the Pelopenesian war—became inevitable. Sparta was helped by Persia who was always eager to divide the Greek city-states. The war ended in the defeat of Athens (after the famous battle of Aegospotami in 404 BC), Sparta reigned supreme for some time, but by the middle of the 4th century BC all the Greek city-states remained hopelessly divided.

King Philip of Macedonia

Taking advantage of the disunity of the Greek city-states, King Philip of Macedonia invaded. With the exception of Sparta he conquered all the Greek city-states. He prepared a plan for a united Greece and to fight the common enemy—the Persian empire. Before he could execute this plan he was assassinated.

Alexander, the Great

He was succeeded by his 20 year old son, Alexander the Great, in 336 BC. Fortunately for Alexander, his father had left behind a highly disciplined and well-trained Greek army. He had been tutored by no less a philosopher than Aristotle himself. Alexander, like his father, loved Greek culture. Soon after he came to the throne, a revolt broke out in his own kingdom. Alexander mercilessly crushed it. The Greeks felt bold and revolted thinking that Alexander was a mere boy, but he mercilessly put down the revolt and destroyed Thebes city completely. The house of the famous poet, Pindar, was spared by Alexander as he admired his great works. Alexander became the undisputed leader of Greece, and the Greeks got ready to fight the Persian Empire under his able leadership. At the head of a large Greek army of 35,000 soldiers, he marched against the Persian Empire and defeated the Persians in three successive battles at Granicus (334 BC), Issues (333 BC) and Arabela (331 BC) Phoenician cities and Egypt came under his control. He built the city of Alexandria at the mouth of the River Nile. After the conquest of the Persian Empire, he invaded India from the north-west and defeated King Porus at the battle of Hydaspes (326 BC). He and his army marched to the mouth of the River Indus and from there sailed across the Arabian sea. He set up his capital at Babylon in 324 BC. Alexander's successful march against Asia has remained without a parallel in world history. Unfortunately, Alexander died at the age of 33 (323 BC) without bringing about a proper fusion of Greek and Asiatic cultures. Soon after his death there occurred a civil war among his competing generals to take control of his vast empire. After forty years, the civil war ended resulting in the division of his empire into three parts: (1) Egypt to remain with Ptolemy, (2) Large part of Asiatic empire of Alexander to remain with Seleucus, and (3) Macedonia and Greece to be under the control of Antigonus.

The Hellenistic Civilisation

Alexander's great conquest deeply affected the course of world history. He enabled the Greek culture to spread throughout the length and breadth of his empire by founding seventy cities. He and his soldiers married Persian women and worshipped Persian gods. He encouraged Greek merchants to trade with the Asiatic countries and encouraged Greek immigrants to settle in Asiatic cities. From this happy union between the west and the east, there developed Greek-Oriental or Hellenistic culture. The main centre of this great culture was the city of Alexandria (Egypt). It also became a great commercial centre. Here the Ptolemies (Greco-Egyptian rulers) set up a world famous museum and library for scholars to visit. The library had a rich collection of 700,000 volumes of Papyrus scrolls embodying knowledge in all fields. The Ptolemies also built an observatory to help the astronomers to make important discoveries.

Greek Language

The Greek language became extremely popular in the entire eastern Mediterranean world. All the rulers of these countries popularised the Greek language among their subjects. Businessmen, students and merchants all learnt this language and improved their prospects. Greek literature came to be appreciated very much by scholars and students. Scribes made copies of old Greek literature.

Scientific Discoveries and Inventions

The Hellenistic civilisation which flourished for nearly three centuries produced great scientists who made many discoveries and inventions. The famous mathematician, Euclid of Alexandria (born around 300 BC), expounded his theorems of geometry so well that they are studied even now. Geography became a subject of study and geographers made maps of the countries. One of the most famous geographers was Eratosthenes (276 BC-194 BC) who accurately measured the circumference of the earth which was said to be 25,000 miles (his small mistake being a difference of 200 miles) without any scientific aid or instrument. He also produced maps with longitudes and latitudes, founded scientific chronology, and devised a method to identify prime numbers. Archimedes of Syracuse (287 BC-212 BC) is well-known to us for discovering the principle of specific gravity. He discovered it while taking bath and was so overjoyed that he ran naked into the streets crying 'Eureka, Eureka' (I have found it, found it).

He constructed many machines by using pulleys and screws. A machine was used to launch ships and catapults for hurling large stones. Hipparchuss was a great astronomer of the 2nd century BC. He believed that the earth revolved round the sun and predicted solar and lunar eclipses accurately. He also invented plane and spherical trigonometry.

Ancient Greece

Art and Architecture

Hellenistic art and architecture flourished in almost all the cities founded by Alexander. The most prominent structure of the time was the Pharos or light-house of Alexandria rising to a height of 400 feet. Other public buildings included libraries, theatres, palaces and baths. Paintings and sculptures were patronised by the wealthy nobles and merchants. Among the beautiful statues, the most famous was Venus de Milo.

Philosophers

The contact between the west and the east brought about new philosophies. There were philosophers known as cynics who urged people to hate politics, power and wealth. The most famous among them was Diogenes of Sinope (412 BC-323 BC). There were others who came to be called as stoics who urged people to have patience, fortitude and courage and accept misfortunes as natural. The leader among the stoics was Zeno of Citium (334 BC-262 BC). There were the epicureans who told people that there was no rebirth and they should enjoy life to the utmost.

Decline

The Hellenistic civilisation declined after three centuries of prosperity. Unfortunately, there existed glaring inequalities. A few became rich and enjoyed all the pleasures of life while the poor became poorer. Slavery continued. Free men had no work and slave-labour became common. The poor and the unemployed found life miserable. The Greek city-states vied with each other and fought among themselves. Thus, the Hellenistic civilisation declined and the Romans found it easy to conquer the Eastern Mediterranean.

Lesson Review

1. Why is the 'Age of Pericles' described as the Golden age in the history of Greece?
2. Write a note in not more than 10 sentences on the following:
   (a) Compare and contrast between the city-states of Athens and Sparta;   (b) Persian Wars;
   (c) Olympic Games.
3. Explain the influence of geographical factors in the shaping of early Greek History.
4. Locate on the outline map of Greece the following:
   (a) Athens   (b) Sparta
   (c) Mediterranean Sea   (d) Mt. Olympus
   (e) Gulf of Corinth   (f) Marathon
   (g) Thermopylae

13

JAINISM

The sixth century BC is considered as one of the important epochs in the history of India for the reason that it gave birth to two great religions—Jainism and Buddhism. This age was marked by religious turmoil since the Hindu religion had lost its pristine glory and simplicity and degenerated into an amorphous cult. The priestly class—the Brahmanas—arrogated to itself a position of pre-eminence and interpreted the sacred lore only to the few. Performance of sacrifices and meaningless rituals were given more prominence than finding a path to attain salvation. A layman lost his sense of devotion and attachment to God due to such services rendered by the Brahmanas. In these circumstances, many felt disgusted and took to ascetic way of life as advocated in the sacred scriptures like the *Aranyakas* and the *Upanishads*. There was also a terrible reaction to Brahmanical Hinduism especially coming from the Kshatriyas.

In the meanwhile a few religious orders were founded by the wandering ascetics or hermits. These wandering ascetics were known as *Shramanas* or *Parivrajakas*. Then came the Samkhya school founded by Kapila. He did not believe in the existence of God and his philosophy wielded considerable influence on Mahavira and the Buddha. The new religious orders did not gain much popularity and they became defunct.

However, there emerged two new sects which gained immense popularity. They were Jainism and Buddhism. Both were founded by men who belonged to the Kshatriya class. They led the revolt against the imposition of Brahminical religion by the priestly class and also against the perpetuation of caste system.

Parsvanatha (8th century BC)

Jaina tradition says that its religion is as old as the human race. It also claims to have produced 24 *Tirthankaras* (saints). The first twenty Tirthankaras (Rishaba being the first) appear to be legendary characters. However, the last two, namely, Parsvanatha and Mahavira, are historical figures. Parsvanatha seems to have lived 250 years before the birth of Mahavira. He was the son of king Asvasena of Benares. He became an ascetic at the age of 30 and the sect he founded gathered a large number of followers called *Nigranthas*. Parsvanatha insisted on his followers the practice of four great virtues. They are (a) Satya (Truth), (b) Ahimsa (non-injury to life), (c) Aparigraha (non-possession of property) and (d) Asteya (non-stealing).

Early Life of Vardhamana Mahavira
Vardhamana Mahavira was the 24th and the last Tirthankara according to Jaina traditions. He was born around 540 BC in Kundagrama, a suburban of Vaishali (the capital of Videha). His parents were Siddharatha and Trishala. Trishala was the sister of Chetaka, a prominent Lichhavi prince of the time who ruled the Vaji confederation. Being noble by birth, Vardhamana was brought up in the midst of luxury. He married Yasoda and subsequently a daughter was born. She was named Anojja or Priyadarsana.

Mahavira

Soon after the death of his old parents, Vardhamana took the consent of his brother to renounce the worldly life. He left home in his 32nd year and became a monk. He discarded his clothes (*Digambara*) and spent the next twelve years of his life in meditation and self-inflicted tortures with the object of achieving perfect knowledge (keval-janana). At the end of this period he succeeded in becoming a *keualin* (omniscient). Vardhamana came to be known as *Jina* (conqueror) and Mahavira. Vardhamana Mahavira spent the rest of his life in preaching his doctrines to the people of Magadha, Anga, Mithila and Kosala. His religion attracted a large number of followers, and among them were kings, powerful nobles, wealthy merchants and house-holders. He lived till his 72nd year and passed away at Pawa, near Patna. Mahavira was a contemporary of the Buddha but they never met.

The Teaching of Mahavira
The followers of Mahavira were called *Nigranthas*. Even today many of them consider him not as a founder of a new religion but as a great reformer. Mahavira began his preaching career to reform the sect founded by his predecessor Parsvanatha. Besides the four vows prescribed by Parsvanatha for his followers, Mahavira added the fifth, i.e., the observance of Brahmacharya (chastity).

One of the main facets of Jainism is the belief in soul and Karma. Mahavira declared that every element is a combination of material and spiritual factors. The former perishes but the latter does not. An individual is subject to a series of life and death. To liberate the soul from the bondage of karma, it is necessary to destroy the latter. This can be achieved by an individual by practising the five vows, namely, Satya, Ahimsa, Aprigraha, Asteya and Brahmacharya.

In addition to observing the above five vows, a true Jain should also follow the three-fold path (called Ratnatraya) to attain "the pure and blissful abode (Siddha Sila)". They are the right belief, right knowledge and the right conduct. By right belief he meant belief in Jainism and by right knowledge the liberation of soul. The right conduct implied the strict observance of the five vows in the day-to-day life of an individual. The doctrine of non-injury is also one of important tenets of Jainism. Mahavira emphasised that not only human-beings, birds and beasts have souls but also the plants, metals, water and wood. Therefore an individual should avoid harming these things. An individual should conquer his senses and lead life of austerity and self-mortification.

Mahavira did not believe that the universe was created by God or make any reference to Him. Change is a natural phenomenon. Birth and death are natural and applicable to men and matter.

Mahavira also rejected the Vedic principles as unimportant and condemned the sacrificial rituals performed by the brahmans. He believed in the freedom of women and allowed them to join his order as Sarmini and Sravikas.

Religious Literature

The teachings of Mahavira are contained in the fourteen old texts called *Purvas*. Towards the end of 4th century BC a great famine broke out in Bihar which led to thousands of Jainas heading towards Mysore led by Bhadrabahu. Those Jainas who stayed behind convened a council to compile the Jaina texts. They are twelve in number and called *Angas*. About the sixth century AD another council was held in Valabhi to bring about the final collection of all Jaina scriptures and put it in writing. They were written in Prakrit language.

Svetambara and Digambara Jains

When Bhadrabahu returned to the north with his followers he found his coreligionists clad in white (Svetambaras) despite the injunction. But Bhadrabahu and his followers strictly adhered to the old rule and remained nude (Digambaras). The Digambaras refused to acknowledge the canon drafted during their absence and adhered to the principles enunciated in the 14 Purvas. The schism in the Jaina religion might have occurred sometime during the first century AD.

Spread of Jainism

Several classes of Angadharas spread the teachings of Mahavira after his death. As earlier mentioned, Jainism got the royal patronage and counts great kings like Chandragupta Maurya, Bimbisara and Samprati as its chief patrons. After the decline of the Mauryan Empire, Jainism spread to western and southern parts of India. Jaina monasteries were built during the rule of Sakas Ksatraps and Rajputs in western and northern India. King Kharavela of Kalinga was a great patron of Jainism. The Satavahanas, the Gangas, Chalukyas, Rashtrakutas and Hoysalas who ruled the south also patronised Jainism.

Its Contributions

The impact of Jainism on Indian culture is profound and worthy of mention. It propounded a new philosophy called "Syadvada" which aims at achieving the welfare of the individual on the one hand and the community in which he lives on the other. Although the principle of Ahimsa was known to Hinduism, it was Jainism which brought about its universal acceptance. The idea that plants have life in them was proved beyond doubt in the early years of the present century.

Jainism rendered great service to humanity by not recognising the caste-system and established the principle of equality. Even women were considered an important section and their freedom was advocated by no less a person than Mahavira.

Jaina religion gave stimulus to vernacular literatures. The early Jaina literature was in Prakrit. Mahavira had preached his doctrines in the language called Ardhamagadhi, a language known to many people in his days. It was in this language that the 12 angas came to be written. But the unique contribution of Jainism to literature was giving birth to the Apabhramsa language. Jaina works produced during subsequent centuries were in all vernacular languages including Sanskrit. Some of the most prominent scholars who produced Jaina literature were Hemachandra, Hari Bhadra, Sidha Sena, Nagachandra and Pujyapad. In Karnataka, Jainism made considerable progress and under its influence many Jaina works came to be written.

Jainism wielded profound influence on the Indian art and architecture. The followers of Jainism built Jaina temples, monasteries and hospitals. The most popular Jaina temple at Mount Abu was constructed by

Kumarapala, a king who was served by the most noted Jaina author, Hemachandra. Jaina stupas, statues, and carved pillars still exist in Mathura, Gwalior, Chitor, Abu and other places. At Udaigiri and Ellora one sees the cave-temples with beautiful sculpture and architecture. One should not forget the Hathigumpa caves (in Orissa) and the colossal statue of Gomateswar in Sravanabelagola.

Lesson Review
1. Sketch the life and explain the teachings of Vardhamana Mahavira.
2. Write a note on the contributions of Jainism to Indian Culture.
3. Write a brief note on the spread of Jainism.

14
BUDDHISM

Scepticism and religious turmoil influenced the course of events during the sixth century BC in India. Brahminical Hinduism had lost its hold on the common people mainly due to its insistence on the performance of meaningless rituals and sacrifices, and with its vague spiritual speculations. What a common man needed was a simple pathway to attain salvation. The chaturvarna system became rigid and lacked rationale. The priestly class dominated the scene and afraid of losing its position, came in the way of the regeneration of Hindu society. The reaction to this priestly-dominated religion came not from the lower classes but from Kshatriyas. Gautama the Buddha and Vardhamana Mahavira both belonged to the Kshatriya clan and they led the revolt.

Early Life of the Buddha
Before attaining the enlightenment the Buddha was known as Siddhartha. He was born in the year 566 BC at Lumbini near Kapilavastu. He belonged to the Sakya clan and his parents were Raja Shuddhodhan and Mayadevi. Mayadevi died soon after the child-birth and Siddhartha was looked after by his aunt and step-mother Prajapati Gautami. Several legends (the *Jataka* stories) have been woven about the childhood life of Siddhartha. Raja Shuddhodhan consulted court astrologers to predict his son's future and they prophesied the greatness of his son in the realm of thought. Worried about his son's monkish predilections, Raja Shuddhodhan got his son married to Princess Yasodhara at the age of sixteen. Prince Siddhartha led his life in luxurious surroundings and did not have much knowledge of the sufferings of life experienced by the common man. After the birth of his son, Rahula, he began to feel uneasy. The visions of sickness, old age and death had great impact on his life. It led to his great renunciation during 29th year of his life.

Great Renunciation
During the next six years of his life, Siddhartha led life of a wandering ascetic and received instructions from two teachers called Alara and Udraka. When the teachers could not satisfy his curiosity regarding life and its purpose, he left them and reached Uruvela (near Gaya). It was there that he practised most severe penances. His thirst for truth remained unquenched and he was reduced to a skeleton. After taking bath in the river Nairanjana, he gave up fasting. He reached Gaya where he sat under a pipal tree in deep meditation. At last his meditation was rewarded with the attainment of supreme knowledge and insight. He was called the *Buddha* (The Enlightened One).

Buddha's first sermon

He spent the rest of his life in preaching his doctrine. He died at the age of eighty at Kusinagara.

Teachings of the Buddha
The Buddha delivered his first sermon at the Deer Park near Benares. This sermon is known as the *Dharmachakra Parivartana* (the turning of the wheel of Dharma). His followers included the five ascetics who had parted his company earlier. He taught his followers to recognise the four "Noble Truths" (*Arya Satya*). The first truth is the existence of sorrow (*Dukkha*). The second truth relates to the main cause of sorrow, i.e., desire (*Trishna*). The third refers to the elimination of sorrow. The fourth truth reveals how sorrow or sufferings can be eliminated by following the eight-fold path.

Ashtanga Marga

It is through the practice of Ashtanga Marga one can attain salvation or eternal bliss. The noble eight-fold path includes (1) Right Views (2) Right Intention (3) Right Speech (4) Right Action (5) Right Living (6) Right Effort (7) Right Mindfulness and (8) Right Concentration.

The Buddha believed in the Hindu doctrines of Karma and rebirth. He explained that by following the eight-fold path the individual soul cuts the cycle of births and deaths and attains eternal bliss or salvation.

The Buddha did not ask his followers to practise penances or austerities on the one hand nor advocated to lead a life full of pleasures. He chose the Middle Path (*Madhyama Marga*) which avoids both the above extremes. Even a householder can follow the eight-fold path and attain salvation.

Buddhist (Sangha) Order of Monks Established

The Buddha rejected the principles of the Vedas and condemned the performance of bloody sacrifices. He denied the existence of God and asked his followers to lead a life of simplicity and purity. He established the Buddhist Sangha where his disciples received instructions and led a life of simplicity and morality. He did not make caste or class distinction before taking them into the fold of the Buddhist Sangha. During the early stages of Buddhism he did not allow women to join the Sangha but a little later they were also permitted. An organisation for the Buddhist nuns was also founded.

Spread of Buddhism

Several factors led to the popularity of Buddhism in northern India. The Buddha was known for his magnetic personality. He explained the doctrines of his religion in *Pali,* a language spoken by the people. He made his teachings popular by narrating them in the form of parables. He kept the doors of his religion open to all, irrespective of caste or class. Princes and paupers vied with each other to embrace this Middle Path. There were no priests, no rituals to be observed and no costly sacrifices to be performed. Even a house-holder can practise the eight-fold path and attain salvation. Finally, the Sangha founded by the Buddha propagated the tenets of the Master after his passing away.

But the most important factor for the popularity of Buddhism lay in the royal patronage it received. Buddhism enlisted the support of great rulers of early times like Bimbisara, Ajatasatru, Emperor Ashoka, Kanishka and Harshavardhana. Emperor Ashoka not only embraced Buddhism but made the religion popular throughout the world by sending his emissaries.

He held the third Buddhist Council. (The first two were held within a century after the death of the Buddha at Rajagriha and Vaishali) at Pataliputra under the leadership of Mogaliputta Tissa. It settled some outstanding disputes and finalised the compilation of Buddhist scriptures. Emperor Kanishka convened the fourth Buddhist Council at Kundalavana (in Kashmir) which prepared commentaries (*Upadesa* and *Vibhasha Sastras*) on the sacred Scriptures. The Sacred Text came to be known as *Pali* Which is divided into three *Pitakas* or baskets. They are the *Sutta Pitaka*, the *Vinaya Pitaka*, and the *Abhidhamma Pitaka*.

Rise of Mahayana Buddhism

The schism developed most probably during the time of Emperor Kanishka. A marked deviation from the practices of the old religion occurred. The simple and revered teacher or the Buddha came to be worshipped as a God. His images were made and prayers were offered to them. The images of the Buddha and the Bodhisattvas adorned the walls of the *Viharas* and *Chaityas*. Sculptors of the Gandhara School of Art made the statues of the Buddha. The *Jataka* stories formed the theme of many of the carvings on the Rock-cut halls and caves. This new Buddhism came to be known as *Mahayana* Buddhism (the Great Vehicle) and it is associated with the name of Nagarjuna, a philosopher of the Satavahana period in Indian history.

Contributions of Buddhism to Indian Culture

Buddhism catered to the spiritual needs of the community by its insistence on chaste and ethical principles of life. The Buddha, like Christ, enjoined upon his followers to return good for evil, truth for a lie and non-enmity for enmity. He advocated restraint and urged his followers to overcome greed and anger. Mercy and kindness for men and animals found a place of honour in the realm of Buddhist thought. Buddhism laid emphasis on the principle of Ahimsa (non-injury). Its teachings had profound influence on great personalities like Emperor Ashoka and Mahatma Gandhi.

Buddhism broke the barriers of caste and class and promoted feelings of social and national unity. It paved the way for political unity of the country under the Mauryan Emperors. Other contributions of Buddhism include the development of *Pali* language and literature and the establishment of centres of learning all over India. The Buddhist monasteries in India in those days served as great centres of learning. In the course of time not only religious texts were taught but also secular subjects introduced. It may not be wrong to say that Buddhism served the educational needs of the community in ancient times.

By far the greatest contribution of Buddhism to Indian culture lay in the development of art and architecture. A large number of ruined monasteries stand today to point out the glory of Indian art and architecture. The Buddhist monks introduced rock-cut architecture. They built their *Viharas* by hewing the rocks. Their artists and architects did splendid work by building the *Chaityas*. Carvings of the Buddha are found on the Chaitya Halls at Karle. The Stupas of Sanchi and Bharhut exhibit their excellent carvings. It may not be an exaggeration to say that early Indian art was profoundly inspired by Buddhism.

Lesson Review
1. Trace the career and explain the teachings of Gautama the Buddha.
2. Explain the contributions of Buddhism to Indian culture.
3. Write a brief note on the spread of Buddhism.

15
HINDU IMPERIALISM

The post-Buddhist India witnessed the growth of Hindu empires. The Kingdom of Magadha gave birth to three great empires in course of time. The Haryanka dynasty produced great rulers like Bimbisara and Ajatasatru. They built a great empire in India and made Pataliputra the seat of their capital. They established a sound system of administration. Besides Hinduism, Jainism and Buddhism also found patronage of rulers and merchants, and in due course of time became popular. Taxila became a great centre of learning. There was considerable progress made in the fields of agriculture and industrial guilds developed. Trade and commerce made headway with the growth of towns like Benaras, Saketa, Rajagriha, Champa, Kausambi, Sravasti and Vaishali. The rulers and nobles patronised art and architecture as revealed in the recent excavations at Rajgir. Pliny speaks of Rome's relations with India.

The Nanda Rule over Magadha

After the fall of Haryanka dynasty in Magadha, the Nanda dynasty established its sway. Its founder was Mahapadmananda. He was a man of low origin. He retrieved his position and honour by destroying many ruling Kshatriya families which were out to destroy him. The Nanda empire extended from the borders of Avanti to Anga. The kingdom of Kalinga might have also come under Nanda control. The last ruler, Dhanananda, (300 BC) turned into a tyrant. The enemies of Dhanananda plotted to overthrow his rule and they turned to Chandragupta Maurya, a former commander of Magadha army, for help. With the help of Kautilya or Chanakya, a brahmin, Chandragupta overthrew the Nanda rule and established his power.

Alexander's Invasion (327 BC)

When the last Nanda ruler was ruling Magadha, Alexander the Great invaded India (327 BC). King Ambhi of Taxila was frightened at the sight of the approaching Greek army led by Alexander. He surrendered without resistance and offered great hospitality to the invader. Ambhi helped Alexander to attack the kingdom of Porus which was situated between the Jhelum and Chenab. The battle of Hydpses witnessed spirited fight offered by King Porus but it was in vain. After the defeat Porus was taken captive and brought before Alexander. When asked by Alexander how he should be treated, Porus replied that he should be treated as one king treats another. Alexander was very much impressed by his personality and asked him to continue ruling his kingdom as his vassal. Alexander continued to march further with his army. He defeated a large number of small kingdoms. When he decided to fight the mighty Magadha kingdom, his soldiers revolted. They felt homesick and wanted to go home. So, Alexander ended his career of conquest and began marching home. On his way back, he died at Susa (323 BC). Although Alexander's invasion did not produce direct results it had its impact on Indian culture. The Indian realised the need for political unity and it enabled Chandragupta Maurya to achieve the same easily. Secondly, the contact with the Greeks opened avenues for Indian trade and commerce with western countries. Thirdly, the Greek influence was felt on Indian astronomy and philosophy.

Chandragupta's Career of Conquest

After assuming power, Chandragupta Maurya embarked upon a career of conquest. During the twenty-four years of his reign he subdued a large number of states and became the master of northern India. He also overthrew the foreign yoke by inflicting a crushing defeat on Seleukos Nikator, one of the generals of Alexander, who was in charge of eastern dominions. After marrying the daughter of Seleukos, Chandragupta Maurya received from him the provinces of Aria (Herat), Arachosia (Kandhar), Gedrosia (Baluchistan) and Paropanisadai (Kabul). Plutarch says that Chandragupta conquered the whole country with an army of 6,00,000 soldiers. Chandragupta's empire extended from Pataliputra in the east to the Hindukush mountains and Herat in the north-west and up to Mysore in the south. According to a Jain tradition, Chandragupta Maurya became a Jaina monk and spent the last days of his life in Sravanabelagola in Mysore.

Bindusara (300 BC-273 BC)

Chandragupta Maurya was succeeded by his son, Bindusara, around 300 BC. He might have ruled the empire for about 27 years. We have no detailed account of his reign. He was described as Amitraghata (slayer of foes). He continued to maintain diplomatic relations with the Syrian king

Antiochos I (son of Seleukos). Deimachus succeeded Megasthenes as an ambassador to the court of Pataliputra. When there was a revolt at Taxila, Bindusara sent his son Ashoka to suppress it.

Emperor Ashoka (273 BC-236 BC) and the Kalinga War

Bindusara was succeeded by his son, Ashoka. According to the Ceylonese chronicles, there ensued a bloody struggle for the throne soon after the death of Bindusara. These works mention that Ashoka killed all his ninety-nine brothers and succeeded to the throne. Known for his extreme cruelty, he earned the nickname, *Chandashoka*. It was in the eleventh year of his reign that Emperor Ashoka fought one of the bloodiest battles in history. As the kingdom of Kalinga did not show its allegiance to the Mauryan emperor, it was invaded. The thirteenth Rock-Edict of Ashoka describes the horrors of this war. Nearly 100,000 were slained and 1,50,000 soldiers were taken captives. The blood of the killed and the injured flowed like a river. This horrible scene left an indelible impress upon the Mauryan emperor. Struck with deep remorse for causing the sufferings of thousands, the emperor decided to turn a new leaf in his life. Unable to bear the anguish, he declared that he would wage no more wars but would try to conquer the hearts of the people by following the policy of *Dharma* (love and compassion). He embraced Buddhism and worked day and night to improve the moral life and material welfare of the masses. The emperor set up personal example of what he was preaching to people. He gave up the pleasures of royal life and undertook journeys to meet the subjects living in the nook and corner of his empire. He was assisted by the *Dharmamahamatras* in achieving the goal of moral and material uplift of the masses. The message of the Buddha was spread to the neighbouring countries. Emperor Ashoka sent missionaries to Egypt, Syria, Macedonia, Cyrene, Ceylon, Lower Burma and Sumatra. The emperor's son Mahendra, and daughter, Sanghamitra, were sent to Ceylon to spread the message of the Buddha and they were successful in converting the ruler of that country into a Buddhist. After the death of Emperor Ashoka, the Mauryan Empire began to decline rapidly. The Mauryan rulers organised sound system of administration.

Mauryan Administration

The empire was divided into five provinces, namely, Prachya and Madhyadesa, Kalinga, Avanti, Dakshinapatha, and Uttarapatha. Their respective capitals were Pataliputra, Tosali, Ujjain, Suvarnagiri, and Taxila. The first province was directly ruled by the emperor from his headquarters at Pataliputra and the rest by his appointed viceroys. The emperor was assisted by a cabinet of ministers and other senior officials. Chandragupta Maurya employed spies and received reports from them about conditions of the people living in different regions of his empire. Kautilya's *Arthasastra* gives an idea about the Mauryan polity. The Mauryan rulers were enlightened despots who followed high ideals of kingship. They discharged their onerous duties like administering justice, giving protection of life and property to their citizens, maintaining age-old customs and traditions, promoting trade and commerce and helping people who were affected by floods and famines. They safeguarded the integrity and sovereignty of our country by maintaining a well-organised standing army of 6,00,000 foot soldiers, 30,000 cavalry, 9,000 elephants and thousands of chariots. The administration of military machine was in the hands of the members of six constituted boards, each looking after one wing of the above plus commissariat.

Similarly, the important capital or cities enjoyed autonomy. Each city was governed by a commission of 30 members which was divided into six boards. Each board was in charge of one or two departments. The departments were industrial and mechanical arts, foreign residents, registration of births and deaths, sales, exchanges, supervision of manufactured articles, collection of taxes on sales. The Greek ambassador Megasthenes describes the administration and social life of Pataliputra in his work, *Indica*.

Social Conditions

The Mauryan emperors promoted religious and social harmony. They encouraged agriculture, industries, trade and commerce. Megasthenes divided the Mauryan society into philosophers (Brahmins), farmers, herdsmen and hunters, traders and artisans, warriors and government officers. Joint-family system was in vogue. Women's position began to deteriorate. The members of the royal family and nobles patronised singing, dancing, acrobatics and theatre. The rulers and nobles were fond of hunting but Ashoka seems to have restrained them from these pastimes. The common public amused themselves with meat-eating, drinking, animal fights and hunting. Slavery prevailed.

Economic Conditions

Agriculture and cattle-rearing continued to be the major occupations of the rural masses. In cities and towns several industries and crafts developed most notably the textiles, carpentry, mine and metallurgy, manufacture of drugs and scents and boat-building. India's premier products were silk-fabrics, linen-cloth, woollen blankets and gold-embroidered clothes.

Inland and foreign trade went on briskly. The contact with west developed after Alexander's invasion enabled traders to send Indian goods to the west. The government built ships and gave these to merchants for hiring the transport of their merchandise. The inland river system also enabled merchants to transport their merchandise by boats.

Religious Conditions

Hinduism maintained its hold on the vast populace of the Mauryan empire although it had to compete with Buddhism, Jainism and several other heterodox creeds. Buddhism received royal patronage under Emperor Ashoka and its ascendancy as a world creed was in the offing. Jainism also made considerable progress in some parts of Bihar, western India and the south. The Jaina tradition mentions that Chandragupta Maurya became a Jaina monk and retired to the south to spend the last days of his life.

Ashoka Pillar

Mauryan Art and Architecture

A number of Ashokan pillars on which his edicts are engraved are not only known for their "beauty and vigour" but also exhibit high engineering and technical skill of the artist. The capital of the Sarnath pillar with the figures of four lions exhibits the artistic excellence of the Mauryans at its best. Ashoka seems to have erected about 84,000 *stupas* all over India, the most prominent being the Sanchi Stupa according to tradition. About Mauryan architecture, contemporary Greek writers make references to the most beautiful and splendidly built palaces at the capital, Pataliputra. Even Fahien, the Chinese pilgrim, who came to India seven hundred years later extols the beauty of these palaces.

Learning and Literature

Learning and literature received great attention of the rulers and the ruled. Taxila, which served as the capital of the Uttarapatha (a Mauryan province), was fast becoming a great centre of learning. Kautilya, the author of *Arthasastra* and minister of Chandragupta hailed from that place. The Mauryan age produced three great works, namely, *Arthasastra* of Kautilya or Chanakya, *Kalpasutra* of Bhadrabahu, and the *Katha Vatthu* of the Buddhists.

POST-MAURYA PERIOD

The Sungas (187-75 BC)
A brahmin *senapati* of the last Mauryan emperor, Pushyamitra Sunga, killed his master on the parade ground in the presence of the army. His *coup* succeeded and he became the master of the central portion of Mauryan Empire, the rest having declared their independence. Among the important events of his reign included the defeat of king Yagnasena of Vidarbha by Pushyamitra's son, Agnimitra (hero of Kalidasa's *Malavikagnimitra*), the Yavana invasions and their defeat, and the revival of Brahmanism. At the same time there was the revival of art as can be seen at Barhut and Sanchi.

Kanva Rule (75 BC-30 BC)
Vasudeva Kanva, a Brahmin minister of the last Sunga ruler Devabhuti, killed his master and succeeded to the Sunga throne. He and his successors ruled the shrunken empire for the next 45 years. It was during this time that the Greeks established their control over the Punjab. About 30 BC, the Satavahanas or the Andhras overthrew the Kanva rule and established their power in the Deccan.

Satavahanas of the Deccan
The Puranas, inscriptions and coins enables us to record the history of the Satavahanas. According to the *Aitareya Brahmana*, the Satavahanas were of mixed blood of Aryan and non-Aryan who established a small kingdom in the Deccan and owed allegiance to the Mauryan Emperors. The first ruler was Simukha. The next great ruler was Satakarni I and in his time the kingdom became an empire with the conquest of Malwa, Vidarbha and parts of the south. The Nanaghat inscription refers to him as *Dakshinapathapati* (Lord of the South) and he celebrated various religious sacrifices to mark his imperial status. On these occasions he gave gifts to the Brahmanas generously. With the death of Satakarni I, the Satavahana power in the Deccan suffered a setback due to the Scythian invasions. The fallen fortune of the dynasty was retrieved by Gautamiputra Satakarni, the greatest of the Satavahana rulers. He ruled the kingdom about the beginning of the second century AD. He built a large empire after destroying the powers of the Scythians (Sakas), Yavanas (Greeks) and Pahlavas (Parthians). His empire extended from the Malwa region in the north to the southern borders of Karnataka in the south. In commemoration of his victory over the Kashaharata ruler, Nahapana, he struck and issued coins in his name. He protected and maintained the four social orders and did

not allow matrimonial relations with the foreigners. He ruled the empire according to the best Hindu traditions. Gautamiputra Satakarni was succeeded by his son, Vasisthaputra Pulamayi who ruled the empire from his headquarters at Pratisthana or Paithan. His brother, Vasisthaputra Satakarni, married the daughter of Rudradaman I, a Saka Satrap (Viceroy). But despite this matrimonial relation, Rudradaman inflicted a crushing defeat on his southern relative. The next great Satavahana ruler was Yajna Sri Satakarni who defeated the western Satraps and conquered their southern territories. After his death the glory of the Satavahanas began to fade rapidly. The Satavahana power vanished about the middle of the third century AD.

Greek Rule in India

While the Sungas tried to stem the tide of the invasions of the Bactrian Greeks, the latter established their kingdoms in the north-western part of India. Demitrios established his sway over Afghanistan, the Punjab and Sindh. One of his successors Menander began his glorious reign after his military conquest of northern India. Although a Greek, he became a great scholar and patron of Buddhism. After his discourse with Nagasena, a great contemporary scholar of Buddhism, he got himself converted to Buddhism. This discussion is covered in a Pali work called *Milinda Panha* (Questions of Menander). Menander ruled India with headquarters at Sakala (modern Sialkot). The next important Indo-Greek king was Antialkidas who ruled the north-western part of India with his headquarters at Takshashila (Taxila). He sent his ambassador, Heliodorus, to the court of the Sungas at Vidisa. Heliodorus became a follower of Bhagavata religion and erected a Garuda pillar in honour of Vasudeva. The Sakas invaded the Greek settlements and the power of the Greeks declined.

Parthians

The Parthians (Pahlavas) revolted against their Seleucid master and set up an independent kingdom. During the third century BC. Mithradates, the Parthian king, invaded Sindh and his later successor, Maues, established a kingdom in the western Punjab. The most famous king of the Parthians was Gondophernes. According to Christian traditions he received Christ's apostle St. Thomas in his country. He and his family became Christians.

Sakas or Scythians

The Sakas were driven out of their homeland by a nomadic tribe called the Yue-chi. Subsequently, they invaded Bactria where they destroyed Greek power. Gradually, they came to India and established three kingdoms, namely, the kingdoms of Mathura, Takshashila and Malwa-Kathiawar. Their rulers governing the first two kingdoms were known as Northern Satraps and the rulers of the third kingdom were known as Western Satraps. The Western Satraps belonged to the Kshaharata race and built a kingdom on the ruins of the early Satavahana empire. They attained glory during the time of Nahapana. But the Satavahana ruler, Gautamiputra Satakarni defeated him and restored the fallen fortunes of his family.

Chashtana and Rudradaman

The next great western satrap, Chashtana, founded a new dynasty and recovered a large part of the lost territory from the Satavahanas. His grandson was Rudradaman who ruled from 130 AD to 150 AD. He probably gave his daughter in marriage to Vasishitaputra Satakarni, Brother of Vasishtaputra Pulamayi. It appears Rudradaman defeated the Satavahanas twice during his lifetime even though he had matrimonial relations with them.

Kushanas

About 165 BC the Yue-chi (Turkish) tribe was driven out of their original homeland on the Chinese frontier. They then settled in the Oxus valley after expelling the Parthians. They got divided and ruled five principalities. It was Kadphises I who welded all of them into a nation. Kadphises I belonged to the Kushan section of the Yue-chi tribe. After attacking and defeating the Parthians he occupied Ki-pin, Kabul and the Indian north-western borderland. He issued copper coins which look similar to those issued by Roman Emperor Claudius. The next ruler was Wema Kadphises or Kadphises II who is credited by the Chinese of having extended his empire into the interior parts of northern India. He embraced Saivism and styled himself as *Mahisavara* on his coins. The subjects in his empire must have enjoyed a prosperous life as can be seen by the gold coins issued by this Kushana emperor.

Kanishka I (Founder of Saka Era)

Kanishka could be described as the greatest among the Kushanas. He was the successor of Wema Kadphises and scholars say that the Saka era of AD 78 began with his reign. According to Chinese historians a Kushan king had fought with the Chinese General, Pan-Chao, sometime during the last quarter of the first century AD and the speculation is rife that the Kushan ruler must be no other than Kanishka I. Again, Hieun Tsang makes a specific reference to the Chinese hostage held in the court of Kanishka.

His Empire

Kanishka built a large empire which extended from Gandhara to Oudh and Benares and included the regions of Jammu and Kashmir, the Punjab, and western U.P. Outside India, his empire included Afghanistan, borders of Sindh and Khotan and Kashgar. The seat of his capital was at Purushaputra or Peshawar.

The people of India often remember this great ruler for having built beautiful monuments and the patronage rendered to Buddhism. He built a wonderful Chaitya (Buddhist abode of worship) at Peshawar which evoked great admiration of travellers in those days. The Kushan sculpture which includes a decapitated statue of the king himself has excited the wonder of many. Kanishka convened the fourth Buddhist Council at Kundalavana (in Kashmir) which was presided over by a great Buddhist, Vasumitra. Ashvaghosha, the learned biographer of the Buddha, was also invited to the council which was to collect all Buddhist manuscripts and prepare commentaries on them. About five hundred monks from all parts of the world participated in the conference. It may be said that Mahayana Buddhism might have made its beginning during the time of Kanishka.

Significance of Kanishka's Reign

Northern India under Kanishka achieved the desired political unity. Although Kanishka showed, great leanings to Buddhism, his coins indicate his eclectic nature. Trade flourished since Kanishka ruled both northern India and central Asia. The age of Kanishka contributed much to the development of art, architecture and literature. The Gandhara school of art reached the pinnacle of glory during the time of Kanishka. The Gandhara sculptors made the beautiful images of the Buddha and the Bodhisattvas.

The Gupta Age

Earliest Rulers

After the fall of the Kushana empire, the political unity of the country was again achieved during the time of Imperial Guptas. Puranas mention the name of Sri Gupta and Ghatotkacha as the earliest Gupta rulers who ruled over the small kingdom of Magadha, as feudatory rulers. The third ruler of the Gupta dynasty was Chandragupta I (320-335 AD) who assumed high sounding and imperial title of *Maharajadhiraja* and consolidated his position by marrying the princess of a powerful ruling family, Lichchavis. Kumaradevi, the Lichchavi princess, added to the prestige and power of the imperial Guptas. It is said that the Gupta era commenced with the accession of Chandragupta I to the throne in 320 AD. At the time of his death, Chandragupta might have built an empire whose territories extended from Allahabad to southern parts of Bihar. Chandragupta nominated one of his sons, Samudragupta, to be his successor. The Allahabad pillar inscription speaks of the career and achievements of Samudragupta. The inscription is a *Prasasthi* (Eulogy) of Harisena, a court-poet of Samudragupta. After assuming power Samudragupta (335-350 A.D.) embarked on a career of conquest. The names of nine kings whom he defeated in northern India is given but unfortunately it is difficult to identify the regions they ruled. Samudragupta's campaigns and annexations of the territories of the defeated rulers had profound effects upon the neighbouring kings. The Malvas of Malwa, the Arjunayanas of Alwar and Jaipur, Yaudheyas of northern Rajasthan, Madrakas of Sialkot, Abhiras of central India submitted to his authority voluntarily. Not satisfied with the conquest of northern India, Samudragupta launched a great campaign to subdue the powerful rulers of south India. He defeated the confederacy of south Indian rulers whose names are Mahendra of Kosala, Vyghraraja of Mahakantara, Mantaraja of Kurala, Mahendragiri of Pishtapura, Svamidatta of Kutura, Damana of Erandapalla, Pallava king Vishnugopa of Kanchi, Nilaraja of Avamukta, Hastivarman of Vengi, Ugrasena of Palakka, Kubera of Devarashtra and Dhananjaya of Kushtalapur. All of them acknowledge the supremacy of Samudragupta and they were asked to continue as feudatory rulers. After *digvijay* over the south, he celebrated the *asvamedha* sacrifice to indicate his imperial status. Samudragupta's fame not only rests on his great conquests but also on his statesmanship. He followed different policies towards the defeated states. He annexed the states of some rulers, exacted tributes from others, and maintained friendly relations with the others. The Emperor's personal accomplishments are many. Some of his coins show that he was an accomplished artist playing upon the lyre. His courtiers called him Kaviraja. The Asvamedha coins indicate his implicit faith in vedic religion. He was a great lover of learning as can be seen from the *Prasasthi* of his court-poet Harisena.

Chandragupta II
Soon after the death of Samudragupta, his son Chandragupta II (380-413 AD) ascended the throne. Before attacking the Sakas in the west, Chandragupta II consolidated his position by matrimonial alliances with the powerful rulers such as the Nagas and the Vakatakas. He married the Naga princess, Kuberanaga. He gave his daughter Prabhavati in marriage to a powerful prince of the Vakataka ruling family, Rudrasena II. The Sakas were foreigners who had settled on the western side of his empire. He considered their presence as a great menace to his empire. He launched a campaign against them with the result that the last Saka Satrap, Rudrasimha

III, was defeated and killed. Thus India was liberated from the occupation of foreigners on her sacred soil. After this conquest, western Malwa and Kathiwar were added to his dominions. The Gupta empire spread from the coast of Bay of Bengal to the coast of the Arabian Sea. This conquest was of great significance since the ports of the west coast were engaged in commerce with the west. Chandragupta II assumed the title, Vikramaditya and Sakari and struck gold and silver coins in his name. The Gupta empire

Gupta Coins

reached the acme of its glory during this time. Many have described his age as the golden age. Fahien, a Chinese pilgrim, who came at this time has spoken highly of efficient system of government and the acts of charity of moneyed classes. In the field of art, architecture and literature the Gupta age stands distinguished. Chandragupta was a liberal patron and his court was adorned by the *Navaratnas* (nine gems meaning nine great and learned men). The greatest among the nine was Kalidasa, the poet *par excellence*. Next comes Dhanvantari, the great physician of the time. The third in line Varahamihira, the great astronomer, the fourth was Amarasimha, the lexicographer, the fifth, Shanku, the architect, the sixth, Kshapanaka, the astrologer, the seventh, Vararuchi, the grammarian, the eighth, Vetalabhatta, the magician and the ninth, Ghatakharpara, probably a poet.

Chandragupta's successor was Kumaragupta who ruled over the empire from 415 to 455 AD. He seemed to have ruled well after observing his performance of the *Asvamedha* sacrifice. However, during the last years of his life, the Gupta empire was subjected to serious trouble by the Pushyamitras living near the Narmada valley. It was Prince Skandagupta who saved the empire from these marauders. Prince Skandagupta next turned his attention to deal with the Huns who were invading and conquering some provinces. His efforts to repel the aggression of the

Huns succeeded and they were expelled from India. After his glorious victory over the Huns, Prince Skandagupta assumed the title, Vikramaditya. His rule ended about 467 AD and subsequently we do not have enough records to trace the Gupta history.

Inscriptions record that the Gupta empire continued to survive despite the troubles from the Huns. Its decline began rapidly from the early sixth century AD. The later Guptas did restore the glory, but only for a short time during the seventh century AD.

Religion

The Gupta age is known for the revival of Brahmanical Hinduism. The emperors revived the vedic sacrifices and protected the four castes. A new feature of the religious life of the people was the Bhakti (intense devotion to God) cult. Religious toleration was another feature worth noticing during that age.

Gupta Age, the 'Gilded age'

The Gupta age is also known for its literary grandeur. It produced great men like Kalidasa and others. The Puranas were recast. In the field of science the Gupta age could boast of having produced great scientists like Aryabhatta and Varahamihira. Narada and Brihaspati contributed to the legal system of the age.

Vardhana Dynasty

Confusion and disintegration of the Gupta empire prevailed in northern India due to the constant invasions of the Huns. It was not until the early seventh century that there was an attempt to stem this tide of disunity and confusion. The Vardhana dynasty which ruled over the kingdom of Thaneswar succeeded in establishing the political unity of northern India. After a series of personal tragedies Harshavardhana came to power in Thaneswar in 606 AD. The nobles of Kanauj offered the crown of late Grahavarman, brother-in-law of Harsha, to Harshavardhana since Rajasri the widowed queen had intention of ruling the kingdom. To what extent Harshavardhana took revenge upon the enemies of his brother-in-law is not clearly known. But he got the assistance of Bhaskaravarman, the ruler of Kamarupa (Assam). Harsha's attempt to conquer the south was foiled by the powerful Chalukya ruler, Pulakesin II. Harsha patronised scholars and Buddhism. Hieun Tsang, the Chinese pilgrim, became his personal friend and guest. He assisted Harshavardhana in holding the Kanauj Assembly where he became the highly honoured guest of the emperor. Harsha also held Prayaga Assembly where the Chinese pilgrim was also present. It was here that Harshavardhana gave away everything to the poor and needy and received his ordinary garments from his widowed sister. Harsha was a great patron of learning and literature. He gave liberal donations to the Nalanda University where scholars from home and abroad received special instructions on Mahayana Buddhism. Harsha was an accomplished writer whose works, *Nagananda, Patnavali* and *Priyadarshika* attained great status in literature.

Early Chalukyas of Badami

In the Deccan, the early Chalukyas played an important role in uniting the Deccan between the sixth and eighth century AD. The most distinguished ruler of the dynasty was Pulakesin II (609-642 AD). He won victories against his neighbours like the Kadambas and the Pallavas and built an empire which extended from the border of Narbada to Cavery. One of his significant victories was against Harshavardhana who tried to conquer the south. However, his tragic end for himself and his empire came when his traditional foe, the Pallavas of Kanchi, invaded Badami under the leadership of King Narasimhavarman I. The Chalukyan empire witnessed confusion and chaos for the next 13 years. Its glory was revived by Vikramaditya in 654 AD. Pulakesin II maintained diplomatic relations with the Persian Empire under Khusrau II. One of the paintings at Ajanta shows the reception accorded to the Persian embassy by the Chalukya king. The Chalukya rulers enriched the culture of ancient India with their patronage of art, architecture and literature. A few paintings at Ajanta and the temples built at Badami and Pattadakal stand as testimony to their encouragement.

Pallavas of Kanchi

In the far south, the Pallavas ruled from the fifth century AD to the ninth century AD. One of their earliest rulers was Vishnugopa of whom there is a reference in the Allahabad pillar inscription. From the sixth century onwards the Pallava rulers became very powerful and blazed a trail of glory. The first ruler, Simhavishnu, might have inflicted crushing defeats on the Cholas, Pandyas and the Ceylonese rulers. The next ruler as Mahendravarman I and with him the Pallava-Chalukya struggle for the supremacy of the south began. Mahendravarman converted himself from Jainism to Saivism. The Chalukya ruler seemed to have gained upper hand in the struggle for supremacy till it was halted by Narasimhavarman I, son of Mahendravarman I. His forces invaded the Chalukya capital, Badami, and it was seized. Pulakesin II lost his life in the battle. The Chalukyas took revenge during the time of Vikramaditya I and Vikramaditya II. In the course of time the Pandyas also attacked the Pallava kingdom and it declined rapidly from the ninth century AD onwards. Aditya Chola defeated

Aparajita Pallava and established a new kingdom in its place during the ninth century AD.

Their Contributions

The Pallavas rendered great contributions to art, architecture and literature. Their cities and towns including the famous Mamallapuram abound with temples, carvings and great works of sculpture. Rock-architecture came to be patronised. The *Pancha-pandava Rathas* (Chariots of Pandavas) are hewn out of rock-boulders. In literature, the kings also contributed. Mahendravarman I was an artist and writer of great repute. He wrote a famous burlesque titled *Mattavilasa-Prahasana.*

It must be noted that Kanchi had been serving as a great centre of learning in the south. Many Vaishnava and Saiva saints imparted instructions and made Kanchi a great religious centre also. Hieun Tsang mentions that there were 100 monasteries and 10,000 priests at Kanchi. Scholars of various hues flourished. They mainly included the Jain, Buddhist, the Vaishnava and Saiva scholars. Vatsyayana, the renowned logician of that time, lived in Kanchi. This great centre of learning attracted even princes like the Mayurasarman of the Kadamba dynasty.

The Cholas of Tanjore

The Cholas of Tanjore came to power soon after the eclipse of the Pallavas in the south. Their origin is shrouded in mystery. They ruled south India from the ninth to the thirteenth century AD. They established their sway over Chola-Mandalam (Chola country) which lies in the region between the two rivers, Pennar and Vellar. The Cholas achieved remarkable progress under one of their greatest rulers, Rajaraja I (985-1014 AD) His great exploits are engraved on the walls of Rajarajesvara temple at Tanjore. He defeated the Cheras, the Pandyas, the rulers of Mysore, the eastern Chalukyas of Vengi and invaded ceylon. His brilliant campaigns on land and sea remain unsurpassed. The Cholas became a great sea-power after the conquest of Laccadives and Maldives.

Rajaraja's Contributions

Besides being a great conqueror, Rajaraja the Great was also a great administrator and patron of art. He introduced many reforms in the administration to serve the cause of the poor and built splendid temples. Being a Saivite he built the Rajarajesvara temple at Tanjavur in honour of God Shiva. His religious toleration is proved by the fact that he gave permission to Sailendra, king of Java, to build a Buddhist *Vihara* near Negapatam.

Rajender Chola's Exploits

Rajendra Chola, son of Rajaraja the Great, succeeded to the Chola throne in 1014 and ruled for about thirty years. He may be described as an illustrious son of an illustrious father. His great exploits included the defeat of the Pandyas, the Cheras, and the Chalukyas of Kalyani. The Chola army led by him marched victoriously up to the banks of the Ganges in Bengal defeating a number of rulers of Kalinga, Orissa and south Kosala on the way. Mahipala, the Pala king of Bengal, was also defeated. On his triumphal return, he built a new capital, *Gangaikondacholapuram.* He also assumed the title, *Gangaikonda.* Not satisfied with the victories achieved on land, he sent several naval expeditions against the Sailendra kings of Java and succeeded in defeating them. Thus the Cholas built overseas empire which included Java, Sumatra, Malaya Peninsula and Ceylon. Like his illustrious father, Rajendra Chola rendered great services to the people by introducing reforms in administration and patronising art and literature. His successors carried on his such good works during the succeeding generations. With the invasion of south India by Malik Kafur the Chola power declined rapidly.

Chola Administration

The Chola emperors were enlightened despots. They divided their empire into mandalas (provinces). They sent members of the royal blood to serve as viceroys. The emperor was assisted by ministers and a coterie of officials as in modern government. Similarly, the viceroys were also assisted by ministers and officials. One of the great features of Chola administration was the local administration of the villages. It was in this field we observe that Cholas followed the principles of democratic government. Their village assembly was democratic in character as it consisted of elected representatives. The Uttaramerur inscription gives an idea of how a village assembly of Uttaramerur consisted of elected members, each elected by the adult voters of one ward and also gives detailed description of the process of election. The village assembly divided itself into committees, each committee consisting of some experienced members looking after one aspect of village affair. Maintenance of temples, agriculture and irrigation, collection of taxes, construction of roads, market regulations and the like were looked after by committees. Thus democratic principles were very much operating in the affairs of the village assemblies. It must be noted that even the Chola emperors respected the decisions of these assemblies.

Other Contributions

The Chola emperors encouraged learning literature, art and architecture. The educational institutions imparted instructions on Vedas, Puranas, Dharmasastras, astronomy, science and various sastras. The Chola artists have created beautiful stone as well as bronze statues of gods and goddesses.

The marvel of Chola architecture can be seen in Tanjavur and other important towns of south India. The Rajarajesvara temple, Brihadesvara temple and Rajendra Chola's Siva temples show the beautiful architecture of the Cholas. The Chola temples are famous for their *Vimanas* (towers), and big courtyards.

There was a widespread prosperity in the Chola Empire due to brisk trade and commerce. The Chola traders maintained commercial relations with China, Malaya, Western Gulf countries and the islands in South East Asia.

The Chola emperors were the followers of either Saivism or Vaishnavism. They built temples in honour of Lord Shiva or Lord Vishnu. They also built temples for many goddesses. The Chola emperors allowed freedom of worship and offered necessary protection to practise one's own religion.

The Chola emperors encouraged Tamil literature. Kamban's *Ramayana* is regarded as a great classic in Tamil literature. Jayagondar wrote *Jiwaka Chintamani*. There were Buddhist scholars who wrote a few works in Tamil. Sanskrit literature also made considerable progress. Thus the Cholas made remarkable progress in many fields and thereby enriched the Indian culture.

The Vijayanagara Empire

In 1336 the Thungabhadra region witnessed the rise of the Vijayanagara kingdom. It was founded by the Sangama brothers Hari-Hara and Bukka with the intention of stemming the tide of Muhammedan invasions of the South and paved way for the glory of Hindu religion and culture. A decade later, a group of feudal lords revolted against the Tughlak regime and founded a Muslim kingdom — the Bahamani kingdom in the northern borders of Vijayanagara. Long drawn battles between these kingdoms became a common feature. Vijayanagara kingdom grew into an empire by stretching its control over the far south, and Krishnadevaraya, of the Tuluva dynasty became its most successful sovereign (1509-29). His reign marks all-round progress, and most notably in art, literature, philosophy and diplomacy. Diplomats and travellers who visited Vijayanagara city have left behind their accounts of peace and prosperity enjoyed by the people. The ruler excelled in literature (himself an author) and his magnificent court was adorned by Ashtadiggajas (eight famous poets). The Portuguese established diplomatic relations and supplied Arabian horses for strengthening the cavalry division of his powerful army. Strong and handsome, he dwarfed other rulers of the country by his generosity and friendliness. Three decades after his death, this assiduously built empire was in trouble, and with the battle of Talikota in 1565 against the Muhammedans it fell. The glorious city lay in ruins, a victim of vengeance.

Lesson Review
1. Trace the career and achievements of Chandragupta Maurya.
2. Assess the greatness of Emperor Ashoka.
3. Write a prefatory note on the expansion of the Mauryan Empire.

16
ROMAN CIVILISATION

PART I

While the ancient Greeks gave the world their idea of democracy, art, philosophy, science and literature, their natural successors, the Romans, added to it their legal system and the art of statecraft. Again, while the Greeks always remained disunited, the Romans showed the way to unity and consolidation. The Greeks tended to be intellectual but the Romans proved to be practical minded. With these contrasts in mind, let us examine the genesis and development of the Roman Empire.

Geographical Factors

Like Ancient Greece, the early history of Rome in Italy was profoundly influenced by geographical factors. The mountains in the north (the Alps) and the seas surrounding on all the three sides have given Italy its natural protection. However, it did not prevent hordes of tribes from entering Italy through the passes. The Apennine mountains run north-south along the eastern coast and hence made it possible for Rome (lying at the centre of the west coast) to dominate over the entire peninsula eventually. Mild climate and fertile soil proved to be congenial for the growth of agriculture. As Italy with Rome faced west rather than east, she was able to gain control over the western Mediterranean world.

Latins and Others

About 1800 BC a group of Indo-Europeans called Italics came to Italy through Alpine passes. One of their tribes was the Latins who settled in Latium, i.e., the central plains of Italy lying south of the River Tiber. They spoke Latin and learned to use bronze. The Latins began to live in small walled villages for protection. They established several such villages in the midst of seven hills near the west coast overlooking the River Tiber. They became trading posts of the Latins and eventually developed into the city of Rome.

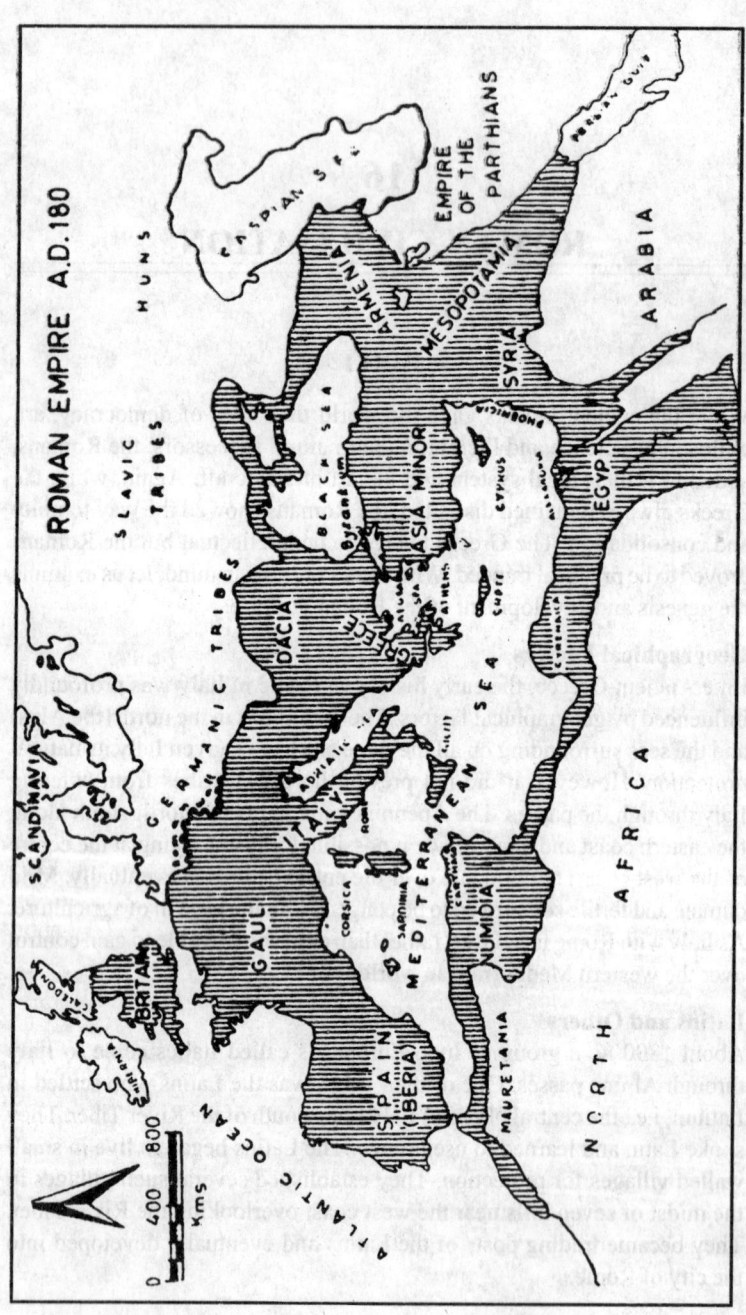

Roman Civilisation

The Latins were not the only people who settled in Italy. There came the Etruscans, a civilised people from Asia Minor, who settled on the land lying north of the River Tiber around 800 BC In the far south of Italy the Greeks had established their colonies. They occupied the eastern part of Sicily also. In the farther north there were the barbaric Gauls.

Etruscan Rule Overthrown

The Latins came under the civilised Etruscan rule for nearly two centuries. From the Etruscans the simple Latins learnt many things like constructing stone-buildings, building arches, draining marshes and using sewage system, predicting future and fighting-formations in war. The Etruscans were eventually driven out by the Latins in 509 BC, and a republic was established.

The Roman Republic was aristocratic in character because only the aristocratic class the patricians enjoyed political, social and economic privileges. Two magistrates known as Consuls, chosen every year from the rank of Patricians (nobles), became heads of the Roman government. The consuls and other officials like the *Praetors* (administrators of Justice), *Aediles* (controllers of city government), *Quaestors* (accountants) and censors (who supervised the list of citizens and their morals) were all chosen for one year by the Assembly consisting of weapon-bearing men. But the most important political body was the senate having about 300 patricians. In times of emergency, a dictator was chosen by the senate for a term of six months. The common people were known as Plebeians who were denied powers and privileges by the ruling politicians. They launched a long historic struggle and finally won some major concessions. Those major concessions for the Plebeians included (1) the right to elect *tribunes* or officials who had the power to veto legislation under consideration by the senate, (2) the right to intermarry with the members of partician family, (3) right to hold public offices, (4) Laws of Rome in the form of *Twelve Tables* (all in writing) as a guarantee of protection against whimsical Patrician judges, and (5) the Assembly or *Comitia* to have power to make laws *which could not be vetoed* by the senate. The fusion between the two classes—the patricians and the plebeians—made the Roman Republic truly democratic in character.

Expansion of Rome

Rome rose as a small city—legends say it was founded by the twin brothers, Romulus and Remus on the Palatine hill in 753 BC—and destiny ordained her to become a big empire after a few centuries. In her early imperial career, she faced formidable enemies such as the Aequians from the east, the Etruscans from the north and the Volscians from the south. Fortunately, all the Latins got united and formed a political league under the leadership of Rome and the attacks of their enemies were effectively repulsed. The Etruscan cities fell one by one to the invading Romans. Then the Gauls, a war-like people from the north, attacked the city of Rome itself and burnt it. The Romans were forced to pay a huge ransom to save themselves. The members of the Latin league broke the union and attacked Rome. So, she had to crush these rebellions.

The Samnites, a war-like tribe inhabiting the highlands of the central Apennines, caused serious troubles to Rome and so she had to wage three wars to crush their power. The result was that she became supreme over central Italy. During the last quarter of the third century BC she had to face formidable Greeks of the south who sought help from Pyrrhus, king of Epirus. Initially suffering setbacks in the war with the Greeks, the Romans, however, succeeded in conquering the south also. Thus, Rome (270 BC) became the mistress of Italy.

Rome's Clash with Carthage

But her troubles were not yet over. A fierce and far more powerful and wealthy foe lay on her southern borders across the sea. Carthage lying on the north African coast just opposite Sicily grew as one of the most powerful and wealthy Phoenician colonies. Her powerful fleet dominated over the western Mediterranean and her armies gained control over northern Africa, Spain, western part of Sicily, Bardinia and Corsica. She grew terribly afraid of the expansion of Rome and attempted to prevent her from trading with Sicily. The wars between those two great rivals broke out in 264 BC when Carthage occupied Messina, a port in north-eastern Sicily. As the first Punic war was mostly fought on the sea, Rome and attempted to prevent her from trading with Sicily. The wars between those two great rivals broke out in 264 B.C. when Carthage occupied Messina, a port in north-eastern Sicily. As the first Punic war was mostly fought on the sea, Rome suffered a series of defeats at the hands of the Carthaginians. However, learning from experience, the Romans started building better battle-ships to fight the enemy. The war ended after 23 years (241 BC) with Carthage suing for peace and ceding the island of Sicily. After another 23 years (218 BC), the second Punic war began when Hannibal, a famous Carthaginian general, attacked Saguntum (east coast of Spain), an ally of Rome. With an army of 80,000 soldiers, and 300 elephants, Hannibal marched from Spain to Italy through Gaul (France) and the Alps and scored three brilliant victories against the Romans. Unfortunately, he could not capture Rome because he had not brought siege machinery. He avenged the first defeat of Carthage by roaming about in Italy from one end to the other proclaiming himself to be her master. But Hannibal did not get cooperation from the Italian cities and his forces and supplies began to dwindle during 13 years of his stay. The Romans appointed Fabius Maximus as dictator to deal with Hannibal. He adopted delaying tactics to wear out his enemy's patience and also by not engaging in an open fight (hence his title or nickname as 'Cunctator'). The Romans also foiled the attempt of Hannibal's brother to go to the rescue of his brother. Finally they sent a brilliant commander, Publius Scipio, who won a victory against the Carthaginians in Spain. From there he proceeded and attacked Carthage (202 BC) itself. Hannibal had to return home to save his people but he was defeated in the battle of Zama. Carthage sued for peace and paid a heavy penalty. She lost Spain, paid heavy war indemnity and agreed not to wage any war against Rome.

Despite these setbacks Carthage recovered her former glory in about half a century. It must be remembered that Hannibal who fled secured the alliance of powers like Macedonia, Greece and western Asia Minor to fight Rome. But he did not succeed as all these three powers were defeated one by one and conquered by Rome.

Carthage Destroyed (146 BC)

Rome had suffered so much at Hannibal's hands that a section of Romans led by Cato desired nothing short of the destruction of Carthage itself. They cried *Delenda est Carthago* (Carthage must be destroyed). While Carthage was busy grappling with her troublesome neighbours, Romans attacked her. Despite her stout resistance she was defeated and the invading Romans took vicarious pleasure in destroying this most beautiful city. Her citizens were killed or sold into slavery. She became a Roman province. Thus, Rome became the mistress of the Mediterranean world. Her merchants became prosperous. She came into contact with the Hellenistic culture which was much superior to hers. This brought about a marvellous transformation in her own civilisation as later events were to prove. Macedonia and Greece became Roman provinces after the suppression of their revolts by the Romans in 146 BC.

Rise of Dictatorship in Rome

The extremes of wealth and poverty resulted in growing class conflicts and sometimes led to civil wars in Rome. The People's Party was formed to make the Roman government to favour the poor by passing necessary land laws. In the meanwhile the Roman generals began to raise mercenary armies to promote their own selfish interests. Thus, the Roman Republic lost much of its original vigour and vitality and finally paved way for the dictatorship of Julius Caesar.

Julius Caesar

Among the Roman Generals who became famous (as the first triumvirate) were Pompey, Julius Caesar and Crassus. Pompey was known for the conquest of Syria and the Near East and controlled the Roman senate. Julius Caesar conquered Gaul (modern France and Belgium) and Britain and sent frequent reports to Rome about his great victories. Crassus died fighting the Parthians. The victories of Julius Caesar made Pompey not only feel jealous but nervous and so he was ordered to return to Rome minus his army. But Julius Caesar with his loyal army crossed the River Rubicon in 49 BC and marched towards Rome—a most fateful step he took in his life. Being extremely popular with the Romans, Caesar made a triumphant entry into Rome while Pompey and the Senate members fled. But Caesar chased Pompey right upto Egypt where he was killed. Egypt under Queen Cleopatra became an ally of Rome. Although he ruled the Roman Empire like a virtual dictator, Julius Caesar showed respect to the Republican traditions and form of government. After putting down the revolts in Spain and Africa, he inaugurated his rule with a series of reforms. His reforms included improvement in agriculture, reduction of taxes, removal of corrupt and oppressive governors, granting of citizenship rights to the people of Gaul and Sicily, distribution of public lands, inauguration of public-work programmes, improving the coinage system and introducing the Julian Calendar in 45 BC. He had many plans such as to bring about a legal code and construction of a library but unfortunately he did not live to complete them. A few of his enemies led by Brutus (who felt quite jealous of Caesar's popularity with the masses), assassinated him on the ides of March, 44 BC. This incident plunged Rome into a civil war. Octavian, a grand-nephew of Julius caesar, and Mark Antony joined to crush those who murdered Caesar. They were joined by Lepidus, a great politician of Rome, to form a second Triumvirate. They defeated Brutus and Cassius, who were the chief conspirators, at the battle of Philippi in 42 BC. Brutus and Cassius took their own lives and the Roman empire was divided into three parts—the eastern provinces including Egypt came under Mark Antony and the Western provinces were ruled by Octavian. Sicily and Africa came under Lepidus. Unfortunately, Mark Antony fell madly in love with the Egyptian Queen Cleopatra and neglected state affairs. Augustus asked the Senate to depose him and proceeded with his army to defeat Antony. Antony was defeated in the naval battle of Actium. He committed

Roman Civilisation

suicide. Queen Cleopatra also committed suicide by taking the poison of an asp. After her death, the rule of Ptolomies ended and Egypt became a Roman province. Octavian (29 BC-14 AD), in an earlier encounter, had brought about the defeat of Lepidus. So he ruled the Roman Empire as the undisputed master with such titles as 'Augustus' and 'Princeps'—the former denoting his divine status. Outwardly showing his regard for the Republican form of government, Augustus wielded unlimited powers to complete the task left by his uncle.

'Golden age' of Augustus Marked by Reforms

The Augustan age is sometimes described as the 'golden age' in the history of Rome. It was known for peace and prosperity. This was ensured by Augustus since he introduced several administrative and economic reforms. Honest and sincere governors and other officials were appointed in the provinces to improve conditions. They were all paid by the central government. The governors took census of the population in their respective provinces and also maintained records regarding the wealth of the citizens. The latter was carried out in order to bring about a fair distribution of taxes. The emperor kept the poor people happy by supplying foodgrains free during difficult times and provided for their free entertainment. They were encouraged to worship him as god. He undertook public works schemes to bring about the employment of the poor. Augustus spent money lavishly on such public works like construction of public buildings, roads, bridges, amphitheatres and fountains. The most prominent among them were the Coliseum, the large amphitheatre (which accommodated 50,000 people), and the Baths of Carachalla. Construction of highways from the provincial cities to the capital served the dual purpose i.e., facilitating trade and commerce on the one hand and exercising political control on the other. There is no doubt in the saying, "all roads lead to Rome". Rome became the nerve centre of all trade and commerce in the Mediterranean World. Rome rose as a small village on the bank of the river Tiber, and after a few centuries became the world capital. It is no surprise that Augustus could say with pride that he found Rome, a city of bricks and turned it into a city of marble. The Roman Empire under Augustus maintained diplomatic and commercial contacts with a number of countries including China and India. He encouraged arts and literature. Livy, a Roman historian, wrote the *Annals* (History of Rome). Virgil wrote an epic poem, *Aeneid*. Other famous writers who enriched the Latin literature with their important contributions were Ovid, Horace, Pliny, Juvenal and Tacitus. Augustus takes the credit for establishing *Pax Romana* (Roman peace) which lasted for nearly five centuries.

Birth of Jesus (4 BC)
One of the most important events which took place in his glorious reign was the birth of Jesus Christ (4 BC,) in Bethlehem, near Jerusalem. Rome extended the citizenship rights to her provincial subjects.

Successors of Augustus

The successor of Augustus was his son Tiberius who proclaimed himself Roman emperor. Thus the Republic came to an end and the empire witnessed the rule of one man. In its long and chequered history, the Roman Empire was alternately ruled by good and bad emperors. The bad emperors included Caligula and Nero. The latter murdered many including his own wife and mother. He blamed the Christians for setting fire to Rome. In the long list of good emperors we have Marcus Aurelius, a great stoic philosopher who wrote *Meditations*. With his death ended the Age of the Antonines. The general decline of the Roman Empire commenced after the death of Marcus Aurelius. It was to some extent checked by Emperors Diocletian and Constantine. The former divided the empire into two parts, the East with its capital at Byzantium and the west with Rome. Constantine brought about the unity between the two under his control after defeating his counterpart. He shifted the capital of the empire from Rome to Byzantium which was renamed after him as Constantinople. After his death the two halves got totally separated with each coming under an emperor.

Fall of Rome
Numerous causes can be attributed to the fall of the Roman Empire in 476 AD. Among the most important are the following:
1. Constant invasions of barbaric hordes like the Germanic tribes and the Huns,
2. A succession of weak and incompetent emperors,
3. Wide gulf between the rich and the poor and the latter bearing the main brunt of many taxes,
4. Slavery
5. Lack of leadership and discipline in the Roman army.
6. Increasing popularity of Christianity

PART II

THE LEGACY OF ROME

Let us examine what the Romans have bequeathed by way of legacy to the world civilisation.

It is no exaggeration to say that were it not for the Romans, the Greek culture would not have spread to the western world. Directly or indirectly the Romans acted as agents to spread and preserve much of what the Ancient Greeks had left behind as their legacy. It was from the Greeks that the Romans imbibed ideas on religion, philosophy, art and architecture, learning and science. But it is also untrue to say that the Romans copied everything from the Greeks. They showed us the way to important fields such as organisation of central and provincial governments, laws, principles of taxation, citizenship rights, hospital and sanitation systems and the construction of public works like the fountains, theatres, baths, bridges, aqueducts and arterial roads.

Pax Romana (Roman Peace)
The Romans were great builders of an empire whose borders touched all the peripheral countries of the Mediterranean sea (Britain and Mesopotamia to be included). After having achieved this they organised the local and provincial governments in such a way as to ensure peace and harmony among the local populace. This they did by not interfering with the local religions and traditions of the conquered lands. However, to ensure a lasting loyalty to their emperors, the Romans granted citizenship rights to provincial subjects thereby granting them status of equality with the Romans. Border provinces were protected from the invading hordes by constructing a wall and stationing of Roman legions. Able governors were sent to maintain law and order, a fair system of taxation and administer justice. Piracy and banditry were put down so that merchants travelled freely without any fear. A uniform system of currency came into vogue to facilitate trade, commerce and banking. In the course of time all the provinces sent their representatives to the Assembly.

Roman Law
The most lasting contribution of the Romans was made in the field of law. It is no exaggeration to say that their laws had made profound impact on almost all the civilised nations of the world today. The first written code came in the form of Twelve Tables in 150 BC which were inscribed on the twelve tables of bronze and publicly displayed in the forum (market place). Subsequent growth of the Roman Empire and of her commerce made it necessary to enlarge the scope of the Twelve Tables taking into consideration such changes as the rights of foreigners living in the Roman Empire. The Roman Government appointed a special judge, *Praetor Peregrinus,* to look into the matters related to the rights of foreigners living in Rome. Taking the customs and traditions as practised by foreigners into consideration, a new body of laws came to be evolved by the judges who held the above office in succession. This body of law came to be

Colosseum

known as *jus gentium*. Again, in other fields, the rulings of the judges and decisions of the magistrates remained as unwritten laws. The Roman laws came to be completely classified and codified only after a lapse of several centuries. The great Eastern Roman Emperor, Justinian, (527-565 AD) undertook this enormous task and quite succeeded in completing the code named after him—the Justinian Code. As the Roman law proved to be just and humane in character, it was adopted by many civilised nations. To mention a few salient features, the Roman law gave an opportunity to the accused to defend his case. Unless his guilt was proved 'beyond any reasonable doubt' in a court of law he was not punished. Another salutary principle that it adopted was that all citizens, however high or low they may be, were equal before law.

Architecture and Engineering

The Romans excelled all others in the construction of public buildings. They copied the Greek style in the construction of columns or pillars but arches and domes were their inventions. Their Pantheon (temple) at Rome has a dome measuring 142 feet in diameter. The Colosseum (stadium) which was completed around 80 AD accommodated about 50,000 persons who assembled there to enjoy gladiatorial fights or the slaying of the Christians by the hungry lions. Roman emperors built forums, baths, bridges, aqueducts, fountains and 12,000 miles of highways on 372 main routes. The aristocratic Romans were fond of luxurious life. They built beautiful country-mansions and decorated them with good furniture, marble statues, attractive paintings and expensive tapestries. It laid out gardens surrounding their mansions and had goldfish ponds.

Learning and Latin Literature

The Romans were fond of learning. The Greek slaves taught Roman children during the early period. But after some time these teachers were replaced by the Romans themselves. Rhetoric, grammar and logic were taught. At advanced centres of learning, subjects like astronomy, mathematics, medicine were included. These were studied by the children of the wealthy in great Greek centres like Athens or Rhodes.

In literature, the Romans tried to imitate the Greeks. It was during the time of Augustus that Latin literature reached its highest watermark. Before the Augustun age, there were the writings of Julius Caesar (*Gallic Wars* and *Civil War*) and Cicero. With the dawn of Augustan age there began an outpour from Virgil, Horace, Livy Sallust and Ovid. During the next few centuries, the Latin literature was enriched by the writings of Tacitus (a famous historian), Juvenal (a satirist), Plutarch (another famous historian), Seneca (a playwright of tragedies), Marcus Aurelius and a host of others.

Science

The Romans maintained personal cleanliness, and for this purpose they built baths. All their towns and cities could boast of good drainage system. They built hospitals where patients were treated by qualified physicians and given medicines. The greatest physician of the Roman Empire was a Greek by the name Galen. He wrote more than 500 works of human anatomy and physiology wherein he explained the functions of different organs of a human body. The science of surgery also made considerable advance. Operations were conducted, if it was found absolutely essential. Pliny the Elder wrote the *Naturalis Historia* (Natural History), a large "compendium of all known science". Strabo was a great historian and Geographer who gave a good account of the uses of materials. Ptolemy (See Greek history) wrote *Almagest*, a gist of astronomical account of his age. The Julian calendar was prepared by Sosigenes, an astronomer of Alexandria, who calculated the base year as 365.25 days (hence a leap year once in 4 years). It was introduced in 45 BC by Julius Caesar. The Romans borrowed the notation system from the Etruscans.

Religion

The ancient Romans worshipped Gods and spirits at home. They did not build temples. The head of the family offered simple ceremonies to family Gods and spirits. Influenced by the Greeks later, they started having prototype of Greek Gods in different names. God Jupiter was the Sky God whom the Romans considered as Almighty. The most important Goddess was Juno. Mars became the God of War. Ceres became popular with the farmers for this deity gave good crops. Venus became the Goddess of love. Neptune was the Sea God. The Romans observed two important festivals, Lupercalia (February 15th) and Saturnalia (December 17th) with all gaiety. Then there was the festival to honour the great mother of the Gods, Cybele. Mithraism also prevailed. Thus mysticism persisted in the Roman Empire. The Roman Emperors like Augustus and Diocletian encouraged people to worship them like gods. With the teachings of Jesus Christ, Christianity spread among the poor and the helpless.

Philosophy

Although Rome could not produce anything original in the realm of philosophy, she had great thinkers who subscribed to either Stoicism or Epicureanism. The former was found to be better "fitted for the Roman temperament". Lucretius advocated Epicureanism. Among the Stoic philosophers, the most prominent were Panaetius of Rhodes, Seneca of Rome and Emperor Marcus Aureleius. The last wrote *Meditations* in which he has interpreted "stoic philosophy and its place in Roman civilisation".

Conclusion

The Romans played a dynamic part in building a vast empire and within its territories lived people belonging to different races and speaking different languages. Their greatness lay in welding these "listless subjects into a powerful nation". They enriched the world culture with their art, architecture and literature. Their greatest gift to mankind was the Roman law which took final shape under Emperor Justinian as *Corpus juris civilis*. It served as a model to many civilised nations. It should also be remembered that it was in the Roman empire that Christianity grew into great religion.

Lesson Review

1. Trace the growth of the Roman Empire till the days of Augustus Caesar.
2. Discuss the legacy of Rome to mankind.
3. Write short notes on the following: (not exceeding 10 sentences):
   (a) The Plebs vs. the Patricians (b) The twelve tables.
   (c) Christianity in the Roman Empire.
   (d) Punic Wars.
4. (i) How did geographical factors influence the early history of Rome?

(ii) Show on the outline map the extent of Roman Empire under Augustus and also locate the following:
(a) Rome (b) Carthage
(c) Syracuse (d) Apennine mountains
(e) Po river (f) Tiber.

17

RISE AND SPREAD OF CHRISTIANITY

The early Roman religion had not offered any spiritual satisfaction to the Romans. The worship of Pagan Gods became boring and the Romans for a time "sought comfort in Persian, Egyptian and other Eastern religious cults and philosophies". Finally, Christianity offered them high spiritual satisfaction and great ideals to cherish. Christianity laid stress on fatherhood of God and brotherhood of mankind. Further it taught people about human virtues like love, pity, kindness, truth, chastity and honour.

Life of Jesus
The first books of the New Testament and the book of the Acts give a vague and brief sketch of the life of Jesus. He was born a Jew at Bethlehem, a small village near Jerusalem, in 4 BC when Herod the Great was ruling Judea. His father was Joseph of Nazareth (a descendant of King David) and his mother was Virgin Mary. Jesus was born at a time when the Jews were under Roman control and the corrupt rule of King Herod. They were eagerly expecting a promised Messiah who would deliver them from the Roman authority. Jesus lived in the small village-town of Nazareth for nearly 25 years. As a bright boy he could understand and interpret Jewish texts. At that time Judaism and the Mosaic laws were being interpreted in different ways. Controversies abounded in Judaism itself.

The life of Jesus came to be profoundly influenced by his cousin, John the Baptist. John the Baptist was a great preacher who told his people that a Messiah would arrive to deliver them from sinful life. He baptised those who sincerely repented for their sins. As John became popular, the authorities became jealous and executed him. Jesus was also baptised by John in 26 AD. After his baptism Jesus started a new life. He became a wandering preacher. He spent the rest of his life in teaching about the fatherhood of God. He talked about the kingdom of God where there would be justice, love and kindness. He collected a band of followers. As he was preaching to the people of the villages, he conveyed his messages in the form of parables. True to his teachings he led a very simple life and mixed freely with the poor. He always went to help those who were sick and oppressed. All his disciples recognised him as the Messiah and Jesus acknowledged this title. Some of his teachings called into question some of the Jewish laws. He preached to wean men away from following the letter of the Jewish laws. He urged them to follow their spirit. The popularity of Jesus caused alarm and suspicion. King Herod and the pharisees condemned him as a "false prophet". In 33 AD Jesus visited Jerusalem on the occasion of Jewish Passover and gave an opportunity to his enemies to hatch a plot to kill him. Unfortunately the Romans believed that his growing popularity was a cause of public disturbances. Jesus knowingly courted arrest when he assaulted the money-changers and traders in the temple. He celebrated his last supper with his disciples—including Judas Iscariot—the night before his death. When Jesus was praying in the Garden of Gethsemane, the temple guard arrested him. It was Judas, who betrayed the identity of his master by kissing him on his cheek and thereby giving hint to the guard who Jesus was.

His Crucifixion (33 AD)
The Jews handed over Jesus to the Roman governor, Pontius Pilate, and accused him of blasphemy. The Romans levelled the charge of treason. Jesus was executed by crucifixion along with two thieves at Golgotha.

Gospels say that three days after his crucifixion Jesus rose from the dead, and forty days later was seen ascending to the heaven by his disciples. His followers called themselves as Christians (Greek word *christos* means anointed). The followers of Jesus established Christianity based mainly upon his teachings.

Teachings of Jesus
While the Old Testament in the Bible contains everything about Judaism, the New Testament includes the life and teachings of Jesus. Jesus taught that God is the creator of the universe and mankind. He is all merciful and kind to one and all. He further said that men should live like brothers and be devoted to God. Sinners should repent and beg God's mercy. Men should develop noble character by doing good deeds. Jesus insisted that people should do good to even those who did bad things to them. He said forgiveness is a great virtue. While being nailed to the cross, he said, "Father forgive them for they know not what they do".

He asked his followers to despise wealth and other comforts of life. To the poor and suffering he promised the kingdom of God where there would be justice, love and plenty. He asked his followers to develop

Christian virtues like brotherly love, compassion, righteous living, meekness and humanity. The spiritual message of Jesus to his followers is given in the form of a sermon—the *Sermon on the Mount*. It runs as follows:

"Blessed are the poor in spirit; for theirs is the kingdom of heaven.

Blessed are they that mourn; for they shall be comforted.

Blessed are the meek; for they shall inherit the earth.

Blessed are they which do hunger and thirst after righteousness; for they shall be filled.

Blessed are the merciful; for they shall obtain mercy.

Blessed are the peacemakers: for they shall be called the children of God.

Blessed are they which are persecuted for righteousness sake: for theirs is the Kingdom of Heaven."

Jesus spoke to the people in the villages in an easily comprehensible language i.e., Aramaic—and conveying his messages through parables. His disciples venerated him as the Messiah and the Son of God.

Spread of Christianity

After the crucifixion of Jesus, his twelve disciples known as the Apostles started preaching among the Jews that Jesus was the Son of God and the Messiah; and by appealing to His mercy one can attain salvation. They got many Jews converted. One of the newly-converted Jews was Paul. He was the first to preach the Gentiles (other than Jews) in the Roman Empire. He became extremely popular among the poor and the slaves. Many of them were converted. Paul was arrested and taken to Rome where he was executed about 62 AD. About the same time St. Peter was also executed for preaching Christianity among the Gentiles. Their martyrdom inspired many and the Christian Church was founded in Rome. But the Roman government turned hostile and persecuted the Christians. Despite the persecutions, Christianity gained immense popularity. The Christians refused to worship the Roman Emperor as God, disliked "high taxes and gladiatorial contests" and did not join the army. When fire broke out in Rome, Emperor Nero blamed the Christians for it. Thousands of them were thrown into the arena where they were killed by the hungry lions. But Christianity did not suffer. On the other hand it attracted many who were disgusted with the old Roman religion. When the Roman Empire began to decay, Christianity gathered more adherents. Christianity spread to all parts of the Roman Empire and Asia Minor by the end of the third century. Constantine recognised the importance of Christians and sought their support in winning the contest for the imperial throne. When he succeeded, he issued the Edict of Milan (313 AD) to make Christianity a legal religion in the Roman Empire. He became interested in Christianity and later embraced it publicly. He built a new capital—Constantinople—and dedicated it to the Virgin Mary. All his successors (with one exception) became Christians. Emperor Theodosius abolished the practice of Paganism and made Christianity the sole legal faith in the Roman Empire towards the end of the fourth century. The fall of the Western Roman Empire did not adversely affect Christianity. More and more Romans who became Christians turned to the Church to save them from the dangers of foreign invasions. The Christian Church emerged stronger despite the fall of Rome. The Eastern Roman Empire (known as Bryzantine) witnessed the spread of Christianity among its slave population. Today Christianity, organised under different churches, claims one-third of the world population as its adherents (2.5 billion).

Lesson Review

1. Describe the life and explain the teachings of Jesus Christ.
2. Write a note on the spread of Christianity by Paul and Peter.

18
RISE AND SPREAD OF ISLAM

PART I

Arabia before the birth of Mohammed the Prophet

The Arabian peninsula, which gave birth to Islam, is situated in the southwest Asia and exactly lies in between Iran-Iraq and north-east of Africa. The people who inhabited this land were known as Arabs. They were

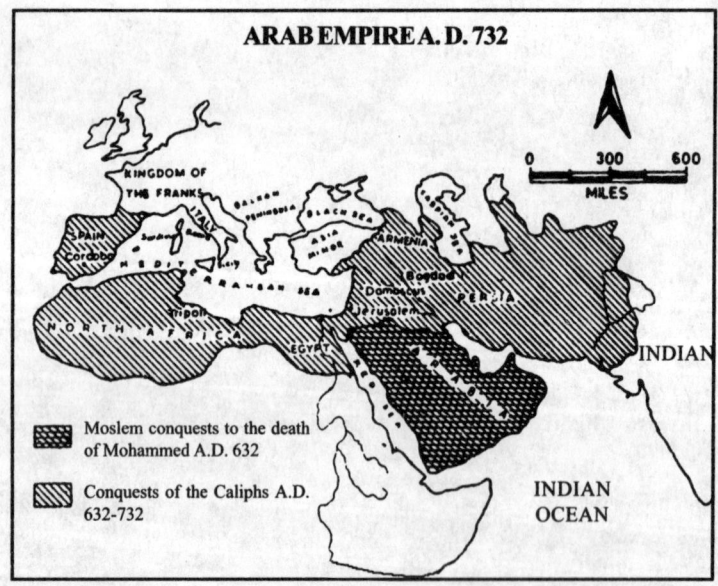

Semitic people, and much of their territory was and is now barren. But lands surrounding a few oases which exist here and there are fertile. Rainfall was negligible and the whole land turned into a desert. At the time of Mohammed's birth it was thinly populated. The Arabs became nomadic

(nick-named as bedouins). They tended camels and used them to carry merchandise from Syria and other upcountry lands to the southern ports and return. They were used to hard life and so quarrels between one tribe and the other were the order of the day. Robbing caravans, plundering cities and bloody wars were all so common because of the absence of a strong central government. Despite these ugly traits, the Arabs were loosely held together by a common faith. The Shrine of Kaaba at Mecca which contained the images of many tribal Gods became a great centre of veneration for the Arabs. Every year, they celebrated the truce of Gods allowing people to come and offer their prayers to the Gods at Kaaba. They exhibited their camaraderie spirit by holding literary and athletic contests. Mecca and Medina became great towns as they were situated near the Red Sea coast with trade routes connecting them.

Life of Prophet Mohammed (570-632)

Mohammed was born at Mecca in 570 AD and belonged to the Hashmite family of Quraishi tribe. His birth was considered auspicious by many because a terrible pestilence which was ravaging Arabia suddenly ended. As Mohammed lost his parents early in his childhood, he was looked after by his grandfather and later by his uncle, Abu Talib. Due to poverty he could not receive any formal education but he was trained to look after sheeps and camels. As a youth he spent most of his time in travelling with the caravans into southern Arabia and Syria. Mohammed was known to many for his honesty and sincerity. They called him 'Amin'. In his twenty-fourth year he was employed by a wealthy widow-merchant, Khadija, whom he married later. They had two sons (who died early) and many daughters among whom Fatima became popular. She was given in marriage to Ali.

From his early youth Mohammed pondered much on the religious life of his fellowmen. During his travels he met the Jews and the Christians, whose monotheistic ideas influenced him deeply. He spent most of his time in religious meditations. Occasionally, he would visit Mount Hira, near Mecca, for meditation and fasting. Many a time he fell into a trance (ecstatic fits) and uttered words which came to be recorded by his early disciples. Later they constituted a part of the Holy Koran.

It was not until his fortieth year, that Mohammed realised the full impact of the divine messages which he received from God. He also realised that he was the chosen one and therefore had great mission to fulfill. Mohammed as convinced that he had great role to play in spreading the message of Almighty God Allah among his fellowmen. He declared "there is no God but Allah, and Mohammed is his Prophet". Soon he gathered a number of disciples, the friend, Abu Bakr. He started preaching the principles of his new faith to the people of Mecca, but their general attitude seemed hostile. The priests of the Temple of Kaaba were alarmed and they opposed the teachings of Mohammed. His life was in danger and therefore he had to retreat to Medina in AD 622. This retreat to Medina constituted a most important year for Islam and it was called *Hejira* 621-22 (reckoning of a new year in the Muslim calendar). Hijri calendar is lunar-based, consisting of 354 days.

Birth of Islam

It was in Medina that Mohammed could get warm reception to his new faith. He gathered a large number of disciples. Mohammed's fame, and that of his new faith, began to spread rapidly all over Arabia. In AD 630 he captured Mecca whose citizens embraced his faith. Thus Mohammed sowed the seed of a new religion called *Islam* (meaning peace with God) in Arabia, and in the course of time it became one of the great religions of the world. Mohammed died in AD 632. At the time of his death Arabia was practically united under his able leadership, and his followers (Mohammedans) having a great zeal to spread their new faith.

Teachings of Mohammed the Prophet

The new faith which Mohammed preached was called *Islam* which simply means submission to God Allah' and the gist of this new religion is found in the sacred book called Koran or *Quran* (in Arabic meaning recitation). Islam includes religious belief of the Mohammedans, their daily duties and the virtues to be practised.

Mohammed preached that there is one God and that is Allah and Mohammed is his Prophet. God reveals his desires to mankind through his prophets and Mohammed declared that he was the last prophet. He condemned idol-worship. He asked his followers to totally submit themselves to the Almighty and all merciful God Allah without whose blessings no one can enter the paradise after one's death. Those who do not believe in Him would suffer in hell. All those who believe in Him and obey His will should live like brothers. All are equal in the eyes of God.

Mohammed preached that every true believer in Islam has certain duties (*ibadat*) to perform in his life. First, he should profess his faith in God Allah and his messenger, Mohammed, by reciting *la ilah illa Allah, Mohammad rasul Allah* (i.e., there is no God but Allah, and Mohammad is His Prophet). This recital of the creed is called *Kalma*. Secondly, he should perform the *Salat* or recite prayers five times in a day (dawn, mid-day, mid-afternoon, sunset, bed-time). Every true believer should go to the mosque to offer his prayer and listen to the discussion of the Koran.

Thirdly, every Mohammedan should fast (from sunrise to sunset) during the lunar month of Ramzan. Fourthly, all believers in Islam should give alms to the poor. The practice of this virtue is known as *zaqqat*. Finally, a true Moslem should undertake a pilgrimage to the holy city of Mecca at least once in his lifetime. This pilgrimage is known as *Hajj*. Mohammed asked his followers to practise many other virtues like humility, charity, and honesty. Respect for women and parents, kindness to slaves and animals, and avoiding gambling and drinking were also prescribed by the Prophet. Koran also contains rules and regulations on such matters like marriage, divorce and inheritance. For those who faithfully follow the teachings of Mohammed the Prophet, God Allah would reward them with a place in the heaven after their earthly existence. On the day of Judgement God Allah would punish the sinners, evil-doers and infidels by sending them to hell. Thus Islam combined in itself some of the best democratic principles such as equality of man, universal brotherhood and direct communion between God and man. It is no wonder that it became one of the world's great religions in the course of time.

Spread of Islam

Mohammed did not leave any heir or nominate any successor. Therefore, the chiefs of Arabia chose the Prophet's friend, Abu Bekr (632-34), to succeed him. He became the first Caliph or *Khalifa* (successor of Mohammed the Prophet and head of the Muslim theocratic State). During his very short term of rule Islam spread to the neighbouring country, Syria. The next Caliph was Omar (634-44) who was mainly responsible for building a large Islamic Empire. His famous general Khalid brought about the defeat of the Roman Emperor Heraclius and received from him provinces like Damascus, Syria, Palestine and Phoenicia. After that Egypt was conquered. The Islamic empire began to spread towards the east with the conquest of Mesopotamia and Persia. During the next hundred years, the Arabs conquered North Africa and Spain. In the east they conquered Sindh (712 AD). They attempted to capture Constantinople twice (673 and 717 AD) but failed. The Arabs crossed the Pyrenees and entered France but they were defeated by Charles Martel in the bloody battle at Tours in 732 AD. However, the Arabs continued to hold Spain for the next seven centuries. The people coming under Arab subjection were given the choice of either embracing Islam or pay tribute or be condemned to death. The Arabs gained control of the Mediterranean Sea after defeating the Byzantine fleets during the early ninth century. They succeeded in conquering Sicily and southern part of Italy. In due course of time Islam spread to eastern Africa, Malaya, Indonesia, some parts of Western China and India. Muslim traders and missionaries also contributed much to the spread of Islam in many countries of Africa and Asia.

Caliphs Othman and Ali

After the murder of Omar, Othman succeeded as the new Caliph and ruled the Islamic Empire for nearly 12 years. During his time, the real power was exercised by his cousin Muawiyah who belonged to the Omayyad tribe. There was a civil strife which finally led to the assassination of Caliph Othman. Othman was succeeded by Ali who had married the Prophet's daughter, Fatima. Ali's serious rival was Muawiyah, governor of Syria and cousin of Othman, who staged a revolt. A series of battles ensued between the two which finally ended in the murder of Ali in AD 661. Before Ali's sons could assert themselves, Muawiyah declared himself as the Caliph in Syria. But Muawiyah, according to a treaty, acknowledged the claim of Hussain (son of Ali) to the caliphate after his death. Unfortunately, things did not happen the way they should have been. After Muawiyah's death, his son Yezid succeeded to the Caliphate. Quite enraged at this turn of events Hussain left Medina for Kufah to meet his followers. On his way he was murdered with his two hundred followers at Karbala in AD 680.

Sunnis and Shias

Disputed succession and civil strife thus became endemic. It divided the Muslims into two sects—the Sunnis and the Shias. The Sunnis maintain that Abu Bekr and his two successors were the legitimate successors of Mohammed the Prophet. The Sunnis strictly conform to the *Sunna* (custom, usage and form) regarding all matters and look to the Koran for direction. However when the Koran "does not fully and clearly provide direction, the inquirer should seek trustworthy information as to what Mohammed had said on the subject, what his action had been with relation to the subject or what he had approved in others". The Shias hold the opinion that Abu Bekr and his two successors were usurpers. They maintain that Ali was the legitimate successor. The Shias also observe the 'martyrdom' of Hussain (son of Ali) at Karbala during the first ten days of *Muharram*.

The Omayyads and the Abbasids

After the murder of Ali, the Omayyad Caliphate began with the succession of Muawiyah who transferred the capital of the Arab empire to Damascus. It was during the time of his son Yezid that the killing of Hussain and his followers took place at Karbala. One of the great achievements of Omayyads was the conquest of Spain following the landing of their famous General Tarik on a rock now bearing his name (Jabal-al-Tarik meaning 'the mountain of Tarik' or Gibraltar). The Omayyad dynasty remained in power till AD 750 and subsequently it was overthrown by Abbasids (descendants of the Prophet's uncle, Abba). They shifted the capital from Damascus to Baghdad. They followed a ruthless policy of eliminating the Omayyad princes till none survived except Abdur Rahman. He fled to Spain and founded the Omayyad kingdom of Cordova in AD 755. The most celebrated ruler among the Abbasids was Caliph Haroun-Al-Raschid who figures prominently in *The Thousand and One Nights.* His son Mamun also became a distinguished ruler of the Abbasid dynasty. Mamun's death was followed by the rise of independent Muslim states. At the end of the tenth century the Arab empire split into three caliphates—(1) the Abbasids of Baghdad, (2) the Fatimid of Cairo, and (3) the Omayyad of Cordova.

PART II

LEGACY OF ISLAM

Enlightened Autocracy

Like the Roman Empire which was known for its vast size and variety of peoples, the Arab or Islamic Empire included in its fold subjects living in Spain, North Africa, the Middle East and South Asia. The Moslems produced enlightened rulers who did not experience any difficulty in bringing peoples under their subjugation. The most distinguished Moslem rulers of the time were Haroun-al-Raschid and his son Mamun. The Caliphs of the time wielded both spiritual and temporal powers and the people considered them as the true representatives of Mohammed the Prophet. The Caliphs not only worked hard to propagate the new faith but tried to bring about equality and universal brotherhood among Mohammedans. Mohammedans cherish the memory of the glorious reign of Caliph Haroun-Al-Raschid because he was just, wise and humane. He created opportunities for the poor and the downtrodden to live in solace and comfort. Furthermore, he encouraged learning, art, literature, science, trade and commerce.

Learning

The Islamic Empire built by the Arabs could boast of great centres of learning. Baghdad, Cairo, Damascus, Cordova, Seville and Barcelona all became centres of advanced learning with the establishment of universities. The Arab scholars in Baghdad translated all the ancient Greek classics and also the Hindu books on mathematics. Learning came to be patronised by enlightened rulers in the form of awarding scholarships to meritorious students and maintaining libraries with vast source-materials. The meritorious students took full advantage of the patronage and produced great works.

Literature and History

The contributions of Arabs to literature was prolific. They produced the Koran which is ranked as one of the world's greatest classics. They also produced a number of biographies and histories, the most famous being the *Annals of the Apostles and the Kings* written by Al Tabari. Their most entertaining work, if one may call it so, is the *Thousand and One Nights* or the *Arabian Nights* which has remained ever green and ever popular. It has now been translated into many languages. In poetry, Omar Khayyam's *Rubaiyat* (in Persian) found its place of honour. Saadi composed mythical and philosophical odes known as *Gulistan* and *Bustan*. In writings on Epics, Al Firdausi became quite famous with his *Shahnama* (Book of Kings) which was dedicated to Sultan Mohammed Ghazni. Another Scholar-Historian, Ibn Khaldun, wrote his masterpiece *Muquaddimah* where he outlined the philosophy of history. The most outstanding philosophers of the age were Avicenna (980-1037) and Ibn Rushid or Averrhoes (1126-1198). The former was a genius who wrote a hundred treatises in different fields of knowledge and his singular contribution to the science of medicine was his work, *Canon of Medicine* (an encyclopaedia on the general practice of medicine). For centuries physicians consulted this standard reference work. In Arab-Spain Averroes wrote commentaries on the works of Aristotle which were translated into Latin by European scholars. His followers, called Averroists, became radical thinkers.

Medicine-Rhazes (865-925)

The Arabs contributed much to the progress of the science of medicine. The first to distinguish himself in this field was Rhazes (865-925) who wrote *Al Hawi,* a comprehensive work on the practice of medicine. After Avicenna, Al Hasan of Basra distinguished himself with an original work on Optics (which was later translated into Latin as *Opticae Thesaurus*) which influenced many western physicians. Thus, Arab scholars in medicine raised the status of the science of medicine from medieval quackery.

Exact Sciences

In exact sciences like mathematics and astronomy the Arabs learnt much from the Hindus. They replaced the Roman numerals with their own which originated in India. The Europeans learnt from the Arabs (who were much indebted to India) the mathematical terms like *zero, cipher* and algebraic equations. They made improvements in Trigonometry by introducing tangent and cotangents. They knew the principle of pendulum in physics. Arab Geographers worked hard to make their subject rise to the status of science. Accurate measurements to draw the longitude and latitude were made with the help of other sciences like physics and mathematics.

Their Manufactures
They learnt the art of manufacturing paper and block-printing from China and introduced them to Europe. They discovered many chemicals and knew the technique of preparing alcohol, sulphuric and nitric acids. The art of dyeing clothes were known to them. The work of Muslim craftsmen particularly in handicrafts, came to be very much appreciated. Persian carpets and leather works became world-famous. Their textiles like muslin, gauze and damask attained great fame. They also produced beautifully decorated weapons such as daggers, swords and knives.

Travel and Trade
The Arabs proved to be habitual travellers. They undertook long voyages by land and sea and made notes on what they had seen and heard. Some of the most famous travellers of the period were Alberuni (a famous astronomer, physician, historian and geographer all rolled into one), Ibn Batuta, Al Idrisi, Ibn Hakaul and a host of others. Their travels were followed by extensive trade with the countries such as India, China and the coastal countries of Africa. They bought large amount of spices from the east, diamonds from Golconda, pearls from Ceylon and musks from Tibet. They sold their specialities such as fine rugs and carpets, Baghdad perfumes, muslin, guaze, mohair, damask and fruit-syrups. It is no wonder that Baghdad became a great city and capital known for its fabulous wealth. In a way the Arabs can be called "the Phoenicians of the Middle Ages", since they carried on a brisk intercontinental trade.

Art and Architecture
Like the Romans the Arabs became great builders. Most of their cities were adorned with great palaces, tombs, mosques and other structures. Under royal patronage beautiful buildings came up such as the Al Hambra palace at Granada (in Spain), Alcazar at Seville and the Great Mosque of Baghdad. Their style of architecture included in its fold the dome, the arch and the minarets. As Koran forbade the representation of human beings and animals, the Muslim artists decorated the outer as well as the inner walls of the palaces and mosques with intricate carvings and designs. Mosques and palaces were surrounded by beautiful gardens and fountains.

The Arabs astounded the western world with their outstanding achievements. It was through them that Europe came to know of the treasures of Greek classics and absorbed the knowledge of the civilised orient.

Lesson Review

1. Give a brief account of the life of Mohammed the Prophet. What were his teachings?
2. Write an essay on the spread of Islam and explain its contributions in various fields.

19
THE CRUSADES

Crusades mean holy wars waged by the European Christians from the tailend of the 11th century to the close of 13th century for liberating the Holy Land from Muslim domination. These lands, considered holy on account of its association with the life of Jesus Christ, had fallen into the hands of the Arabs in the 7th century but the Christian pilgrims were permitted to visit. Conditions changed in the middle of the 11th century when the Seljuk Turks overthrew the Abbasid caliphate and began to advance towards Asia-Minor. They defeated Eastern Emperor Romanus in 1071 and conquered the richest province of Anatolia. It appeared as though their next step would be to conquer Constantinople itself.

Causes of the First Crusade
The Seljuk Turks happened to be new converts (to Islam) and adopted a hostile attitude towards the Christian pilgrims visiting the holy places under their control. Tales of harassment and persecutions at the hands of the Muslims (many a time exaggerated) on the one hand and his own capital being threatened on the other made it necessary for Emperor Alexius I Comnenus to appeal to Pope Urban II for assistance. Pope Urban II was deeply disturbed by the tragic tales of the Christian pilgrims. He was also worried about peace and security of Europe which were threatened by the Mohammedans. He gave the clarion call to all Christians of Europe to fight the Turks and recover the Holy Land. In response to his call for a holy war against the Muslims, a number of church officials and nobles gathered at Clermont (France) where the Pope gave his battle cry. Many of his listeners took up the cross and the movement was called the "Wars of the Cross". There was tremendous zeal and enthusiasm on the part of the Christians to join the wars of the cross. The Pope had earlier promised those who joined the crusades remission of sins, protection of the participant's property and eternal salvation in case of death. These crusades gave an opportunity to many deserving and undeserving people to fight

for the cause. Nobles, merchants, knights, crooks and criminals joined with selfish motives.

The First Crusade (1096-1099)
In response to the call given by the Pope, a mob of 10,000 men, women and children led by Peter the Hermit (a monk) and Walter the Penniless (a knight) marched towards Jerusalem. As they were ill-equipped and without money, they suffered untold miseries. Many of them perished on their way, and the rest were slaughtered by the Turks. However, the main army consisting of 30,000 strong men led by powerful nobles proceeded towards the holy land by sea and land. They met at Constantinople, got reorganised and attacked the Turks after crossing the Straits. They succeeded in conquering Jerusalem in 1099 AD. After heavy fighting, they established a feudal Latin Kingdom of Jerusalem under the leadership of Godfrey of Bouillon. A few military-religious orders were set up to defend this kingdom from Turkish attacks. But this kingdom remained in Christian hands till 1187 A.D.

The Second Crusade (1147-49)
The Christian disunity became apparent to the Turks when they fought among themselves. Taking advantage of this opportunity, the Turks captured Edessa, a key outpost of the Christians, in 1144 AD. The Christians were shocked and Pope Eugenius III called on Christians for a second crusade. The Holy Emperor, Conrad III, and the French King Louis VII, led the second crusade but failed to recapture Edessa. The German and French crusaders quarrelled with one another and failed to succeed in their mission. The Turks slowly advanced further and the Christian strongholds fell one by one. Their great Emperor, Saladin, Finally succeeded in capturing Jerusalem in 1187 AD. Saladin was a brilliant Kurdish Emperor of Egypt who united all the Muslims of the Near-East and west-Asia.

The Third Crusade (1189-1191)
The loss of Jerusalem was a terrible blow to the western Christendom and the Third Crusade got under way. The third crusade is considered famous since it included mighty rulers of Europe and their common enemy, Saladin the Great. From the beginning, King Richard the lion-heart of England, King Philip Augustus of France and Emperor Frederick Barbarosa of Germany hated one another. The ill-fated Frederick Barbarosa got drowned while crossing a river in Asia Minor. The French King, Philip Augustus, quarrelled with King Richard and returned home with his troops. So King

Richard the lion-heart with his knights had to wage a fierce war against the Muslims. He was able to recover a part of the coastal regions but could not capture Jerusalem which was ably defended by Emperor Saladin. Emperor Saladin admired the great qualities of Richard and signed a treaty for permitting Christian pilgrims to visit the holy places.

The Fourth Crusade

Pope Innocent III appealed to Christians to undertake another crusade for the recovery of the Holy Land (1202 AD). Unfortunately, this crusade turned out to be most disgraceful for the Christians since they fought not with the enemy but among themselves. They fell prey to the temptations or evil designs of the Doge of Venice. In the end the crusaders plundered Zara and Constantinople (trade rivals of Venice). They failed in their mission and brought discredit not only to themselves but to the entire Christian world.

Children's and other Crusades (1217, 1228 and 1270)

The fifth crusade was called the Childrens' crusade. It was thought, from the bitter experience of the fourth crusade, that children would not be selfish like the adults and they should try to recover the Holy Land. About 30,000 children led by a German youth Nicholas marched towards the Holy Land. They perished on their way due to hunger and disease. There were two more crusades but none of them succeeded in recovering the Holy Land.

Results

Let us examine the effects of the crusades. Firstly, the crusades did not achieve the desired objective—the liberation of the Holy Land from the infidel Turk. It may be said that Islam continued to spread everywhere. The Byzantine Empire began to decline in importance and power and in 1453 its capital, Constantinople, was captured by the Ottoman Turks. The dream of a united Christendom was also not realised by the Popes who constantly called upon Christians to wage the holy wars against the Turks.

Some of the encouraging and positive results of the crusades were as follows:

The crusades hastened the transformation of medieval life in Europe. The crusaders returning from the east brought new ideas and plans after coming in contact with the more civilised easterners. They brought products of the east and popularised them in their native lands. So, there was a constant demand for the products of the east like spices, silks, muslin, sugar, drugs, precious stones, glass and new fruits.

In the wake of demand for oriental products in Europe, the European merchants established trade relations with the East. Italian cities like Venice, Genoa and Pisa controlled the bulk of the trade with the East, and their merchants became extremely wealthy. Small towns lying on the trade routes between the East and the West and Italy and Western Europe, grew in importance. Berne, Frankfurt, Flanders and Warwick became great centres of commerce.

One of the most important results of crusades was the decline of feudalism. Many nobles and Barons had sold their lands and joined the crusade. Many of them died and the others became poor. The power of the remaining nobles was crushed by their kings. National monarchies developed. With the decline of feudalism the serfs became free and they began to migrate to towns.

Crusades encouraged adventurous spirit among the Europeans. They were eager to travel to far off countries mindless of the difficulties confronting them. European merchants were ready to go on long sea-voyages in order to promote trade. One of the famous merchants who went to the East braving all odds was Marco Polo. He was received well and honoured by the Chinese emperor Kublai Khan.

The crusaders were influenced by the knowledge and scientific discoveries of the Orient. They came to know of the Arabic numerals, algebra and oriental philosophy. Some of the articles introduced to the West by the crusaders included paper and the mariner's compass. Scientific works of Aristotle, long forgotten by the West, came to be reintroduced by the crusaders.

Finally, the papacy had its rise and fall during the period of Crusades. Upto the fifth crusade, the papacy was actively involved. Its prestige and power reached great heights. However, its decline followed soon and as subsequent events indicated that papacy was losing its popularity. Influenced by the oriental culture, a few scholars began to increasingly question the infallibility of the Popes and the church. Europeans became increasingly aware of what was taking place on the other side of their continent. Thus crusades precipitated the transformation of medieval life in Europe.

Lesson Review

1. Why and what for were the crusades fought? Discuss the results.
2. Describe the causes for the failure of the Christians.
3. On the outline map show the Holy Land of the Christians and the Latin Kingdoms. And also point out the routes of the crusaders to reach the Holy Land.

20
THE MIDDLE AGES IN EUROPE

The Middle Ages Defined
The term Middle Ages in the history of Europe refers to the period which lay between the fall of Roman Empire and the discovery of America. This is said roughly to cover a span of one thousand years. The early part of the Middle Ages is often termed as "the Dark Age" for the reason that we don't have much knowledge about life and conditions during that time. The Renaissance scholars of Europe like Petrarch also considered it so because the people of that age disregarded the study of Greek and Roman classics. However, for that reason, a student should not ignore this period as one of uncivilised age. The Middle Ages may be further divided into the Early, the High or Central, and the Late.

The Early Middle Ages (476 AD-1000 AD)
During the early Middle Age, Germanic tribes occupied western provinces of the Roman Empire. The Anglo-Saxons conquered England. The Franks occupied Gaul. The Visgoths settled in Spain and the Ostrogoths held Italy. It was during this time of chaos that people fled to the monasteries which were serving as centres of learning. Christianity offered hope to those troubled humanity from death and destruction. While much of western Europe lay at the feet of barbaric hordes, the Eastern Roman Empire managed to flourish. It was subsequently known as Byzantine empire on account of its Greek influence. It was during the eighth century that Europe came to have feudal society. Her trade and commerce had declined, and her cities lost their importance. For a time the Merovingian and Carolingian dynasties tried to unify western Europe. Charlamagne built what later came to be called as the Holy Roman Empire. It was during the seventh century that Islam was founded by Mohammed, the Prophet. Islam united all the Arabs and further paved the way for their cultural advancement. The Mohammedans embarked upon a career of conquest with a zeal to spread Islam. They succeeded in conquering countries of Asia Minor, northern

Africa and Spain. They would have conquered Europe but for the decisive defeat they suffered in the bloody battle at Tours (732 AD) at the hands of Charles Martel.

The High or Central Middle Ages (1001 AD-1300 AD)

Between 1000 and 1300 AD Europe witnessed agricultural prosperity, growth of towns and universities, strong monarchies and the supremacy of the papal authority. It must be remembered that the Holy Roman Emperors tried to establish their supremacy in the Christendom but failed and at the same time papal authority reigned supreme because of the crusades. The investiture contest between the Holy Roman Emperor Henry IV and Pope Gregory VII resulted in the former deposing the latter in January 1076. The Pope retaliated by excommunicating the Emperor in February 1076. Emperor Henry IV had to go to Canossa and wait in humiliation for three days and three nights to receive papal pardon in January 1077. Later, in 1193 Pope Celestine III excommunicated Holy Roman Emperor Henry VI for imprisoning King Richard I of England, a former crusader.

The Late Middle Ages (1301-1500)

Between 1300 and 1500 AD Europe witnessed famous wars like the Hundred Years' War and Ottoman invasions, famines and plague (the Black Death), and the decline of the papacy. With the development of towns and cities in Europe the shackles of feudalism over the serfs began to break. A new entrepreneurial class emerged. A few intellectuals began to challenge the doctrines and practices of the Catholic church. Let us make a definite study of the Middle Ages in Europe.

THE HOLY ROMAN EMPIRE

After the fall of the Roman Empire in 476 AD, its territories came to be occupied by the barbaric hordes. The Visigoths controlled Spain and southern Gaul, the Ostrogoths held Italy, the Vandals north Africa, the Angles and Saxons Britain, and the Franks Gaul. Of these the Franks in Gaul were to play an important role in the early history of Medieval Europe. The first one to unite all the Franks under one banner in Gaul was Clovis I (465-511), founder of the Merovingian dynasty. He came under the influence of his Christian wife. It was not until he won a victory over the Alemanni he decided to embrace Christianity. His conversion to Christianity proved to be a historic event. France, so named after her occupation by the Franks, became a Christian country. Paris became Clovis' capital. The Eastern Roman Emperor accorded his recognition to his rule in France. The successors of Clovis were weak. Violence and disorder became the

The Middle Ages in Europe

order of the day. The royal power came to be exercised by the chief ministers (Mayors of the Palace). The office of the Mayor became hereditary in the famous Carolingian family.

Carolingian Dynasty

Charles Martel (also known as Charles "the Hammer") was the first in this family to achieve great fame. He defeated all his rivals and reunited the kingdom under his able leadership. He is chiefly remembered for defeating the Arabs in the bloody Battle of Tours in AD 732 and thereby halting their advance into Europe. He maintained political relationship with the papacy which served his dynasty well. Charles Martel's son, Pepin, put an end to the Merovingian dynasty by declaring himself to be the king. The Pope readily approved of his action and anointed him king because he needed Pepin's support to drive out the Lombards who were threatening Rome. Pepin helped the Pope by expelling the invaders and subsequently made a gift of the land held by the invaders. Thus began the foundation of the Papal state in Italy.

Charlamagne and His Conquests

The greatest among the Carolingians was Pepin's son, Charlamagne (768-814). He built a large empire after fighting not less than fifty battles with his enemies. Most of the battles he fought were against the Saxons who gave a lot of trouble to his subjects. After gaining success over them he forced them to embrace Christianity. Those who refused were mercilessly killed. He defeated the Lombards in northern Italy and overthrew the king of Bavaria. Bavaria became an internal part of his kingdom. He fought the Moors (Arabs) in Spain and got a strip of land lying south of the Pyranees. It is a fact that he waged wars not only to expand his kingdom into an empire but also to acquire wealth through plunder. At the end of his reign, his empire included, besides France, the present territories of Belgium, Switzerland, Holland, northern Spain, western Germany and northern Italy. He maintained friendly relations with the Pope (Adrian I). At the request of the Pope he drove out the Lombards who were threatening Rome and therefore came to be called the protector of the Holy Sea. On Christmas day in 800 AD, Pope Leo III crowned Charlamagne as the emperor and thereby indicating that he was the natural successor to the extinct Roman Empire. Thus the Holy Roman Empire had its beginning. It may be said that the relation between the Pope, the leader of spiritual power and the emperor, head of temporal power, came to be established on a sound footing.

Administration

Charlamagne organised the administration of his empire on feudal lines. He considered himself as the owner of all lands and divided them into several tracts and gave it to his trusted friends after taking an oath of loyalty. These tracts or divisions of land came to be called as counties, duchies and marches which were governed by Counts, Dukes and Marquises respectively. They enjoyed powers at the emperor's pleasure. He held the general assembly annually in his capital at Aachen to which all members of the nobility attended. Haroun-Al-Raschid, the great caliph, sent his ambassador with a gift—an elephant—to the court of Charlamagne.

Learning

Charlamagne the Great had no time to read and write. In spite of this handicap, he became a great patron of learning. He attracted a large number of great scholars to his court including Alcuin from Northumbria and Theodulf from Spain and caused revival of learning. He opened a school in his palace for own children and that of the nobles where the study of Greek and Latin was encouraged. To every church in his empire was attached a school where monks taught the children reading, writing and arithmetic. Art and architecture came to be patronised by the emperor as can be seen at towns like Ingelheim and Nijmegen.

Laws

Charlamagne passed "a series of laws, called 'Capitularies'" which were faithfully adhered to by all the nobles. He employed the *missi dominci*, special travelling agents, to supervise whether his subordinates in the provinces and districts are faithfully obeying his orders or not. He signed a treaty with the Byzantine Emperor who recognised him as the emperor of Western Europe. At the end of his reign (814 AD) Charlamagne succeeded in unifying all the Germans and all the Christians under one State and one church. After his death, his son Louis succeeded. He was unable to govern his subjects effectively. Family rivalry and powerful church combined to bring about chaos in the empire. Foreigners such as Arabs, Bretons, Normans and Vikings began to frequently attack his empire. Soon after his death the empire was divided into three parts according to the treaty of Verdun in 843 AD. Charles "the Bald" son of Louis, received France, Lothaire the Eldest got northern Italy and Louis received most of Germany and other adjacent portions of Europe. Lothaire enjoyed the title as emperor. By 887 AD the empire had become extinct. It was not until the succession of Otto the Great (912-973) as the king of Germans at Aachen in 936AD, an attempt was made to unify central part of Europe. Otto the Great was crowned as the Holy Roman Emperor by the Pope in 962 AD. This empire which was constantly associated with the Popes existed for nearly a thousand years. The Holy Roman emperors were all Germans by birth.

THE BYZANTINE EMPIRE

Diocletian and Constantine

The Byzantine Empire was the product of the most fateful decision taken by the Roman Emperor Diocletian in 293 AD, to divide his vast empire into two parts for administrative and military reasons. While he ruled the eastern portion, he allowed a co-emperor to rule over the western portion. He thought that this was the best solution to overcome many problems facing the Roman Empire. But his other plan to bring about orderly succession to both the thrones failed and the empire witnessed a civil war. Constantine emerged victorious and became the Roman Emperor. He finally succeeded in reuniting the two parts of his empire. However, he decided to shift his capital from Rome to the east. For this purpose he built a new capital on the old site of the Greek city, Byzantium (on the Bosporus). This new city was named after him i.e., Constantinople. It was built as a Christian city and had a fine harbour. In the course of time, Constantinople became the "Queen of cities" with a population of about a million and enjoying a most flourishing trade in the world. Before he became the emperor, Constantine had emerged victorious in a battle at the Milvian bridge under a Christian cross. So his faith in Christianity grew. He was converted to Christianity in 312 AD. He not only declared Christianity as the official religion in 325 AD, but also dedicated Constantinople to the Virgin Mary.

The emperor enjoyed absolute powers including the appointment of church officials such as the patriarch of Constantinople and other bishops. They were increasingly associated with the administration of the empire. People were led to believe that the emperor was a representative of God. As most of the subjects of the empire were Greeks, this Eastern Roman Empire or Byzantine Empire became Greek in character. Its official language became Greek and Greek branch of Christianity became official.

An Estimate of Constantine

Constantine the Great was a great general and a brilliant administrator. He introduced a rigid code of taxation and tried to bring about a stable system of government and society. He sought to unify the Christian church.

Although his reign was marked by sporadic outbursts of political and religious feuds, he maintained a perfect control over the affairs of the state. Soon after his death (337 AD), his empire was divided between his two sons. The two parts were reunited twice i.e., in 353 and 363 AD. The western part of the Roman Empire came to be frequently attacked by the barbarians towards the end of the fourth century. Its end came in 476 AD, when the German tribes in Italy elected Odoacer as their king. Odoacer deposed Emperor Romulus Augustulus, the last in the line of Western Roman Emperors.

The Era of Justinian

While the Western Roman Empire ceased to exist, the eastern Roman Empire or Byzantine Empire remained in existence for another thousand years i.e., upto 1453. AD. In its long life it fought many enemies like the Persians, Goths, Avars, Arabs and Turks. It was under Justinian the Great (482-565 AD) that the empire attained the zenith of glory. He was a great general, brilliant administrator and a famous builder. He sent his great generals, Belisarius and others, to reconquer much of the lost Roman territory in the west. After a number of battles his generals succeeded in reconquering Italy, northern Africa and southern Spain. A long war with the Ostrogoths broke their resistance and made it possible to occupy Italy. The wars caused heavy drain on the treasury. Unfortunately Justinian was not successful in stemming the tide of Persian invasions on his eastern borders. He was forced to pay tribute to the Persian Emperor Khosru I, and Syria and Palestine fell into the hands of the latter.

Justinian maintained close contact with the Pope and suppressed heresy in his kingdom. He built many churches and sent missionaries to foreign countries. One of the most impressive churches he built was the church of St. Sophia in Constantinople, the largest in the eastern hemisphere. A part of the city which perished on account of fire was rebuilt. Constantinople was expanded and beautified. He revised the system of taxation.

Justinian Code

But his everlasting fame mainly rests on his Code. He appointed a commission for the "collection of all imperial edicts and common law into four works which together formed the *corpus juris civilis* (body of civil law), later called 'Justinian's code'." The four works refer to the Code, Digest, Institutes and the Supplement. The Justinian Code served as a model and influenced the legal systems of many civilised nations in Europe. It was improved upon by Napoleon during the early nineteenth century when he gave his *Code Napoléon*.

The Middle Ages in Europe 145

Decline of Byzantine Empire
It was after his death that his empire became Greek in character and spirit. Greek replaced Latin as the official language. The empire became very much reduced in size as one province after another was lost to the foreigners. The Lombards conquered Italy, and the Slavs took the Balkan provinces. The Arabs conquered North Africa and Spain. The Persians conquered Asia Minor and threatened Constantinople itself. The successors of Justinian tried their best to check the tide but failed. There was a short revival of the past glory when the Byzantine kingdom came under the Macedonian dynasty. The Muslims were thrown back and the borders of the kingdom were expanded during the 9th, 10th and 11th centuries. It was during this time Christianity got split into separate branches—Roman Catholic and Greek Orthodox. The Byzantine empire fell in 1453 AD when the Ottoman Turks captured Constantinople.

Contributions of Byzantine Civilisation

Theocratic State
The Byzantine emperors wanted to build an empire and bring about unity of all the Christians living in the western and eastern parts of Europe. They styled themselves as representatives of God and appointed church officials to be in charge of some administrative departments.

Architecture and Art
In the field of architecture and art, the Byzantine civilisation made distinctive contributions. The church of St. Sophia with its massive central dome measuring 31 metres (100 ft.) in diameter is the most impressive monument. The interior walls of the church are adorned with impressive religious paintings or mosaics of coloured glasses. By any standard this impressive church is surpassed only by the St. Peters in Rome. The Byzantines became famous for producing beautiful jewellery and decorated armour. Their manuscripts also contain miniature paintings.

Law and Literature
The greatest achievement of the Byzantine Empire is undoubtedly the Code of Justinian. Emperor Justinian appointed legal experts to compile and classify all the Roman laws. They are in the form of four important works. The Code mainly includes the statute law or imperial ordinances which were in force then. The Institutes contain "a critical analysis of law". The Digest comprise the opinions of judges and jurists on many legal issues. The Novels or the Supplements include modifications and additions to the Code. The Justinian Code brought all the prevailing laws

upto date in a neat fashion. It was made easy for lawyers for quick consultation on any given legal issue. The Code constituted the essence on which the government and the laws of the country relied upon for its functioning. There is no doubt that it continued to serve as a model to many legal systems of European countries. When the Barbarians were destroying the Roman Empire, "Byzantium became the repository of classical learning". Her writers worked hard to prepare "encyclopaedias of old knowledge", and started critically analysing the works of Greek philosophers like Plato and Aristotle, and writing commentaries on them. Historians wrote the history of the Byzantine Empire and thereby left to posterity interesting details about life of the people and their achievements.

Centres of Learning

Byzantine Empire could boast of great centres of learning such as Constantinople, Alexandria, Athens and Antioch. Public and private libraries in these centres attracted great scholars. They went there to pursue their studies and research in subjects like mathematics, medicine, surgery, chemistry, geometry, astronomy and others. One of the famous scholars of the Age was Leo of Salonica. He was a great mathematician who solved difficult problems in geometry and astrology. It may be remembered that when the Ottoman Turks captured Constantinople (now Istanbul) in 1453, the Greek scholars of that city fled to Italy and other European countries. It was their zeal to revive classical literature which gave fillip to Renaissance in Europe.

Spread of Christianity

Byzantine emperors rendered great service to Christianity by spreading it among the Slavs namely the Russians, Bulgars and the Serbs. All of them accepted the doctrines of the Greek Orthodox Church. They developed their script on the lines of the Greek model. It is necessary to note that from the seventh century to the middle of the eleventh century there occurred a iconoclastic controversy between the Pope in Rome (head of the Roman Catholic Church) and the Byzantine Emperor. The latter and the Patriarch of Constantinople did not recognise the supremacy of the Constantinople. The Greek Orthodox Church became independent. The Greek church emphasises the metaphysical rather than physical aspects of Christ and has its own liturgical practices. Easter became the great holy day rather than Christmas.

Trade and Commerce

Constantinople became a great centre of trade and commerce due to its central location between the East and West. All trade routes between the

East and the West touched Constantinople. It served the west with products of her own as well as that of the east. Her ships carrying merchandise reached all ports of Europe. All this trade between the East and the West came to a standstill when the Turks captured it in 1453 AD, under the leadership of Mohammed II. With the fall of the city, the Byzantine Empire ceased to exist. As the land route to the east remained blocked by the Turks, the west had to seek new sea-routes to get Asiatic goods.

Estimate
As noted above the contributions and influence of Byzantine Empire had been quite immense. When much of Western Europe had succumbed to the invasions of barbarians, the Byzantine Empire protected and preserved the legacy of Greco-Roman civilisations. She did much to spread Christianity among the uncivilised Slavs. Her missionaries, particularly the two brothers, Cyril and Methodius, rendered valuable service to make Christianity popular among the Slavs. In art and architecture, Byzantine's influence over the rest of Europe during the age of the Renaissance remained conspicuous. When Constantinople fell into the hands of the Turks, Byzantine scholars fled to Italy and other parts of Europe carrying with them copies of the old Greek and Roman classics. Thus, they paved the way for the coming of the age of the Renaissance.

MEDIEVAL CITIES AND GUILDS

Conditions in Europe after the Fall of Roman Empire
After the fall the Roman Empire a number of cities and towns in Europe began to pale into insignificance. A few towns or cities which enjoyed natural protection of the sea or the rivers or the swamps survived the holocaust. Fortunately, towns like Paris, Marseilles, Tours, Naples, Florence, London and Winchester had grown commercially important since the old Roman days. They survived despite the decline of the Roman Empire because they lay on the trade routes. During the Early Middle Ages, which is sometimes described as the 'Dark Age', trade in some of these towns did not flourish. Gangs of bandits roamed on the main roads harassing travelers and merchants. Merchants could not carry on trade because they had to pay heavy tolls on the borders. As precious metals became scarce, trade had to be carried on by barter system. The Europeans lost control over the Mediterranean sea and their place was filled by the Mohammedans. The church looked upon profit-making by Christian

merchants as a great sin and so the Jews flourished as big merchants and money-lenders in Europe. Because of their trade, the Jews came to be hated (known as anti-semitism) by the European Christians.

The whole picture began to change gradually when the invasions of the barbarians stopped by the ninth and tenth centuries and feudalism began to gain a foothold in Europe offering security to the merchants and the common people. Old and new cities began to dot the map of Europe at the beginning of the eleventh century. Some cities began to grow where strong castles offered protection. Others grew around some famous monasteries. Some port cities began to grow along the coast of Italy, France, Spain and England.

Crusades Caused the Growth of Towns
The crusades of the twelfth and thirteenth centuries acted as a great catalyst and transformed life in Europe. Firstly, they indirectly brought about the end of feudalism. The destruction of the power of the nobles allowed towns and cities to play their legitimate role. Secondly, trade with oriental countries gave a fresh lease of life. Thirdly, the crusades gave opportunities to enterprising persons to purchase lands from Barons and establish free towns.

It was however, the trade with the east which gave a great impetus to the revival of the old cities and towns and subsequently to the birth of new towns. The European Christians who got accustomed to the luxuries of the orient demanded oriental products such as perfumes, silks, precious stones, spices, fruits, sugar, glass, muslin and drugs.

Role of European Cities
The Italian cities like Venice, Genoa and Pisa lost no time establishing trade links with the Orient at the time of crusades. Their merchants brought goods from the oriental cities on land and by sea and distributed them to the towns of Europe. In northern Europe, Flanders became a great centre of commerce and exchanged goods with other Baltic countries and England. These two centres in the south and the north, that is Venice and Flanders, catered to the needs of people living inland. So inland trade routes developed and gave rise to the birth of new towns. The Italian port cities maintained contact with the port cities of France (like Marseilles), Christian Spain and England. A number of port cities like Alexandria, Venice, Marseilles, London, Cologne, Hamburg, Nuremberg, Bremen, Lubeck and Bruges along the Mediterranean the North and the Baltic Sea coasts grew in importance. The French and Spanish towns came in contact with the

Moorish towns like Cardoba and Granada. Every medieval town began to hold fairs during religious festivals like Christmas and Easter, and attracted a large number of merchants from far off places like Constantinople. One of such famous fairs was regularly held at Champagne in France where people gathered in large number not only to buy things from the colourful stalls but to enjoy the pleasures and entertainments provided by the city.

Hanseatic League

A group of about seventy German cities formed an association called the Hanseatic League with the main aim of protecting its shipping from the pirates operating in the North and the Baltic Seas. In those days many Norsemen became pirates and preyed upon unwary merchant ships for plunder. The ships belonging to the Hanseatic League sailed in convoys and reached their destination safely. In the course of time the merchants of Hanseatic League became extremely wealthy and powerful and even compelled kings to bow to their demands. The Hansa cities grew enormously rich and cosmopolitan in character.

Political Role of the Cities

It must be remembered that during the height of feudalism many towns and cities sprung up on the territories belonging to the feudal lords. These feudal lords extended their control over them and the people had to pay taxes. The lords were indeed alarmed at the growing wealth of the towns and also for providing shelter to run-away serfs (a run away serf became free if he was not caught after one year and one day). To be free from the clutches of the feudal lords, a town or a city paid huge sums of money as ransom. It received a charter in return which allowed it to have self-government and self-regulation of trade and industry. At the time of crusades many nobles gave charter of freedom to the cities and towns and collected huge sums of money. They required this amount to wage the holy war against the Muslims. After the crusades, the cities and towns helped their respective kings to destroy the power of nobles. Thus they helped in paving the way for the growth of national monarchies in Europe. Even the Popes felt the urge to organise some cities into a league to fight the foreign enemy. One such famous league which was organised for defence was the Lambard League in the twelfth century.

The Rise of the New Middle Class in Towns and Cities

With the growth of towns and cities in Medieval Europe, we see the rise of a new middle Class. They played an important role in making their city wealthy and powerful by working hard. They were educated and broad-minded. They loved freedom and gaiety. It was to them that the ancient

Greek and Roman classics came to be introduced during the later medieval age. The middle-class of townspeople came to be called the *bourgeoisie*. In the course of time the leading members of the middle class took active part in the deliberations of the Town Council. These members came either from the merchant class or from the master craftsmen.

Guilds and Crafts

With the growth of the population of cities and towns, there arose a demand for products and their proper distribution. Merchants and craftsmen formed associations called guilds to control the business of a particular town or city. Guilds came to be formed from the twelfth century. The purpose of the merchant guild was to protect and promote the interests of their members. For example, the merchant guild of a city regulated the quality of goods, prices, weights and measures, working conditions, wages and to supervise business ethics. Each member who joined the guild was bound by an oath taken at the time of his admission. The merchant guilds in the town monopolised trade for themselves, excluded middlemen, prevented unhealthy competition and provided escorts for their travelling merchant-members. As mentioned earlier, the Hanseatic League controlling seventy German cities provided armed-convoys to its travelling members. The merchant guilds rendered great service to the economic development of the towns and cities.

Craft Guilds

When the towns grew big, the craftsmen established their own guilds. In Paris there were more than hundred guilds. Each guild consisted of members or craftsmen belonging to a particular profession like bakers, butchers, weavers, carpenters and so on. The members of the guild were mostly mastercraftsmen who regulated quality, price and supply of their products. They trained boys who worked as apprentices. The boys learnt the craft and opened their own shops in due course of time. The guilds saw to it that they were suitably employed. They opened schools for the children of its craftsmen. The guilds helped craftsmen in many other ways by caring for their needs and providing social security. The guilds joined to help the town or city government in building a great wall for protection from foreign invaders.

Guilds Formed by Towns

Like the merchant guilds and craft guilds, a group of towns also formed their own guild for catering to mutual interests and protection. One such guild was the famous Hanseatic League with as many as seventy German

The Middle Ages in Europe

towns joining. The traders of the member towns opened a number of branches in Russia, Sweden, Denmark and England. Its influence was felt on the countries situated around the North and the Baltic seas.

Decline of Guilds

With the passage of time guilds began to decline in power and wealth. It may be remembered that each guild had practised a kind of monopoly and did not allow competition. Therefore each member of the guild became wealthy and opened a factory. He employed wage-earners and paid them less. Not many journeymen (graduated apprentices) could hope to become mastercraftsmen. When the states grew in power the guilds began to decline. The guild system finally disappeared after the advent of the Industrial Revolution.

MEDIEVAL UNIVERSITIES

Learning in the Middle Ages

A common man in the early Middle Ages hardly cared for book learning. He had no sound knowledge of the classics or anything that happened either in his own country or in the outside world. However, learning came to be encouraged by some wise rulers like Emperor Charlamagne and the church. Every church and monastery ran a school. Priests and monks taught students. But church schools only encouraged those subjects which were directly related to religion or creating religious outlook. They were designed to train students to become priests.

But conditions began to improve from the eleventh century. People became interested in education because it provided a means for securing important positions in the services of the church and the state. With the growth of towns and cities, children started attending schools attached to the church.

Early Universities of Europe

The demand for higher education grew when the western Europeans came in contact with the Byzantine and Muhammedan civilisations. It led to the birth of centres of advanced learning called universities in Europe during the thirteenth century. Universities were associations composed of masters and students. The University of Bologna was the earliest to be set up in Europe followed by others like Salerno, Paris, Heidelberg, Montpelier, Naples, Oxford, Cambridge, Toulouse and Salamanca. Young men crowded the portals of these universities and listened to lectures delivered by famous scholars. The university of Paris was undoubtedly the biggest with about 50,000 students attending lectures at one time in all the four faculties—Arts, Canon Law, Medicine and Theology. Peter Abelard, a famous teacher and scholar (incidentally the founder of this university), attracted a large number of students to his faculty—the faculty of Theology. His book, *Sicet Non* ("Yes" and "No") was banned by the church authorities because he advocated not to rely too much on quoted authorities on religious questions. Salerno's medical faculty and Bologna's law faculties similarly became famous all over Europe. During the twelfth century the University of Oxford in England commenced working. By about the end of the thirteenth century there were about nineteen universities in Europe with famous teachers such as Peter Abelard and scholars like Roger Bacon, Thomas Aquinas and Albertus Magnus.

The Church dominated the academic life of the community, and Saint Thomas Aquinas (1225-1274) was a leading philosopher and theologian who championed the cause of scholasticism.

Universities in those days had no big buildings to boast of as in modern days. Many a time students sat on the floors and copied a text (books were scarce) which was slowly dictated to them by their professor with his explanations and notes. Their knowledge was tested by their teacher in classroom-discussions and debates.

The study of liberal arts was stressed as in the Ancient Roman schools. They included subjects like grammar, rhetoric, logic, geometry, arithmetic, astronomy and music. It is only after completing the study of these subjects students were allowed to study law or medicine or theology.

The Bachelor of Arts was the first degree obtained by a student after successfully completing his study including thorough examination within three or five years. Those who were qualified to teach from among the Bachelor degree holders received their Master's degree after some years. This degree entitled them to become permanent teachers. A few universities also awarded Ph.D. (Doctor of Philosophy) degrees to outstanding scholars.

Student's Life

Students did not merely attend the universities to acquire knowledge but wanted to prepare for a career. They had to suffer many hardships for the universities could not offer physical and material comforts. Despite these hardships, the students were devoted to studies. But the students in those days, like their modern counterparts, used to have newcomers, made fun of teachers, composed limericks and frequently fought with other rowdies.

The Middle Ages in Europe

By way of conclusion, one can say that medieval universities played an important role as centres of higher education and culture. In addition to providing many competent teachers to kindle interest among students in liberal arts, theology, philosophy, law and medicine, they served as a forerunner to the Renaissance in Europe.

Lesson Review

1. Trace the rise and development of the Holy Roman Empire in not more than 40 sentences.
2. Write a note on the Medieval cities and Guilds (40 sentences).
3. Describe what you know of Medieval Universities and of Medieval Scholarship.
4. Locate at least 10 cities or towns that you know of on the outline map supplied to you. Also show some important medieval trade routes.
5. Show the extent of the Empire of Charlamagne on the Map of Europe and locate the important towns and cities therein.

21
FEUDALISM IN EUROPE

One of the most important developments of the Middle Ages in Europe was the advent of feudalism. It "developed out of a need to stabilise a society based on decentralised political power". It began in France following the death of Emperor Charlamagne (814 AD) and spread to many parts of disturbed Europe. It was not established by any king or emperor as such but grew as a response to the chaotic conditions created by the barbarian invaders.

Definition

As feudalism appeared in a variety of forms, it is difficult to define it exactly. One may accept Stubb's definition when he describes it as a "complete organisation of society through the medium of land tenure in which from the king down to the lowest land owner all are bound together by obligation and defence...".

Evolution of Feudalism

Feudalism was not a new thing or phenomenon since it developed in Ancient Egypt when the old kingdom declined. It prevailed in the Homeric Age. It also existed in a vague fashion in the Roman society when a wealthy landlord surrounded himself with clients. It also developed among the Germanic tribes in the form of an institution called *Comitatus*. Brave lads associated themselves with a powerful chief who provided food, shelter and the weapons, to them. But during the middle of the tenth century it assumed a definite shape.

After the death of Charlamagne, central Europe was torn by a civil strife and frequent invasions by the Northmen of Scandinavia, the Magyars of the east and the Moors (Arabs settled in Spain) of the south. Lawlessness and disorder became the order of the day and there was no security to life and property since the central government had collapsed. The kings ruled only in name but could not command the loyalty of their subjects. It was under these conditions that relations between the people and the king underwent changes and gave rise to the birth of a new class called nobles.

Feudalism, A System of Land Tenure

In theory the king owned all the lands in his kingdom and the nobles considered him as their overlord. He divided the land of his kingdom into many regions. Keeping the main region under his control he gave away the rest to his nobles on condition that they took the oath of loyalty and agreed to render military service. Thus, the nobles became his vassals and the king overlord. The land given to the nobles was called fief or fiefdom. The vassal became the virtual owner of the fief and governed it effectively. The vassal himself could not look after the whole fief himself and so gave away parts of it to his friends who agreed to become his vassals. This subdivision of land into parts and their distribution is called sub-infeudation. These lesser vassals were either barons or knights. The lesser vassals had to pay 'homage' and render service to his lord, that is the noble. At the lowest rung of the ladder remained the serf (agricultural labourer) who owned the smallest bit of land and cultivated it. His life and property came to be protected as long as he pleased his master by rendering personal service. The church also owned lands and in the place of a noble there was the bishop.

Homage Ceremony

The second most important element in feudalism is the vassalage. The vassalage started usually after going through a ceremony called 'homage'. The tenant kneeled before his lord barehead and declared himself to be his 'man' or vassal. He took a pledge to serve his liege-lord for life, promised specified number of fighting men (forty days in a year), and agreed to attend the latter's court. He further promised to pay for his lord's ransom (in case the lord is captured by his enemies) and also to bear a part of the expenses incurred at lord's daughter's marriage or when lord's son was knighted. In return the lord promised the vassal his protection and justice, and invested him with the rights and privileges over the fief given to him.

Age of Chivalry

The warriors were known as knights. They agreed to serve one powerful noble or the other and received from him a small estate (say a village). At the time of his knighthood, a squire kneeled before his lord and received a light touch with sword on his shoulders and on his head. The knight promised loyalty to his lord. When the influence of the church increased, the knight took an oath of loyalty to the king, promised to protect the church and save the honour of women. During the age of chivalry, the knights played an important role in the society by discharging their duties faithfully. They volunteered and raised troops to fight the crusades. The knights rode on a horse fully equipped with weapons of war such as the sword, lance, and dagger, and in times of war or combat or tournaments he was fully protected with such thing like shield, armour and helmet.

Feudal Life

As noted above the king had limited powers and hardly came into contact with all the subjects of his kingdom. Loyalty of his subjects were divided. As the king's army was so small he depended upon his nobles or vassals. His revenue came mostly from his own domain. In course of time his nobles became powerful. They levied taxes, set up courts, issued currency maintained army and protected their subjects in their own domain. They built castles which were surrounded by moats. The castles protected not only the noble and his family but also his subjects in times of war. Often the nobles fought with one another. Feuds among the knights were common. Life for the common man was full of risk.

We may say that the manorial system constituted the economic basis of the feudal society. The lord's estate and castle and that of his subordinates formed the 'manor'. Sometimes the lord of the manor was a bishop. The lord lived with his family, servants, guards, fighting men and his serfs. As the castle was built on a small mound and well protected by a surrounding moat filled with water, it afforded necessary protection to the people in times of danger. The outer wall of the castle had gateways with drawbridges. A drawbridge was used for dual purpose, that is to keep out the enemy and allow people to cross the moat. This was done by raising it or lowering it if need be. Outside the castle lay the village where the peasants lived in small huts. Each village had a mill, a blacksmith's shop, a church and a small house of the priest. Beyond the village boundary lay the cultivated field, meadows and woods. One-third of the cultivated lands—sometimes scattered here and there—belonged to the lord. The rest of the land belonged to the peasants. Each peasant owned several strips of land—good and bad—scattered around the manor. The meadows, woods and common land belonged to the lord and his peasant. They were used for grazing of the animals and collection of firewood. Three-field system was in vogue. In the three-field system, a peasant divided his land into three parts and cultivated barley, rye and wheat in two parts. The third part was kept fallow. Next year he cultivated in the first and the third parts and the second remained fallow. In this manner, each part lay fallow once in three years. This was done to restore the fertility. Each peasant grew vegetables, kept poultry and tended cows. As mentioned earlier each peasant or a serf who worked in the fields was a tenant of the lord. Peasants and serfs commended themselves to the service of their lord. So they were bound to the lord's land, and used a part of his land for their own needs. Whenever there was dispute, the lord settled the dispute in his court. Each peasant or serf received protection from the lord and for this he had to (a) work at least three days for free on the lord's land, (b) give the lord a part of the revenue of his own land, and (c) make payment for getting the corn ground and baked into bread at the lord's mill and oven respectively. The serf's position was pitiable as he was neither a freeman nor a slave. He was bound to serve his lord throughout his life despite his miserable condition. He attended the church on all Sundays where the parish priest looked after his spiritual needs. Thus a manor remained as a self-sufficient economic unit by itself with a barter system. Spices and salt were probably the only things which they got from outside. Whenever famines broke out, peasants and serfs died of starvation. It was not uncommon for a peasant to witness the destruction of his field when the enemies attacked his village or by a party of nobles hunting in his fields. Thus the lot of the peasant or the serf was miserable.

Decline of Feudalism

But conditions began to change slowly from the middle of 14th century. A plague commonly known as the Black Death began to spread over the whole of Europe and took a heavy toll of one-third of European population. In England the Black Death decimated half of the population. Peasants were not prepared to work in the fields till their wages were raised. It may be remembered that wages were paid in money currency in those days. The peasants' revolt in 1381 in England did not succeed but the rulers tried to mitigate the sufferings of the serfs and the peasants by voluntarily raising their wages. But in other parts of Europe the peasants and serfs continued to suffer from many disabilities till the outbreak of the French Revolution (1789).

While it is difficult to defend feudalism for its ugly aspects like the bondage of the serfs and the existing inequalities in the society, nevertheless, it provided the necessary stability to a society at a time when Europe was constantly being invaded by the barbarians. Feudalism provided the means of defence and a source of livelihood to those affected by foreign invasions and "supplied a rough and ready method of administration." But in the course of time it became obsolete and useless and inflicted heavy burden on the underprivileged.

Lesson Review
1. Define the term 'Feudalism and discuss its evolution in the Medieval Europe.
2. Write a note on the Feudal Customs and Manners.
3. Give a rough sketch of the Lord's manor in medieval times.

22
THE CHRISTIAN CHURCH IN MEDIEVAL EUROPE

No other institution wielded so much influence on the people of Medieval Europe than the Christian Church. It did the most wonderful work of preserving the past culture and worked to spread it. At a time when the people were troubled by constant invasions of the barbarians, the Christian church gave shelter and catered to the spiritual needs. Pope Leo I went so far as to persuade the great Hun leader, Attila, to withdraw his forces from Italy. The Catholic Church assumed an important role in the lives of the people for its many services rendered at such times like baptism, confirmation, confession and penance, marriage and the last rites performed before and after the death of a Christian.

Other factors which increased the influence of the church were the wealth it possessed in the form of lands and buildings, the services of the educated clergy and its alliance with the state. The authority of the church remained unchallenged for a couple of centuries. To revolt against the church was a very serious matter and even the kings feared to incur its wrath.

Monasticism
In the early days of the Roman Catholic Church, the most important work was to spread the teachings of Christ. The barbarians had to become civilised and Christian. In this mission, the Christian monks played a notable part. The monks lived in monasteries. They lived together but away from the war and turmoil that was ravaging Europe. They tried to fashion their lives on the lines set by St. Benedict. St. Benedict's rule was that monks should take three vows, namely, to lead a life of chastity, poverty, and obedience. The Benedictine rule also enjoined upon the monks to elect one among them as an Abbot and love manual labour. The monks built many churches in Europe. St Benedict, it must be remembered, had founded a beautiful monastery in Monte Cassino (in southern Italy).

He also encouraged monks to take up social and intellectual work such as tending to the sick and the poor and teaching children at schools. In keeping with the Benedictine tradition, monks opened schools and hospitals. They made copies of the Holy Bible and Greek and Latin classics. A few of them started writing. St. Augustine, the bishop of Hippo (north Africa), wrote one of the most original works of the time titled *The City of God*. Following the monastic movement began by St. Benedict, there was the Cluniac movement with its headquarters at Cluny in Burgundy. Its leading monk, Hildebrand, became the Pope—Pope Gregory VII. There were other orders of monks called the Carthusian and Cistercian. They were known to have led a life of poverty and asceticism. The most famous of the Cistercian order was St. Bernard, Abbot of Clairvaux in France, who "encouraged mysticism and contemplation". During the 13th century two new kinds of wandering friars (monks)—Franciscans and Dominicans—began to travel all over Europe. The founders of these two orders were St. Francis of Assisi (1181-1226) and St. Dominic (1170-1221) respectively and both urged their followers not to possess any property. Their main mission was social work. They must wander, preach people in their native tongue, and uplift the poor.

During the time of crusades, a few military orders of the knights—such as the Knight Templars, the Knight Hospitallers, and the Knights of the Teutonic Order—attached themselves to the cause of the Church and tried to liberate the holy places from Muslim control. Some of the monks took up missionary work at the instance of the Popes. St. Augustine undertook the missionary work of converting the Anglo-Saxons in England. Earlier, St. Patrick had gone to Ireland to convert the Irish people to Christianity in 444 AD. Pope Gregory II sent St. Boniface to Germany to carry on his missionary work. He founded the Carolingian Church and became a martyr at Frisia in 754 AD.

Medieval Church and Papacy

The Roman Catholic Church became really universal with hundreds of churches being set up all over Europe. The bishops assisted by a number of priests served the spiritual needs of the community. In the course of time the bishop of Rome claimed to be the leader of the christendom. It may be noted that St. Peter was the first bishop of Rome who was "entrusted with the keys of heaven". With the fall of Rome due to the invasions of the barbarians, the church began to play the role of super-government in western Europe. This became evident when medieval papacy was founded by Pope Gregory the Great (540-604 AD) in 590 AD. He was elected as the Pope when Rome was being attacked by Lombards, and the law and order

The Christian Church in Medieval Europe

situation there had become bad. Using his position and office, he restored law and order in Rome and showed his ability in matters like administration and diplomacy. He founded the Papal authority over temporal affairs and sent missionaries to Britain and Germany to spread Christianity. Papal authority and prestige reached great heights from the accession of Pope Gregory VII in 1073 AD, to the early fourteenth century.

Church Vs. the State

The Church increased its authority under the Popes in manifold ways. It performed all the ceremonies, kept records, set up its own courts and tried and punished heretics. It opened schools, libraries and even settled disputes over legal matters. Naturally its encroachment over state matters caused great concern to the monarchs or emperors. The Pope became the central figure in the dispute over the appointment of bishops and other church officials. This is known as the investiture conflict. Pope Gregory VII prohibited the appointment of bishops by kings and emperors and claimed himself to be the supreme arbiter over temporal and moral disputes. The Holy Roman Emperor Henry IV became angry and announced the deposition of Pope Gregory. Pope Gregory retaliated by declaring that Henry IV was no longer the Emperor and excommunicated him. This rift ended in the humiliation of Emperor Henry IV. When he went to Canossa to seek Pope's pardon, the Pope made him to wait for three days in the cold outside his castle. After receiving the pardon, the Emperor regained his power and position. Then he turned his wrath on the Pope and made him flee from Rome. King John (1199-1216 AD) of England was compelled to seek pardon and submit himself as vassal to the most powerful Pope Innocent III (1198-1216 AD). It is no exaggeration to say that Pope Innocent III became a virtual ruler of Europe. In himself he combined the talents of an eminent jurist, gifted administrator and astute politician. The papacy declined from the early fourteenth century on account of internal squabbles, weak and immoral successors, and the rise of national monarchies. The decline began when the French king Philip IV succeeded in deposing the Pope, appointing his own candidate at his place and forcing him to stay in Avignon (France) as his subordinate in 1309 AD.

Lesson Review

1. Discuss the growing influence of the Medieval Church in not more than 20 lines.
2. Write a note on the quarrel between the Church and the State.

23

MEDIEVAL INDIA, CHINA AND JAPAN

Zahiruddin Mohammed Babur

The early sixteenth century saw chaotic situation prevailing in India. India was divided into several independent states, each at war with the other. Political disunity in northern India attracted the attention of Zahir-ud-din Mohammed Babur, a fugitive prince of Farghana. He became the undisputed master of Afghanistan after his attack and capture of Kabul and Ghazni in 1504. After having failed to recover Samarkand Babur turned his attention to the conquest of India. Conditions in the Lodi Kingdom of Delhi had turned from bad to worse since the ruler, Ibrahim Lodi, faced innumerable revolts from his disaffected nobles. The Afghan rulers of Bengal, Malwa and Gujarat also hated the Lodi Sultan of Delhi. Alam Khan Lodi, the uncle of the Sultan, claimed the Delhi throne but after failing to secure the same, invited Babur to invade India. The ruler of the most powerful Rajput kingdom of Mewar by the name Rana Sangrama Singh also assured Babur of his assistance if he were to attack the Lodi Kingdom.

Babur

Babur marched at the head of an army of twelve thousand disciplined soldiers and conquered the Punjab. After its conquest he proceeded towards Delhi. He fought the most significant battle on the plains of his Panipat in April 1526 against the numerically superior forces of Ibrahim Lodi. The Afghan army led by Ibrahim Lodi perished. Ibrahim Lodi lay dead on the battlefield and Babur became the ruler of Delhi. He occupied Agra and laid the foundation of Mughal rule in India.

Babur's occupation of Delhi and Agra, and his intention to stay in India permanently, enraged Rana Sanga of Mewar. Hostility and war between the two became inevitable when Rana Sanga gave refuge to Alam Khan Lodi and supported the cause of Mahmud Lodi for the Delhi throne. Babur fought Rana Sanga in the battle of Khanua (1527). The Rajput army was routed and its leader Rana Sanga, who was badly wounded, was forced to retire. The Mughal victory over the Rajputs was total and Babur became the undisputed master of Delhi. In 1528, Babur attacked Chanderi and captured it. The Afghans, who felt thoroughly humiliated after their defeat by a foreigner, rallied round under the leadership of Mohammed Lodi and challenged Babur in 1529. Babur fought them on the banks of Ghagara and inflicted a crushing defeat. Thus, all his enemies were subdued. Babur died in December. 1530 after nominating his eldest son, Humayun, as his successor to the Mughal throne.

Humayun

The premature death of Babur created difficulties for his inexperienced son. Humayun had to consolidate the gains that his father had left for him. His brothers and relatives were extremely jealous, cruel and cunning. The Afghans waited for their opportunity to recover the throne of Delhi. In the end Humayun lost his throne to Shershah and went into exile in 1540. He stayed in Persia for nearly 15 years. After the death of Shershah the Afghan empire began to decline of account of internal feuds. Taking advantage of the dissensions, Humayun conquered all the territories from Peshawar to Lahore in May 1555. Then he occupied the Punjab. He fought and defeated Sikander Shah in the battle of Sarhind. When Sikander Shah fled, Humayun occupied Delhi in July 1555. Then he added Agra and Sambhal to his small kingdom. He died in January 1556. Bairam Khan, a close friend of Humayun, crowned Akbar as the successor at Kalanaur on 14th February 1556. Akbar, son and successor of Humayun, was fourteen years old when he ascended the throne. During the lifetime of his father he had worked as the governor of Ghazni. He helped his father during his last days in consolidating the Mughal rule in Punjab. As Akbar was too young, Humayun allowed his friend Bairam Khan to act as his son's guardian. It may be remembered that just before Humayun captured Delhi, it was contested by all the Afghan rulers. A minister of Sultan Adil Shah by the name Hemu captured Agra and Sambhal and laid claim to the throne of Delhi soon after the death of Humayun. Hemu succeeded in capturing Delhi and assumed the title 'Maharaja Vikramaditya'. Akbar convened a council of war at Jalandhar where his nobles advised him to retreat towards Kabul. But Bairam Khan advised Akbar to reject their advice and urged his ward to attack Delhi. Akbar faced Hemu on the plains of Panipat in November 1556. When the battle started, an arrow struck one eye of Hemu and he fell down unconscious. Feeling the absence of their leader, Hemu's army lost courage and fled. Hemu, was taken captive. While Akbar hesitated to kill the wounded Hemu, Bairam Khan felt no pity in cutting off his head with his sword. Bairam Khan wielded power and influence as *vazir* of the empire for nearly four years. During this period Akbar began to expand and consolidate the territories of his kingdom. When Bairam Khan proved to be overbearing, and his loyalty in doubt, Akbar ordered for his voluntary exile.

Akbar

Akbar

Akbar's great desire was to bring about the political unity of India under Mughal supremacy. Therefore he sent messages to the independent rulers of northern India to submit to his authority and pay tributes. When many of them refused to respect his authority; the Emperor declared war against them.

Knowing the nature and character of the Rajput rulers of his time, Akbar adopted a wise and conciliatory policy towards them. He was able to secure their loyalty and affection by recruiting many brave Rajputs into his army and diplomatic service. More than all he married a Rajput princess of Amber and respected her religious rights. But the chief of Mewar, Maharana Pratap raised his banner of revolt. Akbar defeated him in the famous battle of Haldighat (sometimes compared to the Battle of Thermopylae) in 1576 but could not destroy Mewar's spirit of independence. The Sisodiyas continued to resist Mughal authority in their kingdom till the last days of Akbar.

Establishment of Mughal Paramountcy in India

Between 1558 and 1561, Akbar conquered Malwa, Gwalior, Ajmer and Jaunpur. He took Gondwana in 1564 after defeating Rani Durgawati. He conquered Bengal during the same year. He established his supremacy over Gujarat in 1569, Orissa in 1592, Kabul in 1585, Kashmir in 1586, Sind in 1591 and Baluchistan in 1595. By about 1600 Akbar extended his sway over a part of the Deccan which included Khandesh, Berar, part of

Ahmednagar and forts of Burhanpur, Daulatabad, Asirgarh and Ahmednagar. Realising that without the cooperation of the Hindus, it would be difficult to have political stability he altered his religious policy from those of his predecessors.

Akbar's Religious Policy
He befriended the Hindus by abolishing the detested taxes such as the *Jeziya* and the poll tax and extended to them his policy of religious tolerance. Although he was illiterate he always summoned various theologians to hear about and discuss the principles of many religions. He finally founded a new religion which he believed would be acceptable to one and all in India. It was *Din Ilahi*. He took the first step towards achieving Hindu-Muslim unity in our country.

Administration
Akbar divided his empire into 12 provinces or *subahs* and appointed Subahdars to rule over them. Each subah was divided into sarkars and each sarkar subdivided into parganas. Every officer of the state held a civil and military rank and provided fighting men and supplies to the Mughal Emperor. The centre was headed by the emperor who enjoyed unlimited authority. The emperor took the assistance of the Prime Minister (Vazir), Mir Bakhashi, the Chief Sadar, the Chief Qazi, the Muhtasib, the Khan-i-Saman, the Daroga-i-topkhana and Daroga-i-dak-chauki in carrying out the day-to-day administration.

Estimate of Akbar
Both the Hindus and the Muslims began to look upon Akbar as a truly national king. Akbar was also a social reformer who tried to do away with such social evils like the *sati*, infanticide and child marriages. In the words of Edwards and Garrett, "Akbar had proved his worth in different fields of action. He was an intrepid soldier, a great general, a wise administrator, a benevolent ruler, and a sound judge of character. He was a born leader of men and could rightly claim to be one of the mightiest sovereigns known to history..."

Jehangir
Akbar's son, Jehangir, continued his father's policy of conquest and annexation. Mewar, Bengal, Kangra, Ahmednagar and Bijapur all submitted to his authority. Jehangir married Nurjehan, a most beautiful and highly intelligent lady who became a *de facto* ruler. She managed affairs of the empire very efficiently which caused jealousy among many of the emperor's opponents. It was during Jehangir's reign that Captain Hawkings an English envoy, came with a letter from King James I of

England seeking permission for trade in 1608. His visit was followed by the appointment of Sir Thomas Roe as ambassador to Mughal court in 1616. Jehangir gave permission to the English company to establish its factory at Surat. Guru Arjundev (the sixth Guru of the Sikhs) was executed under the order of Jehangir.

Shahjehan (1628-58)
Jehangir died in 1627 and Nurjehan attempted to place her son-in-law, Prince Shahryar on the Mughal throne, but her brother foiled her attempt and succeeded in placing his own son-in-law, Prince Khurram (Shahjehan) on the throne in 1628. Shahjehan suppressed the revolts of the Bundelas and the Subahdars of the Deccan. He extended the Mughal authority to the Deccan by destroying the power of the Nizamshahis of Ahmednagar and compelling the rulers of Bijapur and Golconda to accept Mughal suzerainty. He drove the Portuguese out of Hughli for their nefarious acts concerning women belonging to his palace.

The age of Shahjehan is considered by some historians as the golden age in the Mughal history on account of marvellous constructions. Mughal architecture and art reached the height of its glory during his time. He built Taj Mahal at Agra in the ever-loving memory of his deceased wife, Mumtaj Mahal. The other Mughal monuments which stand to his credit are the Diwan-i-khas, Diwan-i-am, Moti-Masjid and Lal-Qila (Red Fort). Shahjehan's peacock throne was a cynosure of all eyes in those days. When Shahjehan fell ill in 1658, all his four, sons contested for the throne. Aurangzeb eliminated all his rivals, one by one, by a *coup de grace,* imprisoned his ailing father and ascended the Mughal throne in 1658.

Diwan-i-khas

Aurangzeb

Aurangzeb turned into a religious bigot and alienated the sympathies of many non-Muslim communities such as the Hindus and the Sikhs. Hindu temples were destroyed and the Sikh Guru, Tegh Bahadur, was executed at the orders of the Mughal Emperor. In 1679, Aurangzeb reimposed the *Jezia*. Thus the Hindus could no longer look upon him as a national king but as misguided fanatic. So his empire was shaken by a series of revolts staged by the Sikhs, the Satnamis, the Rajputs and subsequently by the Marathas under the leadership of Shivaji.

Shivaji

Aurangzeb expanded Mughal dominions by adding a part of Assam after the defeat of Ahoms. He also put an end to the rule of Shia rulers over Bijapur and Golconda. Since the Maratha leader Shivaji proved to be elusive and dangerous to his empire in the Deccan, king Aurangzeb came down to the Deccan to deal with him. Crowning himself as *Chhatrapati* (king of kings), Shivaji continued to pose a serious threat to Aurangzeb's empire despite the latter's several engagements with him. The result was that the Mughal Emperor lost many men. The endless war with the Marathas sapped the strength of his empire. The death of Shivaji and the weak rule of Sambhaji did not deter the will of the Marathas to carry on their struggle of freedom. Aurangzeb died in 1707 without achieving his goal. The decline and fall of the Mughal Empire followed soon after his death.

CHINA

Ming Dynasty (1368 to 1644)

In 1368 the Chinese were successful in driving out the Mongol conquerors who had occupied their land for nearly a century. An inmate of a Buddhist monastery, Ming, was able to establish his control over China. The Ming dynasty was in power in China from 1368 to 1644 AD. The rulers of this dynasty were able to recover partly the lost frontiers of old China. They encouraged geographical explorations. Their naval expeditions succeeded in establishing contacts with distant countries such as Cambodia, Cochin, Siam, Sumatra, Java and the islands near the African coasts. Influence of China overseas reached great heights.

Advent of the Europeans

It was during the time of the Mings that the Europeans established their contacts with the Chinese. The Portuguese were the first to step on the Chinese soil (1514). They set up their establishment at Macao during the second half of the sixteenth century. The Spaniards also went there in 1575. In 1604 the Dutch followed their example. The English reached the shores of China in 1637. Following the footsteps of the European merchants, the Christian missionaries reached the shores of China to propagate Christianity. Foremost among them was the Jesuit father, Francis Xavier, who propagated Christian faith and died off the coast of Kwantung in 1552. His body was brought to India and laid to rest in the Church of Bom Jesus in Old Goa.

Contribution of the Mings

The Ming emperors revived the old Chinese traditions. They tolerated Buddhism but turned their attention to revive the teachings of Confucius. They opened schools and encouraged religious and secular literatures. They established an imperial academy, and scholars were given help to write poetry and dramas. The civil service examination was also introduced. The emperors encouraged wise men and scholars to compile encyclopaedias. One of their greatest achievements was the codification of Chinese laws. The last few Ming rulers were weak and incompetent. The northern people, called the Manchus, began to enter China. They succeeded in overthrowing the Ming dynasty and declared the son of their chief as the new Emperor of China in 1644.

Manchu Emperors (1644-1911)

Under the Manchu emperors the Chinese empire was expanded to the greatest extent possible. The most prominent Manchu emperors were Kang

Hsi (1661-1772) and Chien Lung (1736-1796). They encouraged art, architecture, literature and learning. Many outlying regions of China such as Korea, Mongolia, Tibet, Burma and Indo-China all came under their sway.

It was during the Manchu rule that the westerners came to China for the purpose of trade. Although they were welcomed in the beginning, the Chinese did not like their behaviour later. The work of the Christian missionaries also caused anxiety to the Manchu officials. So all the foreigners were expelled. However, when the Manchu rule began to weaken, the foreign powers returned to exploit China. The Opium War (1839-42) which broke out between England and China resulted in a disastrous defeat of the latter and paved way for further exploitation.

JAPAN

Japan consists of four main islands, Hokkaido, Honshu, Shikoku and Kyushu. All of them are spread in the north-south direction off the coast of Korea. The Sea of Japan separates these islands from the rest of the north-east coast of Asia. The early history of Japan is full of myths and legends. Japanese believe that their islands were born after the union of God Izanagi and Goddess Izanami. They also believe that Jimmu, the grandson of the Sun Goddess, became the first emperor of Japan. The association of Sun Goddess with the rise of Japan made many people call her "the land of the Rising Sun". During the early centuries of the Christian era, Japan was ruled by several ruling clans. The most important among them was the clan of the Japanese Emperor. Each clan worshipped a common ancestor and was ruled by a common chieftain. All the clans recognised the supremacy of the Japanese Emperor. Each ruling clan had established a feudal type of government. The Japanese society also became feudal from the eighth century AD.

Early Chinese Influence on Japan

The Chinese influence spread to Japan during the period of Han dynasty. Her travellers and merchants began to establish contacts with the Japanese. The Japanese learnt the art of writing from the Chinese. The Chinese works of Confucius inspired many Japanese writers, poets and philosophers. During the period of Tang dynasty the Buddhist monks of China entered Japan and established Buddhist monasteries. Shotoku Taishi, a Japanese emperor of the Nara Period took personal interest in the spread of Buddhism in his country for which he is described as "Ashoka of Japan". After a considerable influence from China, the Japanese began to make much progress towards the path of civilisation. Japan produced two chronicles, *Kojiki* and *Nihon Shoki* during the early eighth century AD. Japanese poetry came to be cultivated and an anthology, *Manyoshu,* became a classic.

The Heian Period (794-1185)

The Heian period in Japanese history witnessed the shifting of the seat of the Japanese capital from Nara to Heian-Kyo or Kyoto. The new capital was associated with the Heian culture which was largely an improved model of the Chinese with necessary Japanese modifications. The Japanese court became known for its splendour and glory. Sculpture, fine-art, calligraphy, poetry, construction of Buddhist monasteries, laying of beautiful gardens all came to be patronised and encouraged. The most romantic composition of the era was *Genji Monogatari.* A cultured and aristocratic society developed on the model as one witnessed in France during the time of King Louis XIV. Among the powerful clans which existed during this time, the most notable was the *Fujiwara.* It rose from humble beginnings from the 10th century and reached great height of popularity and prestige in the 11th century. The Japanese emperors married their daughters to its members and so this clan became powerful. The Fujiwara clan gave Japan the most efficient administration and produced great diplomats. When Fujiwaras fell from power, Japan came to be ruled by two powerful military clans, namely, Taira and Minamoto. Both struggled for paramountcy and the Minamoto clan led by Yoritomo eventually succeeded.

Yoritomo becomes the Shogun

Yoritomo ruled a major part of Japan, and the Japanese emperor recognised this fact and appointed him as *shogun* (general). His followers were rewarded with money and lands. Yoritomo as shogun became the virtual ruler of Japan from 1192. This government of General Yoritomo (the Shogunate) practically came to rule Japan from its headquarters at Kamakura. Yoritomo's government came to be called also as the *Bakufu* (tent government). Japan came to have a liking for military tradition from this period onwards.

Hojo's Administration

After Yoritomo's death, his successors were superseded by his wife's family, the Hojos. It gave Japan a clean and efficient administration. The Hojo period was known for spiritual fervour. The Mongol armies of Kublai Khan invaded Japan in 1274 and 1281 but the Japanese drove them out. After the defeat of the Mongols the Hojo rule became unpopular and

Ashikaga Takauji joined the Japanese emperor in bringing about the end of their rule. After that, Ashikaga Takauji declared himself the Shogun (military commander) and installed a puppet on the throne in 1338 AD. But after about a century the Ashikaga Shogunate (1338-1573) began to face stiff opposition from the provincial houses of Japan. The long civil war continued with many rival houses putting up claim for the imperial throne. This Ashikaga Shogunate could not exercise effective control from its capital, Kyoto.

Advent of Europeans
One of the most important features of this period was the rise of the military caste the *Samurai*. Another important feature of this period was the spread of Zen (austere form of Buddhism) culture. The learning and art of China began to influence Japan. Japanese trade and industry began to grow. The feudal society of the provinces merged with the new civilian society of the imperial capital, Kyoto. It was during the disturbed period of the Ashikaga Shogunate that the Europeans reached Japan. The first to arrive on the shores of Japan were the Portuguese (1543). They were followed by the Jesuits led by St. Francis Xavier who spread Christianity there. The Portuguese entered into trade relations with the feudal lords and introduced musket. The Japanese began to have the first glimpse of Western superiority. However, the Shogun became afraid of the rapid spread of Christianity and the prospect of "Spanish conquest" and ordered for the expulsion of all foreigners. He closed the doors of his country to all foreign trade. Japanese were not allowed to go abroad. But the Japanese link with west was continued through the Dutch after 1641 and they were confined to the islands of Nagasaki and Deshima.

Tokugawa Shogunate (1603-1868)
Oda Nobunaga destroyed the power of Ashikaga Shogunate in 1573 but he was assassinated in 1582. His work of unifying Japan was continued by his commander, Toyotomi Hideyoshi. He waged a war against Korea and after his death power passed into the hands of Tokugawa Ieyasu. He became the Shogun in 1603 and established peace and unity all over Japan.

He resurveyed the lands of Japan and regulated taxes. He kept his enemies at a distance. The lords or their families were compelled to reside at his new capital Yedo. He organised the defence of the country by constructing forts and appointed spies to assist him. Confucianism was accepted as the official creed. The warrior class (*samurai*) rose to prominence. Next to them in importance were the farmers. After that came the others such as craftsmen and merchants. All foreign trade was stopped. Japan shut herself off from the rest of the world till the arrival of Commodore Perry and his U.S. naval squadron in July 1853.

Lesson Review

1. Explain the importance of the reign of the Mughal Emperor Akbar.
2. Write a note on the following:
    (a) Mughal Administration (b) Mughal Art and Architecture and (c) Literature.
3. How far was Aurangzeb responsible for the decline of Mughal Empire?
4. Trace the role of Chatrapathi Shivaji in building a Maratha Empire.
5. Show the extent of Mughal Empire under Akbar and locate the following places on the outline map:
    (a) Delhi (b) Panipat (c) Ajmer (d) Chittor (e) Lahore (f) Asirgarh (g) Ahmednagar (h) Raigarh (i) Kabul (j) Kandahar.
6. Write a note on:
    (a) The Manchu Dynasty (b) Tokugawa Shogunate. (c) The Ming Code.

24
THE RENAISSANCE IN EUROPE

It is difficult to say precisely when the Middle Ages ended and the Modern times began. Many historians believe that in between these two ages there lay a period of transition—the Age of Renaissance. The term Renaissance is French which simply means rebirth. Many historians used the concept Renaissance to give the impression that it followed "the dark years of the Middle Ages". Now this theory, that the Middle Age was the dark age, is discarded. Currently this term Renaissance is used to denote "a rebirth of Greco-Roman spirit of scientific curiosity and of humanism in arts and letters". The Renaissance became an intellectual movement spread all over Italy; and subsequently pervaded to Western Europe from the middle of 14th century to the end of the sixteenth century. It primarily found expression in the revival of the study of ancient Greco-Roman classics, the revival of art and growth of humanism. Unknowingly the Renaissance scholars and artists breathed a new spirit and enriched, through their contributions, the quality of human life. They enabled people of Europe to develop a new and rational approach towards life.

Factors for the Growth of Renaissance
What were the factors responsible for the advent of Renaissance? The capture of Constantinople by the Ottoman Turks in 1453 AD, is said to have triggered off many things. The Greek scholars there fled in panic with their ancient classics and settled in Western Europe. It was in Italy that they found new patrons. For years the Italian nobles and merchants had received rich dividends on account of the brisk trade with the rest of Europe. Their direct contact with the Arab traders enabled them to import oriental commodities for their final distribution to Europe. It was in the great Italian city-states like Venice, Genoa and Florence that merchants and crusaders "brought back new ideas, as well as spices, perfumes, and other luxuries". The weakness of the church made them bold and encourage new learning. It is no wonder that a large number of merchants,

bankers and few churchmen were associated with the patronage extended to the immigrant scholars and artists. Finally, the invention of the printing press rendered it possible for the rapid spread of Renaissance-scholarship.

Renaissance Scholars

The Renaissance scholars and writers came to be called humanists because they dealt with topics which concerned more with humanity than religion. They wrote not in Latin but in their own native languages. Thus the language of the people attained the status of literature. The foremost among the Renaissance scholars in Italy were Dante (1265-1321), Petrarch (1304-1374) and Boccaccio (1313-1375). Dante, a poet *par excellence* (sometimes known as the "Father of Italian poetry"), came to be widely known for his epic poem *Divina Commedia*. It deals with the journey to the next world. His descriptions of tortures in hell and pleasures in heaven attracted the attention of many. What impressed his admirers most was his fearless thoughts and expressions. Petrarch is now known as "the first modern man, for staging the first humanist revolt against scholasticism. He was the first Italian scholar to arouse the interest of many in the Greek and Roman classics. He carried on the relentless task of searching long-lost manuscripts in ancient monasteries. He wrote his famous Latin love sonnets and lyrics, the most noteworthy being *Sonnets to Laura*. His disciple was Boccaccio who entertained his fellowmen with a collection of love stories called *Decameron*. Political strife and instability prevailing in the Italian states during the 15th and early 16th centuries made Niccolo Machiavelli (1469-1527) write The Prince. It became a well known work and was studied particularly by the rulers and political leaders of the time. In that book Machiavelli suggested any available means—fair or unfair—should be made use of by a ruler to fulfil the goal of maintaining political stability of the state or to keep himself in power. Machiavelli's ideas have since then influenced the minds of rulers and politicians alike even to this day.

Renaissance Art

Thanks to the renowned Medici family, Florence in Italy became a glorious centre of Renaissance art. A large number of famous artists were employed in the creation of works of art. Of these, Leonardo da Vinci (1452-1519), Michelangelo (1475-1564) and Raphael may be considered as outstanding. Leonardo da Vinci was a versatile genius of the age whose works in painting, sculpture, mathematics, botany, geology and hydraulics have earned him a niche in the temple of genius. He even foresaw the coming of flying machines. His immortal works in painting are 'Monalisa' and 'The

The Renaissance in Europe

Last Supper.' He adopted new painting techniques and experimented with oil paints to give his work a fine feeling of reality.

The next artist of great repute was Michelangelo. His paintings decorate the ceiling of the Sistine Chapel in the Vatican. When the Pope commissioned him for this job, he took four years to complete. The paintings are on biblical themes. His most famous work is 'The Last Judgment'. Michelangelo's main interest was sculpture where he remained unsurpassed. Since the time of ancient Greeks none had shown so much interest in carving out human figures to perfection. Michelangelo exhibited his great skill as can be seen in the giant statues of Moses and David. "Grandeur of design, tragic driving force, and deep religious emotion make Michelangelo unique as an artist." One more important work which was assigned to Michelangelo by the Pope was to design the dome of St. Peter's Church which was being constructed then. After very hard work he designed the most perfect dome, a model of which came to be copied later on.

Leonardo da Vinci

The third great artist of the Florentine school was Raphael Sanzio (1483-1520). His paintings, mostly *Madonnas*, have been admired by all for their unsurpassing beauty and calmness. To a viewer his paintings gave not only width and height (two dimensions) but depth (third dimension) also. His most celebrated painting was 'Sistine Madonna'. As an architect he helped in designing the St. Peter's Church. His premature death cut short his otherwise glorious career as a great master-artist.

Venetian School: Titian (1488-1576)

Venice produced her own school of artists. Her artists generally produced landscapes and portraits. The most celebrated painter of Venice was Titian. In his long career (he lived up to 88 years) as an artist he produced more than seven hundred paintings which included portraits of many Popes, merchants, nobles and ladies. He became famous as a realistic portrait painter. His most noted paintings include *Christ Carrying the Cross, Assumption of the Virgin, Bacchus and Ariadne* and *The Rape Of Europa.* Another celebrated Venetian painter was Tintoretto (1518-1594) whose famous works are *The Last Supper of San Giorgio Maggiore, The Crucifixion, Christ and the Adulteress* and *Vulcan Surprising Venus* and *Mars.*

Renaissance Sculpture

Progress in sculpture went hand in hand with paintings. The sculptors mostly followed the techniques of classical tradition. Lorenzo Ghiberti (1378-1455) became famous after producing the "magnificent doors for the Baptistery at Florence". The next gifted sculptor was Donatello (1386-1466) who produced, among other things, his best work, that is the statue of St. George in Florence. Luca della Robbia (1400-1482) produced glazed terracotta figurines. Lorenzo de Medici (1449-1492), the ruler of Florence, had his beautiful garden adorned with finest sculptural works.

Renaissance Architecture

The Renaissance architecture in Italy rejected the Gothic style and imitated the classical architecture of the Greeks and Romans. Round arches, tall columns and big domes became the principal features of architecture. Typical of Renaissance architecture in Italy is the St. Peter's Church in Rome. Its great dome (designed by Michelangelo) rises to a height of more than 400 feet above the ground level. This church is big enough to hold a mass of 80,000 people. Close on the lines of St. Peter's Church we see St. Mark's in Venice and St. Paul's Church in London. What distinguishes Renaissance architecture from classical architecture is the emphasis laid on design and ornamentation. Besides churches, Renaissance architecture found its expression in public buildings and palaces. Brunelleschi (1377 – 1446) designed the Pitti palace in Florence. The other palaces built on the style of Renaissance architecture were the Farnese palace in Rome and the Piccolomini palace in Siena. Renaissance architecture wielded its influence for centuries and "was introduced into the United States by Thomas Jefferson in designing his home".

Renaissance Music

Music in the Middle Ages was religious music or church music. It was to serve the religious purpose. But during the time of Renaissance it was gradually transformed to serve humanity under the influence of humanism. Besides vocal music, instrumental music became popular with the introduction of new instruments such as the harpsichord, the violin and the lute. Orchestral music became popular. Though the Renaissance in music was largely the work of Flemish composers, its popularity increased in the sixteenth century Europe by the Italian composer, Palestrina (1525-1594). He composed about 100 masses. He is considered by many as "the father of modern music" on account of the impact he made on later musical composers. In the course of time Europe witnessed the age of operas (setting the drama to music).

RENAISSANCE IN NORTHERN EUROPE

Britain

Renaissance and the Humanist movement spread beyond the Alps in the fifteenth century. In Britain it began in the fifteenth century and reached glorious heights during the Elizabethan times. It found expression in the work of noted poets, essayists and playwrights. Famous among them were Geoffrey Chaucer (1343-1400) with his work *The Canterbury Tales*, Sir Thomas More (1478-1535) with his *Utopia* (in Latin suggesting the creation of an 'ideal state'), Francis Bacon with his *Essays*, Edmund Spenser (1552-1599) with his *Faerie Queene*, Christopher Marlowe (1564-1593) with his *Doctor Faustus* and Ben Jonson (1572-1637) with drama *Volpone*. But the most prominent personalities in the Renaissance English literature were William Shakespeare (1564-1616) and John Milton (1608-1674). Shakespeare "broke with classical concepts of drama and established an English form". His plays (both tragedies and comedies) reveal two great qualities—his unsurpassed mastery over English language and a deep understanding of human nature and human mind. The advent of English theatre added a new feature to public entertainment in those days. In English epic poetry, John Milton's *Paradise Lost* and *Paradise Regained* still remain unrivalled and unsurpassed.

France

France was also deeply affected by the pervading spirit of Renaissance. Outstanding among her writers who enriched French literature were Montaigne (1533-1592), Francois Rabelais (1494-1553) and John Calvin (1509-1564). Montaigne's *Essays* touch every subject "in a direct and lucid style". Francois Rabelais was a satirical writer whose works *Gargantua* and *Pantagruel* became quite popular. They were satires on the clergy and the educational methods of the time. John Calvin, a leading Protestant Reformer, published his treatise *Institutes of the Christian Religion* in 1536 (see chapter on The Reformation).

Spain

Cervantes (1547-1616) was an accomplished writer in Spanish whose novel *Don Quixote,* set in satirical fashion, ridiculed the customs, notions and manners of the Middle Ages. Humour and sadness are well brought out in this novel. Lope de Vega (1562-1635) became famous as the true founder of the Spanish drama and had great works to his credit. Another noted playwright and poet in Spain was Pedro Calderon (1600-1681). In the field of art, Spain produced famous painters like El Greco (1541-1614), Diego

Velazquez (1599-1660) and Bartolome Murillo (1618-1682). El Greco became famous for "his swirling, angular and statuesque compositions with their use of light...." Velazquez achieved popularity for his portraits. He became the Spanish court painter whose portraits show "realism and superlative handling of colour." Murillo was one of the founders of Sevilla Academy, of which he was the first president. One of his most renowned paintings is *Soult Immaculate Conception* which was completed in 1678.

Holland
Holland produced a great humanist scholar and writer in the person of Desiderius Erasmus (1466-1536). Although he was trained as a faithful priest, he lost no time in ridiculing the church for its "malpractices" and "corruption" in his famous pamphlet, *Praise of Folly*. His criticism was aimed at bringing about reforms in the church. He worked hard to bring about the Latin translation of the Greek *New Testament*. One of the greatest Dutch painters was Rembrandt (1606-1669) whose most famous painting is *The Night Watch*. There were others like Jan Vermeer and Frans Hals.

Flemish School

Even before Italy witnessed Renaissance painting, there was the Flemish school in Flanders which produced great painters like Jan van Eyck (1395-1441) and Hubert van Eyck (1370-1426). They discovered the use of oil painting and its effects on its viewers. They broke away from medieval traditions and became known for "descriptive realism and texture". Jan's painting *Annunciation* became famous as it "gave religious and secular character". Peter Paul Rubens (1577-1640) became the greatest seventeenth century Flemish painter known for his religious themes such as *The Descent from the Cross*. The next noted painter was Anthony van Dyck (1599-1641), a pupil of Rubens, who was patronized by Stuart rulers of Britain. He painted the portrait of Charles I. His distinctive style and touch influenced many of his contemporaries.

Germany
From Italy, Renaissance spread to northern Europe. One of the countries affected by Renaissance was Germany. The Humanist movement had profound impact on German scholars. One of them was Martin Luther who was to lead the Reformation movement during the sixteenth century. He translated the Holy Bible into German. In painting, Matthias Grunewald (1480-1528), Albrecht Dürer (1471-1528), Lucas Cranach, the Elder (1472-1553) and Hans Holbein the Younger (1497-1543) became famous. Matthias Grünewald painted the *Isenheim altarpiece*. Durer was well-known for his wood carvings like *The Four Horsemen of the Apocalypse* and engravings

like *The Four Witches* and *Adam and Eve*. One of his engravings includes the portrait of Erasmus. His masterpieces in painting were *Four Apostles* and *Adoration of the Magi*. Hans Holbein the Younger became famous for his wood engravings and portraits. Being a close friend of Erasmus he painted three portraits of him. Some of his most notable paintings are *The Darmstadt Madonna, The Body of the Dead Christ in the Tomb* and *Portrait of Henry VIII*.

RENAISSANCE AND SCIENTIFIC PROGRESS

Scientific Thought and Scientists

During the thirteenth century there was what was known as the "scholastic controversy" between faith and reason. Siger de Brabant (1240-1280s) and his followers believed that "reason and philosophy were superior to faith, and knowledge from faith". A fierce dispute arose which led St. Thomas Aquinas (1225-1274) to defend the Church by his work *Summa Theologica*. Roger Bacon (1214-94) insisted on scientific temper and "empirical observation". He believed that a man's rational character or behaviour was a "natural law" which "manifested divine insight". His ideas were found to be dangerous and he was imprisoned. He manufactured gunpowder and used magnifying glass. The first half of the fifteenth century witnessed the study of navigation and improvement in navigational instruments such as the mariner's compass. It was not till the sixteenth century that Renaissance made its great impact. The result was a scientific revolution in Europe. It began with the Polish monk as well as an astronomer, Nicolaus Copernicus (1473-1543), who challenged the medieval concept of astronomy based on Ptolemy's geocentric system. After rejecting it Copernicus proposed what is now known as heliocentric system (in his book *De Revolutionibus Orbium Coelestium*) according to which the earth, moon and planets and stars orbit around the sun. Kepler (1571-1630) supported the hypothesis of Copernicus by formulating mathematical laws. He improved upon Copernican theory by saying that the planets revolved round the sun not in circle (as Copernicus believed) but in elleptical orbits. But the final credit of substantiating the Copernican theory with necessary proof went to an Italian astronomer, Galileo (1564-1642). By inventing the telescope and observing the motions of heavenly bodies he could prove Copernicus' theory by and large correct. When Galileo tried to prove that the theory of Copernicus was correct through a book, the Church held inquisition against him for challenging its belief and authority. His book was burnt. At that time Giordano Bruno was burnt as a heretic for propagating the views. Galileo's research in mechanics, paved way for Newton's laws of motion and therefore, he was called "Father of Experimental Science". But the genius of modern science in the seventeenth century was an Englishman, Sir Isaac Newton (1643-1727). In his most famous work, *Philosophiae Naturalis Principia Mathematica,* he explained the laws of motion and propounded the law of universal gravitation. Newton also enriched the field of mathematics with his contributions, which of course, included his newly invented calculus. A century earlier, Rene Descartes (1596-1650), French philosopher and mathematician, introduced "mathematical principles to scientific problems". He invented Analytical Geometry. In the field of medical science William Harvey (1578-1657), an English physician, discovered the circulation of blood in the human body and published it in his book *De Motu Cordis* in 1628. A century earlier to this even Andreas Vesalius (1514-64) made a thorough study of the human body and made dissections. Many of his writings disproved Galen's statements. Bartolomeo Eustachi (1510?-1574) found out tubes in human ears and they are named after him. Antonie van Leeuwenhoek (1632-1723), a Dutch microbiologist, made several single lens microscopes, and his most important discoveries are protists (1674), bacteria (1676) and spermatozoa (1677).

Interest in science began to grow steadily in the seventeenth century with the result that encyclopaedias of scientific knowledge came to be published. The wonders of scientific discoveries and inventions compelled rulers, nobles and the wealthy to advance the cause of science. Thus the Humanist movement of the Renaissance period finally culminated in ushering the age of Modern Science. Were it not for the efforts of scholars like Francis Bacon (1561-1626) (founder of principles of scientific method) science would not have become so popular in the seventeenth century.

It may be remembered that the invention of printing press in the middle of the fifteenth century made it possible to spread the new learning and scientific knowledge.

Lesson Review

1. What do you mean by the term 'Renaissance in Europe'?
2. What factors were responsible for the growth of Renaissance in Europe?
3. Trace the development of Renaissance in art and architecture, literature, music and science.
4. Prepare a table in which you name well-known Renaissance artists, architects, writers, musical composers and scientists and their respective contributions.

25
GEOGRAPHICAL DISCOVERIES

The age of Renaissance fostered a spirit of adventure and a great deal of curiosity among the Europeans. After the capture of Constantinople in 1453 by the Ottoman Turks, the Europeans had no means of getting oriental goods other than depending upon the Italian merchants. Fortunately, the Italians had very profitable trade with the Arabs during and after the crusades. During the late thirteenth century a party of Italian merchants were successful in reaching China—a journey on land which took nearly two and half years. One of them was Marco Polo (1254-1324) who received a warm welcome in the court of the Mongol ruler of China, Kublai Khan. He went to Japan and also reached the Spice islands. When he returned to his native place, Venice, he narrated his thrilling experiences to his friends. Since then the curiosity and spirit of adventure enabled the Europeans to reach far off lands not only by land but also by sea. Marco Polo's visit to the East and his return by sea attracted the imagination of many Europeans. The Christian church thought of converting millions of pagans living in the East. Many merchants began to think about the fourfold profits they would derive by having trade with the east. The rulers of Europe thought of establishing trade contact with the east and thereby increase their power and prestige.

Factors Aiding Geographical Discoveries

Fortunately, many factors helped to realise the ambitions of European rulers and merchants. Of these the most important was the knowledge the Europeans derived about the Mariner's compass and the astrolabe. The former was invented by the Chinese for knowing the direction and the latter in finding their way to reach a particular spot. Secondly, the Europeans began to build better ships which were used for a long journey. The sailors of the late fifteenth and early sixteenth centuries also gained useful knowledge about the winds, tides and currents from the school established by the Portuguese prince, Henry the Navigator (1394-1460).

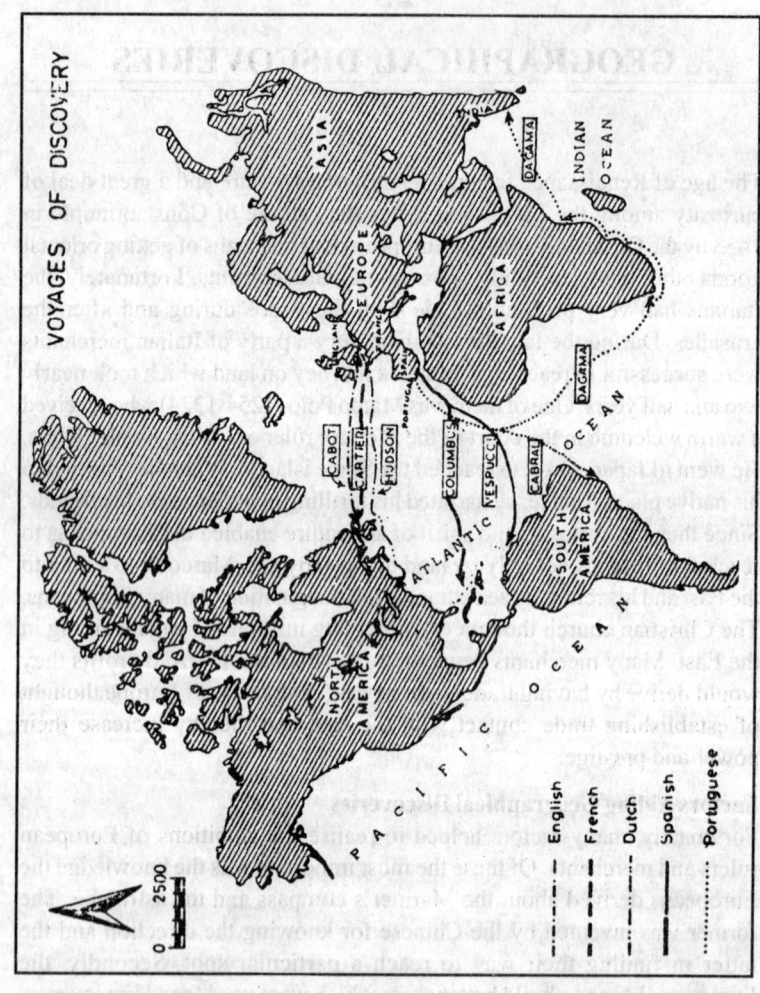

Prince Henry's School of Navigation attracted "the best sailors, astronomers and geographers of Europe" who exchanged their knowledge with others. The school sent annual maritime expeditions along the coastline of West Africa. His navigators discovered the Madiera islands and went as far as Sudan and Senegal. They brought slaves and gold and paved the way for the establishment of Portuguese empire during the next century.

Explorations of Portuguese Navigators
The next few exploits of the Portuguese on sea included the crossing of the equator by Lopo Gonçalves (15th century) and reaching of the Cape of Good Hope by Bartholomew Diaz (1450-1500) in 1488. On July 8, 1497, Vasco da Gama (1460-1524) set sail from Lisbon and followed the route taken by Diaz. Crossing the Cape of Good Hope he sailed along the east coast for a short time. With the help of Arab sailors he found the direction to sail towards India. He reached Calicut on May 20, 1498. Vasco da Gama's discovery of a new sea-route to India was most significant event in the history of not only Europe but Asia also. Two years later, Pedro Álvares Cabral (1467/68-1520), a Portuguese commander, who was sailing down the west coast of Africa, was blown off his course by a storm, and at last reached the east coast of South America. Thus Brazil was discovered on April 22, 1500.

Vasco da Gama

Columbus Discovers the New Continent
In all probability the Vikings were the first to land on the new continent at a time when the Roman Empire was being invaded by the barbarians. After about a thousand years or so, Christopher Columbus (1451-1506), a Genoese sailor, planned to discover a new sea-route to the East. After securing monetary and material assistance from Ferdinand II and Isabella I, the Catholic rulers of Aragon and Castile in Spain respectively, he set sail on August 3, 1492, across the then unknown Atlantic. After a long and difficult voyage he reached an island of the Bahamas on October 12, 1492. He thought that he had reached the shores of India. He called the natives of the Bahamas as Indians. He went to explore Cuba and Haiti. He made three more voyages and explored the islands in the Caribbean Sea. He claimed all the lands that he had discovered for his king and queen. The Portuguese became jealous of the newly acquired lands of Spain and the Pope had to intervene to settle their dispute by demarcating the line of control for each. But the new continent of America that Columbus

discovered came to be called after the name of an Italian explorer, Amerigo Vespucci (1454-1512). He made further explorations of the areas Columbus had discovered and came to the conclusion that it was not India (as Columbus believed) but a new world. It was for this reason that a German geographer "suggested that the New World be called America in Amerigo's honor".

Balboa Discovers Pacific Ocean in 1513
Vasco Nunez de Balboa (1475-1519), a Spanish explorer, went to the new world in search of gold. He reached the Isthmus of Panama and looked over the other side. What he saw was a vast expanse of blue ocean – the Pacific Ocean. Ponce de Leon discovered Florida.

Ferdinand Magellan—His Voyage Round the World (1519-22)
Magellan (1480-1521) who had come to India along with Vasco da Gama was certain that the world was like a globe. He desired to find a westward passage to the east. When the Portuguese ruler turned down his proposal to finance the project, he did not lose hope. He appealed to Spanish King Charles I (grandson of Queen Isabella) who agreed to help him. With five ships and 267 men on board he set sail from Spain in September 1519. He reached the coast of South America and sailed down towards the south. At the tip he passed through the straits which is now known as straits of Magellan. He entered the Pacific Ocean. He lost many good sailors who died due to scurvy and starvation. He reached the Philippines. He was killed in a battle with the natives at Mactan in April 1521. Only one of his voyage ships *Victoria* carrying the survivors reached Spain in September 1522—three years after the ships first set sail. It was a long voyage undertaken to circumnavigate the world.

Hernando Cortez Conquers Mexico (1519)
Hernando Cortez (1485-1547) proved to be one of the greatest Spanish conquistadors of the early sixteenth century. He with his soldiers landed in Mexico and fought the natives called the Aztecs and defeated them. After driving out their ruler, Cortez became the Spanish governor. In 1532, another Spanish adventurer by name Francisco Pizarro (1475-1541) invaded Peru and defeated the Inca ruler. He installed a puppet ruler which angered the Incas. The Incas could not revolt as all their rulers were executed by the Spanish. The Spaniards forced the natives of Mexico and Peru to work in silver and gold mines for their benefit. When there was increasing resistance, the Spaniards began to bring negroes from Africa to work there. The Spanish missionaries converted many natives to Christianity. Thus Spain built a large empire on the new continent.

Geographical Discoveries

Discoveries of English Explorers

Among the many explorers who were trying to find a new sea-route to the east in the late 15th century, there was an Italian by the name John Cabot (1450-1499). He was employed by King Henry VII to discover a north-west passage across the Atlantic to reach India. He set sail in 1497, crossed the Atlantic and reached Cape Breton island (near Newfoundland). Cabot thought that he had reached China. It was his discovery of the east coast of Canada which made the English to claim much of North America. During the last quarter of the sixteenth century, the English explorers like Drake, Gilbert and Raleigh further explored the east coast of North America and laid claims to territories from St. Lawrence to Florida. The English trading company established its outposts in India during the early seventeenth century.

French Explorations

Like the early English explorers, a Frenchman by the name Jacques Cartier (1491-1557) sailed upto the coast of North America for finding a north-west passage to China. He explored Newfoundland and the Gulf of St. Lawrence in 1534. In 1608, another French explorer Samuel de Champlain (1574-1635) founded New France with Quebec city as its capital. French-Canadian Louis Jolliet (1645-1700) and French Jesuit missionary Jacques Marquette (1637-1675) were the first Europeans to discover Mississippi river valley in 1673. La Salle (1643-1687) travelled down the Illinois and Mississippi rivers. Thus, the territory controlled by the French was called New France that included five colonies—Canada, Acadia, Hudson Bay, Newfoundland and Louisiana. The last mentioned was named after King Louis XIV of France.

Henry Hudson and the Dutch Claim

In 1609, the Dutch employed an English explorer by the name Henry Hudson (1565-1611) who tried to find a north-west passage. He discovered the Hudson river and enabled the Dutch to claim the Hudson river region. The Dutch also tried to penetrate through the northern barrier of Iceland but did not succeed. Earlier in June 1596, their explorer Willem Barents (c. 1550-1597) discovered Spitsbergen, the largest island of the Svalbard archipelago (a group of islands) in the Arctic Ocean.

Conflicting Claims Lead to Wars

Each European power laid its claim to extensive areas it had discovered and which was not liked by its rival. So wars were fought among rival European powers on the new continent. For example, the Portuguese fought the Dutch in the East. They became jealous of Spanish possessions on the new continent and posed a challenge. England and France also became rivals on the new continent and carried on wars in Europe and India. In the late sixteenth century England and Spain became bitter rivals and the Spanish Armada threatened to invade England. But the Spaniards were defeated on the sea.

Results of Geographical Discoveries

Let us examine the far reaching effects of these geographical discoveries on the nations of Europe in general and the world in particular. By and large the most far reaching effect was on the European trade and commerce. There was conspicuous shift in the venue of the maritime trade from the Mediterranean region to the Atlantic. Alexandria, Pisa, Genoa and Venice which gained commercial importance during the Middle Ages yielded place to the new commercial centres of Europe like Lisbon, Cadiz, Seville, Antwerp and London. The newly discovered Cape Route assumed great importance on account of the Sea-borne trade between the West and the East till the construction of Suez Canal in 1869.

The discovery of America and a new sea-route to the East introduced a wide variety of commodities hitherto unknown to the Europeans. They were potatoes, chocolate, cocoa, tobacco, quinine, cane-sugar, whale-oil, dyewoods, indigo, tea, coffee and porcelain. The Indian textiles and Persian carpets were in great demand in the European markets.

European explorers brought large quantities of precious metals like gold and silver from the new continent. Mexico and Peru were known for hidden treasures and they were ransacked by the avaricious explorers. With large amount of money in circulation in Europe, employment, wages and the standard of living showed great deal of improvement.

One of the ugliest effects of geographical discoveries was the birth of imperialism of the European powers. The European powers reached the shores of the countries of Africa, Asia and America for the purpose of establishing trade links. Eventually they stayed there as conquerors and masters. These countries were turned into colonies and subjected to political and economic exploitation. Negroes in Africa were taken to Europe, Britain and America and sold in open market as slaves. Colonial rule was established by European powers over their respective colonies with a view to civilise its people. It was during this colonial regime of European powers that Asiatic and African countries witnessed grinding poverty. On the other side, the European powers grew wealthy at the expense of their respective colonies. The industrial revolution in the West hastened further exploitation of the colonies since the European powers needed much of their raw materials.

Other Results

Other results which followed in the wake of geographical discoveries were the changes in the social order of Europe such as the birth of the middle class (*bourgeoisie class*), the rise of absolute monarchy, large scale emigration of people (escaping from religious persecution) and the spread of the activities of Christian missionaries in the colonies. The voyages of the explorers in the long run led to a commercial revolution in Europe. The geographical discoveries paved way for the Western domination of the world.

Lesson Review

1. Write a note on the factors responsible for geographical discoveries.
2. Write an essay on the achievements of Colombus, Vasco da Gama, Magellan, Amerigo Vespucci, Balboa, Cortez and Pizarro.
3. Describe briefly the results of geographical discoveries on Europe.
4. On the outline map of the world show the sea-routes of great explorers and the lands they discovered.

26
THE REFORMATION

Europe witnessed the division of the Christian Church in the sixteenth century after a religious movement called the Reformation. The Reformation was primarily aimed at reforming the Roman Catholic Church. It may be remembered that the Roman Catholic Church was a medieval institution claiming Jesus Christ as its earliest founder, and therefore its sanctity and authority came to be very much respected by all the Christians. However, like other medieval institutions, it developed cracks and became vulnerable. The Popes considered themselves infallible, expected meek obedience to their authority by the people and the state, and any criticism levelled against them was regarded as blasphemous. The kings of Europe often found it difficult to defy the orders of the Church or stop its interference in matters exclusively coming under state jurisdiction. Then how was it that the Church came to be so much discredited in the 16th century?

Decline of the Papacy
Reasons are not far to seek. Pious Christians all over Europe were extremely concerned about the decline in the prestige of the papacy. At one time the successive Popes who were elected were all Frenchmen. It may be remembered that the French influence on the papacy began when the French King forced Pope Clement V to leave his headquarters at Rome in 1309 and stay in Avignon (France). The papacy further declined in consequence of the "Great Schism" when two rival Popes (one in Rome and the other in Avignon) were elected and claimed allegiance from the Christians. To add to this confusion a third Pope was elected in 1409. The Great Schism ended in 1417 but it had caused irreparable damage to the papacy.

During the Middle Ages the Church accumulated vast wealth and owned lands and property. From each Christian house it collected what was known as the "Peter's pence" and also the *tithe* (one-tenth of income). The Pope and the priests lived in luxury and did not strictly conform to the ethics such as celibacy, chastity and exemplary conduct. There was a general laxity in carrying out the ecclesiastical duties. In their struggle for power and pelf they forgot all about the service to be rendered to God and mankind.

State Vs. the Church

The rulers of Europe cast their envious looks on the growing power and wealth of the Church. The wealth of the Church could not be taxed. The Church established its own courts to punish those guilty of religious offences. It frequently interfered in state matters. It did not tolerate criticisms about the way it was functioning, and those who were guilty of it were burnt at the stake.

Rise of Nation-States

The rise of powerful nation-states such as England, France and Spain posed a formidable challenge to the Church's authority. The rulers of these states opposed the supremacy of the Church and considered it as great hindrance to the well-being of their states. After a long struggle these rulers were successful in wrenching some of the powers of the Church, such as nominating the church officials, limiting the jurisdiction of the church courts, controlling the enforcement of papal decrees and levying taxes on church property.

Rise of Secular Attitude

The rise of secular outlook was an important feature of the pre-Reformation period. This secular outlook developed among the people mainly on account of the rapidly expanding commerce and the growth of the cities. Many people believed that there was nothing wrong in acquiring wealth if the world offered them opportunities. Merchants believed in worldly life and thought less of religion. So the changing attitudes of people towards the Church brought about the rise of secularism. Unfortunately, the Church itself had to be blamed because it had lowered its own image by accumulating wealth. The common peasants in Europe looked upon church-taxes with contempt. They believed that if the Church got reformed, they would be able to acquire some of its lands.

Anti-Church Movements

Anti-church movements began to be organised from the early 12th century. The Albigensians and the Waldenses were at the forefront in France. They attacked the church sacraments and priesthood. Under the leadership of successive Popes, crusades were declared to destroy them. In England, John Wycliffe (1328-84), a priest and professor, criticised the worldliness of the clergy and other practices of the Church. He declared that the Bible should be the sole guide to men's spiritual thoughts and conduct. For this purpose he translated the Holy Bible into English. His followers were known as Lollards who became influential. But the Church took steps to curb their activities. John Huss (1369-1415), a Bohemian priest and professor, who condemned the Church for its corruption, was burnt at the stake in 1415. But the anti-church movements did not altogether disappear. In the late fifteenth century, Savonarola (1452-98) established corrupt-free rule in Florence and attacked the corruption of the church with the result that he was hanged and his body burnt in 1498.

Attack by Humanist Scholars
The growth of humanist movement from the middle of the fourteenth century did much to discredit the pretensions of the Church. The humanist scholar Reuchlin "pointed out the inconsistencies of the interpretations of scholastic theologians, made on the basis of a literal use of the text of the Bible". Erasmus, the great humanist scholar, criticized the corruption and behavior of the monks and priests. But he was cautious enough (being a clergyman himself) not to advocate an open revolt against the Church. What he desired most was reforms within the Church. Unfortunately, Pope Leo X, barely understood the danger signal.

Sale of Indulgences
Regardless of the criticisms levelled against the Church, he collected money from the people through his agents to build the basilica of St. Peter's Church. Some of the methods the Pope and his agents adopted were highly questionable according to conscientious Christians. But they kept quiet. In Germany, the sale of indulgences by the Pope's agent, John Tetzel, provoked Martin Luther (1483-1546) to revolt in 1517.

Protestant Reformation in Germany
Luther was born in a well-to-do German peasant family. His father wanted him to become a lawyer but fate decided otherwise. He became a monk. From the day of his initiation, Luther was concerned very much with the attainment of salvation. He was convinced that God alone could help a man to attain salvation. Therefore, he believed that faith in Him would be the only means to attain salvation. He visited Rome in 1511 and was

Martin Luther

shocked to witness the worldliness and "spiritual emptiness" of the Catholic Church. His pent up anger burst forth when John Tetzel started his scandalous sale of indulgences. Tetzel claimed that those who bought the "indulgences" got an automatic remission of their sins by God. Martin Luther, who had then become a professor in the newly started university at Wittenberg, attacked the very concept which lay behind the sale of indulgences by nailing his Ninety-Five Theses on the door of the Castle-Church at Wittenberg. He did not believe in the "Catholic idea of good works as a means of salvation" as implied in the sale of "indulgences" and enunciated the doctrine of "justification by faith". His Ninety-Five Theses got wide publicity in Germany and the sale of indulgences received lukewarm response. The Church officials failed to persuade him to recant his views. Luther wrote letters to the Pope with a view to convince him. Furthermore, he wrote a number of pamphlets to defend his theses. He further championed the right of the individual to seek his own salvation without the assistance of the Church. Christians could take the assistance of the Holy Bible whenever a need arose. In other words, Luther rejected the infallibility of the Pope and the doctrines of the Church. The Pope sent a bull of excommunication declaring Luther as a heretic, which Luther defiantly burnt at a public meeting in Wittenberg.

In 1521, Emperor Charles V summoned Luther to the Diet of Worms to answer charges levelled against him by the Pope. Despite appeals by many of his friends not to attend this congress, Luther did so to defy the Church. The Diet decreed for his arrest. But Luther's protector, Frederick the Wise (Duke of Saxony), saved his life by forcing him to hide. So Luther went into hiding, in a lonely castle for nearly a year where he translated the Holy Bible into German. Before he went into hiding, Luther had urged the German princes to defy the authority of the Roman Catholic Church, exercised through the churches in their respective states. So many German princes of the north lost no time in raising their banner of revolt against the Catholic Church and formed a league to protect Luther. The Lutheran Churches were established everywhere. All the Lutheran states and towns in Germany joined the 'Protest' movement against the Emperor in 1529. Despite many obstacles on his way, Martin Luther was able to spread his convictions through the support of the princes of northern and central Germany, and also with the support of the middle class. But a strong reaction to Luther's religious revolution came in the form of bloody religious conflict dividing Germany into Catholic led by Emperor Charles V, and Protestant led by protestant rulers of Germany. This conflict ended in the Peace of Augsburg (1555). This peace acknowledged the right of a ruler to determine his state religion. Thus, the prestige of the Catholic Church led by the Pope and that of the German Emperor suffered.

Ulrich Zwingli (1484-1531) and John Calvin (1509-1564)
Luther's Protestant movement spread far beyond Germany's borders. His writings influenced many intellectuals, particularly that aspect wherein he held that every individual enjoyed the right to interpret the Bible in his own way. One of them who was influenced by Luther's writings was a young priest in Switzerland by the name Ulrich Zwingli. He became the leader of Protestant movement in Switzerland and organised a new Church in the Swiss city of Zurich. His views spread, and there was a war between Catholics and Protestants in which he was killed (1531). So the Reformation movement in Switzerland received a setback. However, a few years later, a French Reformer, John Calvin (1509-1564), began to effectively lead the Swiss Reformation Movement. He was forced to flee on account of the religious persecution taking place in his country, and finally settled in the Swiss city-state of Geneva. It was here that his religious teachings took deep roots and spread to the neighbouring Swiss cantons. He set up a Calvinist church which enforced strict moral rule on its citizens. His most important doctrine was that of the Doctrine of "Predestination" which he popularised in his book, *Institutes of the Christian Religion*. This doctrine says "that God chooses his own elect", and they live in total righteousness in this world, and "enjoy salvation in the next". Geneva became a great centre of Reformation where the Calvinist doctrines spread through the graduates of the University of Geneva. Many foreigners who studied in this university spread Calvinism to the Netherlands, Hungary, France, Scotland and England. The teachings and doctrines of Calvin were followed by the Presbyterian Church in Scotland (organised by John Knox), the Dutch Reformed Church in Holland, the Churches of Puritans in England and America, and the Huguenot Church in France.

The Reformation Movement in England
Opposition to the Catholic Church and for what it stood had its beginning in the Lollard movement (led by the followers of John Wycliffe) in the fourteenth century. There were other factors such as the influence of Renaissance humanism, and the general laxity and corruption prevailing in the Church that made England ripe for Reformation. Unfortunately, the anti-church movement lacked organisation and leadership. It appeared as though the Reformation movement would not succeed in England. However, it began due to peculiar logic of circumstances. King Henry VIII's (reign

1509-47) marital relationship with his first wife, Catherine of Aragon (who could not produce a male heir), became the cause for the break with the Catholic Church at Rome. His petition to the Pope to grant him permission to divorce his first wife had not found favourable response because Catherine was the aunt of Pope's closest ally, Emperor Charles V. The reason for the impatience of the English king was that he wanted to marry his mistress, Anne Boleyn. Indignant and disappointed at the Pope's refusal, King Henry VIII wore the mantle of leadership of the Reformation movement in England. He got the subservient English Parliament to nullify Pope's power over the Churches in England by its act, the Act of Supremacy. This act made him the protector and the only supreme head of the Church and Clergy of England. After becoming the head of the Anglican Church he confiscated the properties of monasteries and churches. Very few changes were introduced in the doctrines and rituals of the Anglican Church. An English translation of the Bible found its place in every church. During the reign of Henry VIII's successor, Edward VI, the Anglican Church leaned more towards Protestant doctrines. But when a staunch Catholic, Queen Mary (sometimes known as 'Bloody Mary') ascended the throne (1553-58), she unleashed a ruthless persecution of the Protestants. Many of them were driven into exile and about 300 were burnt at the stake. Mary's successor, Queen Elizabeth I (1558-1603), assumed the title of "Supreme Governor" and followed a middle path by avoiding extremes, thereby giving a new direction to the Anglican Church. She was able to restore religious harmony during this period of crisis.

THE COUNTER-REFORMATION

Thus, the Reformation movement shook the foundation of the Roman Catholic Church from the early 1500 and brought about the birth of the Protestant Church. To stem the tide of growing unpopularity, the Roman Catholic Church adopted a series of measures. The Inquisition (the Church Court) founded in Spain began its work of punishing the clergy who were found guilty of corruption, laxity and moral turpitude. In its enthusiasm to suppress heresy by repression, it alienated the sympathy of many, especially of those living in the Netherlands. They revolted against Spain and finally became independent. In the meanwhile, Holy Roman Emperor Charles V convened a conference at Ratisbon in 1541 with the hope of uniting the two churches but his mission failed.

The Council of Trent (1545-63)
In 1545, Pope Paul III convened the Church Council at Trent which met several times between 1545 and 1563. This council took positive steps to refurbish the image of the Catholic Church and also reiterate its authority. They included (1) the Pope is the head of the Church and the ultimate interpreter of the Bible and the church doctrines, (2) the traditional Latin translation of the Holy Bible should be treated as the authoritative version, (3) only the Church has the right to interpret the scriptures and (4) introduced following reforms: (a) condemned and prohibited the sale of indulgences and of the offences of the Church, (b) decided to ensure that church officials were properly educated, trained and disciplined, (c) that sermon be preached in the language of the people, (d) revived the Holy Inquisition to root out heresy, (e) introduced the Papal Index (i.e., press censorship) to prevent publication of any book which goes contrary to the teachings of Catholic faith.

The Society of Jesus Founded by Ignatius Loyola (1534)
The second phase of Counter Reformation began with the founding of different religious orders at the instance of the Pope. The most famous was the Society of Jesus which was founded by a Spanish nobleman, Ignatius Loyola (1491-1556). He had a strange religious experience while undergoing a period of treatment and rest in a hospital after being wounded in a battle. He turned into a missionary after studying the life of Jesus Christ and other saints. He studied theology at Sorbonne University. He established the Jesuit order with only six followers to begin with after taking the consent of the Pope. He and his followers swore to lead a life of poverty, chastity and "service to God and Christianity." The strength of the Jesuit order increased and they all rendered yeoman's service to God and humanity in different parts of the world.

St. Francis Xavier (1506-1552)
One of the Jesuit followers of Ignatius Loyola was Francis Xavier who spent the last 12 years of his life in Japan, India and other parts of Asia. He was raised to Sainthood in 1622. His body is preserved at the Church of Bom Jesus in Old Goa. Thus selfless and dedicated work carried out by these Jesuits went a long way in restoring the grandeur and glory of the Roman Catholic Church.

The Reformation

Lesson Review

1. Write a note on the early movements directed towards the reforming of the Catholic Church.
2. Describe the Protestant revolt led by Martin Luther in Germany.
3. Discuss the Reformation movement led by (1) Ulrich Zwingli in Switzerland, (2) John Calvin in France and (3) King Henry VIII of England.
4. What do you mean by Counter-Reformation? Explain the progress made by it.

27
THE RISE OF THE NATION-STATES IN EUROPE

The concept of Nation-State is of modern origin. It developed probably in the late Middle Ages. Prior to this, people of a particular country thought not in terms of having belonged to a particular country but as a citizen of a particular town or a city. A man who lived in London did not consider himself an Englishman but as a Londoner. Then how did the Nation-States emerge? When feudalism thrived in Europe, the people's loyalty was directed towards their liege-lords. But when any of their lords did not return from the crusades, the kings of Europe began to establish their contacts with their respective subjects. They put an end to the power of the nobles. They used gun-powder (a state monopoly) to destroy castles of the nobles. So by the late Middle Ages the kings of Europe became undisputed masters of their kingdoms.

However, their struggle did not end after crushing the power of the nobles. The Church became a serious rival. Its authority began to increase and sometimes encroach on the jurisdiction of the State. The kings did not like the international connection and loyalty of their respective state churches. A few of them supported anti-church movements. Conditions began to change by the middle of the 14th century. The power of the Church declined. Growth of trade and commerce resulted in the birth of a new middle-class which became a staunch supporter of an enlightened monarchy. Medieval ideas and notions were swept away after the discovery of new lands. Europe witnessed the revival of strong monarchies everywhere which worked for nationalist self-interest.

England, the First Nation-State in Europe
The earliest nation-state to emerge on the European continent was England. The most important factor which gave a sense of identity to the original inhabitants of this island—Britons—was the geographical contiguity. Between 450 BC and 43 AD, the Celts migrated from Central Europe and

settled in Britain and Ireland. In 54 BC, Julius Caesar invaded Britain and exacted tributes. The Romans again conquered this island and ruled her from the first century to the early fifth century AD. When the barbarians invaded the Roman Empire, the Roman army was withdrawn from England. Then followed the invasions of Germanic, Angles, Saxons and Jutes who occupied a part of this island. During the late eighth and early ninth centuries the Danes, who were adventurous sea-faring men, attacked this island. Alfred the Great (849 AD-899 AD), the famous Anglo-Saxon king of England, was able to drive them out. After his death, England came under the rule of King Canute of Denmark (1016 -1035). After Canute's death, the Anglo-Saxons in England recovered their independence. But their independence proved to be short-lived as William, Duke of Normandy (France), invaded England in 1066 AD. He defeated and killed the Saxon King, Harold, at Hastings and became the master of the island for about two decades. In the course of time, the cultures of the two—Anglo Saxon and the Norman-French—came to have harmonious blending and thereby producing the present English culture. King William ordered the survey of all land-holdings in England for tax purpose which was recorded in the *Domesday Book*. His successors were weak, and in 1154 King Henry II ascended the English throne.

Royal Absolutism
Under King Henry II of England royal power increased by leaps and bounds and included the appointment of church officials. He established the common law, appointed itinerant judges, and introduced the jury system. All these were done in order to protect the people of the land from tyrannical rulers. King Henry also made an attempt to gain control over the faction-ridden Ireland, and for that purpose sent his son, John. But John failed because his attitude alienated the sympathy of many chieftains there. Henry's successor was Richard I (the Lion-heart) who remained mostly away from England because of his participation in the third crusade. In order to collect money from the people for the crusade he sold charters of freedom to many towns and cities. Eventually this innocent act paved the way not only for the self-government of the towns and cities but also promoted the spirit of liberty.

Limitations on Royal Power
The next important phase in the development of British political system was the evolution of parliament. When King Richard I was away, his younger brother John tried to seize control of England. A war broke out between John's forces and those loyal to the king. John was compelled to

accept a truce. The king returned to England in 1194, and John was banished. The latter was deprived of all his possessions. Subsequently, the king forgave John and restored some of his lands in Ireland. On Richard's death in 1199, John succeeded him. King John (1199-1216) lost his French possession Normandy following a war with the French monarch Philip II in 1204. To raise revenue for reclaiming Normandy, he resorted to harsh economic measures—heavy taxes on estates and castles inherited by barons, frequent imposition of scutage payments and increased duties on imports and exports—which made him extremely unpopular. His defiance of Pope Innocent III in not recognizing Stephen Langton as Archbishop of Canterbury resulted in his excommunication in 1209. John's excommunication was revoked in 1213 following his recognition of Stephen Langton in 1212. King John made a futile attempt to regain Normandy in 1214. The nobles and barons rose in revolt and forced him to sign the Magna Carta in 1215 at Runnymede. This document secured for them the royal guarantee that their ancient rights and privileges would not be violated. It included (a) freedom from arbitrary arrest and confiscation of property, (b) trial by jury and (c) levy of new taxes only with the consent of the Great Council. The importance of the Great Council which was to become parliament in the later days was recognised by King John. His successor was Henry III who was also a weak ruler. He became unpopular like his father after his intervention in Italian politics. The nobles opposed the king and forced him to sign the *Provisions of Oxford.* It was later followed by the imprisonment of the king in the Tower of London. The leader of the nobles Simon de Montfort convened the meeting of the Great Council in 1265 which included, among others, two knights from each shire and two citizens from each town. In the true sense this was the first Parliament England had (1265). The next ruler was Edward I who needed money for the conquest of Wales and Scotland. So he required the support of all the four groups—the nobles, clergy, townsmen and representatives of shires—for the imposition of new taxes.

Model Parliament (1295)
So he summoned what is now known as the *Model Parliament* in 1295 which also included representatives of the last two groups. He succeeded in conquering Wales but not Scotland. Scots under King Robert Bruce defeated the English at Bannockburn in 1314 and remained free for the next three centuries. The reign of Edward III (1327-1377) witnessed the commencement of England's Hundred Years War (1337-1453) with France (cause being Edward's claim to the French throne), the Black Death (1348-50) and the strengthening of the constitutional position of the Parliament

vis-a-vis the King. Soon after the conclusion of the Hundred Years War, England witnessed a civil war. The House of York (with its White Rose as its badge) and the House of Lancaster (with Red Rose as its badge) fought against each other for the English throne. Therefore this civil war came to be known as the War of the Roses (1455-1485). This thirty years war ended in the victory of Henry the Tudor who belonged to the House of Lancaster.

Tudor Rulers of England

With popular support King Henry VII (1485-1509) suppressed the rebellious nobles and revived strong monarchy in England. He founded a special court called the Star Chamber which was used against the seditious barons. He lowered the expenses of the government and at the same time avoided waging of foreign wars. He encouraged England's trade and commerce with Europe and laid the foundation of a strong navy. When he died, England could boast of her political and economic stability. His son and successor, King Henry VIII (reign 1509-1547) led the Reformation movement by severing his connection with Rome (see Chapter on Reformation). He founded the Anglican Church and became its champion. The British Parliament showed its subservience to royal interests and policies. The short reign of Edward VI (1547-1553) witnessed the acceptance of Protestant doctrine by a majority of the English. His successor was Queen Mary I (1553-1558) who was a devout Catholic. She married an equally devout Catholic, King Philip of Spain, and tried to revive Catholicism in England. The persecutions of protestants and the execution of 300 of its leaders earned her the title "Blood Mary". Her successor, Queen Elizabeth I (1558-1603), avoided the extremes and established Anglicanism as the official religion of England. The Elizabethan Age is rightly considered as the 'Golden Age' in the history of England since it ensured religious harmony, made England an unrivalled sea-power after the defeat of the Spanish armada in 1588, encouraged overseas trade, and caused the birth of Renaissance.

Stuart Rulers

After Elizabeth's death, England came to be ruled by Stuart rulers. As the first Stuart ruler, James I (1603-1625) united the kingdoms of England and Scotland. He fancied himself as the divine representative of God as often expressed in the Latin phrase, *a deo rex, a rege lex* (meaning "the king is from God, and the law from the King"). His absolute despotism alienated the sympathies of the common people. His religious and foreign polices provoked the Puritans (English Protestant-Extremists). A long dispute between the king and the Parliament ensued. His son Charles the First ascended the throne in 1625 and made things worse by imprisoning the opposition members of the House of Commons for opposing him. However, the members of the Parliament asserted their position by forcing the king to accept the *Petition of Right* (1628). Nevertheless, the bitter dispute between the King and the Parliament plunged the country into a civil war. It was fought between the Cavaliers (supporters of the King) and the Roundheads (supporters of the Parliament). Oliver Cromwell's *Ironsides* finally defeated the royal forces at Marston Moor and Naseby. King Charles was taken captive and executed for treason in 1649. Oliver Cromwell ruled as the 1st Lord Protector of the newly formed Commonwealth of England, Scotland and Ireland from 1653 until his death in 1658. The Long Parliament invited Charles II (1660-1685), son of the executed Charles I, to return to England and rule as King. He treated the Puritans with contempt and drove them out of office. The Parliament tried to restrain his power by forcing him to sign the *Habeas Corpus Act* in 1679 which provided for the right of the accused to demand a trial in a court as to why he is being held in prison. The successor of Charles II was his brother James the Second. His short reign (1685-1688) was marked by disputes between the King and the Parliament on the one hand and the king and the Anglicans on the other. When he baptised his newly born son in 1688 as a catholic, the Parliament decided to invite the king's Protestant daughter, Mary (who had married William, King of Holland) to assume power in England. William and Mary accepted the invitation. James II fled, and England achieved the "Glorious Revolution" (sometimes called as the "bloodless revolution") in 1688. Parliamentary control over the King and the Queen was established after the *Bill of Rights (1689)* was passed. Some of the achievements of the "Glorious Revolution" included the end of absolute monarchy, the supremacy of the Parliament, the rise of the middle class and the establishment of a protestant State.

France
With the disintegration of Charlemagne's empire, France was split up into small kingdoms each ruled by a powerful noble. Feudalism took deep roots, and therefore it took a long time before a strong monarchy could emerge. The powers of the central government began to increase gradually under King Hugh Capet and his successors. The most outstanding among them were Philip II Augustus, Louis IX, Philip IV and Louis XI. King Philip II Augustus (1180-1223) decided to augment his power at any cost. He found that King John of England owned nearly half of France. As a feudal chief, Philip called John who was his vassal to his court. But John did not

oblige him thereby providing an excuse to Philip to conquer most of the English possessions in France. Furthermore, Philip drove out the Albigensians from Toulouse and gained control over it. King Louis IX (1226-1270) extended his power over the nobles by various means and introduced currency and legal reforms. King Philip IV (1285-1314) augmented the royal power further by taxing the Church lands, forcing Pope Clement V to withdraw Pope Boniface VIII's bulls *Clericis Laicos* (papal order that forbade the clergy from paying taxes to rulers without the Pope's consent), seizing the properties of the Knights Templars and calling the first Estates-General to support his policies and actions. During the time of Louis XI (1461-1483) the whole of France except Brittany came under royal control and the nobles could hardly challenge the power of the king.

France fared badly in the Hundred Years' War with England on account of the series of defeats she suffered at the hands of the latter. Her weakness was due to the absence of a strong central government. It was during this time of national crisis that a young peasant girl, Joan of Arc, appeared on the scene. She believed that she was ordained by God to lead the French army to victory. So she coaxed the disowned French King Charles VII to let her command the French army. Under her command the French army won resounding victories against the English and they lifted their siege of the city of Orleans. Her victories paved the way for the establishment of strong monarchy in France under Charles VII (1422-1461) who was crowned King of France at Reims Cathedral in 1429. In the end, Joan was captured by the English and tried for witchcraft and heresy in a Church court at Rouen. She was burned at the stake on May 30, 1431. The French king and soldiers were highly inspired by her great heroism and sacrifice. National feelings ran high and the French drove the English out of their country. Only Calais remained in the hands of the English.

France was deeply disturbed by the religious wars between the Catholics and the Huguenots (French Protestants) in the sixteenth century. However, the political situation improved after King Henry IV of Navarre, a Protestant, ascended the throne of France as the first monarch of the Bourbon dynasty in 1589. He converted to Catholicism in 1593 to thwart Catholic opposition to his rule. He issued the Edict of Nantes in 1598 which granted religious freedom to the Huguenots—ending all internal conflicts. His prosperous rule ended with his assassination by a Catholic fanatic in 1610.

Bourbon Monarchy of France

King Henry IV founded the Bourbon Dynasty whose descendents ruled France until monarchy was overthrown in 1792 (during the first French Revolution). He made France powerful and wealthy. His Finance Minister, the Duke of Sully, averted a possible bankruptcy by introducing necessary reforms. Agriculture, textile industry and the manufacture of silks and linen were encouraged. France sent explorers in search of new lands. French settlements were established in Nova Scotia.

Henry IV was succeeded by Louis XIII in 1610. He was eight years old then but the entire task of administering France fell upon the shoulders of the Prime Minister, Cardinal Richelieu. Besides his contribution to the cause of improving French culture, Cardinal Richelieu worked hard for making France the leader of Europe and the French monarchy supreme. He achieved the first by curbing the power of the Habsburgs (Austrian rulers) in the Thirty Years' War (1618-48), and the second by destroying the power of the nobles and the Huguenots in France. The king appointed *intendents* to govern the provinces and look after the local governments.

Louis XIV (1643-1715) succeeded Louis XIII after the latter's death in 1643, and under his leadership France reached the height of its glory. All powers were concentrated in the hands of one man, and that was Louis XIV who declared "I am the State". The French capital, Versailles (Paris), became the centre of gaiety and culture. He revoked the Edict of Nantes and persecuted the Huguenots. Thousands of them fled to England and other European countries. His famous minister Colbert put the finances of the state in a sound state and encouraged colonisation. But King Louis XIV involved the nation in a number of costly wars with the purpose of extending her natural boundaries. At the time of his death France was heading towards bankruptcy.

Spain

Conquests and occupation marked the early history of Spain. The earliest to settle there were the Iberians. Then Carthaginians invaded and settled in Spain during the 3rd century BC. From the 3rd century BC, to the middle of the sixth century AD, Spain became a part of the Roman Empire. After that the Visigoths invaded Spain and ruled her upto the early 8th century AD. The Mohammedans invaded Spain and ruled her from the early eighth century to 1462. Subsequently the Christian kingdoms grew stronger and the Moors (Mohammedans in Spain) were pushed back. When Ferdinand of Aragon married Isabella of Castile in 1469, Spain witnessed the unity of two most powerful Christian kingdoms. All of Spain was liberated from the Moors in 1492. It was under King Ferdinand and Queen Isabella that Spain witnessed the rise of royal powers, discovery of new lands by Columbus and others and the persecution of non-Christians. They forbade wars among nobles and crushed all opposition to their reign. They kept the Church under their control. During the first half of the sixteenth century Spain was ruled by the Holy Roman Emperor, Charles V. Philip II, son of Charles V, ascended the Spanish throne soon after his father's retirement in 1556. Spain had become the wealthiest nation in Europe due to the inflow of gold and silver from the new world. She became the leading nation in Europe, and her king tried to restore "Catholic unity through the inquisitions". Philip II married the English Queen, Mary. He failed to force the Dutch to accept the Catholic faith. They revolted and became a free nation.

Switzerland

In the thirteenth century, Switzerland constituted a part of the duchy of Swabia. It was then a part of the Holy Roman Empire. Some of the Swiss Cantons formed a league to resist the attempts of the Holy Roman Emperor to suppress them. They succeeded in defeating the Austrians at Morgarten in 1315. In the course of time, the Swiss cantons grew from strength to strength. They won their independence from the Holy Roman Empire in 1648. Since then they have maintained their fierce independence and strict neutrality in the affairs of Europe.

Prussia

The Rise of Prussia Under Hohenzollerns

In the Middle Ages, Prussia (which is now a part of Germany) was a petty state occupied by the Teutonic knights. Over a period of several centuries a number of principalities or duchies grew up around it. Each duchy was ruled by a Duke. The famous Hohenzollerns ruled the Duchy of Prussia from 1618. Earlier they were rulers of Brandenburg, another German duchy. Each Hohenzollern ruler added some bit of territory or the other and thus Prussia expanded to become the strongest state in the whole of Germany. The first famous Hohenzollern ruler who made Prussia strong was Frederick William (1640-88). He was called 'The Great Elector' on account of position and influence in the Holy Roman Empire. He enlarged his kingdom, centralised the government, and built a strong army and navy. His son Frederick I (1688-1713) was accorded recognition as 'King' by the Holy Roman Emperor in 1701. So Prussian kingdom included Prussia as well as Brandenburg. Frederick's son, Frederick William I (1713-1740) succeeded to the throne in 1713 and ruled Prussia for the next 27 years. He introduced compulsory education for all children and built a strong army. He added Swedish Pomerania to Prussia.

The greatest among the Hohenzollern dynasty of rulers was Frederick II the 'Great' (1740-86). From early life Frederick II developed a taste for poetry, drama, music and painting. He admired the French language and French writer Voltaire. Naturally his father thought him unfit to rule the country. But Frederick II proved to be ruthless and autocratic. He took full advantage of the chaotic conditions prevailing in other European states to expand his dominion. He revoked the recognition given to *Pragmatic Sanction* (a declaration issued by Holy Roman Emperor Charles VI in 1713 that recognized the right of his daughter to Habsburg's possessions which included Austria), and invaded Silesia, a part of Austrian Empire, in December 1740. With this began the War of the Austrian Succession. It ended in 1748 with the signing of the Treaty of Aix-la-Chapelle by the competing powers. This war did not achieve its purpose and Frederick the Great retained Silesia. This war of course spread to other continents such as America and India because France and England were rivals there. The treaty of Aix-la-Chapelle in 1748 brought an uneasy peace among the belligerents. So Archduchess Maria Theresa (1740-1780) of Austria began to prepare for another European war, this time seeking the help of the French for her cause instead of the English. Thereupon, the English switched their support to the side of Frederick the Great of Prussia. The Seven Years War began in 1756 on the European continent and spread to America and India since Britain and France were rivals there. The war came to an end by the treaty of Paris which was signed in 1763 by all the participants. The war resulted in the recognition and approval of Prussia's claim and annexation of Silesia. Austria felt very much humiliated. Prussia became a great power in Europe. The power of the French began to decline rapidly both in America and India. The English victory in this war was due to the leadership displayed by her War Minister, William Pitt, the Elder. The English Generals Robert Clive and James Wolfe played an important role in the victories achieved in India and Canada respectively.

Taking advantage of the weakness of Poland, several European powers were eager to bring about its disintegration. Frederick the Great of Prussia played a dynamic role in the first partition of Poland in 1772. He took the western half of that unfortunate country.

Enlightened Despotism
As an enlightened despot, Frederick the Great encouraged agriculture, commerce and industries. He welcomed the Huguenots of France who fled their country to escape persecution. In fact it was due to their labour that Prussia's industries flourished. What France lost Prussia gained. He

codified the laws of the country and gave a clean and efficient administration. He took special interest in maintaining a strong and efficient army. He granted full religious toleration to his subjects and patronised art, literature and music. Voltaire, the French philosopher and writer, became a great favourite of Frederick the Great. To sum up, Prussia under Frederick became a model state in Europe.

Austria

The Habsburgs of Austria

The Habsburgs who ruled Austria for centuries belonged to a very old and wealthy family. Due to a series of marriage alliances they could add vast territories to their dominion. In 1273, one of their family members by the name Rudolph was elected as the Holy Roman Emperor. Rudolph became the ruler of Austria. The power and prestige of the Habsburgs increased when Charles V became the Holy Roman Emperor. He not only ruled Austria, but also Spain and her overseas empire. With the outbreak of Protestant revolt, his position became shaky, and he finally abdicated his throne in favour of his two sons, Philip II and Ferdinand. Philip II ruled Spain and her empire and Ferdinand ruled Austria. The former lost much territory, wealth, and influence due to his Catholic outlook. The Austrian Habsburgs also lost much prestige during the Thirty Years War (1618-1648). The treaty of Westphalia (1648) which ended this war resulted in the Habsburg recognition of the independence of Switzerland. The power of Austrian Emperor came to be very much reduced. Frederick the Great of Prussia took full advantage of the weakness of the Habsburgs of Austria and snatched away the rich province of Silesia from the Austrian Empire.

Russia

Geographical Factors

Most of European Russia is situated on the great plain spreading from Central Europe in the West to the Ural Mountains in the east. Much of this plain in the north is in the Tundra region which experiences long and extreme winter and a very short summer. Therefore, human habitation in this region had become impossible. But the southern part of the Russian plain enjoyed a fair climate and became suitable for human habitation. Thus, geographical factors such as the extreme climates and barren lands of the North kept Russia isolated. The South enjoyed a mild climate and had black fertile soil. Therefore, many Slavic tribes settled in this region during the time of the decline of the Roman Empire. Since the Russian rivers such as the Dnieper, the Don and the Volga all flow towards the south, many village communities of the Eastern Slavs settled on their banks. When the Norsemen invaded Russia, they set up the kingdom of Novgorod. They expanded their dominions to the south, but in the long run they were absorbed by the Slavic subjects. During the tenth century the Christian missionaries from Constantinople spread Christianity in and around a flourishing town, Kiev. Since then the southern subjects of Russia kept in close touch with Constantinople.

During the middle of the thirteenth century Russia witnessed the invasions and occupation of her territory by the Mongols, a nomadic tribesmen from the steppes of Central Asia. It may be remembered that under their great and mighty ruler, Chenghis Khan, they had overrun China, Turkestan, Persia and Mesopotamia earlier. The Russians suffered untold miseries at the hands of the invaders who occupied their land for several centuries.

Russia Under Czars

When the Mongol hold over Russia weakened on account of their internal troubles, a prince of Moscow called Ivan III (1462-1505) refused to pay tributes and declared his independence. He annexed Novgorod and its neighbouring states into his kingdom. He was also known as Ivan the Great. During the second half of the sixteenth century, Russia was further expanded by Ivan IV (1547-84), the first Czar of Russia. He was also known as Ivan the Terrible. He began his career as a good ruler but later became a tyrant. He was known for his frayed tempers, madness and merciless killings of innocent people. He drove his peasants to serfdom by giving more powers to the Boyars (landlords). Russian peasants were not allowed to leave their homeland. Ivan's successors were weak and so the country passed through difficult times. Finally the national assembly elected Michael Romanov (1613-1645), a grand-nephew of Ivan the Terrible, as the new Czar of Russia in 1613. He was the founder of the Romanov dynasty which ruled Russia till the outbreak of the Bolshevik Revolution in 1917.

Peter the Great (1682-1725)

One of the greatest rulers of this dynasty was Peter I or Peter the Great. He ascended the throne when he was ten years old. He grew to be sensitive, intelligent and hardworking. He despised the backwardness of his country and the attitude of the people. Determined to uplift his country from terrible backwardness, he undertook a journey to learn about the progress made in Western Europe. On his return (which was precipitated by the revolt of his palace guards), he introduced several reforms. He struck terror into the hearts of his subjects by summarily executing those rebellious guards. None had the temerity to challenge his authority since that time.

Westernisation of Russia Under Peter

Foreign engineers, ship-builders and artisans were invited to construct schools, hospitals, dams, dockyards and factories in Russia. He compelled the Russian nobles to adopt western style of dress, manners and etiquette. He compelled Russian women to overcome their shyness and appear in public. He simplified Russian alphabet and introduced a uniform currency. Furthermore, he raised a large standing army and built a powerful navy. To bring about rapid westernisation, Peter founded a new capital city called St. Petersburg in 1703. It served as Russia's "window on Europe."

Foreign Policy

The main thrust of Peter's foreign policy was to secure for Russia the ice-free ports in the north and the south. Joining the side of Denmark and Poland, he fought a long and bloody war against Sweden (The Great Northern War, 1700-1721) and succeeded in securing the sea-coast lying between Prussia and Finland. It was on the marshy lands of the Baltic Sea coast that he built his new capital. Peter also fought against the Ottoman Empire and captured Azov (a town near Sea of Azov) in 1696. He had to cede this town to the Turks after his defeat in the Turkish War (1710-1713). His victorious military campaign against the Persians (1722-23) secured for him the southern and western coasts of the Caspian Sea.

The other changes Peter introduced were the introduction of a new calendar, western system of counting, establishment of printing press and bringing the Greek Orthodox Church under his personal control. Subsequently the Greek Orthodox Church came to be known as the Russian Orthodox Church.

Catherine II or Catherine the Great (1762-1796)

Thirty-seven years after the death of Peter the Great, Russia witnessed the accession of Queen Catherine or Catherine the Great whose rule proved to be most momentous. She was a German princess who married Peter III. When he turned insane, Catherine got him murdered so that she could rule the country. Her rule proved to be more autocratic than that of Peter the Great although she considered herself to be an enlightened despot. Some of her internal reforms included the revised code of laws, construction of hospitals and orphanages, patronage to artists and writers, opening of schools and academies and the adoption of French language and manners for her court. However, all her reforms came to mean nothing to the teeming millions of Russian peasants and serfs. She kept the Church firmly under her control.

Foreign Policy
Under her able leadership Russia followed an aggressive foreign policy. It yielded rich dividends as Russia gained territories from both Poland and Turkey. Quick in grasping the political situation in these two countries, she decided to strike. Poland was Russia's western neighbour, and the situation there was chaotic after the death of her king, Augustus III. So, Catherine lost no time in persuading the nobles there to elect one of her own courtiers Stanislaw II August Poniatowski (1764-1795) to the Polish throne. When the people of Poland revolted against her interference she got the revolt crushed. She later joined Prussia and Austria in bringing about Poland's partition. The three partitions of Poland (in 1772, 1793 and 1795 respectively) reduced the size and wealth of that country to such an extent that she no longer existed. Russia under Catherine the Great received more than half of the territories of Poland, and her borders touched the frontiers of Austria and Prussia.

War With the Turks
While attacking the insurgent Poles, Russian troops violated the borders of Turkey. It led to a war between these two great powers. Catherine succeeded in defeating the war-weary Turks. The Turks signed the Treaty of Kuchuk Kainarji in 1774 and surrendered to the Russians Azov and its adjacent territory. In 1784, she got from the Turks, the Crimean peninsula. Again in 1792, the Turks ceded to her the lands along the Black Sea and the right to protect the Christian subjects of the Ottoman Empire. Russia also got the right to free navigation through the Straits of Dardanelles. It is no wonder that she was called by many historians as Catherine the Great.

Lesson Review
1. Trace the rise of England as a nation-state.
2. Explain how French monarchy became popular and strong from the 12th century?
3. Describe the rise of Prussia as a nation-state.
4. What were the reforms of Peter the Great aimed at westernising Russia?
5. Is it correct to say that Catherine the Great completed the work of Peter the Great?

28
AMERICAN WAR OF INDEPENDENCE

After the discovery of the new continent, colonies of different European powers such as Spain, England, France, the Netherlands and Sweden had sprung up everywhere. For example, Spain had established her colony in Florida. French settlers established colonies in Northern America which were called as New France (Canada) and Louisiana (U.S.A). The British colonies—in all thirteen in number—sprang up on eastern sea-coast of the present U.S.A. These British settlements were promoted by chartered companies and were approved by the British Crown. Jamestown in Virginia became the first British settlement in 1607. The main reasons for the peoples of Europe and Britain to emigrate were trade and religion. For example, the Jamestown settlement was started as a commercial venture by the Virginia Company. Religious enthusiasm of the Pilgrim Fathers who fled persecution in England was also responsible for the spread of a number of settlements. Fifty years after the foundation of Jamestown, the English established a number of colonies.

Development of 13 English Colonies

The Pilgrim Fathers came to America and established colonies (in the New England area). They sought civil and religious autonomy from their mother-country, and made the Mayflower compact as the basis of their new government. The southern colonies such as Virginia and Georgia developed due to the rapid spread of tobacco and cotton cultivation. The landlords there were typical English Squires who employed slaves. The Quakers and Catholics developed Pennsylvania and Maryland colonies respectively. Pennsylvania was founded by William Penn (a quaker) where the residents were "free to worship as they pleased". Lord Baltimore who set up the colony of Maryland exclusively for Catholics also allowed Protestants to settle there. The Dutch set up new Amsterdam as a trading post. When the English defeated the Dutch in 1664 and captured New Amsterdam, they renamed it as New York. Part of the colony of New York became New Jersey. The colony of Delaware was founded by a Swedish company and ultimately fell into the hands of the English. The colony of Connecticut was founded by some people of Massachusetts who desired more religious freedom and political voice than they were getting in their own colony. Men from Boston founded the colony of New Hampshire. With the exception of Connecticut and the Rhode Island, all other colonies had governors who were appointed by the king or proprietors. Each governor was assisted by a council. Each colony had an assembly consisting of elected representatives which voted for approving local taxes and local laws.

All the colonies required British protection as the French across the northern border, and the Red Indians from the West, constantly posed a threat. The British governors could afford to give that protection to the natives of the thirteen colonies. By the middle of the eighteenth century the thirteen colonies had a population of about one and half million. The natives of the 13 colonies had no reason to complain because their representatives voted to levy taxes without outside interference.

British Mercantilist Policy

When the colonies grew in size and importance, the British government felt keen on establishing control over them. Firstly, the British King appointed governors to rule over them. The salary of the governor was to be borne by the colonial exchequer. Secondly, the British merchants were interested in deriving benefits from a policy which Britain was to adopt arbitrarily and implement it in her colonies in America. This policy was called the mercantalist policy. A series of mercantilist regulations were passed by the British Parliament which restricted the scope of colonial exports and imports. For example, the colonists were made to sell their goods only to the English merchants and to buy foreign goods after paying duty at an English port. Furthermore, the colonists were not to compete with the English manufacturers. Opposition to these mercantilist regulations was widespread and the colonists resorted to smuggling of goods. Taxes were also evaded by the colonists. Some of the merchants in the colonies maintained their trade contacts with the enemies of Britain.

It was this measure of political and economic independence enjoyed by the colonists which Britain sought to curb, not for selfish reasons, but out of dire economic compulsion. The change in English colonial policy took place in 1763, that was after the Seven Years' War (1756-63) in Europe. Britain finally achieved victory over France and her allies, and from the former she received Canada after signing the treaty of Paris.

However, the long war strained her slender resources to such an extent that her government started imposing heavy duties on her manufactured goods. It was this domestic constraint that compelled her to change from the lenient policy she was pursuing towards her colonies to a somewhat severe one.

When the French lost Canada to Britain after the Seven Years' War, the colonists heaved a sigh of relief. They no longer feared a French attack on their colonies. It was this change in the situation which gave them courage and self-confidence. They began to boldly articulate their views. However, the British government under King George III, was not prepared to give them a large measure of independence. On the other hand, it tried to exploit the colonies in order to save itself from a financial bankruptcy.

Conflicting views arose when Britain tried to make good her financial deficit by levying taxes on the colonies. It was argued that since Britain protected the colonies during the Seven Years War, she felt it justified that the colonies should share a part of the financial burden. But the colonists replied that the war on the continent had been fought and financed by them and therefore the mother country should not impose taxes. Furthermore, they argued that their colonial assemblies alone had the right to tax them.

Enforcement of Mercantilist Regulations

King George III began to assert his position and forced the cabinet to secure parliamentary sanction for imposing new taxes on the colonists. The royal officials in the colonies were ordered to strictly enforce the mercantilist trade regulations. For proper enforcement of trade regulations the British government sent troops to America. British agents were authorised to check smuggling and search private residences on suspicion.

Britain also ordered settlers not to move beyond the traditional border on the western side lest they provoke the Red Indians. This order made the fur traders and small farmers in the colonies angry. Businessmen also became disturbed as they hoped to buy western lands at a cheap price.

Sugar Act (1764)

The British Parliament passed the Sugar Act in 1764 by which duty was imposed on molasses imported by the colonists. The colonists tried to smuggle molasses but their activities were curbed. There was considerable resentment since the tax was imposed by the British government. Its objective was to compel the colonists to contribute towards meeting the expenses of British troops stationed in the colonies.

Stamp Act (1765) and Its Repeal
During the next year, George Grenville (the British Prime Minister), introduced a new measure, the Stamp Act, by which the colonists were required to register various legal documents, wills and licences by affixing revenue stamps. The British Parliament gave its consent as the amount of revenue to be raised was not big, but the colonists reacted very strongly. They raised a storm of protest. Heaps of stamps and the effigies of stamp collectors were burnt, and there were riots in New England and New York. The Stamps Act Congress which was composed of the representatives of nine colonies met at New York and passed a resolution stating that British Parliament had no right to tax the colonies without their consent. The British government made a hasty retreat and repealed it. However, it insisted on its right to tax the colonies. On hearing that the Stamp Act had been repealed, mobs in the colonies became overjoyed and ceased their agitation. In fact, the agitation was mainly directed not so much against the revenue to be raised through the purchase of stamps as on the right of the British government to tax them. Secondly, the agitation brought about the unity of all the nine colonies as apparent from the meeting of the Stamp Act Congress.

Townshend Acts (1767)
The Grenville ministry yielded place to Pitt's ministry. Its Chancellor of Exchequer Charles Townshend passed a series of acts, which included the Townshend duties act that proposed duties on colonial imports of glass, lead, paint, paper and tea. By another act called New York Restraining Act, the New York assembly was forbidden from passing any new laws before complying with the terms of the Quartering Act of 1765. The Quartering Act required the colonies to provide food, shelter and meet other expenses of the British troops stationed there. Besides raising a storm of protest, the merchants of Boston, Philadelphia and New York resorted to the boycott of British goods. It may be remembered that the non-importation agreement of colonial merchants, and the activities of the Sons of Liberty (a group of American patriots), had compelled the English merchants to ask their government to repeal the Stamp Act earlier. Some colonial enthusiasts advocated home-made manufactures of all kinds so as not to rely on Britain for imports. Townshend died and his place was taken by Lord North. To break the unity of the colonists, Lord North repealed all Townshend duties except on tea. The presence of the British customs commissioner in Boston enraged the colonists. In 1770, an altercation between a mob and the British soldiers resulted in the latter firing at the former, killing five and injuring many. Samuel Adams, an American politician and revolutionary, described this incident as the "Boston Massacre."

Boston Tea Party (December 16, 1773)

The tax on tea was retained for two reasons. Firstly, the British government wanted to retain its right to tax the colonies despite constant opposition from the colonists who raised slogans like "No taxation without representation", and "taxation without representation is tyranny". Secondly, Lord North tried to help the East India Company to dispose of its large stock of tea by selling them to the colonists. As usual there was popular opposition to this move and leaders in the colonies tried to prevent unloading of tea at the colonial ports. At Boston harbour, the activists of the Sons of Liberty disguised themselves as Mohawk Indians and stealthily made entry into the East India Company ships and threw all the chests of tea into the water. The news of the 'Boston Tea Party' spread like wild fire, and under pressure from the American patriots the consignees in Charleston, Philadelphia and New York refused to receive their tea shipments.

King George III and his prime minister, Lord North, took retaliatory steps. By a series of acts (Coercive Acts of 1774) they withdrew the charter granted to Massachusetts colony, put Boston harbour under quarantine, and banned political meetings there. Colonists accused of crimes were to be tried in England. The Quebec Act (1774), passed by the British Parliament, recognized the Catholic religion in Canada and brought territory between the Ohio and the Mississippi under the governor of Quebec. This act was therefore viewed as a coercive act by the American colonists as it checked their westward expansion. It proved to be one of the major causes for the outbreak of the American Revolution (1775-1783). Quebec was invaded by the forces of the American Continental Army in September 1775.

The First Continental Congress (1774)

British retaliation roused the anger of the colonists. The colonial assembly of Virginia took the first step in issuing a call for a Continental Congress to deal with the intolerable acts of the British government which endangered the liberties of every colony. Accordingly, the First Continental Congress met in September 1774 in Philadelphia. It included delegates from all the colonies except Georgia. George Washington, John and Samuel Adams, and John Jay, who were to play an important role in the early history of the United States of America, were among those who participated in the Congress. They sent a petition to King George III to redress their grievances, formed a "Continental Association," with the purpose of stopping all trade with Britain, and agreed to meet again during the next spring. In Britain, leaders like Lord Chatham and Edmund Burke, who were sympathetic to the American colonists, appealed to their government to repeal the Coercive Acts. But King George III's government remained adamant.

Skirmishes at Lexington and Concord (April 19, 1775)

The First Continental Congress had approved steps to be taken to prepare for war. The people of Massachusetts gathered arms and ammunition and trained minutemen to fight. In Boston, British General Thomas Gage sent troops to capture ammunition stored by minutemen at Concord. When the troops arrived at Lexington, conflict ensued resulting in the death of eight minutemen. British troops advanced towards Concord and destroyed what little military supplies they found. On their way back to Boston, the British troops were fired upon by the minutemen (American militiamen ready to fight at a moment's notice) resulting in over 250 British casualties.

Declaration of Independence (4th July 1776)

A few weeks after the battles of Lexington and Concord, the Second Continental Congress met in Philadelphia (May 1775). The Congress included delegates from all the colonies except Georgia. They adopted the Olive Branch Petition on July 5, 1775, and sent it to Britain on July 8, 1775. It asserted loyalty of the colonists to the British crown in a final attempt to avert war. The Congress also released a document titled, *Declaration of the Causes and Necessity of Taking Up Arms* (July 6, 1775), which described the reasons for the colonists taking up arms. Britain answered the Olive Branch Petition with the Prohibitory Act (1775) which closed the colonies to international trade. The Second Continental Congress, which first met in May 1775, approved the invasion of Quebec province. The Battle of Quebec (December 31, 1775) ended disastrously for the colonists. Thomas Paine's pamphlet *Common Sense*, published in January 1776, advocated independence for the colonies from the corrupt British monarchy. The Second Continental Congress decided to sever relations with the mother country by appointing a committee to draft a formal declaration of American Independence. Thomas Jefferson drafted the Declaration of Independence which was proclaimed on 4th July, 1776. It included, among other things, a list of omissions and commissions of the government of King George III, and asserted the colonists' "certain inalienable rights, that among these are life, liberty, and the pursuit of happiness". In the end the solemn declaration mentioned, "we therefore...solemnly publish and declare, that these United Colonies are, and of Right ought to be Free and Independent States...."

The War

The Second Continental Congress appointed General Washington as the commander of the Continental Army and began to raise necessary resources for the continuation of war. Washington commanded ill-equipped and poorly trained soldiers numbering 19,000 and was pitted against 32,000 trained British soldiers led by William Howe. Howe defeated Washington at the Long Island and captured New York. But Washington did not lose his courage. He recrossed the icy river of Delaware on a snowstorm Christmas-night and captured Trenton from the Hessians. He followed up this victory with another at Princeton. The war entered a new phase when Lord George Germain accepted a plan to isolate the New England by sending a force of 8,000 soldiers under the command of General Burgoyne who was to come down from the Hudson Valley to New York to join Gen. Howe. This plan did not work out the way it was intended. Firstly, Burgoyne found it difficult to reach the south because of the difficult terrain and weary soldiers. Secondly, Gen. Howe left New York for the south not knowing that he was to meet Burgoyne. He went southwards, defeated Washington again at Brandywine Creek and Germantown, and occupied Philadelphia. In the meanwhile, Gen. Burgoyne was defeated at the battle of Saratoga and finally surrendered in October 1777. The defeat of the British at Saratoga proved to be a turning point in favour of the colonists. The French foreign minister believed that the American colonists deserved assistance from a friendly country. So France joined the war on the American side in 1778 to help them in winning the war, and at the same time derive satisfaction of avenging her defeat by Britain in the Seven Years' War. France lent money and sent her volunteers to America. The French navy also played a decisive role during the crucial stages of the war. Soon Spain and the Netherlands were also at war with Britain as allies of France. The League of Armed Neutrals (Russia, Denmark and Sweden) assumed hostile attitude towards Britain. Thus, Britain was alone in her fight against the rebellious colonists who were thousands of miles away from her. Lack of communication and fresh reinforcements weakened the British army which had the problem of effectively controlling the territories it had conquered. In Britain, the Whigs condemned the attitude of King George III towards the colonies. General Washington spent the most bitter winter at Valley Forge. His army starved and its morale was very low. The British won several victories in the south in 1780. But in October 1781, the British army in the

Washington   Lincoln

south led by General Cornwallis was surrounded by the American and the French armies. Unable to extricate himself from this predicament, Cornwallis with his soldiers surrendered to Washington at Yorktown. It was the most important event in the course of the war. The war continued till 1783 even though Britain was weary. Britain lost the war because her leaders were unable to direct it efficiently. Secondly, she had lost her supremacy on the seas due to French intervention. Thirdly, she was fighting on the foreign soil which lay thousand of miles away. Fourthly, her commanders committed many blunders. In the end, one must also give due credit to General Washington for having ably led the colonial forces to victory.

Results of the War
In 1783, the British signed the Treaty of Paris (1783) by which she recognised the independence of the 13 colonies. The treaty included the delimitation of territory ("from the southern boundary of Canada to the northern boundary of Florida and from the Atlantic to the Mississippi").

One may say that American War of Independence was an event of great importance in the history of mankind. The long struggle of the colonists against the royal tyranny ended. Ideals enshrined in the Declaration of Independence were put into practice. The Americans chose a republic in the place of monarchy and built a truly democratic state.

Thirdly, the American Revolution had its impact on the French who groaned under tyrannical monarchy. When the French volunteers led by General La Fayette returned to France from the colonies they sowed the seeds of revolution on their native soil, thus, paving the way for the outbreak of the French Revolution in 1789.

King George III and his government stood very much discredited in the eyes of the people. Despite the advice given to King George III about following a policy of restraint towards the colonies, he remained adamant (he was mentally deranged). So royal interference was kept at a low level henceforth.

In the end, the mercantilist theory, that colonies exist for the benefit of the mother-country, came to be very much criticised. Britain changed her policies towards the other colonies considerably.

Lesson Review

1. Trace the causes which led to the outbreak of the American war of Independence.
2. What were the important results of the American war of Independence?
3. On the outline map of North America show the 13 British Colonies and locate the places where the important battles were fought.

29
THE FRENCH REVOLUTION (1789)

Towards the closing years of the 18th century Europe was shaken by the French Revolution—considered by many historians as the most important landmark in human history. The revolution which occurred in 1789 swept away the existing political institutions and aimed at establishing a more egalitarian society and responsible government than what existed before. The Revolution began with the siege of Bastille on July 14,1789 and continued until the rise of Napoleon Bonaparte to power. Let us examine the causes which led to the sudden overthrow of the French Monarchy in 1789.

Political Causes

Royal absolutism, as witnessed during the glorious period of Louis XIV, came to an end with his death in 1715. His great-grandson, Louis XV, who ascended the throne at the tender age of five, neither had the capacity nor the ability to govern the country effectively. France drifted towards chaos by involving herself in numerous wars. Mindless of the financial burden that would fall upon the poor peasantry, she fought the wars of Austrian succession and the seven years war with the result that she lost her empire. Poor peasants who could not pay the taxes were sent to prison and those who spoke against royal despotism and tyranny also suffered. King Louis XV never evinced keen interest in governing the country but engaged himself in the pursuit of worldly pleasures. When his ministers tried to discuss with him the serious problems of the state, he said, "After me, the deluge". He sadly neglected the affairs of the state and appointed his favourites to important offices. The treasury was empty after the wars, and the king remained, as usual indifferent. He also adopted a policy of repression by imposing curbs on the freedom of the press and speech. The king did little to alleviate the sufferings of the common people. Louis XV's successor was Louis XVI. He was twenty years old when he came to power. He was intelligent and well-intentioned. But he had no will to carry out some bold reforms to set right the deteriorating conditions prevailing in France. His judgement was influenced by flattering courtiers and his ill-advised queen, Marie Antoinette.

Unfortunately, France had no uniform code of laws. A law which was regarded as just and fair in one province was not so in another. Nepotism and corruption in every government department further alienated the sympathies of the people.

The Bourbon monarchy discarded the practice of consulting the Estates-General on state matters since the days of Louis XIII. They thought that it served little purpose. In the absence of the Estates-General, the kings of France arrogated powers for themselves but were advised by able chief ministers like Cardinal Richelieu, Mazarin and finance ministers like Colbert. However, towards the end of the eighteenth century, King Louis XVI was mostly advised by incompetent ministers.

Marie Antoinette

Social Causes

Invidious distinctions and unjust privileges marked the character of the French society. The society was divided sharply into three estates or classes. The first estate was constituted by the higher clergy like the archbishops, bishops and the abbots who governed the church of France.

The First Estate (the Church)

The Church owned one-fifth of the cultivated lands in France and enjoyed great influence with the Government. Like the nobles, the higher clergy was also exempt from paying most of the taxes. With the nobles they supported absolute monarchy. The Church collected *tithe,* a tax from the people for providing community services. It also maintained institutions of learning. The lower clergy lived in miserable conditions.

The Second Estate (the Nobles)

There were about 80,000 families in France who belonged to the nobility—the Second Estate. Even though feudalism declined in France since the days of Richelieu, the nobles continued to enjoy all the privileges such as non-payment of most of the taxes, avenues to higher positions in the French administration, and income from various feudal dues of the peasants. It may be noted that most of the nobles were absentee landlords. This idle aristocracy became parasitic, and the peasants felt that they were being unjustly taxed.

The Third Estate (the Common People)

The bulk of the French population belonged to the third estate. They were the middle class members, the peasants and artisans. The educated middle-class, which consisted of merchants, lawyers, teachers, doctors and others, was conscious of the inequalities in the social order and unfair and oppressive taxes resorted to by the despotic monarchy. The government hardly cared for their welfare. It was from them that the main thrust for the revolution came. The peasants complained of overburdening taxes which reduced them to penury. After paying taxes to the landlord, the church and the state, a poor peasant could hardly make both ends meet with 18 per cent of his income. He was further subjected to humiliation when the nobles destroyed his field while hunting animals. The French artisans complained of the regulation of trade-guilds which favoured their masters and left them with meagre income.

Economic Causes

The French system of taxation was both unjust and unfair despite the fact that peasants in the neighbouring countries suffered much more than them. Nevertheless, French peasants suffered due to oppression of the tax-farmers and uncertain imposition of the taxes. The privileged classes did not pay most of the taxes and the burden was naturally shifted on the shoulders of the poor peasants.

Intellectual Awakening

It is said that ideas govern the world and they come from the philosophers. France produced great philosophers during the eighteenth century. Voltaire became internationally famous as a great writer and critic whose style and pungent criticism were inimitable. It was through his plays and writings that he launched his bitter attacks against the existing institutions like the church and the state. He made fun of the eccentricities of the nobles. Writing about Voltaire (1694-1778), Macaulay says, "Of all the intellectual weapons ever wielded by man the mockery of Voltaire was the most terrible."

While Voltaire would have liked enlightened despotism, Montesquieu (1689-1755), a good student of constitutional government, preferred constitutional monarchy in France such as the English type. He summed up his ideas of new kind of government in his important work *De l'esprit des lois*. It was in this work that he popularised the theory of separation of powers, and of its exercise by three branches of government—the legislative, the executive and the judiciary. If this is done, he argued, there would be no tyranny, and the liberty of the individual could be safeguarded.

Probably the greatest French philosopher of the age was Jean Jacques Rousseau (1712-1778). In his *Social Contract,* he explained that the king and his subjects are parties to a contract, and therefore if the king does not rule the people according to their general will, he loses their loyalty. The people have every right to overthrow the monarchy under such circumstances. Rousseau was advocating popular sovereignty theory. His writings cast such a spell on his admirers that they were ready to revolt against the oppressive monarchy. Diderot was another intellectual of the time who prepared an *Encyclopaedia* containing the latest knowledge. He exposed the rotten system of administration in France and suggested several remedial measures.

The Role of the King

When the American colonists revolted against the oppressive rule of the mother country and won a resounding victory at Saratoga, the French government decided to help them with men, money and materials. It caused a serious strain on the finances of the country and cast a heavy burden on the poor peasants. After the success of the American Revolution (1783), the French volunteers returned to their homeland and sowed the seeds of the revolution. The king ought to have reduced the expenses of the royal

Siege of the Bastille

household and wisely dealt with the financial crisis. But, this was not to be because the queen and her advisers always came in his way. Turgot was appointed as the Minister of Finance to suggest remedies. He advised the king to tax the privileged class. He was summarily dismissed at the instance of the queen. The financial crisis reached threatening proportions, and the government defaulted payment of salary to the armed forces. Unfortunately, France witnessed near famine conditions in 1788 with the result there was serious food shortage. Coupled with this, there was unusual and severe winter in 1789. It was at this critical juncture the king was advised by his courtiers to summon the Estates-general (French Parliament) to get approval for further dose of taxation.

Course of the Revolution
When the Estates-general was summoned, the king ignored the importance of the Third Estate (600 representatives elected by the common people) and tried to consult the representatives of the three estates separately. The representatives of the Third Estate advised the kings to bring together the representatives of all the three estates at one place for discussion of state problems. The king discarded their advice. Subsequently, it led to a quarrel between the king and the representatives of the Third Estate. They, along with a few representatives from the other two estates, took a pledge (Tennis court oath) not to return home till the drafting of the new constitution was completed. The new constitution was to be framed to limit the powers of the king. When the king dismissed Finance Minister Jacques Necker on July 11, 1789, rumour spread that he might dissolve the National Assembly too. An unruly mob in Paris stormed the medieval prison fortress of Bastille—a symbol of royal despotism—on July 14, 1789, and set the prisoners free. The royal power was weakened further when the revolutionaries drove out royal officials from Paris and established their own government in Paris—Paris Commune (1789-1795). The king summoned troops to frighten the Paris mob. It led to further escalation of mob fury. Hungry women of Paris marched to the royal palace of Versailles and demanded bread. When there was no proper response, the mob entered the palace and ransacked it. They forced the king, the queen and their children to live in Paris. The National Assembly completed the drafting of the constitution in 1791. According to this new constitution the king's powers came to be reduced. Laws were to be made by the Legislative Assembly, and members of this assembly were to be elected by tax-paying citizens. The king was not happy with the civil constitution of the clergy. However, he gave his consent to abide by the laws of the new constitution. Looking at the tense situation prevailing in the countryside (where the peasants rose in revolt against the nobles) and also a possibility of a war breaking out with Austria on the borders, the king thought it fit to flee the country. In June 1791, he attempted to flee with his family, but was

apprehended at the border town of Varennes. Thus, ended the hopes of the Moderates who desired a constitutional monarchy. The Extremists gained ground in popularity and power. It led to the deposition of the king and his subsequent execution (1793). France was fast drifting towards a war with her neighbours as their monarchs were shocked on hearing about the execution of King Louis XVI. A total anarchy prevailed with the new constitution being set aside. The National Convention which met in September, 1792, began to draft a new constitution. It abolished monarchy and declared France as a Republic. Thereafter, it established a Committee of Public Safety which was headed by the extremist leaders like Danton and Robespierre. These leaders enjoyed unlimited authority. The Girondins, who were moderates, were executed and the reign of terror began (September 5, 1793-July 27, 1794). France witnessed the guillotining of thousands of nobles and innocent men who had supported monarchy. Among the famous women who were executed were Queen Marie Antoinette, Madame Roland and Madame du Barry.

Constitution of 1795

After the death of Robespierre, the moderate elements gained predominance in the National Convention. The National Convention framed a new constitution for France in 1795 according to which the executive powers were vested with the Directory of five persons who were to be advised by a legislative body consisting of two chambers. When there was royalist uprising in Paris against the new constitution, troops were ordered to crush it. A Corsican youth named Napoleon Bonaparte took charge of the command, and after a 'whiff of grape-shot' dispersed the unruly mob which was about to attack the National Convention. This young officer was destined to rule France from 1799 to 1815.

Results of the Revolution

During its ten year course the French Revolution brought about far reaching changes. Firstly, it destroyed the vestiges of feudalism and liberated the serfs. Secondly, it established a constitutional monarchy which also disappeared in due course of time. The declaration of the Rights of Man came to be included in the new Constitution as an article of faith. The nobles and the Church lost their property and their lands were distributed to the peasants. Slaves in the French colonies were set free. The watchwords of the French Revolution such as Liberty, Equality and Fraternity reflected the coming of a new democratic and social order in Europe.

Thirdly, the revolution roused national feelings. The common people were prepared to die for the sake of protecting the gains of the revolution. The French Citizen-militia fought the enemies on the French borders.

The French Revolution (1789)

Finally, the French Revolution had a lasting effect on the people of Europe in the 19th century. Those who were groaning under the tyranny of foreign rulers, derived their inspiration from the French. Europe was convulsed by frequent revolutions aimed at overthrowing oppressive governments. The revolution asserted the political supremacy of the middle class. In the ensuing chapters one learns about the way in which the Italians and Germans overthrew the oppressive regime of Austria and achieved unity.

Lesson Review

1. What were the causes of the French Revolution of 1789? Trace its results.
2. Write a brief note on the course of the French Revolution (1789).
3. Write short notes on:
   (a) Mirabeau   (b) Robespierre
   (c) Role of King Louis XVI.

30
NAPOLEON BONAPARTE

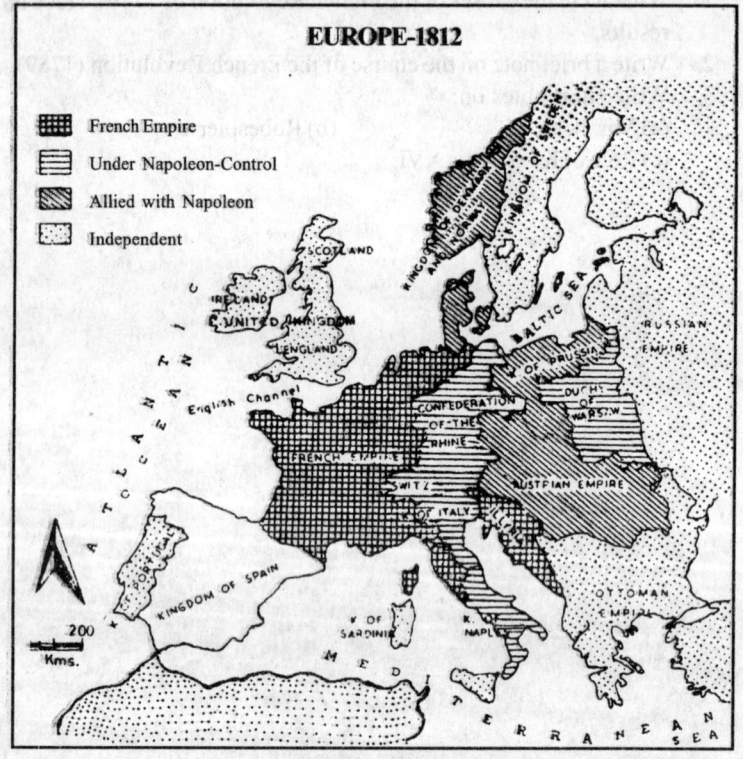

Napoleon Bonaparte, who guided the destiny of Europe for nearly 15 years, was born at Ajaccio in the island of Corsica in 1769. His parents were Italians and he spoke French with a foreign accent. He attended military schools at Brienne and in Paris. Children of French nobles who attended these schools treated him with contempt since he belonged to a poor family. When he was sixteen, Napoleon joined the French army. When the revolution broke out he supported the Jacobins. When the British attacked Toulon, Napoleon went to its rescue and succeeded in driving them out. He was arrested after the fall of Robespierre and sent to prison. He would have been guillotined but for a quirk of fate. He impressed the Directory with his timely and effective action against the royalist mob which threatened to attack the National Convention. He rose high in his career because he knew one of the Directors, Paul Barras. Another Director by the name Lazare Carnot was so impressed by Napoleon's military ability that he appointed him as the commander of the Italian expedition.

He found his soldiers ill-fed, ill-equipped and lacking morale and courage. Despite these handicaps, Napoleon, by his exemplary courage and conduct, turned them into highly disciplined soldiers. He gave them a sense of purpose. By a master-stroke of stratagem he drove the Austrians out of Southern Italy. His brilliant victories against the Austrians compelled the Austrian Emperor to sue for peace. Dazzled by his brilliant victories, the Directory asked him to undertake the task of defeating Britain, an ally of Austria. Napoleon convinced the Directory that Britain could be subdued only if her economy was throttled. For this it was necessary to attack Egypt. The French army under Napoleon set sail to Egypt and the Egyptians were defeated in the Battle of the Pyramids (July 21, 1798). However, Napoleon received a serious setback when Lord Nelson destroyed the French fleet at Aboukir Bay in the Battle of the Nile (August 1, 1798). Leaving his army in the lurch, Napoleon made a secret exit and returned to France. He received a hero's welcome and he blamed the Directory for his failure. After overthrowing the Directory following a *coup,* (1799), Napoleon declared that France would be governed by the Consulate (1799-1801) consisting of three Consuls. He became the First Consul and later consul for life. The French gave their consent to all these acts of Napoleon because they found at last a man who could give France political stability. France was threatened by another coalition of European powers with Britain and Austria at the forefront. Napoleon swiftly responded to the situation. He compelled the Czar of Russia to withdraw from this coalition. He struck at the Austrians in Italy and defeated them. Britain sued for peace—the peace of Amiens in 1802. This peace gave enough respite to Napoleon to

Napoleon Bonaparte

turn his attention to the domestic problems of France. Napoleon established numerous satellite republics in Italy, Germany and Belgium. He obtained Louisiana territory in Northern America from Spain as a compensation for the loss of Canada after the seven years war. Riding the crest of a wave of popularity, he was voted Consul for life by the French people in a referendum held in August 1802. On December 2, 1804, Pope Pius VII crowned Napoleon the Emperor of France.

Napoleonic Wars

Napoleon's ambition was to unite the countries of Europe, and make France its leader. But his enemies were equally eager to bring about his downfall. So the brief respite ended and the war between France and powers of European coalition continued from 1803. Napoleon planned to make a direct attack on Britain and started organising a powerful fleet for this purpose. However, he changed his mind. He attacked Austria and captured Vienna. He brought about the end of the Holy Roman Empire and himself became the king of Italy. He routed the combined armies of Austria and Russia in that splendid Battle of Austerlitz (December 2, 1805) which marked the climax of his career. Britain under the leadership of Prime Minister William Pitt gave up her attempt to contain Napoleonic supremacy over Europe. By 1810 Napoleon had reached the apogee of his glory. Russia and Prussia turned into his allies after the Treaties of Tilsit (July 1807). Napoleon appointed his brothers as kings. Louis became the king of Holland; Joseph, king of Naples; and Jerome as king of Westphalia. Napoleon divorced Josephine since she could not give him a son and married Marie Louise, daughter of the Emperor of Austria. Not satisfied with keeping Europe under his control, he imposed the Continental System—through his Berlin and Milan decrees—to prevent Britain from carrying on trade with allies of France and neutral countries. However, he had gone too far. Britain retaliated by issuing Orders in Council (1807) which prohibited British, allied and neutral ships from conducting business with France and its allies. Russia broke her alliance with France and Spain revolted. He invaded Portugal in 1807 as it disregarded the Continental System, and thereafter conquered Spain in 1808. His brother Joseph became the king of Spain. Napoleon marched against Russia for breaking the treaty of Tilsit. At the head of a large army [consisting of 600,000 soldiers] he marched right upto Moscow (Battle of Borodino; September 7, 1812) to find it totally deserted. The Russians followed the scorched-earth policy towards the invader. To make things worse, the Russian winter set in. Starvation and severe cold destroyed the bulk of Napoleon's army and he made a hasty retreat. Taking advantage of Napoleon's debacle, his enemies took full advantage. In the meanwhile, the Spanish revolted and received assistance of the English troops led by the Duke of Wellington. The Austrians, the Prussians and the Russians combined their might and inflicted a crushing defeat on Napoleon's army in the Battle of Leipzig (October 16-19, 1813). On April 6, 1814, Napoleon abdicated his throne and his enemies offered him lenient terms. He was banished to the island of Elba. The allies nominated Louis XVIII as the king of France. Napoleon did not wish to remain away from France and so he secretly escaped from Elba (February 26, 1815) and landed on the French coast. He gathered an army and reached Paris. He declared himself as the emperor of France and determined to challenge his enemies on the battlefield. The final battle was fought on June 18, 1815, at Waterloo, a few miles away from Brussels. It ended the career of Napoleon. The allies condemned him to exile, and he spent the rest of his days as a prisoner of the British in the far-off island of St. Helena. He passed away in 1821.

His Lasting Achievements

Code Napoleon
More than the meteoric rise and astonishing military career, Napoleon's place in history largely rests on his Code of Laws—Code Napoleon. It may be remembered that France had no uniform code of laws for effective administration and political stability. It was this long felt need that compelled Napoleon to undertake the arduous task of framing a code of laws. The code, simple in its form, was the work of a genius and it touched every aspect of French life. Subsequently, it served as a model for other European countries. The code reflected the aspirations of the French who wanted to build a new society. Along with the Napoleonic Code, two other codes, namely, the criminal and commercial, were introduced to bring about social and economic stability.

Concordat (1801)
Ever since the promulgation on the Civil Constitution of the clergy, the relation between France and the Vatican had undergone severe strain. Napoleon perceived that much of rural folk in France were staunchly Catholic. Therefore, he felt that he would win their sympathy if he established friendly relations with the Pope. He made friendly overtures to the Vatican and got encouraging response. Negotiations with the Pope ended in a treaty called the Concordat. The Pope's right to invest the symbols of office and spiritual powers to his church officials in France came to be recognised, subject to the prior approval of the government. Napoleon also conferred some favours on the Protestant Churches and the Jewish Synagogues.

Bank of France (1800)
It may be remembered that France had been plagued by a serious economic crisis since the outbreak of the revolution in 1789. It was Napoleon's desire to tackle this serious problem on the one hand, and to secure the support of the prosperous middle-class for his wars on the other, which led to the founding of a national bank in France. Taxes were levied on the basis of one's ability to pay. Corruption was put down to a great extent. But during the last few years of his career as French Emperor he frequently resorted to levying indirect taxes to sustain the wars he was waging.

Public Works
Napoleon paid great attention to public works. He granted funds on a liberal scale for undertaking public works. He personally evinced keen interest in the beautification of great cities such as Paris. No wonder Paris became the most beautiful city in Europe full of public buildings, public parks, beautiful bridges across its numerous canals and tree-lined boulevards.

New Educational System
The educational system in France also received its due attention from the Emperor. He devised a new system to discipline the young minds to serve the goals he himself set for, in order to glorify the state. He weaned the schools away from the church control. He founded public schools which paid attention to the development of mind and body. Napoleon founded the Imperial University in 1808 to meet the growing demands of young scholars. He also founded an Academy of Science to encourage scientific pursuits. He took pride in attracting scholars and scientists to some of the academies he had opened. He encouraged scholars to study the ancient history of Egypt soon after his Egyptian campaigns.

Legion of Honour (1802)
Napoleon began rewarding the most highly talented French citizens with Legions of Honour. As the most coveted award, they were given to great scientists, soldiers, artists and men of letters as a mark of recognition of their outstanding services to the state. Besides a citation, they carried a cash award.

Overseas Empire for France
Napoleon tried to build an overseas empire for France. He compelled Spain to cede the territory of Louisiana in Northern America to France for the purpose of building an empire there. However, his plan did not succeed as he sold it to the U.S.A. during the presidency of Thomas Jefferson.

Centralisation of French Administration

The most important reform of Napoleon was to reorganise the system of administration. The characteristic feature of his reform in this field was centralisation. He appointed all the officers of the state, and also the prefects in the provinces, and gave some autonomy to the city municipalities. All the officers of the provinces and at the centre were appointed taking into consideration their loyalty to the Emperor, moral integrity and efficiency.

From the above, it is evident that Napoleon, coupled with his personal ambition, tried to consolidate the achievements of the revolution. He gave France its political stability at the most critical juncture of her history.

Importance of Napoleonic Era

Napoleon described himself as the "Child of the Revolution". He proved to be one of its most ardent advocates. All foreign states controlled by him had to copy the model of French institutions. It was because of this, many subject-states under French control improved their systems of administration. However, when the French rule became oppressive, it paved the way for the rise of nationalism.

It may be remembered that Napoleon had indirectly brought about the unification of Germany and Italy by creating several satellite republics in them. But when he started his engine of oppression, they started revolting. So it may be said that Napoleon was defeated by the very forces—spirit of nationalism and democracy—which he created.

Napoleon tried to build a United States of Europe with France as its leader. He sought to achieve this by his spectacular military exploits. It was he who founded the idea of militarism and modern diplomacy in the nineteenth century. It was not until the rise of Bismarck that a strong military-state like Germany was able to play an important role in the history of modern Europe. In a way Napoleon became the precursor of Bismarck.

Lesson Review

1. Trace the career and explain the achievements of Napoleon Bonaparte.
2. Describe the causes which led to the downfall of Napoleon Bonaparte.
3. On the outline map of Europe trace the boundaries of Napoleonic Empire in 1812.

31

CONGRESS OF VIENNA
(SEPTEMBER 1814-JUNE 1815)

With the exile of Napoleon to the island of Elba, the European rulers heaved a sigh of relief. They could attend to the task of reshaping the geopolitical map of Europe undisturbed and those who caused the fall of Napoleon were eager to share the spoils. Prince Metternich, the Chancellor of Austria, convened the Congress of European Powers in Vienna. It was the first of its kind in the diplomatic history of Modern Europe wherein all the concerned powers affected by Napoleonic wars attended. Kings, Prime Ministers and diplomats from several countries came to Vienna and participated in the discussions which were held for several months. To make their task less boring, Prince Metternich arranged for their recreations. Vienna was then known for its gaiety and splendour. Music and dance enlivened the atmosphere followed by banquets held in honour of many foreign dignitaries. The Congress discussed various issues, prominent among them were territorial settlements, restoration of balance of power, and mechanism to prevent French domination in the future. The Final Act of the Congress of Vienna, after much deliberation, was signed on June 9, 1815.

Role of Prince Metternich
Prince Metternich, a diplomat *par excellence,* set upon himself the task of undoing the work of Napoleon. In other words, he wanted to "turn the clock of history backward" i.e. to the pre-revolutionary days. To begin with he got the consent from his other partners to remake the map of Europe on the basis of two important principles: (a) the principle of legitimacy and (b) the principle of compensation. All the representatives along with Metternich opposed the idea of revolutions and upheld the cause of royal absolutism and efficacy of the old order.

The Principle of Legitimacy

Napoleon had dethroned many kings of Europe and they were eager to recover their positions. As agreed upon, the peacemakers decided to restore them to their original positions. Accordingly, Bourbon monarchies were restored to France, Spain and the kingdom of the two Sicilies. Louis XVIII, who had fled France on the return of Napoleon from Elba, became the king of France. Among the other dynasties which were likewise restored were the House of Braganza in Portugal, House of Orange in the Netherlands and the House of Savoy in Sardinia. The Pope got back his papal states in Italy and the German rulers (who lost their positions on account of the creation of the Confederation of the Rhine by Napoleon) also got back their kingdoms.

The Principle of Compensation

The peacemakers began to deal with the second issue—how to reward the victors and punish the culprits. France was found guilty beyond all doubt but her new foreign minister, Talleyrand, argued that his country should not be punished for what Napoleon did. In other words, he pleaded that France was not guilty but Napoleon was. In the end the allies decided that France should surrender all the territories she had acquired after 1792. The peacemakers were happy that monarchy was restored there and hoped to surround that country with powerful neighbours. For this purpose, Austria was made strong with new additions. She got the Italian provinces of Lombardy and Venice in addition to Illyria. She also got the control of the Confederation of the German States. Russia continued to retain Finland. She also got a major part of the Grand Duchy of Warsaw. Prussia received Pomerania and a part of Saxony as her share of spoils. Britain received Malta, Ceylon, Trinidad, Heligoland, Mauritius and the Cape of Good Hope. For losing her colonies, Holland was compensated with Belgium. Sweden which joined the allies against Napoleon was rewarded with Norway partly for her support and partly for her loss of Finland to Russia and Pomerania to Prussia. Turkish possession in the Balkans remained undisturbed. Not knowing that they had acted with purely selfish motives; they felt happy that they had in effect brought about a lasting territorial settlement. They firmly believed that they were ushering in an enduring peace and looked forward to a bright era in the history of mankind.

Alliance Systems

To ensure that the peace of Europe, which they supposedly thought that they had established, should not be rudely disturbed either by a revolution similar to the one France had in 1789 or by an upstart like Napoleon, the leading powers of Europe, Austria, Prussia, Russia and Britain entered into an alliance—the Quadruple Alliance. It was directed against France. The representatives of the Quadruple Alliance agreed to hold meetings at regular intervals to consider measures for "the maintenance of peace in Europe".

Laying stress on the practice of Christian virtues on the part of the European rulers in dealing with their respective subjects, Czar Nicholas I proposed the Holy Alliance. He appealed to all the Christian rulers of Europe to join his proposed alliance. Despite their unwillingness, many Christian rulers gave their tacit consent so as not to offend the Russian Czar. Britain kept out of this alliance. In the end Prince Metternich created a system whereby an individual ruler, troubled by internal revolts, could receive help from his neighbours to quell the same.

Spirit of Nationalism Suppressed

Let us examine the work of the architects of peace. Critics have pointed out that the peacemakers conveniently ignored the spirit of nationalism that was prevailing while remaking the map of Europe. They foisted incompetent rulers upon unwilling subjects. They readjusted boundaries of nations irrespective of the national sentiments. States became mere pawns on the chessboard and the peace makers moved them from place to place. In their enthusiasm to encircle France with powerful neighbours so as to keep her on constant check, Austria was made strong at the expense of Italy and Germany. Catholic Belgians came under Protestant Dutch rule, and the unwilling Norwegians came to be controlled by Sweden. Likewise many decisions of the peacemakers were made not out of consideration of necessity or propriety but on grounds of expediency.

Metternich System Supported the Reactionary Rulers

Secondly, the Congress of Vienna by its decision to restore unpopular monarchies in certain countries gave its tacit consent to carry on their royal despotism. It allowed reactionary tendencies to develop in the face of Popular outcry. Depending on the support offered by the Metternich system, many rulers became reactionaries. They suppressed popular uprisings, gagged the press, and curbed other forms of liberalism. To sum up, the Metternich system, by its opposition to popular aspirations, went about the wrong way in maintaining peace in Europe. Therefore, much of its work collapsed by the middle of the nineteenth century.

The peacemakers failed to take note of the spirit of nationalism in countries like Italy, Germany and Belgium. They frowned upon the legitimate demands of people to have a parliament and a constitution and tried to suppress them by letting loose their engine of oppression. Liberalism in Europe during the nineteenth century rose like a tidal wave and engulfed the reactionary rulers. The main merit of the Metternich system was that it could maintain peace and order throughout Europe for nearly half a century. It was the precursor to the League of Nations.

Lesson Review

1. Discuss the principles on the basis of which the peacemakers of the Congress of Vienna brought about the territorial settlements.
2. What were the territorial settlements made by the Congress of Vienna?
3. Comment on the settlements made by the Congress of Vienna.

32
INDUSTRIAL REVOLUTION

The mass production of consumer goods with the help of the newly invented machines ushered in a new era in the history of mankind. It was during the eighteenth century that Britain and Europe witnessed this kind of transformation. This transformation in the method of production—from man-made to machine-made—is called the Industrial Revolution. The Industrial Revolution went through many phases during the last two hundred years.

Origin of Industrial Revolution
It originated in Britain due to many factors. It may be remembered that Britain was principally an agricultural country before the advent of Industrial Revolution. However, she also made rapid strides of progress in trade and commerce. Napoleon had once declared contemptuously that Britain was "a nation of shopkeepers". Many factors were responsible for the advent of Industrial Revolution. Among them the most important are the availability of raw materials, scarcity of labour, a fully developed banking system, and the birth of a new entrepreneurial class. Fortunately, Britain had a large number of semi-skilled workers who were always available to take up extra work. Again Britain had large amount of coal and iron which were available at a cheap cost. The Royal Society of London encouraged scientific discoveries and thereby created a favourable climate for the onset of Industrial Revolution. New inventions and new methods of production went hand in hand. Over a span of a hundred years Britain's countryside witnessed the rise of factories.

Features of Industrial Revolution
The Industrial Revolution proved to be a silent revolution. It was marked by a gradual change. First of all, it was confined to the textile industry. John Kay invented the 'Flying Shuttle' in 1733. Operated by hand, it increased the speed of the weaving of cloth. This invention was followed

by another called 'The Spinning Jenny' by James Hargreaves in 1767. Hargreave's Jenny spun eight threads at one and the same time. He kept his invention a secret for sometime thinking that this would create retrenchment of workers. In 1769, Richard Arkwright invented a spinning frame called a 'Water-frame' because it used water-power in the place of man-power. As water-frame was too big to run at the home of the worker, factories were built. In the meanwhile, Samuel Crompton invented his 'Spinning Jenny' in 1779 combining the good qualities of the 'Spinning Jenny' and the 'Waterframe'. The 'Spinning Mule' spun hundreds of threads at a time and produced either fine or coarse thread. Since the method of weaving was not improving in tune with the manufacture of threads, the inventors began to pay attention to this problem. In 1785, Reverend Edmund Cartwright invented the 'Powerloom' which wove cloth quickly. This machine was driven by a big water-wheel. The next invention was that of Eli Whitney's 'Cotton Gin', a machine which was used to separate the seeds from the cotton. So during the span of half-a-century the textile manufacturing industry in Britain changed from hand-made to machine-made. During the next half century colourful cloth was produced when the new methods of bleaching, dyeing and printing were discovered. In 1846 the 'sewing machine' was invented to stitch clothes by an American named Elias Howe.

Spinning Jenny

Iron and Steel Industry
The other industry which was affected by the Industrial Revolution was the iron and steel industry. For making machines iron was used. Since a long time people were in the habit of smelting the iron ore in brick furnaces by using the charcoal as fuel. The iron produced by this process was brittle. So it had to be reheated and impurities removed. Finally coke was used to produce iron. The blacksmiths hammered it into different shapes according to their convenience. But the whole process was very laborious and costly. Henry Bessemer discovered a faster and cheaper method of producing steel in 1856. Subsequently, iron and steel were used in making all the machines. Textile and metal industries were started in many towns in Britain

like Sheffield, Birmingham, Manchester, Liverpool and London. The factory system came to stay in Britain.

Coal-Mining Industry

It may be remembered that wood was used in place of coal as fuel. When coal or coke was used for producing stronger iron, coal mining became necessary. Coal was available at far cheaper rate and people began to

Steam Engine

make use of it instead of wood. Fortunately, Britain had large coal reserves, and so coal-mining became one of the largest industries.

The Invention of Steam Engine by Newcomen and James Watt

The British mine owners were faced with the problem of water seeping into the mines. They employed labourers at high cost to pump this water out. A British engineer named Thomas Newcomen made the first steam engine and used it to pump the water out of the mine. But this consumed too much fuel. After a few years, a young Scottish inventor by the name James Watt redesigned the steam engine so as to make it produce more power and consume less fuel. His new invention was patented in 1769 as it proved to be a great success not only in mining industry but also in others. So water power was replaced by steam power in many industries such as the textile and steel.

Factory System in Britain

The invention of numerous machines including that of the steam engine and their utilisation by wealthy capitalists revolutionised the organisation of industries. Only rich men could buy machines and house them in a large building which became a mill or a factory. Many workers were required to run the machines for which they were paid meagre wages. People who were without jobs in the villages began to drift towards these factories located in small towns. The workers started living in huts near the factory where they were employed. So the factory system replaced the old medieval guilds. In the course of time these small towns where the factories were located became big cities with population bursting at their seams.

Industrial Revolution

Revolution in Transport

While the factory system produced goods for mass consumption at a rapid rate, it was also found necessary to transport these goods by a faster means to the far off distribution centres in the country. An American by the name of Robert Fulton invented a steam boat called *Clermont* in 1807. The Clermont covered the distance of 150 miles from New York to Albany on the Hudson river in 32 hours. A few years later a number of steam boats appeared carrying cargoes on the rivers and the coastline. In 1838, a trans-oceanic steam-boat *Sirius* crossed the Atlantic in 18 days.

An English engineer George Stephenson built the first public railway line, and with his son Robert Stephenson designed an advanced steam locomotive called *Rocket*. It completed its 40 miles journey from Manchester to Liverpool in an hour and half in 1830. Between 1830 and 1870, Britain added about 13,500 miles of railroad.

McAdam Improved the Road Construction

France led other countries in the construction of roads and canals. In the U.S.A. canals were dug to link important rivers and lakes. River transport there assumed great importance. In Britain, an engineer by the name McAdam showed how smooth and hard-surfaced roads can be built on which vehicles can move without jolts. When these macadamised roads— roads built as per his method —were completed the stage-coaches carrying number of passengers moved fast. They covered fourteen miles an hour.

Revolution in Communication System

Along with quicker means of transport, the means of communication also improved conspicuously. Samuel Morse, an American, invented telegraph to send messages in 1844. Messages were sent by means of telegraph wires. In 1876, Alexander Graham Bell invented the telephone. This new instrument carried human voice on wire from one end to the other. In 1866, Cyrus W. Field laid the Trans-Atlantic undersea cable connecting the U.S.A. with the European continent. Guglielmo Marconi invented the Wireless Telegraph in 1896, and he succeeded in sending signals across the Atlantic for the first time in 1901. Based on his theory, radio broadcasting and television were introduced.

Significance of Industrial Revolution

Let us examine the significance of Industrial Revolution. It may be remembered that man since prehistoric age has been trying to make his life comfortable by devising better tools and implements. He made use of animals for his work. He tried to improve his life through means of knowledge. He understood the working of the forces of nature. However, it is only in the last two centuries that he has been able to invent complex machines and find out new sources of power. Power-driven machines began to produce large amount of goods to satisfy the needs of the community. Mass production increased not only the wealth of the country like in Britain where Industrial Revolution began but also improved the standard of living of the people. Through improved means of transport and communication, man has been able to build a new society and civilisation. Thus, Industrial Revolution made it possible for man to build a civilised world.

Spread of Industrial Revolution

The industrial revolution began to spread from the place of its origin—Britain to the European continent. France too was affected by it but the Napoleonic wars put a stop to this temporarily. After the defeat of Napoleon the industrial revolution continued. The defeat of Napoleon in Waterloo gave a new impetus to Britain to rise as a great industrial and commercial giant. By the middle of nineteenth century, Germany also made rapid strides of industrial progress. On the eve of the First World War, Germany rose to great heights of power after having made tremendous industrial progress. The other countries of Europe also felt the impact, and in due course of time, they too achieved industrial progress. The U.S.A. achieved industrial progress by leaps and bounds soon after the Civil War. At the end of the 19th century she emerged as a great power. India, as the colony of the British, also began to make industrial progress especially from the time of Lord Dalhousie. He introduced railways and telegraphs. British capital was encouraged and the British industrialists invested money here. The textile industry made remarkable progress. Jamshedji Tata opened a steel factory to make India self-sufficient in steel. The other industries were started in the private sector.

Japan and the Industrial Revolution

One of the Asiatic countries which made marvellous industrial progress during the last decades of the nineteenth century and the early decades of the twentieth century was Japan. After Commodore Perry's visit she realised that it would be of no avail resisting the advent of western civilisation. Japan realised that the key to the West's superiority lay in its scientific and technological progress. So, she began to increasingly copy western methods and models and in the end became a highly advanced country. No doubt that she is now competing with such highly industrialised countries as the U.S.A and West Germany.

Industrial Revolution

Effects of Industrial Revolution

In the West the Industrial Revolution produced good and bad effects. Firstly, it transformed the life of the people in the towns and cities. Factories produced consumer goods on a large scale. They were made available at cheap prices. Factories provided employment to many. The general standard of living of the people improved. In the long run, however, these good effects faded and the ugly aspects became manifest.

The capitalists and entrepreneurs invested their capital, built factories, and purchased raw materials. They employed cheap labour. They purchased machines which produced goods on a large scale. They earned huge profits and enjoyed a better standard of living. While the capitalists or in other words the middle class enjoyed life, the conditions of the labour class turned from bad to worse. Men, women and children who were employed in factories got meagre wages. They had to work for longer hours and could not complain for fear of being dismissed. They lived in squalor. A great novelist of that time was Charles Dickens who described the pitiable conditions of the poor in Britain. In villages, cottage industries suffered a serious setback on account of the competition with machine-made goods. Many of them became unemployed and they went to the overcrowded cities in search of employment.

Man's social life was affected in many ways. In a family the husband and wife had to work hard to make both ends meet. Sometimes their children were also employed. All of them received low wages. Women no longer depended upon menfolk for money. Many a time the absence of parents at home had its impact on the children. They became delinquents. As machines were not properly fenced, there was danger to the life of a labourer. Unhygienic surroundings left them in poor health. Slum areas in cities where the alarming increase in growth of population. While the rich became richer, the poor poorer.

The exploitation of the labour class by the rich middle class (sometimes known as the bourgeoisie) continued unabated. The middle-class easily influenced the government in order to safeguard their vested interests. The capitalist middle-class enjoyed the levers of power because they elected the members of the parliament, bribed the government officials and did a lot of lobbying for favourable legislation. Unfortunately, the labour class did not have access to power despite its numerical superiority.

Workers' life was not only affected by the working conditions imposed on them by the capitalist class but also by the policies of the government. Therefore, the workers demanded certain political rights such as the right to franchise. They also demanded that their trade unions be recognised so that they could fight for their rights, the most important being collective bargaining. The conflict between the capitalists and the workers led to strikes and lockouts. It was in these circumstances that socialism took its birth. Socialism advocated the bridging of the gulf between the rich and the poor by improving the conditions of the workers. However, it was not until Karl Marx, the German philosopher, coined the word, 'socialism' that attained great popularity with the working class. Karl Marx introduced the doctrines of 'scientific socialism'. With Frederick Engels he wrote the *Communist Manifesto* wherein he gave clarion call to the workers of the world to unite for they had "nothing to lose but their chains". Subsequently Karl Marx wrote *Das Kapital* in which he talked about the class war, exploitation of workers by the capitalist class, labour theory of value and advocated the establishment of the Socialist State. He appealed to the workers to remain united everywhere, take over the charge of government by force, confiscate the property of the rich and establish the socialism state which would be run by the *proletariat* (workers). It was on these lines that Lenin organised the October revolution in Russia (1917) and established a Communist or Socialist State. It became the first Socialist or Communist State in the world.

Karl Marx

Lesson Review

1. What factors were responsible for the outbreak of Industrial Revolution in England? Trace its development in the cotton textile industry.
2. Write a note on the progress made by the following: (a) iron and steel industry (b) coal-mining industry and (c) the transport system (d) revolution in communication system.
3. Describe the effects of the Industrial Revolution in Europe.
4. On the outline map of England locate the industrial towns and cities and point out their importance.

33
REVOLUTIONS IN LATIN AMERICA

By 'America' we not only mean the United States of America but also many other countries situated in the continents of North and South America. It includes Canada, and many other countries which are referred to as 'Latin America'. Latin American countries are those which are situated to the south of the United States. There are about twenty Latin American countries whose cultures were mainly influenced by either Spain or Portugal. Except Brazil, all the others have Spanish speaking population. Almost all the people of these countries are Roman Catholic by religion. Situated to the south of the US is a large Latin American country by the name Mexico. Long ago, two of the great civilisations, the Maya and the Aztec, flourished here. Mexico is rich in soil and mineral resources. The Spanish conquistador, Hernando Cortes, with his followers landed on the Mexican coast and swiftly conquered the empire (1519) built by the Aztecs. The Spaniards ruled this country for about three centuries. Soon after the conquest of Mexico, another Spanish adventurer, Francisco Pizarro, invaded Peru. He killed the Inca ruler and established the tyranny of Spain. The natives were heavily taxed and forced to work on the farms of the rich Spanish settlers. In the course of a few centuries, the Spanish colonies spread across Central and South America.

Portugal became a serious rival to Spain in due course of time. A Portuguese ship sailing under skipper Cabral was blown off its course from the African coast and reached the coast of Brazil. In the course of time Brazil became the only Portuguese colony in Latin America. A few colonies were also set up in South America by the British, French and the Dutch. A few islands in the Caribbean also were occupied by the European imperialists.

Causes of Revolts in Latin America
The Spanish and the Portuguese brought their armies to Latin America to quell the revolts of natives. The greed of the Spanish and the Portuguese

knew no bounds. The natives were forced to sell all their goods to their conquerors at cheap price and buy goods brought to them by their masters at high cost. The mineral resources of their country like gold, silver, tin, copper and oil were exported to enable their masters to become rich. Moreover, the Spanish and Portuguese treated their subjects with unmitigated harshness. Finally, the American war of independence, the French Revolution of 1789, and the Napoleonic wars inspired the natives of these Spanish and Portuguese colonies to raise the banner of their independence.

When Napoleon appointed his brother, Joseph, the king of Spain, the Spanish colonies in America refused to recognise him as such. Mexico, Venezuela, Peru, Argentina and Chile declared their independence one after another. Fortunately, they enjoyed a profitable trade with Britain and the latter offered them her naval protection. However, with the restoration of King Ferdinand VII to the Spanish throne by the Treaty of Valençay (1813), the independence of the Spanish colonies was in danger. King Ferdinand VII could be described as one of the most reactionary rulers of Europe at that time. The return to harsh Spanish rule was galling to the subjects of the colonies in South America.

Course of Revolutions

A series of rebellions broke out from Mexico to Argentina in the early part of the nineteenth century, and the Spanish King sent his troops to quell these revolts. The liberation movements were strong and so the Spanish troops failed in their mission. The native revolutionaries drove them out of their colonies. Despite his initial setback, the Spanish king continued to send his troops to the colonies year after year with the hope of eventually recovering them.

Francisco De Miranda, a Venezuelan patriot played a most prominent role in the liberation movement of his country. In the end he was caught by the Spaniards who made him to suffer by imprisoning him in a dark cell. Miranda died a martyr to the cause of independence of his country in 1816. His unfinished task was carried out by another great patriot, Simon Bolivar (1783-1830). Bolivar fought the Spanish forces for nearly 15 years and finally achieved the independence of Venezuela. Along with Venezuela, Columbia, Ecquador and Panama also became free.

Jose De San Martin

In the meanwhile, another patriot of Argentina, Jose De San Martin led a revolutionary movement against the Spanish government and he was joined by Simon Bolivar. Martin was successful in liberating Chile. Subsequently, he gained another victory over the Spanish which resulted in the liberation of his motherland, Argentina. In a short time the other Spanish colonies, Peru and Bolivia, were set free by Martin and Bolivar.

Father Hidalgo, a priest, led a national movement for the independence of Mexico. Most of his followers were simple peasants. Although his struggle failed and he was executed by Spanish authorities, his inspiring leadership was unforgettable. A couple of years later, the national movement gained momentum and the Spanish governor was expelled. The Mexicans declared their state as a republic. With the exception of a few islands in the Caribbean sea, Spain lost all her colonies in South America.

With the extension of Napoleonic control over Portugal, the royal family fled the country and settled in Brazil. So Brazil became the headquarters of the Portuguese authority, and for quite sometime, the Brazilians enjoyed many privileges. However, after the Napoleonic defeat, the royal family left for Portugal and Brazil came to be treated as a colony. It was this reversion to the old status that the Brazilians disliked because they lost all the privileges. Therefore they rebelled. The eldest son of the Portuguese king, Dom Pedro, became the leader of the revolutionary struggle. The Brazilians declared their independence and chose Dom Pedro as their emperor in 1822. This empire continued till 1889, and in that year, the Brazilians established a Republic.

The Monroe Doctrine

The Monroe doctrine of 1823 discouraged the European powers from political interference in the affairs of the independent countries of South America. So Spain and Portugal practically lost all hopes of recovering their colonies. Many of the newly independent countries in South America were unfortunate in losing their democratic set up and frequently came under the spell of ruthless dictators. Changes in government became the normal feature in their political system. A typical example was Mexico, where within fifty years time "there were fifty seven changes of government...".

Lesson Review
1. Give a brief summary of the causes and course of Latin American revolutions.
2. On the outline map of South America show the different Latin American countries and their respective capital cities.

34
NATIONALISM IN EUROPE IN THE NINETEENTH CENTURY

Both the French Revolution of 1789 and Napoleon Bonaparte failed to achieve their objectives. The former turned into an anarchy and the latter, who considered himself as a saviour, turned into a worst type of dictator. Moreover, the Congress of Vienna tried to set the clock backwards. It looked as though the peacemakers had done a commendable job—the establishment of a durable peace in Europe. However, as subsequent events were to prove that they had done was a mere patchwork to stem the surging tide of nationalism.

Revolution in Spain, 1820

The first crack appeared on the fabric woven by the peacemakers of Vienna when the Spaniards revolted against their king, Ferdinand VII. After coming to the throne, he re-established the old and made conditions miserable to his subjects. But the revolution did not succeed because Metternich and his allies sent a French army to quell it. Thousands of Spanish revolutionaries were executed or driven out of the country. The Spanish king's oppressive rule also provoked the subjects living in the Spanish colonies to revolt in Latin America. They proclaimed their independence after driving out the king's governors. The Spanish king sent his troops year after year to punish them but did not succeed in his mission.

Greek War of Independence (1827)

Soon after the suppression of the Spanish revolution, there appeared another. This time Greeks staged a revolt against their Turkish overlord—the Ottoman Emperor. The Greeks were very much influenced by the national and liberal movements spreading all over Europe. They also expressed a strong desire to secure either independence or self-government. Their national sentiments found a form for expression—*Philike Hetairia*. It was a Society of Friends' formed to organise a mass movement to secure independence. Its members hoped that the Christian nations of Europe would sympathise with their aspirations. Russia atleast expressed her great sympathy not only with the Greeks but also on other Balkan subjects of the Turkish Empire. When the Greeks revolted, the Turkish emperor perpetrated great atrocities on them which put the Christian nations to shame and Russia tried to take advantage of the situation. It was specifically to prevent Russia from gaining any predominant position in the Balkans that European powers intervened. They compelled the Greeks and the Turks to come to an agreement. These events culminated in the signing of a treaty at London in 1827, by England, France, Russia. In 1829, the Sultan of Turkey was forced to recognise the independence of Greece. Thus Greek nationalism witnessed its triumph.

Belgian Independence
It may be remembered that Congress of Vienna gave Belgium with predominantly Roman Catholic population to Holland which was Protestant. These two kingdoms merged to form the kingdom of the Netherlands. The Belgians hated the Dutch king because he was Protestant and also for imposing the Dutch language on them. Encouraged by an uprising in France in 1830, the Belgians too rose in revolt against their Dutch master. The Belgian rebels soon drew up a constitution and invited a German prince to rule over them. Fortunately, Britain and France gave their recognition to their independence. Austria and Russia were too busy to go to the assistance of the Dutch king. So by this curious coincidence of favourable events, the Belgians secured their independence. Belgian neutrality was guaranteed by big powers like Britain, France and Prussia in 1839.

July Revolution in France (1830)
In France there was another revolution because Charles X, successor of King Louis XVII, tried to establish "the old regime". He began to invoke the 'divine right' theory of kingship. He suppressed the freedom of speech and press and violated the constitutional laws of the country. He began to rule by royal ordinances. Therefore the revolution broke out in 1830 and he was forced to flee the country. The people chose Louis Philippe, the Duke of Orleans, to rule the country.

Revolutions in other Parts of Europe
Revolts broke out in many parts of Italy and Poland, but they were all crushed by Austria and Russia respectively. In Germany, the rulers took drastic steps to stem the tide of liberalism. The university students and teachers were demanding many constitutional rights. They held Wartburg

festival to express their national feelings. Austria looked upon all these activities with great concern and compelled the German rulers to crush these liberal tendencies.

THE UNIFICATION OF ITALY

Although Italy happened to be the home of Renaissance, it was a divided country. Numerous kingdoms had risen out of the ashes of the Roman Empire. Each was ruled by a Duke and the country suffered much because of their rivalry. It was this fact which pained Machiavelli who wrote *The Prince*. Italy began to play a minor role in the European affairs because she was dominated by big powers like Austria, Spain, and France. So when Napoleon conquered Italy, the Italians began to regard him as a liberator. But when his oppressive rule started, they began to detest him. After the downfall of Napoleon, the Congress of Vienna presided over by Prince Metternich considered Italy as a mere "geographic expression". The principle of legitimacy was applied and Italy came to be divided. The Pope received his papal states. The king of Sardinia got back his kingdom consisting of Piedmont and the island of Sardinia. The Spanish king recovered the kingdom of the two Sicilies (i.e., Naples and Sicily). Austria annexed Lombardy and Venetia to her empire. Small duchies in northern and central Italy were revived and they were mostly ruled by Austrian princes. Out of all the rulers, only two were Italians, and they were the Pope and the king of Piedmont. Both lacked patriotism so as to bring about the unification of Italy. Thus Italy lost her sense of identity, and remained, as Metternich had said earlier, as "geographic expression". Austria was able to dominate the whole Italian peninsula by suppressing all liberal and nationalist ideas. She appointed spies and resorted to brutal repression whenever people revolted.

The Rise of Nationalism in Italy

Nationalism may be described as a strong feeling of love and loyalty which people have towards their own country. But this feeling was lacking among the Italians in the early stages of the Italian unification. The first movement towards attaining freedom from foreign rule was started by the 'Carbonari Society'. It was a secret society formed mainly by charcoal-burners and hence the name *Carbonari*. They organised revolts in 1821 and 1830 but they were brutally suppressed by Prince Metternich. The revolts foiled because the '*Carbonari*' were divided on the issue of the form of government to be established if they succeeded in gaining freedom. The task of unifying the Italians for grappling major issues facing the country became more difficult because of excessive parochialism.

This stupendous task fell on the shoulders of three great giants of the unification movement—Giuseppe Mazzini, Count Cavour and Garibaldi. The first played the role of a prophet, the second that of a statesman and the third of a brave soldier-cum-patriot.

Mazzini (1805-72)

Mazzini hailed from Genoa which came under the control of Piedmont. From his early childhood he was quite concerned about the fate of his country. He always dressed himself in black garments fancying himself as a mourner. He gave up everything in order to fight for the liberation of his country, He joined the Carbonari which was the only revolutionary

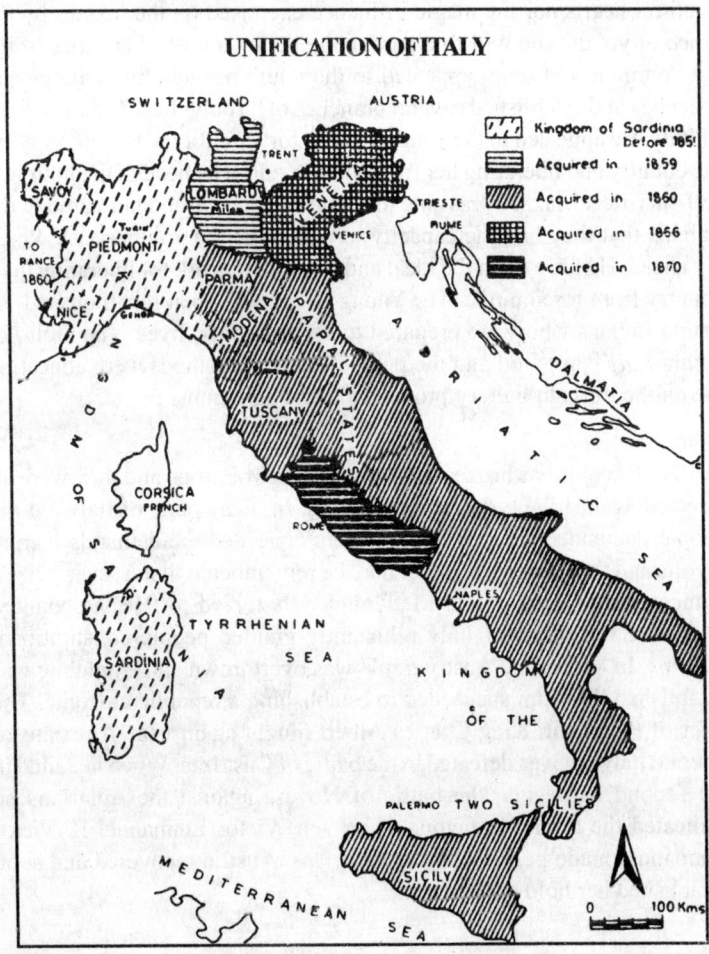

organisation. He was arrested and imprisoned in 1831. Mazzini was disappointed at the attitude of the Pope and the ruler of Piedmont because they were the only Italians who could have done something to liberate and consolidate the country. As such he decided that if Italy became free, it should become republic.

"Young Italy" Movement

Soon after his release he founded a new organisation called "Young Italy". He firmly believed that young men of Italy could easily bring about the liberation of their motherland. He declared "Place youth at the head of the insurgent multitude; you know not the secret of the power hidden in those youthful hearts nor the magic influence exercised on the masses by the voice of youth. You will find among the young a host of apostles of the new religion". Mazzini appealed to the youth through his writings and speeches and established several branches of "Young Italy" in all corners of Italy. He appealed to the youth to come forward for the task of unifying the country and liberating her from foreign rule. The need of the hour was self-sacrifice. Mazzini was able to create confidence and faith among the Italians that they had the capacity to undertake the arduous task which lay ahead. He gave them the ideal and strength to work for liberating their country from foreign rule. The Young Italy began to attract thousands of young Italians who were prepared to sacrifice their lives. The motto of *Young Italy* was "God and the people", and its methods were educating the public through literary propaganda and agitations.

1848 Revolution

In 1848 Revolutions broke out in many parts of Europe and they were all directed against the tyrannical monarchs. In many parts of Italy too the people demanded reforms. Some rulers conceded the demands fearing revolts and the others refused. It may be remembered that Austria herself witnessed a revolution and Metternich was forced to flee the country. Therefore the rulers of Italy reluctantly granted people constitutional reforms. In Venice the Austrian rule was overthrown and a republic was established. Mazzini succeeded in establishing a republic at Rome. The ruler of Piedmont, King Charles Albert fought against the Austrians to liberate Italy but was defeated in the battle of Custozza. When he failed in the second battle i.e., the battle of Novara against the Austrians he abdicated the throne in favour of his son, Victor Emmanuel II. Victor Emmanuel made peace with the Austrians. Austria recovered and soon established her hold on Italy.

The Pope recovered Rome with the assistance of the French troops. Mazzini was forced to flee. He remained as an exile in Britain. But he continued to direct the national movement in Italy through secret correspondence. The failure of 1848 revolutions in Italy, though disappointing to many, made Italians more determined in achieving their goal. King Victor Emmanuel was ready to support the national movement.

Cavour (1810-61)

King Victor Emmanuel II was fortunate in having a leader of great calibre like Cavour to work for his kingdom. Cavour belonged to an aristocratic family in Sardinia. As the founder of a reputed newspaper *Il Risorgimento*, he urged the king to take the lead in liberating Italy from the Austrian control in 1848. Undaunted by the defeat Sardinia suffered at the hands of the Austrians, Cavour decided to work for the unification of Italy. He got elected to the Assembly and made speeches calculated to improve the state of affairs in Piedmont and Sardinia. The king was deeply impressed and he subsequently appointed Cavour as the Prime Minister in 1852. Before Cavour emerged on the political scene, the Italians believed in the popular slogan "*Italia Fara da se*". (Italy will look after herself). But Cavour was not convinced about this because of the failure of the 1848 revolution. He firmly believed that the kingdom of Piedmont and Sardinia was too small a power to strike a blow on the mighty Austria. So he was convinced that his kingdom could fight only if a foreign power helped her. He also realised that his kingdom should make enormous strides of progress before she could take upon the task of rallying other states to fight for freedom.

He devoted his energies to make his state—the kingdom of Piedmont and Sardinia—a model in all respects. He encouraged modern agriculture and rapid industrialisation. He followed the policy of free trade. A network of canals was built. Roads, bridges and railways were laid to facilitate trade and bring economic prosperity. He introduced British system of budget and methods of taxation. He established a "free church in a free state". The Piedmontese army was reorganised.

He was waiting for an opportunity to take active part in international affairs. It was in 1855 that he decided that his state should join the Crimean war. The war was fought between Britain, France and Turkey on the one side and Russia on the other. Although Cavour's state had no self interest involved in the outcome of the war, even then Cavour thought that this was the way he should secure the sympathy of France and Britain for Piedmont by joining their side. Piedmont played its role in the success of the allies and she was invited to participate in the Congress of Paris in

1856 after the defeat of Russia. It was in this Congress Cavour appealed to the big powers like France and Britain about the need to give support to the unification of Italy. He eagerly looked forward to secure the support of France since the French Emperor Napoleon III was once a *Carbonari*. The French Emperor was moved by the appeal for support to Piedmont in bringing about the unification of Italy. But it was not until an unsuccessful attempt made by Orsini (an Italian bandit) to kill him that Napoleon took decisive steps to help Piedmont.

Emperor Napoleon III sent a message to Cavour to meet him at Plombieres and accordingly in July 1858 the two great leaders met secretly to discuss how France could be of assistance to Piedmont in the unification of Italy. The French Emperor agreed to militarily assist Piedmont if Austria attacked her. It was also agreed that France would get Nice and Savoy in return for French support. After this secret agreement with France, Cavour lost no time in provoking Austria to a war (1859) by creating border incidents. As anticipated, Austria declared war on Piedmont and Cavour sought help from the French Emperor. With French military assistance the Piedmontese troops achieved success in the battles of Magenta and Solferino. These battles resulted in the liberation of Lombardy from Austrian rule, and if the war had continued for some more time Venice too would have achieved freedom. But that was not to be because the French army was withdrawn by the orders of the French Emperor. Cavour was so much disappointed that he even thought of committing suicide. What compelled Napoleon to change his mind remains a mystery but he signed an armistice agreement with Austria by which he stopped his hostility. Austria was to give Lombardy to Piedmont and the terms of the armistice came to be ratified later by the treaty of Zurich. When Austrians left Lombardy, the people of Parma, Modena, Tuscany and Romagna rose in rebellion against the Austrian rulers and decided to merge their respective states with Piedmont. The French Emperor gave his consent to their desire and for which he received Nice and Savoy from Piedmont.

Role of Giuseppe Garibaldi (1807-1882)

One of the most romantic figures in the nineteenth century Italy was Garibaldi. He is described as "the sword of Italian Unification". Garibaldi was a disciple of Mazzini. He was a native of Nice. He was a born patriot and subsequently joined the 'Young Italy' founded by his master. He helped his master in organising many revolts. When his plot to overthrow the king of Piedmont failed in 1833, he was forced to go into exile. He spent the next twelve years in South America where he helped the Uruguayans to fight against the tyranny of the Brazilian rulers. It was there that he married Anita "who shared his dangerous life in the saddle and in the battlefield". He gathered a large number of loyal volunteers who were ready to sacrifice their lives for his sake. He returned to Italy in 1848 to help Mazzini to attack Rome and establish a republic there. But the mission ended in failure and he was forced to leave Italy in 1849. After his exile ended in May 1854, he lived on the island of Caprera. In 1859, he assisted Piedmont in her war with Austria and won victories against it. Although Cavour did not like his methods he wanted to make use of him. When the Sicilians staged a revolt against their foreign ruler, Cavour secretly urged Garibaldi to undertake the task of helping the rebels. So commenced one of the

Garibaldi

most daring exploits of Garibaldi—the liberation of Sicily and Naples. He left for the island of Sicily in May 1860 with his followers called Red-shirts. When Garibaldi landed in Sicily with his Red-shirts (1150 men), the Sicilians eagerly welcomed him and joined him in overthrowing the Spanish-Bourbon monarchy. He overcame the feeble resistance offered by the troops of King Bomba. The Spanish rule ended there. Encouraged by his success, Garibaldi managed to cross the narrow straits of Messina under dangerous circumstances and liberate the people of Naples from the yoke of Spanish rule. From there Garibaldi began to march towards Rome to liberate the people from French-supported Pope. Frightened at the prospect of alienating the sympathies of the French Emperor Cavour appealed to his king, Victor Emmanuel II, to forestall Garibaldi's attack on Rome. At the head of an army the king invaded the papal states and occupied Umbria and the Marches. From there he proceeded to meet Garibaldi. Garibaldi could have become a dictator by his own right over southern part of Italy but he proved to be a patriot *par excellence*. He surrendered all the territories he had conquered to King Victor Emmanuel II and refused all rewards and riches. He shed tears when his native place, Nice, was handed over to Emperor Napoleon III. He retired to lead a farm life in the island of Caprera. In 1861, Victor Emmanuel II was crowned as the king of Italy and a parliament was summoned to meet at Turin. Cavour died without seeing Rome and Venice being united with the rest of Italy.

Venice United with the Rest of Italy (1866)
On the eve of Austro-Prussian war in 1866, Bismarck, the Iron-Chancellor of Prussia, promised Venice to the Italians if they opened a new front

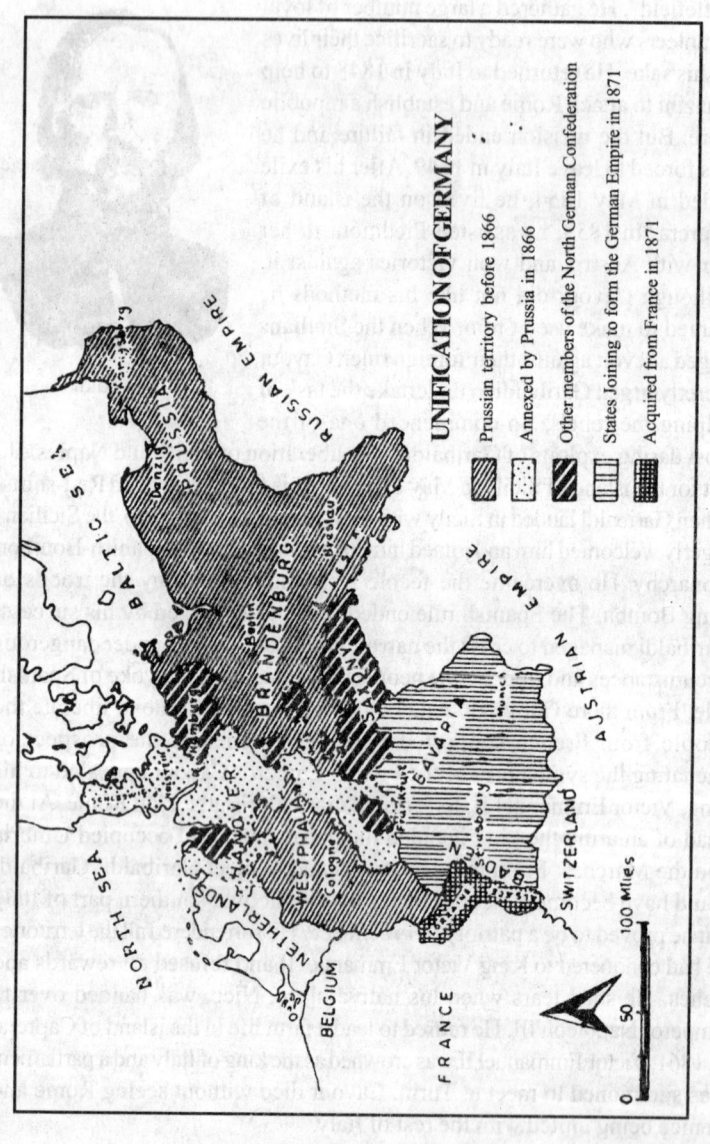

against Austria. Accordingly, the Italians fought the Austrians when the Austro-Prussian war broke out. However, they were defeated. But the Prussian troops inflicted a crushing defeat upon Austria at Sadowa (July 3, 1866) and the peace of Prague was concluded. Austria was forced to part with Venice to the Italians. Only Rome, held by the Pope remained to be liberated.

Rome Liberated in 1870
When the Franco-Prussian war broke out in 1870, Emperor Napoleon III was forced to withdraw the French troops from Rome. In the absence of French protection, the Pope who held Rome could hardly resist the merger of Rome with the rest of Italy. Thus, all parts of Italy were liberated and united. Mazzini's dream that Italy should remain a Republic did not materialise. Italy chose constitutional monarchy. The Pope began to live in the Vatican after having lost his control over Rome.

UNIFICATION OF GERMANY

Before the advent of Napoleon, Germany happened to be a congery of more than three hundred petty and independent principalities each ruled by a prince. It was Napoleon who welded them as 38 states. It was his oppressive rule there which roused national sentiments to a high pitch. After his downfall, the Congress of Vienna established a loose kind of confederation. It also provided for a Federal Diet which was to consist of the representatives of 38 German rulers. The Diet was to be presided over by the Austrian delegate. After making this arrangement, the Congress of Vienna hoped that they would not encounter troubles. The ruler of every German state was a sovereign in his own territory and therefore opposed every move of the liberals to bring about the unification of Germany. A few German states like Hanover and Holstein were governed by foreign kings and they were least expected to support national movement.

Rise of Nationalism
Under such circumstances the initiative to rouse national consciousness lay with the university students and teachers. The University of Jena took a leading part in spreading the national movement. The students and teachers held Wartburg festival which, among other things, was aimed at expressing their national sentiments. Metternich was alarmed at some of the events happening in Germany, particularly the murder of a Russian spy, Kotzebue. He summoned a meeting of the ministers of important German states at Carlsbad to take steps to suppress the national movement. It was here that resolutions were passed and they were announced in the

form of decrees (1819). Austria began to exercise her magisterial powers through a commission of investigation. The commission was to investigate about plots and conspiracies hatched by disgruntled German patriots to overthrow the confederation.

Zollverein (Customs Union)

Before 1817 Prussia had a customs house in each district and they hampered free flow of goods from one corner of the state to the other. In order to encourage free flow of goods, the Prussian government got an act passed by which Tariff Reforms were introduced. The Tariff Reforms converted Prussia into a Free Trade area. To see that other German states also did likewise, Prussia levied heavy transit duties on tariff goods coming from them. The other states agreed to join the Customs Union of Prussia. With the exception of a few German states and Austria. Almost all joined the Customs Union of Prussia. Thus, Prussia took upon herself a leading role in bringing about the economic union of German states in 1837. This economic union was called as *Zollverein* and it paved the way for the political unity.

The 1848 Revolution in France

The French Revolution of 1848 had its impact on Germany also. As Austria herself witnessed an uprising, the Germans took advantage of the chaotic situation and rose in rebellion against their rulers. The liberals in the country took lead in holding elections and the Frankfurt Assembly met. The Frankfurt Assembly began to draw up a new Constitution for the whole of Germany and offered the crown to the Prussian king, Frederick William IV. The Prussian king rejected the offer for he knew that if he accepted it there would be a war between his state and the Austrian Empire. In the meanwhile, the Frankfurt Assembly failed to achieve its objective and the national movement was suppressed. The liberals in Germany were deeply disappointed, Austria regained its control over all the German states. However the king of Prussia made a final attempt through his minister, Radowitz, to bring about the union of German states under his leadership. But this attempt did not succeed since the Austrian Emperor was firm in his decision about not losing his control over all the German states. The king of Prussia was forced to give up his attempt by the Agreement of Olmütz in 1850. The old German Confederation was revived and Austria reigned supreme.

King William I of Prussia (1861-1888) and his Iron Chancellor, Bismarck (1871-1890)

The last stage in the unification of Germany began with the rise of Otto von Bismarck. The leadership in the unification movement passed from the German liberals to a highly conservative Prussian 'junker' who always believed in strong monarchy. Bismarck's appointment as Chancellor by the new Prussian king came at a time when the Prussian Parliament, dominated by liberals, refused to grant money to introduce military reforms. The deadlock began 1862 when the king insisted that he be allowed to reorganise the Prussian army whereas the liberals stood for constitutional reforms. Dejected at the attitude of the Parliament, the king decided to abdicate. However, he was dissuaded from doing so by his close advisers Von Roon (War Minister) and Moltke (the Prussian General). At their request, the king finally summoned Bismarck, who was then in Paris, to return and handle the political crisis.

Otto von Bismarck belonged to the landowning German aristocracy, the 'junkers'. He was a staunch conservative and had no sympathy for parliamentary democracy. He was a firm believer in a strong and enlightened monarchy. He believed, like the king, that Prussia's greatness depended upon her military force. He possessed an iron will and tenacity of purpose which helped him in overcoming many a crisis. Fortunately, Prussia discovered the right man to guide her destiny for the next twenty-eight years.

'Blood and Iron' Policy

After being appointed as chancellor by the king, Bismarck addressed the members of the Prussian parliament about the need of the hour. He cautioned them saying that "Not by speeches and resolutions of the majorities are the great questions of the day to be decided, but blood and iron". In a characteristic way the Prussian parliament decided to defy him but Bismarck dealt with it severely by arresting many of its opposition leaders. The Prussian government forcibly collected taxes to enable the government to undertake necessary reforms in reorganising the Prussian armed forces. Bismarck was convinced that Prussia alone had the capacity to lead all the other German states, and if she has to achieve the unification, it has to be through means of war against the enemies of German unification. He realised that Austria was the principal enemy which had to be defeated in a war. Within four years of his coming to office, Bismarck made strenuous efforts along with Roon and Moltke to keep the armed forces well-trained and well-equipped. Prussian army began to possess a new weapon, the breech-loading needle gun. This was to enable it to remain invincible.

War with Denmark (1864)

In 1863, the new Danish king declared a new constitution by which he annexed German-populated Schleswig into his own kingdom and established closer ties with Holstein, a member of the German Confederation. By this act he violated the protocol signed at London in 1852. Prussia had always looked upon these two duchies as rightfully belonging to her. So Bismarck planned his strategy in such a way that Prussia should involve Austria in a war with Denmark, and after victory, pick up a quarrel with her over the sharing of the spoils. Immediately he called upon Austria as the leader of the German Confederation to join Prussia in sending a combined military expedition against Denmark. Austria and Prussia sent an ultimatum to the king of Denmark to withdraw his new constitution, and upon his refusal, sent a joint expedition in 1864. The combined forces of Austria and Prussia inflicted a crushing defeat upon Denmark and her ruler signed the treaty of Vienna in 1864. As per the terms of the treaty the king surrendered his control over these two German duchies to Austria and Prussia. Bismarck was convinced that his Prussian troops had proved their superiority and he can look forward to another promising performance by them if a war were to break out with Austria.

Friction over the Spoils of War
The question arose as to who should have control over these two duchies. Austria proposed that the Duke of Augustenburg should assume their control. But Bismarck was not willing. There was about to be a war between Prussia and Austria but it was averted following the Gastein Convention (August 20, 1865). By this convention, it was agreed, pending final settlement of this issue, Austria should administer Holstein and Prussia should control Schleswig. Prussia should also get the duchy of Lauenburg. Thus Bismarck was able to eliminate the claim of the Duke of Augustenburg and succeeded in keeping his pressure on Austria. Austria was not happy about this arrangement and secretly supported the cause of the concerned Duke. In the meanwhile, Bismarck was making diplomatic preparations to isolate Austria in case a war broke out. Russia proved to be friendly as he supported her when she suppressed the rebellious Poles in 1863. Then he turned his attention to secure the neutrality of France in the event of a war with Austria. So Bismarck offered to Emperor Napoleon III of France, who had then suffered a set back on account of his Mexican adventure, prospects of a future compensation were he to remain neutral if Austro-Prussian war broke out. Napoleon was overjoyed, and even imagined that he could gain advantages if the war prolonged. So Napoleon assured Bismarck of France's neutrality. Bismarck turned his attention to Italy to secure her military cooperation. For this purpose, he promised the Italian

ruler the state of Venetia were he to succeed in a war with Austria. He also knew that Britain would not take sides.

Austria was not happy with her precarious possession, the German dominated Holstein. So she supported the claim of Duke of Augustenburg and asked him to raise this issue in the German Diet. This step was a clear violation of the Convention of Gastein. The Prussian troops occupied Holstein and Prussia proposed for the elimination of Austria from the German Confederation. In response, Austria supported by other German States declared war on Prussia. Bismarck convinced the Prussians that the war was defensive.

Austro-Prussian War (1866) and Results

Being the leader of the German Confederation, Austria got the support of most of the German states to meet the challenge of Prussia. However, the Prussian troops led by Moltke was able to overcome all the resistance. In the meanwhile, the Italians opened another front and created panic in Austria. The war was over within seven weeks with Prussia scoring splendid victory over her enemy in the battle of Sadowa. Although there was a clamour to march and capture Vienna, Bismarck discouraged this move. He offered lenient terms to Austria by the treaty of Prague. Austria recognised the dissolution of the German Confederation. Austria was excluded from the German political system. Venetia was ceded by Austria to Italy. Prussia annexed the two duchies of Schleswig and Holstein, Hanover, Hesse Cassel, Nassau and free city of Frankfurt-on-the-Maine. All the German states lying north of the river Maine were to join the North-German-Confederation formed and led by Prussia. However, the southern states wished to remain independent and Bismarck gave his tacit consent. It was this generous attitude which made these southern states sign military convention with the North-German Confederation. Bismarck's spectacular success silenced all the liberals at home.

Franco-Prussian Relations

Emperor Napoleon III was rudely shaken by Prussia's victory at Sadowa. It caused great disappointment to him because he could not take advantage or secure compensation for remaining neutral during the course of Austro-Prussian war. He put up his claims frequently for compensation and Bismarck turned it down. Prussia's rise alarmed the French, and a French Marshal by the name of Randon said, "It is France who has been defeated at Sadowa". There was national outcry that France should somehow take revenge. Bismarck was also making preparation for a likely war with France as that would fulfil his main objective—the annexation of southern German states into North-German Confederation. These German states lay in between France and North-German Confederation, and in the event of war between France and Prussia they would have had to opt for France or Prussia.

Bismarck's Diplomacy

As before, Bismarck secured the neutrality of Russia. This time he promised that in the event of a war with France the Czar could repudiate a few clauses of the Treaty of Paris concerning the Black Sea. Austria remained friendly with Prussia because the latter had offered generous terms in the treaty of Prague. Britain's neutrality was taken for granted. Thus France remained isolated.

Events Leading to Franco-Prussian War

The throne of Spain fell vacant and the Spanish Statesmen offered it to Prince Leopold, a relative of the Prussian king. Bismarck forced the prince to accept it which he had rejected it earlier. The news of his acceptance provoked France and she demanded the prince's rejection. Not satisfied with this, France ordered her ambassador to see the Prussian king to get official confirmation and further, to secure an assurance that his relative would not again offer himself as candidate. The king granted an interview to the French ambassador and whatever transpired was communicated to Bismarck through a telegram. Bismarck cleverly abridged the Ems telegram in such a way so as to give the impression that the French ambassador was insulted by the Prussian king. The French emperor felt deeply humiliated and the war became inevitable. It was at this juncture that Bismarck exposed the French Emperor's greed for other's territories. So the southern German states were left with no option but to join the North German Confederation.

French Defeat at Metz and Sedan

The French emperor was equally eager to fight Prussia since his prestige was sagging at home, and the press and the opposition were vehement in crying for revenge. France declared war and mobilised her troops to the border. Prussia had been making preparations for war earlier and its forces crossed the French borders and defeated the French army at two important places, Sedan and Metz. At both the places the French armies surrendered. The Emperor himself was taken prisoner at Sedan. The Prussian army proceeded towards Paris to force a new treaty upon the newly formed Republican government.

The Treaty of Frankfurt (1871)

Paris put up a stiff resistance to the invaders but it was of no avail. She finally surrendered. France signed the humiliating treaty of Frankfurt by which she ceded Alsace and a part of Lorraine to Prussia. She agreed to pay 200 million pounds as war indemnity in instalments, and till its final settlement, agreed for Prussian-army-occupation of her soil. To add insult to injury, Bismarck crowned King William I of Prussia as the emperor of united Germany in the famous Hall of Mirrors at Versailles. Thus, Bismarck achieved the unification of Germany through his matchless diplomatic skill and premeditated wars.

NATIONALISM IN THE AUSTRIAN EMPIRE

Prince Metternich of Austria failed to notice two great forces—nationalism and liberalism—operating in Europe, and by his organised system sought to destroy these very forces at every manifestation. The much despised Metternich system sought to suppress the legitimate aspirations of the peoples, be it political unity or demand for constitutional government. His reactionary system could not survive for long. In 1848, Austria herself was deeply disturbed by a revolution and the famous architect of the Concert of Europe had to flee. Shortly, however, the new Austrian Emperor, Francis Joseph I, succeeded in quelling these revolts and establishing order. Political stability was of utmost importance and urgent necessity since Austrian Empire had subjects belonging to various races and speaking different languages. But the new emperor's troubles were not yet over since the Magyars led by Kossuth revolted and declared their country independent. But when the newly declared state of Hungary started treating the Slavs badly, the latter supported Austria's hands and subsequently the Austrians took the help of the Russian troops to recover Hungary. So it was due to internal differences among the people of Hungary which gave an opportunity to Austria to suppress her newly won independence in 1849. Hungary became a vassal state of Austria and the latter was keen to establish a strong hold on the former.

Quarrel between Hungary and Austria

It was in 1860 that Austrian statesmen realised that they could not go on holding Hungary under their iron rule. There was the need to liberalise their hold on Hungary by giving her some amount of autonomy. So they drew up a charter or diploma in 1860 and restored Hungary to pre-1848 status. By this Charter, Hungary got her Diet (Parliament) and her districts and towns came to have autonomy. It was through this charter that the

Austrian statesmen sought to reconcile their differences with the Hungarians. When the Magyars expressed their deep dissatisfaction and created trouble for Austria, she introduced the February Patent (constitution of the Austrian Empire) by which even the autonomy granted under the 1860 charter was withdrawn and the iron rule over her was clamped. The new constitution which Austria adopted hardly provided for any freedom or autonomy for Hungary. Hungary refused to send her deputies to the Austrian Reichstag. The Hungarians under Ferenc Deák maintained that theirs was a separate nation since a long time. If the Austrian Emperor wanted to rule over it he must take an oath to uphold the fundamental laws of Hungary and wear the crown of St. Stephen.

The 1867 Compromise between Austria and Hungary

The strained relations and the political deadlock continued till 1865-66. However, conditions changed when Austria was defeated by Prussia after the seven weeks war. Austria was humbled and she was in a demoralised state. She was more than agreeable for a compromise with Hungary since she had lost her leadership over the German states by the Treaty of Prague. Austria needed the support of Hungary, and her statesmen including the Emperor finally arrived at a compromise with the Hungarian leaders. After taking the approval of the parliaments of Austria and Hungary, the Austrian Emperor Francis Joseph I was crowned the constitutional ruler of Hungary. Thus, Austria-Hungary came to have dual monarchy and both states were considered equal. Austria-Hungary had a common ruler, two separate Parliaments and administrations, and a joint ministry for three important departments *viz.*, finance, war and foreign affairs. Although the dual monarchy seemed to be the best solution under the circumstances, there were several obstacles coming in the way of proper cohesion. The statesmen of Austria sought to overcome this by diverting the attention of the people. They tried to achieve this by showing keen interest in the Balkan affairs. The Balkan peninsula had become a hot-bed of political rivalry among the nations situated there. It attracted the attention of big powers sometimes. The Austro-Hungarian dual monarchy disturbed the political balance of this region by advancing its own interests. For example, the Congress of Berlin had entrusted the administration of Bosnia and Herzegovina to Austria-Hungary. Serbia was eager to unite all the Slavs under her leadership. She was encouraged in her enterprise by Russia who had her own axe to grind in this region. However, Austria-Hungary was not prepared to lose Bosnia and Herzegovina even though the population of these two states belonged to Slav race. The hatred between

Nationalism in Europe in the Nineteenth Century

Austria and Serbia intensified when the Austrian Archduke Ferdinand and his wife were assassinated in Sarajevo by a Serb on June 28, 1914. Subsequently this event led to the outbreak of World War I.

Agitations and Redressal of Grievances

The grievances of the Irish began to increase in the nineteenth century and they frequently resorted to loud and noisy protests. There was bitter hatred between the Irish Catholics and the British. It was in this atmosphere that Irish nationalism grew. Bowing to the popular demand, the British passed in 1829 the Catholic Emancipation Act which gave the Irish Roman Catholics the right to hold offices and also to get elected to the parliament. Forty years later the Church of Ireland was disestablished by the British Parliament. In 1873, the Irish nationalists formed the Home Rule League, a political party, which agitated for 'Home Rule'—a self-government for the Irish within the United Kingdom of Great Britain and Ireland.

Land Reforms

During the late 19th and early 20th centuries, the British Government began to improve the lot of the Irish peasants by introducing necessary land reforms. The British government led by Prime Minister Gladstone passed several measures mainly to check the harshness of landlords on their Irish tenants and when they failed his government purchased lands from the landlords and later sold it to the poor peasants at reasonable rates. To purchase these small plots, the British government advanced loans to the tenants. In addition to these concessions, fair rent and fixity of tenure provided the much desired relief to the farmers.

Home Rule Bill

In order to pacify the Irish, Gladstone proposed the Home Rule bill in 1886 but it caused a split in the liberal party. Subsequently, he was forced to resign. The same bill came up before the parliament in 1893 and again it failed. In 1914, the Home Rule bill was passed by the British Parliament but there was resistance to it by the Protestant minority in northern Ireland. Again this bill was opposed by the 'Sinn Feiners" a secret society formed by some Irish firebrands, who believed in violence and desired nothing short of total independence of Ireland. Before this issue could be solved, the world war broke out in 1914 and the law was not enforced.

The 'Easter Rising' and Division of Ireland

During the war the extreme Irish nationalist members of the Sinn Fein (meaning *we ourselves*) rose in rebellion with the assistance of the Germans. They urged their compatriots not to pay taxes to the British and resist them by all means. The British sent their special troops called the "Black and Tans" to stamp out this rebellion. During the next few years the Sinn Feiners carried on terrorist attacks and guerilla warfare and the British caught many of their leaders and executed them. However, when the war ended the British government showed interest in settling this Irish problem. In 1920, Lloyd George, the British prime minister, got the Government of Ireland Act passed by the British Parliament which split Ireland into two parts. The Protestant dominated northern Ireland with six counties in it (now called Ulster) became a part of the United Kingdom. The twenty-six southern counties where Roman Catholics were in great majority got the dominion status and a separate parliament and came to be known as the Irish Free State (Eire). The Irish Free State was to remain as a part of the British Empire and owe allegiance to the British crown. The Irish Free state protested at the division of Ireland but accepted the compromise treaty in 1921. The compromise treaty included that if Ulster desired to join the Irish Free State it could do so at any time. But Ulster desired to remain with Britain.

The Irish Free State (Eire) Under Eamon De Valera

In 1932, an American-born Irishman named Eamon De Valera became the prime minister of the Irish Free State. He was a radical and under his leadership, the Irish Free State took the next few steps to become free from the British yoke. The oath of allegiance to the British king was dropped and the payments of tribute to British government ceased. The British government protested but the Free State stood firm.

Lesson Review

1. Describe the role of Mazzini, Cavour and Garibaldi in the unification of Italy.
2. Describe how Bismarck brought about the unification of Germany.
3. Write a note on the following: (a) Greek war of Independence (1827), (b) Belgian independence, (c) Nationalism in the Austrian Empire (d) Irish nationalism.

35

THE EASTERN QUESTION AND BALKAN NATIONALISM

In 1453, the Ottoman Turks captured Constantinople and began to extend their sway over the south-western part of Europe and the northern coast of the African continent during the next two centuries. They reached the acme of power during the middle of the seventeenth century. They had conquered all the lands which lay between them and Austria. They attacked Hungary, and after its conquest, laid siege to Vienna during the middle of the sixteenth century under the leadership of Sultan Suleiman the Magnificent. At his juncture the Holy Roman Emperor got help from the king of Poland and defeated the Turks. He drove them out of Vienna. The Turks continued to threaten the Roman Empire till the last quarter of the seventeenth century. It was late in the seventeenth century that the Turks suffered from a series of defeats which caused the beginning of their decline.

Unfortunately, the Balkan peninsula, which once formed a part of the Eastern Roman Empire, remained as an integral part of the Turkish Empire. The Sultans of Turkey subjected the Christian population of this region to an undiluted despotism and misrule. When a fresh wave of nationalism and liberalism swept over the western part of Europe in the early nineteenth century, the Christian subjects of the Balkan peninsula also longed to be free from the tyranny of the Turkish Sultans.

Meaning of the "Eastern Question"

The Congress of Vienna in 1815 failed to realise the aspirations of the Christian subjects living in the Turkish empire and the peacemakers decided not to disturb her territorial sovereignty. It was in one of the meetings of the later Congresses that Czar Nicholas described the Turkish empire as the "sick man of Europe". Ever since the days of Peter the Great, Russia had been eager to bring about the downfall of the Turkish Empire and expand her own empire. It was not until the early decades of the twentieth century that she found opportunities to take steps in this direction. However, there were other European powers, especially Britain and France, who were equally eager to thwart Russian attempts to bring about the liquidation of the Turkish Empire mainly to maintain the delicate balance of power in Europe. Britain was concerned about the threat Russia was likely to pose if she conquered Turkey, and further expanded her dominions towards south Asia. So three aspects dominate what is popularly called the "Eastern Question", namely the decline of the Ottoman empire, the rise of Christian nations in the Balkans against the Turkish master, and the conflicting ambitions of big powers and their intrigues.

Balkan Nationalism on the Rise

The inhabitants of a small country, Montenegro, were the first to rise in revolt against their Turkish master and in 1799 succeeded in liberating themselves after driving out the Turks from their country. The next to revolt against the Turkish Sultan were the Serbs who were supported by the Russians. They succeeded in securing self-rule but lost that status in 1812 because the Sultan reasserted his control. It was not until 1830 that the Serbs regained their independence.

The Crimean War (1854-56) and the Treaty of Paris (1856)

The next country to become free from the Turkish yoke was Greece. As noted in one of the earlier chapters, she became independent in 1829 as per the treaty signed in London. The next phase of the Eastern question began in the 1850s. The decay of the Ottoman empire attracted the attention of Czar Nicholas who was eager to kill "the sick man of Europe", and acquire places of strategic importance such as the control of the Black Sea and the straits and also the vast territories of Turkey. In 1844, the Russian Czar proposed to British statesmen to divide the Ottoman empire among themselves but he got no ready response. Britain was eager to maintain the balance of power in Europe and she did not want to see Russia growing stronger at the expense of Turkey. Therefore, the Russian Czar decided to go it alone and staked his claims for the protection of Christian subjects in the Holy Land then under the control of the Sultan. Russian troops occupied the Danubian principalities and provoked the European powers. The result was the Crimean war which broke out in 1854. Britain, France and Sardinia went to the assistance of Turkey. The principal battles were fought on the Crimean peninsula. They were Alma, Balaclava and Inkerman. The unbearable Crimean winter of 1854-55 took a heavy toll and the rate of British casualties increased due to neglect of wounded soldiers. It was in these circumstances that Florence Nightingale rendered yeoman's service and reduced the casualty-rate from 44 per cent to 2 per cent. Finally, Russia was beaten in 1856 and she sued for peace. The Treaty of Paris (1856) forced the Russians to give up their claim of protecting the Christian subjects in the Holy Land. In its place the Sultan was forced to give his assurance to treat his Christian subjects with sympathy and introduce reforms. The Black Sea was neutralised. So Russia was prevented from having any influence in that area. The allies hoped that they had brought a lasting peace. But subsequent events proved how hollow this treaty had been as none of the concerned powers bothered much about carrying out their obligations.

"Pan-Slavism" and Russo-Turkish War (1877-78)

The Sultan again commenced his tyranny on the Christian subjects and Russia did not give up her old ambition of conquering Turkish territory. She began to encourage national movements in the Balkans ("Pan-Slavism") in order to bring about the overthrow of Turkish rule there. The Sultan's reluctance to introduce any of his promised reforms and his failure to offer relief measures to the famine-stricken Balkan provinces—Bosnia and Herzegovina—caused lot of anger and discontentment. The Christian inhabitants revolted in 1875 and they were supported by Serbia and Montenegro. Then the trouble spread to Bulgaria whose inhabitants also rebelled against the Sultan. The Sultan sent troops to quell these revolts and the Turks carried out large scale massacre of the Christian subjects. Russia intervened on behalf of these Balkan countries. The Russo-Turkish War (1877-78) ended in the defeat of the Sultan who sued for peace. The signing of the Treaty of San Stefano (March 3, 1878) by the Sultan resulted in a tilt in the balance of power towards Russia. According to this treaty, the Sultan recognised the independence of three Balkan nations, Montenegro, Serbia and Rumania. A new state of Bulgaria emerged which was to be under the protection of Russia. Russia got additional territories from Turkey. This treaty caused great alarm and jealousy among other major powers, such as Britain, Austria, France and Germany.

Congress of Berlin (1878)

Disraeli, the British prime minister, threatened war against Russia if the demand for the revision of this treaty by a Congress was not accepted.

Bismarck, the Iron Chancellor of the German Empire, played the host and convened a Congress of powers related to this dispute at Berlin in 1878. Russia meekly submitted to this revision as she was not prepared for another European war. As per the revised peace terms (a) Russia surrendered to Turkey some territory she had taken, (b) the size of Bulgaria was reduced and granted autonomy, and (c) to maintain parity with Russia,

Britain got the island of Cyprus, and Austria received the provinces of Bosnia and Herzegovina. So Bismarck took credit for helping avert a likely European war by bringing about amicable settlements among the disputing parties. However, the nationalistic conflicts in the Balkan region continued despite many initiatives to bring peace there.

Political Turmoil
Neither Russia nor the newly born Balkan nations were happy. These nations encouraged revolts against the Sultan in the territories controlled by him in order to extend their boundaries. Sometimes they frequently fought among themselves to extend their boundaries. Another factor which kept this region in a perpetual state of tension was the hatred of Serbia towards Austria-Hungary for administering the Slav-populated Bosnia-Herzegovina. Serbia coveted these territories very boldly for they were populated by serbs. Russia was encouraging Serbia in her grand design of conquest of this area.

Young Turk Revolution (1908)
Disgusted with the corrupt and inefficient rule of the Sultan, a group of soldiers and intellectuals who called themselves "Young Turks" succeeded in seizing power in 1908. The Sultan was forced to grant a series of reforms to his own subjects, and further agreed to rule the empire according to a constitution. Some of these reforms included parliamentary democracy, freedom of the press and speech and limited powers to the monarch. These developments caused deep concern among the subject nationalities in the Balkans. But when they heard that the Young Turks were bent upon "Turkification" of all the subjects of the Ottoman Empire, they became restless. The word "Turkification" meant the adoption of Turki language and culture by all the inhabitants in the Ottoman Empire. The Christian subjects as well as the Arabs were not prepared to accept this plan and therefore got ready to oppose it tooth and nail.

Break Up
The first Balkan country to break away from the Turkish hold at this time was Bulgaria. She took advantage of the chaotic situation prevailing in the Ottoman capital following the 1908 revolution and declared her independence. Her ruler assumed the title of a king. Austria-Hungary suddenly annexed the two Balkan principalities of Bosnia and Herzegovina which provoked Serbia. Russia felt humiliated because Austria duped her in the bargain with the result that the straits were not allowed to be open for Russian warships. At the same time she was not prepared to support Serbia if there was a war between the latter and Austria-Hungary. In the meanwhile, Austria tried to appease Turkey by offering cash-compensation

for annexing Bosnia and Herzegovina. As none of the European powers were ready to support Turkey against Austria, the former accepted this offer.

The Italo-Turkish War (1911-12)

In 1911, Italy regarded the moment ripe and declared war on Turkey. She coveted Tripoli and Cyrenaica, both belonging to Turkey. While the war continued, Greece, Serbia and Bulgaria formed the Balkan League to protect themselves from future Turkish onslaughts. Turkey was alarmed at the prospect of a prolonged war she had to wage. So she sued for peace in 1912 and signed the Treaty of Lausanne. As a result of this treaty, Italy received Tripoli.

The First Balkan War (1912)

While the Balkan league was preparing itself for a war with Turkey, it was Montenegro which declared war on Turkey. She asked the members of the Balkan league to join her. The members of the Balkan league joined her in October 1912 with the result the Turks were defeated in all the engagements. Finally, she sued for peace, and on May 30th, 1913 signed the Treaty of London. After signing this treaty, Turkey lost almost all her possessions in Europe which she had ruled for more than five centuries. She was able to retain Constantinople and a small strip of territory along the coast. Bulgaria got much of the Turkish territory and not satisfied with it caused another war.

The Second Balkan War (1913)

Bulgaria's relations with Rumania, her northern neighbour, got strained because the latter demanded a small strip of territory. When Bulgaria refused to grant this demand, Rumania declared war on Bulgaria. Turkey joined Rumania and subsequently Serbia, Greece and Montenegro also joined the fray. All these powers defeated Bulgaria and she agreed to sign a treaty. The Treaty of Bucharest was signed by her on August 10, 1913. According to the treaty, Turkey got back the city and fort of Adrianople. Serbia and Greece got large chunks of Bulgarian territories. Rumania which started the war received the territories which she had earlier demanded from Bulgaria. The Bulgarians were thus humiliated and their bitterness towards her oppressors increased.

Balkan Crisis as a Prelude to the World War I

The major powers in Europe watched these developments in the Balkans with their fingers crossed. Many peace initiatives failed and bitter hostilities continued unabated. Serbia was backed by Russia regarding the claims over Bosnia and Herzegovina, and Austria-Hungary was not prepared to cede them at any cost. Thus Serbia's desire of annexing the two principalities dashed to the ground. As subsequent events proved, this situation led to the outbreak of the World War I.

Lesson Review

1. What do you mean by the 'Eastern Question'? Trace its development.
2. Write a note on the following: (a) Berlin Congress, (b) Balkan wars.

36
MODERN IMPERIALISM

The rise of modern imperialism began in the nineteenth century. The European powers extended their control over the countries of Asia and Africa after defeating the respective native powers. The outbreak of the industrial revolution in Britain and its subsequent spread over western Europe resulted in the growing demand for raw materials and new markets. It was to meet these twin demands, and also to achieve political prestige, the European powers eagerly looked forward to acquiring colonies in Asia and Africa. European merchants of the early centuries had come to Asiatic countries particularly for trade. The native powers allowed them to carry on trade on their soil. However, subsequent events provided ample opportunities to these foreigners to establish their sway over the natives. Political disunity of the country and internal rivalry among the native states attracted the attention of the foreign powers. Adept in political machinations and intrigues, the foreign merchants sought to take advantage of the political turmoil. They finally managed to subjugate the native powers and build empires.

Among the many Asian countries which came to be dominated by the European imperialists in general and the British in particular, mention must be made of India and China.

British East India Company's Wars
After the fall of the Mughal empire, there was a political vacuum and the Marathas did struggle to fill this void. They did not succeed and so the country consisting of big and small sovereign states, lacked political unity and a strong leader. The Mughal empire continued to exist as a shadow of its former self. While the Portuguese were satisfied with establishing small colonies in Goa, Diu and Daman, Dupleix the governor of the French East India Company dreamt of establishing a French empire in India. The Anglo-French rivalry of the early 18th century resulted in the three Carnatic wars. Dupleix's dream vanished and the French in India were totally defeated by

the British. The Seige of Arcot (1751) by Robert Clive (later became Governor of Bengal between 1757-1760 and 1765-1766) marked a turning point in the military fortunes of the British. The three Carnatic wars not only resulted in the defeat and ignominy of the French, but paved the way for the English to have sway over the Carnatic region. After his victory over the French, Robert Clive became a hero. He was sent to Bengal to deal with the Nawab Siraj-ud-daula, who according to some English writers, had caused the so called "Black Hole tragedy". Clive hatched a plot to dethrone him and finally forced him into a battle—the battle of Plassey in 1757. Clive won the battle easily as Mir Jafar, the commander-in-chief of Siraj-ud-daula, betrayed his master by changing sides soon after the battle began. Siraj-ud-daula fled the battlefield but he was subsequently caught and killed. Clive rewarded Mir Jafar with the nawabship of Bengal. The new nawab learnt to his regret that the Company officials were making too frequent a demand for money for him to satisfy. Finding Mir Jafar to be good for nothing, Company officials made his son-in-law, Mir Kasim, to take over the nawabship. Mir Jafar was forced to retire. Mir Kasim, the new nawab, discovered that the British company officials were secretly engaged in dubious trade practices by misusing the *dastaks* and causing heavy drain to his treasury. He desired to put a stop to it by catching the culprits. It became the main cause of another war—the battle of Buxar. The Mughal emperor and the nawab of Oudh went to the rescue of nawab Mir Kasim, but the British led by Major Munro inflicted a crushing defeat upon the allies at Buxar in October 1764. Mir Kasim became a fugitive, the nawab of Oudh fled to the Rohilla country, and the Mughal emperor came over to the side of the English. In the meanwhile Clive was raised to the peership and sent to Bengal to deal with the political situation. According to the Treaty of Allahabad, the nawab of Oudh was restored to his position on condition that he ceded Kora and Allahabad. These territories were given to the Mughal emperor Shah Alam, to maintain his royal dignity. In August 1765, the Mughal emperor issued a *firman* granting the Company the *diwani* of Bengal, Bihar and Orissa. In return for this favour, the Mughal emperor was promised an annual sum of rupees twenty-six lakhs. Thus, the English Company became a virtual master of the largest province in India. Lord Clive established a double government which was later abolished and Warren Hastings (1774-85) set up a new system of administration in India. The Regulating Act of 1773 vested authority in the hands of the Governor-General and his Council and set up a Supreme Court at Calcutta. The new Governor-General made an attempt to codify the Hindu and Muslim laws. The Company thereafter stood forth as the

Diwan and took charge of the responsibility of collecting the land revenue through its own collectors.

Wars in the South

The governors of Bombay and Madras embroiled the Company in wars with the Marathas and the Mysore rulers respectively. As things were not going in favour of the Company, the Governor-General felt inclined to take over the matter into his own hands. It was due to his effective intervention that the prestige of the Company was saved. It may be remembered that Hyder Ali of Mysore had almost succeeded in expelling the English from the Carnatic but the English bought some more time by concluding a humiliating treaty with him.

Expansion of British Empire

Lord Cornwallis (1786-93) defeated Tipu Sultan of Mysore in the third Anglo-Mysore war and inflicted a humiliating treaty. He took the Sultan's sons as hostages. Cornwallis entered into a new treaty with the ruler of Oudh. Lord Wellesley (1798-1805) aimed at establishing British paramountcy over India and for this purpose prepared a plan—the subsidiary system of alliances—to coax native powers to get British protection. The Nizam, followed by the Peshwa and the ruler of Tanjore, joined this alliance. Tipu refused to sign the treaty and so a war—the fourth Anglo-Mysore war—was forced on him. He fought the English bravely and perished in 1799. Thus the Company established sway over Mysore, Malabar and the Canara districts. Wellesley's rule witnessed enormous expansion of British power. The Maratha leaders, Holkar and Sindhia, were forced to sign the subsidiary treaty after the second Anglo-Maratha war. Lord Hastings (1813-1823) fought the Marathas and put an end to their power. The Rajput rulers were forced to acknowledge the paramountcy of the British. The rulers of Malwa, Bhopal and Bhundelkhand also became the allies of the British company by signing the Subsidiary treaty.

William Bentinck [Governor-General of Bengal (1828–33) and Governor-General of India (1833–35)]

The 'Forward policy' of the British had its respite during the governor-generalship of Lord William Bentinck. Being a staunch liberal, he made the British rule popular with his reforms.

Bentinck's Radical Reforms

The most radical change that he brought about was the introduction of Western system of education. The Persian and Sanskrit languages lost their position of pre-eminence, and their place was taken over by English. The other reform was the abolition of *sati* by law.

Lord Dalhousie (1848-56) and Annexations

The power of the British East India Company reached its pinnacle during the time of Lord Dalhousie. The second Anglo-Sikh war was fought (1848-49) and the Punjab was annexed to the British territory in March 1849. The second Anglo-Burmese war was fought in 1852 and the British annexed Pegu. To bring Indian territories belonging to the native rulers under British control, Lord Dalhousie enforced a doctrine called the 'Doctrine of Lapse'. By the application of this doctrine, he annexed states like Satara, Udaipur, Jhansi, Nagpur and Sambalpur into the British dominions for the sole reason that the rulers of these states had no natural heirs to succeed to the respective thrones. He annexed others also but they were not approved by the Company authorities. Peshwa Nana Saheb lost his pension and title soon after the death of his father, ex-Peshwa Baji Rao II. Even the Mughal emperor would have lost his title had not the Company authorities intervened. Dalhousie's treatment to the ruler of Oudh had no parallel. Oudh was taken over by the British on account of misgovernment even though it was not a dependent state like others. So in a moral sense the application of Doctrine of Lapse was wrong and roused the indignation of many rulers like Rani Laxmibai of Jhansi and Nana Saheb who staged a revolt in 1857. One may say that the great uprising of 1857 was the direct outcome of Dalhousie's policy towards the native states. In 1885-86 the British waged the third Burmese war and annexed upper Burma. Britain also got Malaya with its capital, Singapore. Britain fought the Afghan wars to safeguard her interests in India from a likely danger coming from Russia. Finally, Britain and Russia came to an agreement on their spheres of influence in south Asia before the first world war broke out.

CHINA

The thrilling adventures of Marco Polo, an Italian traveller of the late 13th century, brought for the first time some knowledge of east to the European countries. Marco Polo recorded his experiences of China-visit in a book. This attracted the attention of many Europeans. The Europeans realised that China was definitely more advanced than any of the leading European countries. So they were eager to visit China. However, travel to China on land became more risky since the fall of the Mongol Empire. It was then that Portuguese explored the possibility of finding a new sea-route to China. They finally succeeded in their mission during the sixteenth century. It may be remembered that China had enjoyed her splendid isolation for a number of centuries. But that was to end temporarily due to constant flow of foreigners and Christian missionaries. The Portuguese, the Dutch, and the English merchants visited this country with the hope of establishing trade. The Chinese produced many things of which tea, silk, porcelain and art objects were in great demand in western countries. The Christian missionaries started arriving in China. They began mass conversions which resulted in religious conflicts. The foreign merchants, soldiers, and missionaries constantly had their bickerings which disgusted the Chinese. When their unseemly behaviour annoyed the Chinese, the government ordered all the foreigners to leave their country. Canton was the only port where the foreign merchants were permitted to carry on their trade.

Opium Wars

It was not until the middle of nineteenth century—when the power of the Manchu Emperors had declined considerably—that the Europeans succeeded in getting the doors of China opened for trade. The Chinese demanded silver for many things purchased from them. Many ships of the British East India Company carried silver and Indian-grown opium to China and got in exchange silk and tea. The harmful effects of the consumption of opium by the Chinese alarmed the government and it passed orders banning the import of opium. However, the English merchants encouraged the smuggling of opium into her territory. It was this act of treachery that led to the First Opium War (1839-1842). The British forces attacked the Chinese ports. The Manchu government, being too weak, was unable to defend itself. It sued for peace. Treaty of Nanking (August 29, 1842), among other things, included the opening of five more ports for foreign trade and the ceding of Hongkong to the British. In 1857, the Sino-British relations got strained due to the insult of the British flag and the murder of a French missionary. The Anglo-French joint expedition again humbled China for the second time (1857) and the Chinese were forced to offer more concessions. An additional dose of concession included the opening of six more Chinese ports to the foreign merchants. The Chinese government guaranteed protection to European citizens and the personnel of foreign diplomatic missions. The westerners could travel freely anywhere in China. Similar concessions had to be offered to other foreign powers such as Russia, Germany, Japan and the U.S.A. Each of these powers began to dominate China in some way or the other. For example, France began to extend her sphere of influence over Indo-China. Similarly, Germany, Russia and Japan began to covet some territory or preferred to extend their influence over some part of China or the other. The Germans, ensconced themselves in the Shandong Peninsula. Russia looked upon North Korea and also both sides of the River Amur as her possessions.

Sino-Japanese War (1894-1895)

In the meanwhile, Japan was emerging as a great Asiatic power and began to covet the entire Korean peninsula. Unfortunately, Korea owed only nominal allegiance to China and the latter's weakness was fully exploited by Japan. China and Japan both claimed this territory as theirs with the result a war broke out on August 1, 1894. The Japanese proved more than a match to the Chinese in modern methods of warfare and the use of weaponry. China was easily defeated. She had to give up her claims on Korea and pay a vast sum of money as war indemnity. China also gave away a few islands on her sea coast, the most noteworthy being Formosa. Japan annexed Korea in 1910. The Sino-Japanese war exposed China's weakness, and the foreign powers were eager to cut her vitals (a historian has described this as 'cutting of the Chinese melon') for their benefit. The British snatched the Chinese port of Weihaiwei and the Yangtse river valley. The Russians extended their sphere of influence over Manchuria while the Germans got 'exclusive rights' over the Shandong Peninsula. Japan succeeded in acquiring the Liaodong Peninsula and would have got southern Manchuria also but for the intervention of powers like France, Germany and Russia. These powers intervened on the pretext of saving China but had an ulterior motive. France got some territories in Indo-China, Russia received Port Arthur and other concessions, and Britain expanded her Indian borders to the Burmese side.

U.S.A. Advocates 'Open Door Policy' with Regard to China

The process of dismembering China would have been completed had not the U.S.A. intervened. The American statesmen had been extremely busy dealing with their own domestic problems. Till late in the nineteenth century they did not know whatever was going on round the world. By the end of that century, the U.S.A. emerged as a giant and looked forward to establishing close economic ties with a number of countries. She found her western neighbours to be too greedy where China was concerned. Seeing that her merchants in China were being discriminated, and also being disappointed at being excluded from having her sphere of influence in China, the U.S.A. advocated what is called the 'Open Door Policy'. This policy was espoused by the U.S. Secretary of State, John Hay in 1899. Britain supported this policy which included the respect to China's territorial integrity and independence by foreign powers and equal opportunity in China for the commerce and industry of all nations. The other nations accepted this policy "in principle". Thus China was saved to some extent from being conquered or losing her sovereignty and independence like India.

JAPAN

Japan is a group of four main islands which is situated off the north-east coast of China. Like her great neighbour she kept herself aloof from the rest of the world for a long time. Her contact with the Europeans began when Francis Xavier, a Jesuit priest, arrived with some missionaries during the sixteenth century. After that, merchants and missionaries arrived frequently. They received a warm welcome in the beginning. The activities of the Christian missionaries annoyed the Japanese, a majority of whom were followers of Shintoism. A large segment of the Japanese society had also embraced Buddhism. So the Japanese government expelled the foreigners in 1615 as China had done. Only one island port was kept open for foreign trade. Thus Japan got into a self-imposed isolation for the next two centuries.

It was not until 1853 that Japan opened her doors to the westerners. This came as a sequel to Commodore Perry's visit to the Japanese port of Yokohama. Perry's powerful fleet frightened the Japanese. Perry delivered a letter of the President of the U.S.A. to the Japanese government and promised them that he would return next year to collect a reply. The letter contained a proposal for a commercial treaty between the U.S.A. and Japan. When Perry returned to Japan after several months, the Japanese government agreed to sign a commercial treaty with the U.S.A. Subsequently, Japan signed similar treaties with the other major western powers. Japanese government gave its consent to westerners to move freely and reside in her territory. They were also permitted to trade freely. Perry's visit to Japan had far reaching consequences in the sense that Japan decided to learn the secrets of western superiority.

Meiji Revolution

One of the most important results of Perry's visit to Japan was the internal political revolution called the Meiji Restoration. The power of the *Shogunate* (military dictatorship) fell and the people had to recall the young emperor, Mutsuhito (1867-1912) to rule the country. The young emperor assumed reins of power and piloted his nation to great heights of industrial and technological progress. At the turn of the century, Japan astonished all powers by its rapid strides of progress. This was possible because she chose to westernise herself. The Japanese realised that the superiority of the West lay in their progress in science and technology and their application. So the Japanese government encouraged sending promising and brilliant students to Western countries to learn the scientific and technological know-how. Japan also invited foreign industrialists and scientists to set up industries and laboratories on her soil. In the course of time, Japan shed its feudal features and accepted the ways of modern civilisation. Like the other imperialist countries, Japan too looked forward to establishing colonies. Her efforts bore fruit in this direction soon after the Sino-Japanese war of 1894-1895. She was considered a big power in the world by Britain during the early years of the 20th century. The friendship between Japan and Britain culminated in a defence treaty—the Anglo-Japanese Treaty of 1902. This Anglo-Japanese alliance was directed against a common enemy, Russia. Russia had given enough trouble to Japan and both quarrelled over the control of Manchuria. In the Russo-Japanese war of 1904-1905, Japan inflicted a crushing defeat upon Russia. Russia had to cede Port Arthur and other territories plus giving up some concessions in southern Manchuria to Japan. The defeat of this giant at the hands of puny Japan surprised the whole world. Japan emerged as a world power.

Lesson Review

1. Trace the rise and growth of the rule of the British East India Company in India.
2. Explain the circumstances which led to the political and economic exploitation of China by the western powers.
3. Describe Commodore Perry's visit to Japan and its aftermath.

37
WESTERN IMPERIALISM IN AFRICA

Africa is the second largest continent in the world with a total area of 11,700,000 square miles. This continent enjoys a wide variety of climate and soil. It is rich in mineral deposits such as diamonds, gold, copper and iron ore. Because of its immense size and hostile climate, its interiors remained unexplored for a very long time. During the late fifteenth century, the Portuguese established a few trading outposts along Africa's west coast. Following the footsteps of the Portuguese, other European powers like Spain, Holland and others established their own trading posts. However, it was not until the middle of nineteenth century, that the interior lands of Africa came to be explored. The greatest among the early explorers was a British missionary, David Livingstone. Finding that the natives of Africa, mainly negroid in stock, were very backward and uncivilised, he made it his goal to bring them under the civilising influence of the West. The next great explorer was an American journalist, Henry M. Stanley who explored the Congo region. His thrilling adventures in Africa excited many merchants and businessmen who were eager to exploit the resources of that continent.

Partition of Africa
Stanley's exploration of the Congo basin impressed King Leopold II of Belgium. He was the first to take the initiative in organising an international conference for the purpose of civilising the people of the African continent. He appointed Stanley as his agent and promoted a company to acquire the Congo basin. But the French laid their claims to a part of Congo and so they had to be satisfied. The land lying north of the river Congo was ceded to the French. The natives of Leopold's Congo suffered a great deal as the population of each village had to pay heavy taxes. They groaned under his tyranny. His scandalous rule attracted the attention of the other European powers. They lost no time in condemning his atrocities. The king, who looked upon the Congo region as his personal property, was forced to

turn over the same in 1908 to the Belgian Parliament. It was then that reforms in Belgian Congo region were introduced.

The success of Leopold's venture in Congo encouraged other European trading companies like the British and the French to set up trading outposts in Africa. They put forward claims to the Niger valley. After a struggle, Britain won. The French took northern part of Africa. Britain also got the Cape Colony from the Dutch in 1815. But the Dutch farmers called the Boers did not like the British. They moved northwards and established two republics called Transvaal and the Orange Free State. They settled there, but when gold was discovered in Transvaal the British began to move there. The hostilities between the Boers and the British resulted in a war called the Boer War in 1899. The Boers were defeated. The British acquired some more territories in the course of time. All lands conquered were grouped together and named as the Union of South Africa (1910).

By about 1914, Britain emerged as the greatest imperialist power in the African continent. She realised the importance of acquiring Egypt soon after the construction of the Suez Canal (1869). The Egyptian ruler was encouraged to borrow money from Britain to improve the Egyptian economy. In the meanwhile, Britain bought a majority of the shares in the Suez Canal company and thus obtained its control over its administration. The shrewd British prime minister at that time was Disraeli and he gradually began to exert his pressure over the ruler of Egypt. The Egyptians resented the British influence and revolted in 1882. This revolt was put down and thereafter the British influence grew. On the eve of the First World War Egypt became a British protectorate. After this the British gradually moved southwards towards Sudan. The Muslim fanatics were defeated and Sudan became a part of British empire. But France also put forward its claim to Sudan. However, the differences between the British and the French were settled. The British "Empire builder", Cecil Rhodes, thought of acquiring all the territories from Egypt in the north to the Cape Colony in the south. But the Germans upset his plans. However, the British extended their control over Uganda, British East Africa (Kenya) and a part of the Somaliland. Cecil Rhodes established the colony of Rhodesia (present day Zimbabwe and Zambia) in southern Africa, which was named after him. Britain also established the colonies of the Gold Coast and Sierra Leone along the west coast of Africa.

After the fall of the Ottoman Empire, the European powers were eager to establish their control over its satellite states in northern Africa. France took Algeria during the time of king Louis Philippe (1830-48) and later annexed it. It was from there that France began extending her sway over other neighbouring territories like Tunisia, Morocco and West and Equatorial Africa. France also set up her colonies in Senegal, Somaliland, Madagascar island and part of the Guinea coast.

Spain acquired a part of Morocco, Canary islands, Rio De Oro and Rio de Muni. Italians upheld the French claim over Morocco against that of the Germans and France allowed Italy to occupy Libya in return following Italy's war with Turkey. Italy had earlier acquired Somaliland facing the Indian Ocean and Eritrea facing the Red Sea. In 1896, Italy's attempt to conquer Ethiopia failed miserably.

Germany entered the race for colonies in Africa as the last-minute competitor. She could manage to acquire large chunks of territory in West Africa where she set up colonies like German South West Africa, German Cameroons and Togoland. On the eastern side she acquired Tanganyika (German East Africa). She quarrelled with France twice over latter's attempt to establish her protectorate over Morocco, and on both occasions there might have been a war. However, these situations were averted.

The Portuguese, who were the first to show interest in Africa, acquired Angola and Mozambique. The acquisition of colonies in African continent was not without rivalry on the part of the European powers. All of them wanted to subjugate the natives of Africa and exploit the resources for their selfish ends. The African continent offered mineral and natural resources to European powers. Moreover, it had and has a "fantastic variety of wildlife". It may be said that only Ethiopia and Liberia remained unsubdued by the European powers. Otherwise almost all the parts of Africa were colonised by European powers. It was only after the world War II that many of these colonies became independent.

Lesson Review

1. Explain briefly the factors which led to the colonisation of Africa by the western powers.
2. What do you mean by "Scramble for Africa"? Explain its effects.
3. On a map of Africa show the colonies of different European powers in 1914.
4. Write a short note on the following: (a) "Dark Continent" (b) David Livingstone (c) Henry M. Stanley (d) Cecil Rhodes, the Empire Builder.

38
NATIONALISM IN THE FAR EAST

CHINA

In an earlier chapter, Western imperialism in China during the nineteenth century was discussed. Let us examine how Western imperialism in China paved way for the rise of Chinese nationalism.

As mentioned earlier, the United States of America insisted on other imperialist powers to maintain an open door policy with regard to China. This policy indirectly saved her from a possible partition. The weakness of the Manchu government and the danger of a likely partition of the country caused great indignation among the Chinese masses.

Boxer Uprising (1899-1900) and Results
A secret patriotic society under the name of *Patriotic-Harmonious Fists* (the Westerners called it the "Boxers") became popular with the motto 'cherish the dynasty, exterminate the foreigner.' In the course of time, this movement spread with the increasing support of the Chinese officials. Even the Dowager Empress of China gave her support to this movement. The Boxer Uprising was directed against the Western Christian missionaries, the new Chinese converts and the foreign embassy staff. They attacked and killed some Christian missionaries and foreign merchants. They surrounded the compound walls of the western embassies in Peking. The Western powers demanded that the Chinese government should issue immediate orders to its governors to suppress the Boxer Movement. They also sought the help of friendly countries like Japan and the U.S.A. Japan and the U.S.A. sent a joint expedition to relieve the siege of the Western embassies in Peking. They were successful in driving out the Boxers and thus helping the personnel of the Western embassies. The Western powers were angry with the Chinese government for not coming to their rescue at the time of the crisis. They demanded of the Chinese government to dismiss

all negligent officials and asked for indemnity. The Chinese government was helpless and meekly obliged. The Western powers got the control over the Chinese excise and customs. Firstly, the Boxer uprising resulted in riveting the yoke of Western imperialism on the Chinese. Secondly, the Chinese turned their wrath against Manchu government. These circumstances led to the final overthrow of the Manchu government in 1911.

After suppressing the Boxer rebellion, the Dowager empress introduced Western type of reforms. After her death, her successor proved to be unequal to the task of modernising China. Therefore, China remained helpless at the time when the Russo-Japanese war broke out on her soil. The success of Japan, an Asiatic power over mighty Russia surprised the whole world. It convinced the Chinese about the impotence of their own Government in dealing with the western imperialism. The Chinese students and businessmen became increasingly hostile to the Manchu government. They joined the nationalist movements and organised boycotts. The strikes and boycotts became the chief weapons of the nationalists in 1905 and 1908. Most of them were directed against the presence of foreign powers. The Manchu government resorted to large scale repressions. In October 1911, a mutiny broke out in Hankow and Wuchang which resulted in the fall of the Old Manchu dynasty.

Dr Sun Yat Sen

Dr Sun Yat Sen, who led some revolutionary groups against the Manchu government, was chosen as a provisional president of the new Republic. The new Republic was set up with its headquarters at Nanking. Unfortunately, Sun Yat Sen was not acceptable to some other political factions. Meanwhile a civil war broke out. Subsequently Sun Yat Sen volunteered to retire, so that political unity could be brought about. Finally, Yuan Shi Kai was chosen as the first president of the Republic of United China. Yuan Shi Kai was a powerful warlord in China. When he became the president he found that a large number of provincial governments under different warlords defied the central authority. Therefore he took upon himself the task of crushing these overlords and establish the authority of central government. These warlords fought against the centre in 1912 and 1928. It may be remembered that China joined the First World War on the side of the Allies. The European powers were too busy fighting the Germans in World War I. So Japan found an opportunity to press her 21 demands. China was helpless to resist the pressure from the Japanese. She was also unable to receive support from friendly powers. Had China accepted all of Japan's 21 demands, she would not have been able to preserve her independence and territorial integrity. In 1916, Yuan Shi Kai died and China remained practically divided with no central government worth its name existing.

When the peacemakers at the Paris peace conference recognised Japan's control over the Shantung Peninsula, the Chinese nationalists staged angry protests and boycotted the Japanese goods. Finally, Japan agreed to respect Chinese territorial integrity and sovereignty and the latter in return lifted the boycott.

Sun Yat Sen had founded the Kuomintang party (National People's Party or Nationalist Party) in 1912 which worked against Yuan Shi Kai. As such Yuan Shi Kai had imposed a ban on the Kuomintang party. Sun Yat Sen fled to Japan. He returned to China after the First World War and worked against imperial powers who were not giving up their concessions and privileges in China. Russia under the leadership of Lenin gave up many of her concessions and offered economic and military aid to the Chinese nationalists. She also gave training to many of the nationalists in Moscow. One of the prominent leaders who took training in Moscow was Chiang Kai Shek. Sun Yat Sen tried to implement his three vital principles—National Independence, Democracy and Economic Reforms—in the southern part of China where his party had gained control.

Sun Receives help From Russia

Soon after the death of Sun Yat Sen in 1925, General Chiang Kai-shek succeeded to power. He conquered the north China and thereby united the entire country making Peking his capital. For a short time, it appeared as though China's problems were over. China was on its way towards modernisation and Chiang Kai-shek persuaded the Western powers to give up their concessions. The Western powers reluctantly agreed to do so. But Chiang's main trouble started when he quarrelled with the Chinese Communists in 1927. They defied his authority with the result they were forced to go underground. For nearly ten years, Chiang fought his battles with the Communists who came in the way of progress. The Communists were led by Mao Tse-tung who made north western part of China his stronghold.

Undeclared War between China and Japan

However, the Japanese attack and the conquest of Manchuria in 1931 stirred deep national sentiments in the form of the Chinese boycott of Japanese goods. The Japanese retaliated by attacking the port city of Shanghai in 1937. It led to an undeclared war between the two countries for nearly eight years. The Nationalists and the Communists in China forgot their differences for a while. Japan inflicted several defeats upon China which resulted in the former occupying many Chinese regions. Bands of Chinese nationalist guerillas fought the invaders in the interior lands and cut off their lines of communication and supplies. The American government offered loans to the government of Chiang so as to make him withstand the pressure of the Communists on the one hand and the Japanese on the other.

Chinese Revolution (1949)

The corrupt government of Chiang Kai-shek did not last long after the World War II. The vast country remained poor. They had no sympathy for the corrupt government. The Nationalists and the Communists continued to fight for power for nearly four years (1945-1949). The Communists led by Mao-Tse-Tung got economic and military aid from the Soviet Union. The U.S.A. supported the Kuomintang forces led by Chiang Kai-shek. The Communists captured Manchuria and then moved southwards. They inflicted a series of crushing defeats on the Nationalist forces in 1949. General Chiang Kai-shek fled to the nearby island of Formosa. The main land of China thus witnessed the rule of the Communists since 1949. The victorious armies of Mao Tse-tung established the People's Republic of China. Mao Tse-tung became the undisputed leader of China. However, the United Nations recognised only the Nationalist Government's Republic of China (based in Taiwan or Formosa) in 1945. It was only in 1971 that the People's Republic of China took over the permanent seat with veto powers from Republic of China in the United Nations Security Council.

JAPAN

The Meiji restoration constitutes the most important landmark in the history of modern Japan. It ended Japan's century old isolation and also broke down the power of the Shogunate. The new emperor, Mutsuhito, resumed full authority and ably led his country in the task of modernisation. The Japanese adopted Western political system with some minor adjustments. They had a constitution which provided for a bicameral legislature with limited powers. All the authority was vested in the emperor.

Economic Reforms

The Japanese realised that the secret strength of western superiority lay in modern industrialisation. As a first step, the Japanese Government abolished feudalism. The emperor encouraged the rapid industrialisation of his country. Hundreds of Japanese scholars and scientists were sent abroad to acquire scientific and technological knowledge. Western engineers and scientists were invited to Japan and extended their cooperation for the modernisation of the country. Within three decades Japan built modern railroads, set up modern banking system, organised foreign trade and established a stable currency. There was remarkable improvement in the postal system of the country.

Educational System

Japan also adopted Western educational system. A large number of schools, colleges and universities were established. The public school system was encouraged. The teaching of English language was also encouraged.

Re-organisation of the Japanese Forces

Japan reorganised her infantry forces on the lines of the Prussian model. Her navy copied the model of the British. Large sums of money were spent on modernisation of Japanese armed forces. It was due to this added strength that Japan was able to think on the lines of conquest. Fortunately, Japan had undergone the process of industrial revolution.

Japanese Imperialism

Several factors were responsible for Japan turning into an imperialist country. Growing population, limited land, paucity of raw materials, and a search for market were responsible for turning Japan into an imperialist country. Imitating her Western counterparts, Japan looked forward to establishing her own colonies in Asia. The weakness of the Manchu government in China attracted her attention and she put forward her claim on Korea which was owing allegiance to China. In the ensuing struggle (1894-95) for Korea, China was defeated with the result she gave up her claims. Japan received a huge war indemnity and a few islands including Taiwan (formerly Formosa) from China. At the turn of the 20th century, Britain, for her own reasons, developed intimacy with Japan which culminated in the Anglo-Japanese treaty. It was directed against Russia. In the meanwhile, Russian ambition in the Far East, particularly Manchuria, posed a threat to Japan's interests in Korea. Japan tried to settle this dispute with Russia through negotiations but failed. It resulted in a war. The Russians suffered an ignominious defeat at Mukden and came to terms. The Treaty of Portsmouth (1905) was signed by which Russia recognised Japan's interest in Korea, transferred to her the lease of the Liaodong Peninsula, and gave southern-half of the island of Sakhalin. Russia also agreed to evacuate Manchuria. Japan's inherent strength at beating an European-giant like Russia surprised the whole world. Japan's success in this war encouraged other Asiatic countries under foreign rule to demand self-government.

Japan entered the World War I on the side of Britain with the hope of adding more territories to her Empire from her weak neighbour, China. Taking advantage of the preoccupation of European powers during the conflict, Japan sent an ultimatum to China in January 1915 to concede her "Twenty-one Demands". Japan also threatened China with a war if these demands were not accepted. Yuan Shihkai of China privately accepted many of the demands relating to territorial claims and economic concessions. America entered into the Lansing-Ishii Agreement (November 2, 1917) with Japan by which she recognised the special claims of Japan over China. At the Paris peace conference, China and Japan clashed and put forward conflicting claims. Japan's claims over China were upheld by the Peace Conference and China was very much disappointed. Japan was rewarded with the former German territories in China and a large number of islands. After the first world war Japan's prestige as a world power rose to a new height, She secured a permanent seat in the League's Council. Although she looked forward to expanding her empire at the expense of her weak neighbour—China—she was restrained from this course of action according to the terms of the Nine-Power treaty to which she became a party. At the Washington Conference (1921-22) the nine powers including Japan agreed to respect the Chinese territorial integrity and sovereignty. Therefore, for about a decade, Japan did not trouble China.

Lesson Review

1. Write a note on the Boxer uprising in China.
2. Explain the factors which led to the Chinese revolution of 1911.
3. Discuss the events which led to the Communist Revolution in 1949.
4. What do you mean by 'Meiji Restoration'? What reforms were introduced in Japan after this event?
5. Write a short note on: (a) Boxer Protocol; (b) Sun Yat sen; (c) Sino-Japanese war; (d) Russo-Japanese war; (e) The Twenty-one Demands.

39
NATIONALISM IN SOUTH AND SOUTH-EAST ASIA

Persia (Iran)

Persia, renamed as Iran in 1934, was an independent country. However, she came under the influence of Britain and Russia at the close of the 19th century. The Shah of Persia was a friend of both Britain and Russia. After the defeat of Russia at the hands of the Japanese in 1905, Britain compelled Russia to agree to the establishment of the 'spheres of influence' in Persia. Russia was allowed to retain her influence over the northern part of Persia and Britain retained her influence in the South. The central part of Persia came to be influenced by both. After the Russian revolution of 1917, Russian forces withdrew from Persia. The frequent interference of both these imperial powers over Persia caused the rise of nationalism. In 1921, a Persian army officer, Reza Pehlavi, overthrew the government and set up a nationalist government at Tehran. He became the minister of war. He reorganised the Persian Army and assumed dictatorial powers with the sanction of the Mazlis (Persian Parliament). He became independent from the control of the Shah of Persia. When the Shah left the country, the national assembly elected Reza Pehlavi as the new Shah of Persia. Reza Pehlavi introduced several reforms to modernise his country. In 1934, he changed feudal name of Persia into Iran. In 1934, he changed feudal name of Persia into Iran. He cancelled the right of Anglo-Iranian Oil Company to extract oil. However, Britain persuaded him to agree to a sixty-year lease for the Anglo-Iranian oil company. During the World War II, British and Russian troops occupied Iran and the Shah was deposed for his pro-Nazi sympathies. His son Mohammed Reza Pehlavi was enthroned. As per the agreement of the Teheran conference, the U.S.A., Britain and Russia recognised the independence and territorial integrity of Iran. The British left Iran as per this agreement, but the Russians did not do so. Therefore,

Iran complained to the United Nations Organisation about the continued presence of Russians on her territory (*see* UNO achievements). In 1949, the constitution of Iran was revised and accordingly the Prime Minister exercised his powers. He was made responsible to the Iranian Parliament. Iran witnessed the rise of a powerful prime minister by the name of Mossadegh. He nationalised the Iranian oil companies including the British owned Anglo-Iranian oil company. Britain broke off her diplomatic relations with Iran as the latter had broken the lease agreement. A financial crisis developed in Iran due to the closure of oil companies. An uprising against Mossadegh in 1953 resulted in his deposition and the restoration of the regime of the Shah of Iran. The Shah of Iran came to a settlement with the oil companies and thereby maintained peace.

Afghanistan

Afghanistan, a mountainous and arid region, was inhabited by several Muslim Pathan Tribes. She came to attract the attention of the British statesmen during the second half of the 19th century. When the Russians extended their sphere of influence over Persia, the British were afraid of a possible invasion of India. So, the Russian threat to their Indian empire compelled the British to take interest in the affairs of Afghanistan, which was a buffer state. The British wanted to convert Afghanistan into their protectorate. Caught up between the two great contending powers, this unfortunate country suffered most. The British fought two wars on the Afghan soil to compel that country to join the British camp and keep the Russians out. The two Afghan wars yielded rich dividends to the British as they secured control over Khelat, Quetta and Gilgit. They also retained the control over the newly carved out region called Baluchistan.

Britain and Russia set up a new boundary convention to demarcate the boundary lines of their extending sphere of influence. The aggressive attitude of the British, and their interference in Chitral, caused deep resentment. Revolts against the British broke out in 1897-98. The British suppressed these revolts with great difficulty during the time of Lord Curzon. He formed a new province Afghanistan and named it as the North West Frontier Province (NWFP). This was done to establish better control over that Province and organise efficient administration. The Anglo-Russian convention of 1907 included a broad agreement of their respective spheres of influence in Persia and Afghanistan. The Russians agreed to respect the British control over Afghanistan. Afghanistan protested to Britain regarding her involvement in World War I. She was forced to fight (though reluctantly) the Turkish emperor who happened to be the Caliph.

Provoked by some German agents, the Amir of Afghanistan sent his Army across the Indian frontier but the British forces defeated it. Afghanistan made some progress after 1919. Her Amir, Amanulla Khan, secured the British recognition to Afghan independence in 1921. Both the countries exchanged ambassadors in 1922. He established cordial relations with Persia and Turkey. He accepted foreign technical assistance to modernise his country. Unfortunately, his illiterate subjects were unable to appreciate his zeal for modernisation. He was deposed in 1929 and Mohammed Nadir Shah came to power. However, this unfortunate king did not live long for he was assassinated in 1933. His son, Zahir Shah, ascended the throne in 1933. He introduced reforms such as the new constitution which provided for a bicameral legislature. Afghanistan kept herself aloof from the World War II. She became the member of the United Nations Organisation in 1946.

British Conquest of Burma

The Burmese ruler provoked the British East India Company by claiming the latter's border-territories such as Chittagong, Dacca, and Murshidabad in 1818. His armed provocations caused the first Anglo-Burmese War in 1824. After a protracted and difficult war, the British defeated the Burmese. The Burmese ruler signed the treaty of Yandaboo in 1826. As per the terms of the treaty, the Burmese surrendered Arakan and Tenasserim, paid a war indemnity and received a British resident. In 1852, the Burmese ruler appeared to have ill-treated some British merchants in Burma, and therefore, the British company under Lord Dalhousie fought the second Burmese war. The second Burmese war resulted in the defeat of the Burmese forces. The Burmese ruler was forced to cede Pegu (Lower Burma) to the British. The third Burmese war was also fought in 1885, and again Burma was defeated. She was annexed to the British-Indian empire by a proclamation on 1st January 1886. The British appointed a Lt. Governor in 1897 to administer the Burmese territory. In 1935, it was decided by the British government to separate Burma from India.

Burmese Nationalism

During the World War II, desperate Burmese nationalist group led by Aung Sang left Burma and took military training in Japan. They hoped to expel the British with the Japanese assistance. When Japan conquered Burma during the Second World War, they set up a puppet government. Aung Sang became the Minister of War. After the Japanese retreat from Burma, Aung Sang crossed over to the British side to enable them to re-conquer Burma. When the British were reluctant to grant freedom to Burma,

Aung Sang formed a political party to agitate. After the Labour party came to power in Britain in 1945, it was decided to grant independence to Burma. Assassinations of Aung Sang and several other leading politicians followed. Britain granted independence to Burma and she became a republic in January 1948. The first prime minister of the Burmese republic was U Nu. His government faced internal troubles from the communists and other insurgents. On March 2, 1962, Gen. Ne Win staged a military coup and became Burma's dictator. Burma did not join the Commonwealth of countries. Burma has followed strict neutrality in her foreign ever since independence.

Ceylon

As per the settlement arrived at in the Congress of Vienna (1815), the Dutch gave the island of Ceylon to Britain. Ceylon is an island mainly inhabited by the Sinhalese and Tamilians. In 1919, the Ceylonese became politically conscious and organised a national Congress for the purpose of securing self-government. After World War I, the British granted a partial self-government (including communal electorates) to the Ceylonese. The majority of the Ceylonese were and are Sinhalese and, therefore, they were not happy with the idea of communal electorate. The Donoughmore Commission suggested some more reforms in the electoral system. But, the Ceylonese were not satisfied. During World War II, the British Government promised some more reforms which would come after the conclusion of the war. In February 1948, Ceylon became an independent dominion within the Commonwealth. An extreme nationalist party won the election and came to power in 1956. The new prime minister of Ceylon forced Britain to withdraw totally from this island-nation.

Southeast Asia : Philippines

After the Spanish American War (1898), the U.S.A. received the Philippines islands from Spain. The Americans had no intention of retaining it permanently within her fold. There was resistance to foreign rule from the Filipinos. But the Americans postponed the granting of independence to the Filipinos, till such time they would be fit to receive the same. The United States Government granted self-government to the Philippines and in 1934, passed the Philippines Independence Act. According to this Act, Philippines became a Commonwealth country. Her first president was Manuel Quezon. Philippines was promised full independence after a lapse of 12 years. During World War II, the Japanese conquered and occupied these islands. However, she was reconquered by the American General, Douglas MacArthur. She was granted independence on July 4th, 1946.

The Filipinos preferred a Republican Constitution. Soon after her independence, Philippines began to face a large number of problems—a legacy of Japanese occupation of the Island during the war. Ultimately, a strong government was established under the leadership of President Ramon Magsaysay. He was able to introduce a series of economic reforms. Lands were redistributed among the landless. However, the Filipinos began to rely heavily on the American economic and military aid for improving their economy and defence respectively ever since their independence.

Malaya

The British opened a trading station in Singapore in 1819 and later conquered the interior native. Malaya, mainly populated by Malay Chinese, Tamilians and the Muslims, produced tin and rubber. Singapore, the capital, served as a strategic outpost of the British. The British also extended their control over North Borneo, Sarawak and the Brunei. The first two along with Malaya formed the present state of Malaysia. During World War II, the Japanese forces overran Malaya but the British were able to recover this territory during its concluding years. In 1948, the British faced continuous troubles, particularly from the communist Chinese. The British separated Singapore from Malaya in 1946 and granted a measure of self-government. In the meanwhile, a party led by Tunku Abdul Rahman won the elections in Independent Malaya and he became the prime minister of the country in August 1957. In Singapore, a new constitution was introduced, and after the elections, Lee Kuan Yew, the leader of the Abdul Rahman was not satisfied with the division of Malaya and suggested to the British to establish a united federation consisting of its former colonies, i.e., Malaya, Singapore, North Borneo, Sarawak and the Brunei. Accordingly, the new federation was formed which included all the former British colonies except the Brunei (1963).

French Indo-China (1893)

It was during the time of Emperor Napoleon III (1848-70) that France acquired the Chinese-held New Caledonia, Cochin-China, and Cambodia. She had a few trading centres and colonies in India too. Her empire in Indo-China (1893) began to spread when her Prime Minister, Jules Ferry, undertook an expedition to the Far East. He succeeded in getting the consent of the Chinese government for the establishment of a French Protectorate over the two vassal states of China—Annam and Tonkin. During the next two decades the French Empire in Indo-China expanded further at the expense of two nations-China and Siam. France and Britain came to a settlement regarding their mutual spheres of influence over Siam in 1896. Three years earlier, France had established the union of Indo-China.

World War II and Liberation Movements Vietnam

During the World War II, Japan compelled the French Vichy Government to permit her to use Indo-China as a base for her military operations. In 1944, the American forces aided by the Chinese forced the Japanese to retreat and that was how France regained her colony of Indo-China. However, her troubles were not yet over in this part of the world. The success of Japan in this part of the world during the war inspired a group of revolutionaries called the Vietminhs. Their great leader was Ho Chi Minh. He started a national movement to liberate the area held by France. The French-controlled puppet government led by Bao Dai in Annam was toppled and Ho Chi Minh installed an independent Republic of Vietnam. Subsequently, the French reestablished their control over the northern cities held by the Vietminh forces. But the Vietminh forces led by Ho Chi Minh launched a long guerilla warfare to expel the French despite the stiff resistance offered by 400,000 French-troops. The war seemed unending and terribly expensive for the French who had no hopes of winning. The climax came when the Vietminh forces captured the French stronghold of Dien Bien Phu in 1954. A settlement was arrived at the Geneva Conference, in 1954, that North Vietnam (separated by 17th parallel) should be under the control of the Vietminh and South Vietnam to be under the Bao Dai government temporarily pending the following election for the whole country, in 1956. France set up independent monarchies in Cambodia Laos whose territorial integrity and sovereignty were to be respected by all countries as per the Geneva agreement.

Bao Dai became unpopular and was forced to go into exile. He was succeeded by President Ngo Dinh Diem who had the full backing of the government of the United States. It may be noted that the U.S.A. was alarmed at the spread of communism in Southeast Asia and determined to contain it at all cost. The regime of Ngo Dinh Diem became extremely unpopular for its cruelty and corruption. He refused to hold elections in 1956 according to the Geneva agreement and in this he was supported by the U.S. government. Had elections been held, Ho Chi Minh would have undoubtedly won. Disgusted at the attitude of Ngo Dinh Diem, the nationalists in South Vietnam formed the National Liberation Front (NLF) and sought the assistance of the Vietminh forces to liberate the country. It exercised its control over certain areas in South Vietnam with the support of the people. The Diem's regime became very unpopular and he was murdered in 1963. The government of South Vietnam was led by weak military rulers who were supported by the United States Government. To prevent South Vietnam from falling into the hands of the Viet Cong (soldiers of the NLF), the American government carried on a proxy war. Presidents Johnson and Nixon got their feet dragged into this quagmire and unfortunately they could not perceive that the NLF supported by the Vietminh was waging a war of liberation. The Americans could not see the end of the tunnel and finally signed a peace agreement with the Hanoi government in January 1973. With the withdrawal of American advisers from South Vietnam, the Saigon government had no chances of survival. It fell into the hands of communist forces (North Vietnamese) in April 1975. A socialist republic was established on July 2, 1976 with Hanoi the Capital.

Thailand

During the second half of the nineteenth century, Siam (now Thailand) was flanked by two great powers—France and Britain. However, her king kept these two powers at bay. He kept them in good humour by granting economic concessions and also played one against the other. Both these powers came to an agreement regarding their spheres of influence in 1896. The Japanese overran this country during World War II. After the war she became a free nation and joined as a member of the UNO in 1946. Monarchy was established and Thailand joined the U.S. sponsored SEATO, for protection from the threats of her communist neighbours like China and Vietnam.

Indonesia

After World War II, the Indonesians in the islands of Java and Sumatra declared themselves free from the Dutch rule with the Japanese support and elected their own President, Sukarno. But the Dutch were not prepared to easily give up their former colony. They came with full force to take over it. But the Republican Indonesians were prepared to fight. The Dutch tried to pacify them by offering political concessions. After a period of lull which was followed by mutual distrust and recriminations, the Dutch tried to settle the issue of colonial status by force of arms. But their attempts were stiffly resisted and the matter came before the United Nations Organisation. The UNO sent its team of negotiators, and the Dutch were prepared to grant a kind of dominion status to Indonesia under the Dutch crown. But the Republicans had by then become so strong that they simply declared their total independence in 1950. The Dutch, however, retained the Western half of New Guinea (Western). It became a "bone of contention" between the Indonesians and the Dutch for about a decade. In 1963, the Dutch ceded this part of their empire also to Indonesia.

Nepal Ruled by King Mahendra

Like Thailand, Nepal, a Himalayan kingdom, had remained free from foreign domination. The ruling dynasty changed in 1951, and a Hindu ruler, King Mahendra, started governing the kingdom. He maintained cordial relations with the powerful neighbouring states like China and India.

INDIAN NATIONALISM

The origin of Indian nationalism is traced to the Great Uprising of 1857—an episode derisively described by the British historians as a mere 'Sepoy Mutiny'. Although it failed to achieve its objective, the consequences were far reaching. This episode in the history of our struggle for independence rudely shook the British Government and Queen Victoria admitted the omissions and commissions of the British East India Company. Her proclamation was followed by constitutional reforms. The Act of 1858 ended the Company's rule in India and the transfer of all of its powers to the British Crown. However, the brutal suppression of this uprising left too deep a scar on Indians to heal easily. It kept reminding them of their subjections to the whims of an alien rule.

The Legacy of the British Rule

The benefits of the British rule to the Indians were many. Among them the most important was the Western system of education. It transformed the very outlook of the middle class Indians. The educated middle class was influenced by the philosophy of the British liberals and they eagerly looked forward to the achievement of self-rule. The West's achievements in science and technology highly impressed the Indians. The spread of English language and literature was achieved through its adoption as a curriculum in schools and colleges. The learning of English not only enabled a person to get a job in the civil service but also provided a common platform for exchanging of ideas. The introduction of rail and road transport broke down the geographical barriers and enabled the Indians to travel to the nook and corner of India. The introduction of postal system during the time of Dalhousie was a great leap forward in the means of communication and was followed by the telegraph system. Another boon of the British to the Indians was the evolution of the administration of justice. The industrialisation of the country began slowly from the middle of the nineteenth century. Finally, the most splendid contribution of the British to the Indians was the organisation of an efficient system of administration. The rule of law brought all the Indians together on an equal footing and thereby made them conscious of their identity and equality.

Factors Responsible for the Rise of Nationalism

Despite these benefits, the Indians were not happy on account of what one may call as the British acts of omissions and commissions. India became a helpless victim of the British imperialism. Lord Lytton's Afghan war was expensive and without any justification. While famines ravaged this country taking a heavy toll, the Viceroy held a lavish Delhi Durbar for the native princes just remind them of their subjection to the British Queen. He further caused deep humiliation to the Indians by gagging their press. The Indians were prohibited from carrying weapons for self-protection. Indian economy had no chance to improve itself, particularly after wilful neglect of agriculture and denial of protection to the village industries. Educated unemployment rose to great height, and to make matters worse there was the flow of gold to Britain. The free trade policy adopted by the British administrators wrought its havoc upon Indian economy.

Pioneering work in reforming the Hindu religion and its caste-ridden society was taken up by Raja Ram Mohan Roy. He founded the Brahmo-Samaj with a view to cleanse the Hindu society and religion of evils, and for that purpose he advocated the abolition of the dreadful custom of "Sati" and the study of western science and literature. His Brahmo Samaj infused a sense of nationalism among its followers. Swami Dayanand Saraswati founded the 'Arya Samaj' (1875) with a view to bring about a cultural, social and political homogeneity among the Indians. His motto was 'India for the Indians'. He exercised a "great nationalising influence on his followers". Swami Vivekananda started the Ramakrishna Mission in memory of his master (Swami Ramakrishna Paramahamsa). A large number of its branches all over the world spread the teachings of Swami Ramakrishna. The Ramakrishna Mission set up many schools, colleges, hospitals, orphanages and dispensaries. Swami Vivekananda rendered great service to the cause of Hindu religion by explaining its subtleties to the westerners. The Prarthana Samaj and the Theosophical Society also contributed much to the awakening of self-respect and nationalism among the Indians. The Indians began to crave for emancipation from foreign rule.

Raja Ram Mohan Roy

The vernacular press in India played a dynamic role in awakening the masses and also identified the economic problems facing the country. It urged the British government to find solutions. It donned the garb of an adversary with its penchant for criticism. It took up the cause of the poor and the downtrodden and demanded justice. It enlightened the public on many political and economic issues and drew attention to the existence of many social evils in our country. It exposed the many acts of omissions and commissions of the British government and enlightened the public on how they would be affected.

The Illbert bill controversy at the time of Lord Ripon further alienated whatever sympathy the Indians had for the British. A chance to right the wrong and keep the Europeans on a footing of equality with the Indians was foiled by the British jingoists. To the educated Indians it appeared as though the goal of self-government was "not a luxury but a necessity". It did not take much time for the educated Indians to unite for the cause of self-government. A giant step in this direction was taken by Mr. Allan Octavian Hume, an ex-I.C.S. officer, when he laid the foundation of the Indian National Congress in 1885. Its first session was held at Bombay under the presidentship of W.C. Bannerjee. The Indian National Congress represented the Indian masses, and in due course of time attracted the cream of intellectuals in India. It tried to safeguard the interest of the Indians, and in its annual sessions, demanded representative bodies, separation of the executive and judicial functions, trial by jury, pruning of military expenditure, reduction of taxes, and simultaneous conducting of ICS examinations in England and India. Appropriate resolutions were passed for this purpose and submitted to the Government of India. During the formative years the Congress received encouraging response from government officials, but later on the government became suspicious.

Lord Curzon's Regime (1899-1905)

The Indian Councils Act of 1892 was passed but it failed to satisfy the Indian National Congress for the reason that instead of giving representative bodies it provided for consultative councils. All further demands of the Congress fell on deaf ears of the British government. The regime of Lord Curzon (1899-1905), despite its administrative efficiency, was detested by many Indians. Curzon believed in the 'Whiteman's burden theory' and hardly bothered to understand the national mood. His high-handed actions like the officialisation of the Calcutta University, and reducing the autonomy of Calcutta Corporation to a farce, evoked loud protests from Indians. His reactionary regime ended with the partition of Bengal which provoked the Indians as never before.

Rise of Extremism

The partition of Bengal had its impact on the Congress. It widened the rift between the Moderates and the Extremists which ultimately led the latter to leave the party itself at the annual session held at Surat in 1907. The extremists were led by Lokamanya Bal Gangadhar Tilak who called for a halt to the cringing attitude of the Congress in its dealing with the British government, and recommended an agitational approach to get the grievances of the Indians redressed. The movement against the partition of Bengal became strong and, in Bengal, it took the form of boycott of the British goods. The *Swadeshi* movement received a generous support from the Congress. In Maharashtra, Tilak whipped up a propaganda against the British misrule through his fiery speeches and writings. He published a paper, *Kesari*, which fanned national feelings. Tilak organised Ganesha festivals and trained the youth to prepare for great sacrifices. He was found guilty of sedition in the Rand murder case and sentenced to long imprisonment in Mandalay.

Further Developments

The Congress's demand for self-government was rejected by Lord Minto but constitutional changes were brought about by the Indian Councils Act of 1909 (popularly known as Morley-Minto Reforms). The worst feature of this Act was the introduction of the separate electorates, and it was a deliberate attempt on the part of the British not only to drive a wedge between the Hindus and the Muslims but also to take the wind out of the sail of the ongoing national movement. The Moderates in the Congress could not make much progress, and their stalwarts, Sir Pherozeshah Mehta and Gokhale died. There was a reconciliation between the Extremists and the Moderates in 1915. Tilak was released early on account of his ill-health. Shortly after his return from Mandalay prison, he joined Mrs Annie Besant in starting the Home Rule movement in 1915-16. The Home Rule movement was started on the model of Irish movement and it gathered the support of the public. Meanwhile, the Congress patched up its differences with the Muslim League (1913) and both demanded the British to grant self-government in 1916 (Lucknow Pact). It may be remembered that World War I was in its crucial stages, and in August 1917, Mr Montagu, the Secretary of State for India, declared his offer of responsible government. He came to India and conferred with the Indian Viceroy, Lord Chelmsford (1916-1921), about the necessity of ushering in another dose of political

Lokamanya Tilak

reforms. Their discussions ended with the publication of a report—Montagu Chelmsford Report—which formed the basis of the Government of India Act of 1919. During these years political unrest took a violent form, particularly in states like Bengal, U.P. and Punjab, and the British government resorted to repressive measures.

Jallianwala Bagh Tragedy

In April 1918 the Rowlatt committee submitted its report on the nature of criminal conspiracies against the British government. It suggested certain steps to stem the tide of violent activities by the revolutionaries. On the basis of its recommendations the British passed the Rowlatt Act which restricted the freedom of our people. The agitation against the enforcement of the Rowlatt Act by the British spread everywhere. One such peaceful protest held in the Jallianwala Bagh near Amritsar met with unusual and unexpected British brutality. General Dyer, the British Police Chief, ordered his constabulary to open fire on the innocent mob which had assembled to listen to their leaders. Hundreds were killed and the Punjab Governor continued to terrorise the people of that state with his wanton brutalities. The Jallianwala Bagh Tragedy deeply shocked the people of our country, and in protest, Rabindranath Tagore renounced his knighthood. The anti-British feelings rose to a very high pitch, and Gandhiji entered the political arena to take up cudgels for this country against the British.

GANDHIAN ERA

Born in Porbandar (Gujarat) on 2nd October, 1869, Mohandas Karamchand Gandhi went to London to qualify himself for the bar. He became a barrister-at-law and went to Natal (South Africa) for practising his profession. He was shocked at the racial discrimination practiced by the White South African government against the coloured and therefore took up cudgels against it for securing civil rights for the Indians. He adopted a novel approach—the *satyagraha*—to ventilate the grievances of the native Indians. After his struggle in South Africa he returned to India in 1915. From the early years of his political career he came under the influence of G.K. Gokhale whom he called his political guru. He launched his satyagraha movement for the abolition of the indenture system for recruiting Indian labourers for the other British colonies. The British yielded. He scored another victory against the British by means of satyagraha movement at Champaran when they agreed to redress the grievances of the Indigo cultivators. Another movement organised at Khaira also succeeded. So,

Gandhiji took up the cause of the poor and the downtrodden and struggled for their emancipation. He "brought politics from the drawing rooms of the educated middle class to the humble homes and fields of the peasantry". He supported the British in their war efforts but warned them that their tyranny in India—referring to Rowlatt Report—would be resisted at all cost. The Jallianwala Bagh tragedy shook his conviction regarding the British sense of justice and fairplay and he prepared himself to launch an epic struggle against the British misrule which he described as 'satan' (*shaitan*). With the backing of the Congress he launched the Non-cooperation movement (1920-22). He awakened the masses with his call to boycott courts, legislatures, educational institutions, British goods and the like and urged the Indian elite to discard British titles, if any. Gandhiji also extended his full support to the *Khilafat* movement organised by the Muslims in India in order to bring pressure upon England to change her policy towards the Turkish Sultan after the World War 1. He went to Gujarat and launched satyagraha (non-violent protest) at Bardoli in 1922. The constructive side of the Non-cooperation movement included the adoption of *swadeshi,* removal of untouchability and Hindu-Muslim amity. The Non-cooperation movement spread all over the country and the British administration was paralysed. The British government was in serious trouble and in its usual way resorted to repressive methods. The situation for the British worsened with the outbreak of a rebellion by the Moplahs in the Malabar region of Madras Presidency (1921) and the Akali movement in the Punjab (early 1920s). When the Non-cooperation movement, which was non-violent, turned violent resulting in the deaths of some police personnel in Chauri Chaura (U.P.), Gandhiji felt extremely sad and gave a call to halt this movement. He undertook a fast and later he was arrested and sent to prison. His followers, Motilal Nehru and C. R. Das, were disappointed at the cessation of this movement while it was in full swing. They formed a new party called the Swarajya Party. The 1919 Act came into force in 1921. In the ensuing elections, the Swarajya Party won some seats. Their motto was to wreck the constitution from within. Congress was disappointed with the Government of India Act (1919) since it neither provided a responsible government at the centre nor was Diarchy (government by two independent authorities) functioning satisfactorily in the provinces. Separate electorates were continued. Motilal recommended a revision of this Act and the British appointed the Muddiman committee for this purpose.

All-White Simon Commission Boycotted

In 1927, the British government appointed a committee under the chairmanship of Sir Simon to look into the working of the constitution provided by the Act of 1919 and suggest measures for improvement, if any. Accordingly, Sir Simon arrived with his team but the Congress boycotted this commission since it did not include a single Indian. But the Commission continued its work despite the boycott and submitted its report to the government in 1930. Meanwhile, the Congress took the initiative to convene an All-Party Conference at Delhi in 1928 to discuss the question of a new constitution for India which would give a fully responsible government. The All-Party Conference appointed Motilal Nehru as the chairman of the committee and asked him to submit a report. The Nehru Committee suggested that the Dominion status should be the political objective. The Congress gave an ultimatum to the British government to give a constitution based on the Nehru Report at a date not later than December 1929. As there was no serious response from the British side, the Congress declared that the Nehru Report had lapsed. In its Lahore session, it accepted Jawaharlal Nehru's resolution declaring that *poorna Swarajya* (total independence) be the goal. Under the presidentship of Jawaharlal Nehru Congress got ready to launch several movements—the boycott of central and state legislatures and the launching of the Civil Disobedience Movement. Gandhiji again assumed the leadership of the freedom struggle.

Gandhiji: Dandi March

Gandhiji's Dandi March

Gandhiji started his Civil Disobedience Movement with the famous 'Dandi March,' a journey undertaken from Sabarmati Ashram to the Dandi Beach by walk to break the salt law as a token of his protest against the imposition of tax on salt. The Dandi March attracted nation-wide attention and similar movements were started elsewhere also. Millions participated in this movement, and as usual, the British government resorted to oppressive methods. Gandhiji and other national leaders were arrested and sentenced to jail. Thousands of followers were also sent to prison. Congress boycotted the First Round Table Conference held in London in 1931. It was convened to discuss the future constitutional set-up in India.

The Gandhi-Irwin Pact (1931) and the Communal Award

The First Round Table Conference ended in failure mainly because the largest political party in India, the Indian National Congress, did not participate in it. So Lord Irwin, the Indian Viceroy, summoned Gandhiji undergoing prison-sentence and reached an agreement with him. As a part of the agreement, the British government released all the prisoners and withdrew the ordinances, and on his part, Gandhiji withdrew the Civil Disobedience Movement. Congress agreed to participate in the next Round Table Conference. It was a matter of pride for Congress that the British government recognised its "status and authority to speak for political India". Gandhiji attended the Second Round Table Conference as the sole representative of the Congress but found that the British statesmen were suspicious and conservative. He failed to convince the British regarding the right method to solve the communal problem. The attitude of the British was unhelpful and he returned to India very much disappointed. The British made the matter worse by announcing the 'Communal Award'. Seats in the legislatures were distributed on the basis of caste and creed. The Congress boycotted the Third Round Table Conference. On the basis of the discussions held in all the three conferences the British government prepared a White Paper which resulted in the legislation of the Government of India Act of 1935.

The Act of 1935 and the Origin of Pakistan Movement

The Government of India Act of 1935 provided autonomy to the British provinces and installed a dyarchy at the centre. The Congress was not happy at the way the Act sought to establish a federal set up. What it desired was a new constitution to be drafted by a truly representative Constituent Assembly. The Act came into force in 1937. Congress formed ministries in seven provinces (U.P., Bombay, Madras, C.P., Bihar, Orissa and NWFP) and joined the coalition ministries in Sind and Assam. The Muslim League failed to secure a majority in any province. Congress practically ruled the whole country with the exception of the Punjab and Bengal. However, its rule was a short-lived one. It may be noted that the Muslim League secured 110 seats out of the 482 Muslim seats in the eleven provinces and so peeved about it. As Congress had Hindu members in majority, the Muslim League began to have its own apprehensions at the prospect of Muslim minority coming under Congress rule in many states. It issued statements regarding the atrocities committed by the Hindus everywhere and about the bias of Congress Ministries.

Mohammed Ali Jinnah

Mr Jinnah, the leader of the Muslim League, began to advocate the theory that the Muslims in India constitute a separate nation and he began to work towards this end. The Muslim League held its session at Lahore in 1940, and under Jinnah's leadership, demanded a new homeland for the millions of Muslims living in the Punjab, NWFP, Kashmir, Sind and Baluchistan.

Muslim Poet, Mohammed Iqbal

It may be remembered that the idea of a new homeland for the Muslims in India was propagated by the famous Muslim Poet, Mohammed Iqbal, in 1930.

When the World War II broke out in 1939, the British Viceroy declared India's participation in it on the side of the British without even informing the Central Legislature or the Congress party. The Congress Party executive immediately ordered the Congress ministries in all the states to resign as a mark of protest. Accordingly, Congress Ministries resigned.

Jinnah

Failure of Cripps' Mission

In 1942, pressure mounted on the British government to bring about the end to the political stalemate. President Franklin Roosevelt made a fervent appeal to the British Prime Minister, Winston Churchill, to find a political solution to India's struggle for independence. The British Prime Minister dispatched Sir Stafford Cripps on a mission to India in 1942 to consult Indian leaders on certain constitutional proposals. If accepted by our leaders it would be implemented at a later date. As Cripps' proposal assumed a form of a promise of the British to be implemented after the war (incidentally, the fortunes of the British in the war were at its lowest ebb), Gandhiji aptly described Cripps' proposal as "a postdated cheque", and somebody added "on a crashing bank". Congress rejected Cripps' proposal and it was followed by the rejection of the Muslim League. The Muslim League reiterated its demand for a separate Muslim State, 'Pakistan'. Soon after the failure of Cripps' mission, war clouds began to hang over India also. The British had suffered a severe drubbing at the hands of the Germans, and the Japanese had conquered by March 1942 most of South-East Asia and were knocking at the doors of India. Gandhiji quite rightly felt that while Britain could not save herself from her enemies, there was no point in holding on to India. Japanese submarines began to move menacingly in the Bay of Bengal.

'Quit India' Movement (May, 1942)

So Gandhiji launched his greatest movement to drive the British out of India. He appealed to the good sense of the British to 'Quit India' as their presence in this country was inviting a Japanese invasion. Failing to get satisfactory response, he launched the greatest movement in his life, the 'Quit India' movement. The agitation spread all over the country and the British government was paralysed. Thousands were arrested including the leaders of Congress and houses had to be hired by the government to turn them into jails as all their prisons were full. Large scale violence followed after the arrest of Gandhiji and other leaders. Very much pained at the course of events, Gandhiji undertook a fast in February 1943. He was not released despite his illness. In the midst of this political turmoil, another great tragedy struck India. The devastating Bengal famine took a very heavy toll of lives. Gandhiji asked Jinnah to accept the formula put forward by Sri. C. Rajagopalachari on the issue of a separate state for Muslims. But Jinnah rejected this offer and it appeared that he wanted Pakistan on his own terms and conditions.

Wavell Plan and Simla Conference (1945)

In 1945, Wavell, the British Viceroy in India, put forward his plan to end the deadlock between the Congress and the Muslim League. But even this plan did not bring about amity between Congress and the Muslim League as the latter insisted on its right to nominate Muslim members to the Viceroy's Executive Council at the Simla Conference.

Subhas Chandra Bose and I.N.A.

The story of India's freedom struggle is not complete without a reference being made to the heroic saga of Subhas Chandra Bose. Subhas Bose left the I.C.S. and joined the Congress. But his differences with the Congress made him to leave it and form what is known as the Forward Bloc. As the British were watching his activities, he had to leave the country secretly. He reached Berlin and discussed the question of India's independence with the Nazis. Thereafter he went to the Japanese-occupied Malaya and Burma and organised the Indian National Army (I.N.A.) by recruiting the Indians there. His aim was to invade Indians with his I.N.A. and liberate her. It may be noted that the I.N.A. conquered Manipur and Aishevpur thus covering an area of 10,000 square miles. The I.N.A.'s attempt to liberate India failed and a number of I.N.A. soldiers were captured by the British. About this time, Subhas Bose was supposed to have died in an air-crash. A few of the I.N.A. soldiers like Shah Nawaz, Dhillon and Sehgal, had earlier deserted the British army and joined the I.N.A. They were tried by a court-martial and sentenced to death. Jawaharlal Nehru pleaded their case at the time of their trial. They were released.

Cabinet Mission (1946)

In 1945, the Labour Party came to power in England after the general elections. It was in favour of India's independence. The labour government sent to India a Cabinet Mission to solve the political deadlock. The members of the Mission held meetings with the leaders of political parties and thereafter held a conference in Simla. In this conference, the leaders of Congress and the League failed to arrive at a compromise. Despite the disagreement between two major political parties in India, the Mission submitted its own proposal or plan in May 1946. It rejected the demand for Pakistan for various reasons. It recommended a Union of India consisting of British and princely ruled states. It provided full autonomy to all the states and the Union was to deal with subjects like defence, foreign affairs, communications and revenue matters. It also provided for a Constituent Assembly to frame a new Constitution for India. After the promulgation of the new Constitution, the British government was to give up its powers of paramountcy. The Cabinet Mission urged the necessity of forming an Interim Government. At the Meerut session of Indian National Congress a resolution was passed urging the British to convene the Constituent Assembly for drafting a new constitution and declared India as an independent and sovereign republic.

Jawaharlal Nehru was invited by the Viceroy to form the Interim Government and he did so in September 1946. Although the Muslim League was called upon to join the ministry, it did not do so. However it changed its mind soon and agreed to join. The Muslim League was not happy at the turn of the events, that is the rejection of Pakistan by the

Cabinet Mission, and so plunged the country in chaos by fomenting communal riots. The Muslim League refused to join the Constituent Assembly. Prime Minister Attlee's statement on 20th February about British Government's definite intention to transfer power not later than June 1948 undermined the Cabinet Mission's insistence on the necessity of maintaining the unity of India. It encouraged the Muslim League to organise large scale disturbances in India. The Labour Party Government in Britain appointed Lord Mountbatten as the Viceroy

Jawaharlal Nehru

and he came forward with his plan to solve India's political problem. He convinced the Congress leaders of the inevitability of the partition of the country after explaining Jinnah's adamant stand. Accordingly, India was divided. India, that is Bharat, became free on 15 August 1947. Pakistan was born on 14th August 1947. The leaders of the Congress requested Lord Mountbatten to continue his work in India as the first Governor-General of Independent India. India's new Constitution came into force form January 26, 1950 and on that day she became a Sovereign Democratic Republic.

Lesson Review

1. Write a detailed note on any two of the following:
   (a) Nationalism in Iran; (b) Burmese Nationalism; (c) Anglo-Russian Convention; (d) Liberation movement in Indo-China; and (e) Indonesia's struggle for independence.
2. Describe the role of Gandhiji in India's struggle for independence.

40

EMERGENCE OF THE U.S. AS A WORLD POWER

Early Years of the New Republic and President Washington (1789-97)

Soon after the success in its war of independence, the colonies became states. They were united and governed as per the provisions of the articles of confederation. A Constitutional Convention was set up in 1787 to draft a new constitution for the U.S.A. It was headed by George Washington. Most leading revolutionaries and lawyers were associated in 1789 and came into force from that year. The Americans chose to remain under a republican form of government headed by an elected president for a fixed term. Washington's nomination became the obvious choice and he was chosen as the first president of the U.S.A. During the early years of the republic he paid attention to achieve a more perfect union of the states. The financial stability of the new republic also became his main concern. The Jay treaty was signed with Britain even though the interests of the country suffered. Financial stability of the country was brought about by Alexander Hamilton, secretary of the treasury, who introduced various economic reforms. The two-party system in America developed, with Hamilton favouring a strong federal union and Thomas Jefferson (Washington's Secretary of State) championing the cause of Anti-Federalism. The parties founded by them came to be known as the Federalist party and the Anti-Federalist party respectively. In modern United States, the Republican Party has adopted many principles of the Federalist Party, and the Democratic Party that of the Anti-Federalist Party. In the long run, the two-party system laid deep foundation for the smooth functioning of the democratic political system of the country.

Expansion of U.S. Territory
Under President Jefferson, the U.S.A. doubled the area of its then existing territory with the purchase of Louisiana territory from Napoleonic France.

The entire territory along the sides of the Mississippi cost the U.S.A a sum of $ 15,000,000. A large number of her citizens began to migrate as far as the Rocky mountains with the purpose of settling.

The War of 1812 and Its Results

When France and Britain were engaged in a conflict, the U.S. maintained her strict neutrality. Despite her observance of neutrality, her commercial interests with Europe suffered because of naval blockades. Failing to get Britain respect her rights on the seas, America fought a war with Britain, called the War of 1812. Neither party gained any final victory and subsequently both agreed to end their hostilities. The war had its telling effect on the U.S.A. The war infused a new sense of national unity and self-confidence. The Americans no longer depended upon Europe for improving their economy. The American government launched various schemes of its own to strengthen its economy. A protective tariff was introduced by an enactment of American Congress with a view to protect "infant industries". The westward movement accelerated fast and eleven more states were admitted into the Union. With improved means of transport and communication, America was poised to achieve new heights of prosperity. During the time of President Madison western Florida was annexed. In 1819, Spain sold Florida to the U.S.A. The west began to play an important role in the life of the country.

Monroe Doctrine

In the foreign policy area, the U.S. took the first step to stem further tide of European interference and colonisation of the American continents by enunciating what is called the Monroe doctrine. Embodied in a message sent to Congress, President Monroe (1817-25) warned European powers that their further interference in Spanish colonies and attempt at colonisation could be considered as unfriendly acts towards the U.S. His declaration implied the supremacy of the U.S.A. over the whole American subcontinent. Further his warning had salutary effect on European powers. A popular candidate of the west, Andrew Jackson, was chosen as President in 1829. He was a man of the masses and a "People's President". The 'Jacksonian Democracy' represented the fulfilment of some of the aspirations of a common man.

Controversial Issues which Divided the Nation

During the ensuing years what troubled the politicians and statesmen most was the spread of slavery. Whether the new states which desired to join the Union should be slave-free or slave was the question which raised heated controversy between the North and the South. Unfortunately, the northern and the southern states could not see eye to eye on many matters. Two crucial issues which divided the country and plunged it into civil war were the new tariff proposal before the congress and the question of slavery.

The North-South Differences
One may as well note how these two controversial issues affected the North and the South. The northern states were comparatively prosperous than the southern states due to rapid industrial progress and trade. The new tariff proposal helped them in accelerating their progress. However, this development was adversely affecting the South. The southern states were generally backward. They depended on agriculture. They imported many agricultural tools and other necessary products from abroad. If the new tariff bill became the law, the imported products would cost more. Secondly, the northerners shunned slavery and treated its existence as a blot on the fair name of their country. They were vehement in their argument that the newly formed states which desired to join the Union should be slave-free. The southerners did not like any of these arguments. To them, the slaves constituted a vital segment of their economy. Without slave-labour, agriculture in the south would suffer. The argument that slavery should not be permitted, constituted a great threat to the south. These controversial issues became highly politicised to such an extent that a civil war became inevitable. The Republican party was founded by the northerners who hated slavery and its extension to other territories.

Abraham Lincoln and Civil War (1861-65)
In the 1860 presidential election, Abraham Lincoln of the Republican Party was chosen president. The new president was an advocate of the abolition of slavery and soon after his election, the southern states seceded from the union. They formed a confederacy of their own to fight the union, and the nation plunged into a civil war. Since the South forced a war upon the Union, Abraham Lincoln made a proclamation for the emancipation of slaves. The war dragged on for four years, and at the end the South capitulated.

The civil war speeded up the economic revolution of the country on an unprecedented scale. The war efforts geared up the country's efficiency in industrial production. Between 1861 and 1890, the country made enormous strides of progress in the fields of agriculture and industries. In the South there was despair and a period of reconstruction began. It took a few decades for the southern states to recover from the wounds inflicted by the civil war and join the mainstream of national life.

Further Expansion of U.S.A

A few thousand Americans drifted towards Texas, then a part of Mexico, and settled there. The Texans opposed the dictates of Mexican government and thereafter the former revolted and declared their independence in 1836. Texas applied for admission into Union (U.S.) but had to wait for a number of years. In 1845 she got the admission and became a state of the U.S. The annexation of Texas by the U.S. directly led to a war with Mexico. After winning this war, the U.S.A. received a vast area lying towards the west of Rio Grande river. This included the territory of California. In an earlier development Britain, which disputed the claims of U.S. in the Oregon territory, submitted herself to a peaceful settlement in 1846. The Gadsden purchase was made by which some territory near the south-west coast became a part of the U.S. So by the middle of the 19th century, the U.S. had grown from the original thirteen states to nearly 48 states, and spread from the seaboard of the Atlantic in the East to the Pacific seacoast in the west. In 1867, fishing in the Bering Sea by the Americans necessitated the purchase of Alaska from Russia at a cost of $ 7,200,000.

American interests in Cuba developed during the last decade of the nineteenth century. The Spanish tyranny over the Cubans evoked great sympathy among the American public. Relations between Spain and the U.S. became strained, and an American ship, *Maine,* was blown up under mysterious circumstances in the harbour of Havana. Acting upon the wishes of American Congress, President Mickinley declared war on Spain in 1898. After the defeat of Spain, her government signed the treaty of Paris by which her colonial rule in Cuba ended. Furthermore, she surrendered Puerto Rico, Guam and the Philippines to the U.S. As a compensation to her territorial loss, Spain received from the U.S.A. a sum of twenty million dollars. It may be remembered that during the course of the war, the U.S. also occupied the Hawaii islands. Alaska and Hawaii became the last two states to join the U.S. So the American national flag has fifty stars, each star representing a state. During the early years of the present century, the U.S. built the Panama canal and extended its control over its zone. It was not until she joined World War I on the side of the Allies, that her enormous strength became evident to the world.

Lesson Review

1. Trace the factors which led to the rise of the U.S. as a world power.
2. Show on the map of the U.S. the territories annexed by the U.S. from time to time.

41
WORLD WAR I

The early years of the twentieth century witnessed uneasy calm in Europe. Nationalism was at its peak with peoples of various countries demanding a share in the running of their government. Monarchies were beset with a number of problems since people had taken to the path of agitations. The Russians were unhappy since the Czarist dictatorship had rendered little service to them. A revolution broke out in 1905 but it was easily suppressed.

Nowhere had nationalism risen to such monstrous proportion as in Germany. To a large extent Bismarck was responsible for this narrow outlook. He gave the Germans a strong feeling and extolled about their martial virtues. He played upon their pride and fears of a possible attack by France which was eager to take revenge. The Germans began to hate the French since it was from their quarter that they had to fear much. What would happen if France, supported by other major powers in Europe attack Germany? These fears kept the Germans united and national sentiments rose to a very high pitch. It was because of this national unity that Germany could achieve rapid strides of economic progress.

Bismarck's Plan to Keep France Isolated

The defeat of France, and her subsequent ceding of Alsace and part of Lorraine to Germany, had given great amount of joy to Bismarck. But this great statesman was not without worries. He realised that his newly created German Empire may have to run the risk of another war since France was crying hoarse with *revanche* (revenge). Therefore, he concentrated his attention on how best he could protect the German Empire. He sought to achieve this first, by keeping France politically isolated through diplomatic means and secondly, by binding other major European powers to Germany through military alliances. He took the first step in this direction by creating a league of the three emperors—of Russia, Austria and Germany—which existed till 1878. But after the Congress of Berlin (1878) Russia withdrew from the League and cleared the way for a military alliance between Austria and Germany (1879). In 1882, Italy joined this alliance thus making it into Triple Alliance. Italy had her own reasons for taking this drastic action. She was disappointed when France annexed Tunisia into her empire, a territory which she coveted most. She hoped to acquire more territories with the help of her new friends. Bismarck did not give up his hope of securing the alliance of Russia. He revived the league in 1881, and again in 1887 with the Reinsurance Treaty of three great powers—Russia, Austria and Germany. However, after his resignation, circumstances compelled Russia to drift from the German camp and join the opposite side.

While Bismarck's diplomatic manoeuvres politically isolated France, his successors did not show the same skill to achieve this objective. The new German emperor did not bother to improve his relations either with Russia or for that matter with Britain. The foreign policy of the new German emperor alarmed both Britain and France. It paved the way for reaching an understanding between them—*entente cordiale* in 1904—on how best to meet the threat posed by Germany to their interests. In 1907 Russia and Britain signed a convention by which they reached a broad understanding on the problems dividing them. It was not until England and Russia reached an understanding that the Triple *entente* was formed to contain German expansionism. So on the eve of the Great War, Europe remained divided into two military camps and also with daggers drawn against each other.

Colonial Rivalry Heightens Jealousies

Notwithstanding the above, there were other factors which exacerbated the feelings of hatred among the powers in the rival camps. Of them the colonial rivalry takes the first place. It may be remembered that the European powers had almost entered into a race for establishing colonies in Africa and Asia in the middle of the nineteenth century. Britain established the largest number of colonies in Africa followed by Belgium, France, Portugal, Spain and Holland. But Germany's entry into this race as a last-minute addition, and the way she set about establishing colonies covering millions of square miles of area, frightened the others. It looked as though Germany was upsetting the applecart of Britain.

Economic Imperialism of Britain and Germany

The late nineteenth century witnessed another peculiar phenomenon—the international trade rivalry, particularly in South America. The two giants, namely, Britain and Germany, clashed to capture the markets of South American Republics. It may be noted that for a considerable time Britain had enjoyed a monopoly, and the entry of Germany in South America seemed to threaten her interests. Cut-throat competition between German and British businessmen in these countries created intense hatred and paved the way for a conflict.

Armament Race

Another factor which seemed to disturb international peace was the race for armaments. Britain and France had every reason to be concerned with Germany's growing military strength. It appeared as though Germany was getting ready for a war. She began to increase her naval strength by constructing battle ships with a view to achieving parity with Britain. The Kiel Canal was dug more deeply so as to enable battleships to enter the inlet.

International Crises

A series of international crises kept the world on tenterhooks. Germany did not like Britain and France to partition north Africa among themselves. The French claim over Morocco was opposed by the German emperor. He came to Tangier and recognised the independence of Morocco and of her Sultan. He insisted that all powers should have equal opportunities of trade in that country. But France was adamant, and Germany sent a gunboat *Panther* to the Moroccan port of Agadir to force her opinion. War between France and Germany seemed imminent. However, this Agadir Crisis (July 1911) passed off peacefully.

Balkan Wars Created Tension

The Balkan wars kept the Near East of the European continent in a perpetual state of tension. The emergence of Serbia as a conspicuous power, and its dispute with Austria-Hungary over Bosnia and Herzegovina, made the matters worse. Serbia received moral support from her big neighbour, Russia. Serbia's hatred of Austria reached a high pitch since the latter had annexed Bosnia and Herzegovina into her empire—a territory inhabited mostly by the Serbs.

Murder of Crown Prince of Austria

The murder of Archduke Ferdinand (the crown prince of Austria) and his wife on the streets of the Bosnian capital, Sarajevo, by an unknown Serb engulfed the world into a great conflict.

Backed by Germany, Austria issued an ultimatum to Serbia for apprehending the criminals (who were hiding in Serbia) and handing them over to the Austrian authorities. Serbia rejected the ultimatum but sent a reply, and after the stipulated time, Austria attacked Serbia. Russia mobilised her troops to defend Serbia and warned Austria of serious consequences. Germany entered the arena to defend Austria and shortly all the powers in the hostile camps were automatically drawn into the war. Turkey and Bulgaria joined the war on the side of Germany. Italy left the triple alliance in 1915 and joined the opposite camp with the hope of recovering Italian territories under Austrian control.

Course of the War

The Great War was fought on three continents (Europe, Asia and Africa) with deadly weapons causing heavy toll of lives and large-scale destruction. Trench and tank warfare became common. The war was mostly fought on the continent of Europe. Germany derived all the advantages of an assailant. She won many battles. But her offensive was finally halted on the French soil when the British army came to France's rescue. The war continued for nearly four long years. The unrestricted submarine warfare launched by Germany to crush Britain hurt even the U.S.A. A number of ships belonging to the Allies were seized by the German navy, and a big passenger-liner *Lusitania* carrying hundreds of American and European passengers was sunk. The Germans also encouraged Mexico to attack the United States of America. All these factors led President Woodrow Wilson to urge American Congress to declare war on Germany. It may be remembered that about this time the Bolshevik Revolution broke out in Russia, and Lenin had signed a peace treaty (Brest-Litovsk) with Germany to mark the cessation of Russia's hostility. The entry of the U.S.A. into the Great War (1917) brightened the prospects of victory to the Allies. Subsequently, the Germans were pushed back and the German Emperor, Kaiser William II, lost hopes of winning the war. He abdicated his throne and fled to Holland. The German army signed the armistice agreement on November 11, 1918, to mark their surrender to the Allies. The allies of Germany had earlier suffered defeat at the hands of the *entente* powers.

Results

The Great War took a heavy toll of lives. It is roughly estimated that about ten million lives were lost and twenty million people must have been wounded. There was a large scale damage to civilian property. The war cost the people $200 billions. A large variety of deadly weapons such as incendiary bombs, grenades and poison-gas were used. Tanks, submarines and aircrafts were also used. Secondly, the Great War wrought its havoc on the economies of the participating countries. It may be remembered that about 25 nations had joined the Allies at the time of the outbreak of the war. The victors felt the devastating effects of the war even before its cessation. All these nations were burdened with huge debts. Germany and her allies suffered most since they had to pay heavy sums to the victorious

Allies as reparation debts. Thirdly, Germany was forced to sign the Treaty of Versailles on 28th June, 1919. It was a dictated peace, and Germany had by then become too weak even to protest. She lost everything. Austria-Hungary signed the Treaty of St. Germaine. Hungary signed the Treaty of Trianon with the Allies in 1920. Bulgaria had accepted the terms of the Treaty of Neuilly in 1919. Turkey, which sided with Germany during the war, signed the Treaty of Sèvres in 1920.

Treaty of Versailles—Its Humiliating Terms to Germany
As per the terms of the Treaty of Versailles, Germany lost Alsace and Lorraine to France, Eupen and Malmedy to Belgium. Schleswig to Denmark, some territory to Poland and agreed to Danzig city remaining free. She lost all her colonies to the victorious Allies. Her army was restricted to a force of 100,000 soldiers—just enough to maintain her severely depleted territory. Conscription in Germany had to be abolished. The Rhineland was demilitarised. Her naval strength was restricted to bare minimum, and the construction of battleships and submarines came to an end.

Germany was forced to accept the war guilt, and therefore, had to pay a very heavy sum—estimated at about 20 billion gold marks by 1932—as war indemnity to the Allies. The statesmen belonging to the victorious Allies paid lip-sympathy to Germany's plight and promised her that they would also eventually disarm.

Beneficial Results of World War I
Some of the beneficial results of the World War I included the destruction of the autocratic monarchies in Germany, Russia, Austria-Hungary and Turkey, and the birth of new states such as Poland, Czechoslovakia, Finland, Rumania and Yugoslavia in Europe. In Russia, the Czarist dictatorship came to an end after the outbreak of the Russian Revolution in 1917. As a matter of fact the First World War precipitated the outbreak of Russian Revolution. Nationalism in Europe witnessed its final triumph. The last, but not the least, outcome of the World War 1 was the emergence of the United States of America as a world power.

Lesson Review
1. Trace the causes of the World War I. Mention its results.
2. Write a short note on:
    (a) The Treaty of Versailles   (b) Wilson's 14 points

42
RUSSIAN REVOLUTION (1917)

One of the most important landmarks in the history of the world is the Russian Revolution. To understand the Russian Revolution of 1917 in proper perspective and dimension, a student has to comprehend the tyranny of the Russian Czars on the one hand and the appalling backwardness of that country and its subjects on the other. One may remember that Russia was once a landlocked country with no access to the sea. Most of her territory which lay in the north was uninhabitable due to extreme cold and barrenness of the soil. But in due course of time, and thanks to the services of Peter the Great and Queen Catherine, Russia extended her borders towards the Baltic region in the north-west and the Black Sea coast in the south. Some of her explorers went farther east and reached Siberia. Thus Russia gained large tracts of territories in northern Asia and her eastern border touched the Pacific Ocean. Although Russia became bulky in size due to constant acquisition of territories, she was not making progress to the extent her western counterparts did. In the Russian empire lived many European and Asiatic peoples speaking different languages and following customs of their own. For example, there were the Poles, Lithuanians, Latvians, Estonians, Finns, Germans, Swedes, Rumanians, Tartars, Mongols, Armenians, etc. In the European side of Russia, many followed the Orthodox Christianity. There were also many others who belonged to the Roman Catholic Church, the Protestant Church, Judaism and Islam. It was the autocracy of the Czars that held these different nationalities together.

The Czarist Autocrats
The reforms of the Czar, Peter the Great, and Czarina Catherine had not been able to help Russia to attain a standard of living comparable to that of any of the western European countries. For this the Russians had to be blamed since they remained illiterate, ignorant and pitiably poor. Besides, Russia had no middle class worth the name that could take up the leadership of organising a revolution as in the case of France in 1789.

Adding to their miseries, they inherited a political system which did little to alleviate their sufferings. The Russian Czars enjoyed unlimited authority. This autocracy was supported by the nobles on the one hand and the church on the other. The nobles enjoyed all privileges and power. They occupied all key positions in the administration. They owned large estates. The Russian Orthodox church was fully controlled by the Czar and the priests acted as his agents. With two most powerful institutions backing the Czar it is no wonder that he became the "Autocrat of all the Russians". Czar Alexander I (1801-25) began his regime as a liberal but was later influenced by the staunch reactionary, Metternich. So he could do little to reform his administration. Czar Nicholas I (1825-55) had no sympathy for western liberalism and crushed revolts at home and also in Poland. He resorted to repressive measures such as the censorship of the press and letting loose of police brutalities. When there was a revolt in Poland in 1830 he withdrew their constitution and appointed cruel Russian officials to look after that country. He joined the rulers of Austria and Prussia in his fight against liberalism which was spreading to many parts of central Europe. In 1849 he helped the Austrian ruler to quell the people's revolt in Hungary.

Czar Alexander II (1855-1881)
The defeat of the Russians in the Crimean War proved that the Czarist autocracy was no match for industrial nations like Britain and France. When Nicholas I died in the midst of the Crimean War, his son, Alexander II, came to power (1855-1881). He is described as the "Reforming Tsar". He signed the peace treaty to end the Crimean War (1856) and introduced liberal reforms. He gave the Poles the right to self-government. One of the most important reforms that he carried out in his country was the liberation of millions of serfs. In 1861 he drew up a programme by which the serfs became free and owned plots of agricultural land. However, they were made to pay sums of money every year to compensate the landlord for the loss of his land. His reforming zeal annoyed the nobles who warned him about the dangers entailing his liberal reforms. The Czar realised this during the latter half of his reign when he was confronted by a series of revolts. The Poles staged a new revolt in 1863 and it had to be crushed. After that the Czar lost much interest in reforms and started his reactionary rule. The change in the Czar's attitude disappointed many young and educated men. They came under the influence of radical ideas. They resorted to violence with the hope that the Czar would relent. However, the Czarist tyranny continued. Many officials were killed by the terrorists and a wave

of oppression began. Even the Czar was not spared. He was assassinated in 1881.

Reactionary Rule of Alexander III (1881-1894)

Alexander III became the ruler of Russia in 1881. To avenge his father's murder, he let loose the engine of oppression. He tightened the press censorship and ordered arrest of all suspected persons who opposed his rule. He adopted a plan called "Russification" which, among other things, included pure loyalty to the Czarist regime. "One Czar, one church, one language" became the slogan of the day. Educational institutions were supervised by Russian officials and harsh penalties were inflicted on those who criticised the government. In these circumstances, no opposition to the autocratic rule of the Czar was possible and so many young men joined radical parties which preached terrorism. The Nihilists were the first to play the role of striking terror by killing the agents and officials of the Russian Czar. The government hunted them down ruthlessly. Those caught were summarily executed. Czar Alexander III encouraged a movement called "Pan-Slavism" which aimed at encouraging nationalism in the Balkan countries where Slavic people lived. Russia was looked upon by the Slavs of these countries as their 'big brother'. The Pan-Slav movement became handy and served as a means to expand the Russian influence in the Balkan countries.

Industrialisation

At the close of the nineteenth century, the Russian population had doubled and her economic conditions turned from bad to worse. To solve some of the major economic problems such as unemployment and poverty, the Czarist government launched a new programme of industrialisation. The government borrowed large sums of money from the industrially advanced European countries and the U.S.A. The industrialisation of Russia which began in the late 1870s no doubt resulted in the employment of many and the development of modern industry. However, in the long run, it created other serious problems such as exploitation of labour and bad living conditions.

Reign of Czar Nicholas II (1894-1917)

Despite the progress achieved in the construction of railroads, introduction of new industries, and tapping of her natural resources, Russia remained as feudal as she was at the beginning of the nineteenth century. The conditions of the working class remained as hopeless as ever. The government headed by Czar Nicholas II (1894-1917) continued to remain as oppressive as the earlier ones. The common people began to hate him and his notorious minister, Prince Rasputin. The latter was the devil personified and cast his evil spell on the Czar and the Czarina. Popular discontentment rose to a new height when Russia was defeated by a tiny Asiatic country, Japan, in the Russo-Japanese war (1904-1905). The Czarist government stood exposed for its ineptitude at the way the Russians suffered a humiliating defeat and signed a disgraceful treaty with Japan. In the wake of this defeat a large number of secret revolutionary parties sprang up. The Social Democratic Party was most radical in its character. The Social Democrats turned to catch the attention of industrial workers in Russian cities and their moral mentor was Karl Marx.

1905 Russian Revolution

The disastrous defeat in the Far East culminated in the outbreak of riots in the cities and district towns. The Russian peasants rose in revolt and burnt the homes of their rich landlords. In the meanwhile, the people marched in the streets of the capital to the royal palace to submit a petition containing their grievances but the Czar was in no mood to entertain them. The royal guards opened fire and hundreds were killed. This horrible incident sent a wave of shock throughout the country. The news of the death of hundreds of Russians provoked the workers in the cities to go on a general strike. The industrial workers' strike spread throughout the country and the Czarist government became seriously concerned with the worsening crisis. The Czar was frightened at the halting of the country's wheels of progress and finally yielded. He bowed to the demands of the common people and introduced many reforms such as the freedom of press, speech and assembly. He recognised the trade unions and cancelled arrears of land payments by the peasants. However, the most important step that he took was the promise to hold elections for the Duma (Russian Parliament). But soon after the royal troops returned from the Far East the Czar began his oppressive rule. The Duma demanded liberal reforms and an end to royal tyranny. It was dissolved. The next one which met made a similar demand and it also suffered the same fate. The Czar revised the election rules in such a way that only the loyal upper class representatives were voted to power. The new Duma meekly submitted to the wishes of the Czar. Thus, the revolution of 1905 failed. His autocratic rule over his unhappy subjects continued as ever before.

The entry of Russia into World War I was an act of crowning folly on the part of the Czar. The country was hardly prepared for war of such magnitude and against such a formidable enemy like Germany. The war weary Russian soldiers could hardly make any progress on the war front. Thousands of ill-equipped and untrained peasants were sent to the war front only to get killed by the highly trained German troops.

Downfall of Czar Nicholas, March 1917, and Provisional Government
Large scale desertions by soldiers and the incompetence of the Russian commanders brought disgrace to the country. The workers in Russia went on strike. Large scale uprisings in all the big cities and towns perturbed the Czar. There was the Hunger March in the capital and the Czar ordered his troops to open fire on them. But the soldiers refused to obey their officers and joined the revolutionaries in hoisting the Red Flag. The Czar was forced to abdicate (March 1917). He, his wife and a number of nobles were killed. The Duma formed a provisional government. The provisional government was headed by a moderate social revolutionary called Alexander Karensky who introduced a number of reforms. But these reforms did not please the radical groups and they soon accused the government of protecting the interests of the bourgeoisie and upper classes instead of the working and lower classes. They set up Soviet councils for workers and soldiers in Petrograd and other important towns. Their next step was to convene an All Russian Congress of Soviets at the capital.

Karensky's Menshevik Government Not Popular
The provisional government was unable to provide radical solutions to some of the acute problems such as the food shortage, redistribution of lands among peasants and unemployment. Furthermore, it wanted to vigorously pursue the war in spite of numerous setbacks. As such, its continuance was abhorred by many and they looked forward to its overthrow by the Bolsheviks whose radical programme looked very promising.

Vladimir Lenin (1870-1924) and Bolshevik Revolution
(November 7, 1917)

When the position of the Menshevik government weakened under the leadership of Karensky and the defeat of Russia at the war seemed imminent, the Bolsheviks under Lenin took full advantage to overthrow this government. Lenin was the son of a school inspector. His life was rudely disturbed when his brother was executed for making an attempt to assassinate the Czar. Lenin became a revolutionary. The Czarist police finally

Lenin

caught up with him. He was arrested and sent to far off Siberia. He escaped from Siberia and became a political exile in Switzerland. It was in 1903 that he became the leader of a more extremist revolutionary group called the Bolshevik party. When Karensky's fall seemed imminent, despite the support he received from the Western countries, Lenin secretly travelled through Germany in a sealed train and entered Russia in April 1917. After setting foot on his native soil he was joined by his trusted lieutenants, Leon Trotsky and Joseph Stalin. They got the support of the Soviet councils of workmen and soldiers. The Bolsheviks under Lenin promised to people "Peace, Land, Bread." It had a great appeal particularly for soldiers, poor peasants and city workers. Being a master tactician and strategist, Lenin made careful preparation for a few months to bring about the downfall of the Menshevik government. He struck on November 7, 1917 which resulted in the fall of the provisional government of Karensky. Lenin established a Soviet Republic (workers' state) and made peace with Germany by signing the Treaty of Brest-Litovsk in 1918. His job of consolidating the Soviet Republic was made difficult by the rich landlords and nobles. They were supported by some of the Western countries. Leon Trotsky, the trusted colleague of Lenin, helped to destroy these counter-revolutionaries with the newly organised Red Guards. As the new leader of Russia, Lenin began to concentrate on the onerous task of building a new socialist order for his country.

Lenin's Early Measures

He came down heavily upon the large landowners and the capitalists and seized their properties. All land belonged to the people. It was distributed to the poor peasants. The factories were taken over by the government and handed over to the committee members elected by workers who were to run it. The banks were nationalised and the depositors lost their money. The new Bolshevik government declared that it would not pay the debts of the previous governments.

Lenin's early measures provoked the rich who created trouble. However, Lenin took steps to curb their opposition with the help of the newly created Red Army. In 1921 the country's economy fared no better than during the Czarist regime. The workers had not proven competent to run factories and so the industrial production dropped to a low level. The peasants started to hoard foodgrains with the hope of securing manufactured goods. The government seized their foodgrains to supply it to the urban population. A severe drought overwhelmed a large part of Russia and millions of people perished. The future of the Bolshevik government under Lenin looked bleak.

Lenin's New Economic Policy (1921-24)

It was at this critical juncture that he declared the implementation of the "New Economic Policy". The New Economic Policy (NEP for short) was the adoption of mixed economy. The Soviet government controlled major industries, trade and banking while the individuals were permitted to sell their foodgrains in the open market. They were also given the permits to open stores and small factories. The Soviet government entered into contracts with foreign governments and capitalists regarding the financing of industrial plants. Trade treaties were concluded with foreign nations. A stable currency was introduced. Russia's economic health improved with the adoption of public and private enterprises. A new constitution was drawn up in 1923.

Joseph Stalin (1879-1953)

Lenin's death in 1924 was followed by a ruthless struggle for power between the two contenders, Stalin and Trotsky. In the end, Joseph Stalin succeeded in eliminating his rival. He assumed charge as the leader of Russia. Subsequently, he became the dictator of Russia. Son of a poor cobbler in the province of Georgia, Stalin attended a seminary with a view to become a priest. As luck would have it, he took interest in the revolutionary doctrines. He was expelled and he became a revolutionary. He was arrested by the Czarist police and subsequently sent to Siberia. When the provisional government assumed power he was released. Subsequently, he joined the Bolshevik party and helped Lenin to organise the Bolshevik Revolution in November 1917. After the Bolshevik Revolution he became the general secretary of the Bolshevik (Communist) party. He made full use of his new position to build up his strength in the communist party. When Lenin died he drove his rival, Trotsky, into exile.

Russia's Five Year Plans

Stalin planned to make Russia an economic giant through the Five Year Plans. The first one commenced in 1928. The Five Year Plans mainly aimed at the modernisation of agriculture and rapid industrialisation. The former was sought to be achieved through large cooperative farms known as collectives which would adopt scientific methods of agriculture. The government would supply the necessary assistance such as modern machinery and scientific personnel. Rapid industrialisation was another hallmark of the Five Year Plan. The Russians had to suffer a great deal since Stalin was a hard task-master.

Russian Revolution (1917)

Lesson Review

1. Discuss briefly the causes of the Russian Revolution. Mention its results.
2. Sketch the role of Lenin in building a Socialist State in Russia.
3. Write a note on the contribution of Stalin to the modernisation of Russia.
4. Write a short note on: (a) New Economic Programme; (b) Treaty of Brest-Litovsk.

43
POST-WAR EUROPE

League of Nations (1919-1946)
One of the covenants of the Treaty of Versailles provided for the establishment of an international organisation to maintain peace and security in the world. The US President Wilson, the author of this idea, felt that such a system was badly needed if the world was to be made safe from future catastrophies. After he returned home he pleaded with the Senate to approve the Versailles treaty but it rejected it. So, the U.S.A. could not become a member of the League of Nations. Germany joined the League of Nations in 1926 and the Union of Soviet Socialist Republics (USSR) not until 1934. However, in 1933 Germany withdrew from the League, and the USSR was expelled from it in 1939. Without the membership of these three important nations, the League had no chance of achieving success. The League had fifty-eight member-nations on its rolls by the beginning of February 1935—the maximum it ever had.

Aims of the League
The League aimed at preventing wars through peaceful settlement of disputes among member-nations. Secondly, it desired to preserve and protect the independence of member-nations by promoting international understanding and co-operation.

Organs of the League
The League set upon itself the task of achieving the above aims through its organs—mainly the Assembly and the Council. To begin with, all those powers who worked for the defeat of Germany and her allies became members. A number of neutral powers also joined the League after receiving the invitation. Germany was not invited to become a member and U.S.A. and Russia also could not join. Each member-nation sent three representatives to the assembly but exercised only one vote. The assembly met from time to time to discuss general problems, and elected members to serve in the other organs.

The League's Council met three or four times in a year and discussed important matters relating to the maintenance of international peace and stability. It consisted of eight members (four Permanent and four non-Permanent members). The Council's important resolutions required the unanimous approval of all of its members to become effective. Whenever acts of aggression were committed by the member nations, the League recommended economic sanctions against them.

The League headquarters were located in Geneva (Switzerland). The members of the League elected the secretary-general to conduct the meetings of the League. Several assistants rendered help to him in conducting the meetings and maintaining the office. He was personally involved in arriving at the decisions the League had to take on many important matters.

The World Court consisted of fifteen judges who were mostly drawn from member-countries. Its headquarters were located at the Hague. The World Court heard appeals from member-countries regarding boundary disputes with their neighbours. The World Court disposed of many cases relating to boundary disputes and thus, prevented the parties from going to war. The decisions of the World Court were binding on both the parties relating to the dispute.

I.L.O

An International Labour Office was established for the purpose of drawing the attention of member-countries to the conditions of labourers and suggest improvements. The International Labour Office worked for improving the conditions of labourers in many countries. It recommended many measures to be adopted by member-countries for improving the welfare of labourers.

W.H.O

The World Health Organisation was founded to improve the standards of health enjoyed by the peoples of many countries. The W.H.O. began to fight malnutrition among children in many countries and also worked for the eradication of many contagious diseases such as malaria, cholera and small-pox. The affluent countries of Europe began to provide funds for research work undertaken by many scientists belonging to W.H.O.

The International Boundaries Commission

The League set up the International Boundaries Commission to adjudicate many boundary disputes brought before it by the member-nations. It rendered great assistance to the League in settling many border problems.

Achievements of the League

One of the major achievements of the League of Nations was that it averted wars for the next twenty years. Countries, large and small, frequently depended upon her for the settlement of disputes. The decisions taken by the League were respectfully obeyed by the member-nations. The following disputes were solved by the League of Nations:

(a) Dispute between Finland and Sweden (over Aland Islands in 1921), dispute between Germany and Poland over Silesia (1921), dispute between Greece and Bulgaria (1925), and dispute between Iraq and Turkey over Mosul oilfield (1926);

(b) It arbitrated in the dispute between Greece and Italy during the Corfu crisis and averted a possible war between Yugoslavia and Albania;

(c) The League successfully supervised the administration of the colonies coming under the Mandate system;

(d) It helped Austria, Hungary and Greece with economic aid and brought about the resettlement of the refugees. It also checked the spread of many diseases. It checked trafficking in slavery and narcotics.

Causes of Its Failure

The above achievements of the League paled into insignificance while it dealt with the real crux of the world problems. The big powers gave cooperation grudgingly to the League. The U.S.A. and Soviet Union remained outside the League of Nations. On many important matters, the League failed to secure the cooperation of big powers. More often than not, the big powers could not arrive at unanimous decisions.

The League had no military force of its own to enforce its decisions on erring member-nations when they flouted the international laws. Therefore, it was unable to prevent aggression committed by member-nations. Italy invaded Abyssinia and the League applied economic sanctions against her. The big powers were unable to go to the assistance of the League. In 1931, Japan invaded Manchuria and refused to withdraw her forces in spite of the League's order. When Japan was branded as aggressor, the Japanese delegate in the League of Nations walked out. Meanwhile, Germany began to rearm herself in 1935 and thereby violated one of the clauses of the Treaty of Versailles. She occupied the Rhineland in 1936 without bothering about the League's reprisals. The League could not act promptly when the Spanish Civil War started in 1936. The League remained helpless when a conflict arose between China and Japan. The

League also failed to bring about a satisfactory disarmament. When the Nazi Germany annexed Austria in 1938, the League could do little to assist that unfortunate nation. It may be said that the decline of the League of Nations began after the economic depression (1929). With the outbreak of the Second World War, the League died a natural death.

Lesson Review

1. Give a brief sketch of the structure of the League of Nations and mention its aims.
2. Write a note on the achievements of the League of Nations.
3. Trace the factors responsible for the failure of the League of Nations.

44
PEACE MOVEMENT IN EUROPE (1919-1939)

The establishment of the League of Nations for achieving international peace may be described as an important landmark in world history. Article 8 of the Covenant emphasised that the maintenance of peace rests upon a reduction of national armaments which should be consistent with the national safety. The task of bringing about a general disarmament among nations was entrusted to the League's Council. Germany was disarmed as a first step in the long way for the attainment of general disarmament among member-nations. Besides the League's Council's attempt to achieve disarmament, a number of other attempts were also made in this direction. One such attempt which became successful was the Washington Conference. It was held from November 12, 1921 to February 6, 1922. The initiative to hold such a conference came from President Harding of the U.S.A. following some feelers sent to him by Britain.

Washington Conference (1921-22)

A widespread fear of an arms race between the powers which defeated Germany and her allies culminated in a common demand for reaching an understanding. Britain sent a note to the U.S.A. that she should agree to a parity with the U.S.A. in the manufacture of armaments. This as well as the necessity to restrain Japan from future incursions into China made the U.S.A. to realise the necessity of holding an international conference for reaching an understanding and disarmament. Besides the U.S.A., Britain and Japan, the other powers which were invited to attend the conference were France, Italy, China, Belgium, Netherlands and Portugal. Although Russia was eager to attend the conference, she was not invited to join in. In an atmosphere of friendly nature a number of treaties and agreements were signed by the concerned members having specific purposes. The most noteworthy were, the Four Power Pact which included the U.S.A.,

Britain, Japan and France; the Five Power Naval Limitation Treaty and the Nine Power Treaty. In the Five Power Naval Limitation Treaty, the concerned powers, especially the U.S.A., Britain and Japan, agreed to maintain a shipping tonnage ratio of 5:5:3 respectively. In the Nine Power Treaty the powers including Japan agreed to respect the sovereignty and territorial integrity of China.

Efforts of the League

Meanwhile France was apprehensive and signed several treaties and agreements with her friendly neighbours as a protection from German invasion. The League's Council too made several efforts to bring about disarmament. It appointed a commission whose draft ran into rough weather though the fourth Assembly unanimously adopted the Treaty of Mutual Assistance in 1923. The fifth Assembly also worked hard and it approved a protocol for peaceful settlement of international disputes. Unfortunately, the Big Powers were reluctant to ratify. Thus the League's effort failed.

Locarno Pact

The German Foreign Minister Gustav Stresemann succeeded in convincing France about the necessity to arrive at agreements to lessen the tension, and at the insistence of France invited Italy, Belgium and Poland to attend a meeting in October 1925. The representatives of France, Britain, Italy Belgium, Czechoslovakia and Poland met at Locarno on a footing of equality.

45
EUROPE BETWEEN THE TWO WORLD WARS

As mentioned earlier, World War I had wrought havoc upon the economies of those who actively participated in it. Unemployment, inflation and food shortage were some of the burning problems faced by the victorious allies as well as the defeated powers. Unfortunately, the democratic governments in Europe were unable to face these challenges effectively. Corruption and nepotism became rampant and people suffered unbearable hardships. So the worsening conditions prevailing in all parts of Europe eroded the faith of the people in the efficacy of democratically elected governments. Therefore, people began to eagerly look forward to such a government, irrespective of its style of functioning, which would solve all their problems. They were eager to embrace communism or even dictatorship if their problems could be solved.

In Russia, the people rose in revolt against the Czar and established a government of the Moderate Socialists. However, even the reforms of the Moderate Socialists did not satisfy the common people. It was overthrown by the Bolsheviks under the leadership of Lenin. When Lenin came to power he introduced radical reforms (*see* Chapter on Russian Revolution).

Fascism in Italy

Post-War Conditions in Italy

As mentioned earlier (*see* the Chapter on the World War I), Italy changed sides—joined the Allies—in 1915 with the hope of gaining additional territories after the war. However, her hopes were dashed to the ground when the Paris Peace Conference turned down many of her demands for additional territories. She felt very much betrayed by the Allies. In addition to the deep frustration, her government was haunted by ever-growing problems of poverty, hunger, unemployment, disease and inflation. The post-war Italian government, was hardly in a position to cope with these serious problems. The Communists and the Socialists encouraged the people to revolt. Riots, strikes and conspiracies became the order of the day. The Italian parliamentary government was too weak to maintain law and order in the country. Italy, at that time, had the misfortune of having too many political parties which caused political instability. There were the extreme nationalists on the one side and the Socialists on the other who always attacked the government for its bunglings. So, between 1920 and 1922 the country was in deep chaos and there was always the "Red Threat."

Benito Mussolini (1883-1945) and the Rise of Fascism

It was during this period of imbroglio that Benito Mussolini assumed power. Two things helped him to rise from his humble position of an ill-provided son of a village blacksmith to that of a Dictator of Italy and these were, his "driving ambition, and a helpful and devoted mother." After a formal university education he entered public life as a socialist activist and a journalist. He suffered a prison sentence for his brazen attack on the government for its Libyan adventure. Subsequently, he became editor of the official Socialist newspaper, *Avanti! ("Forward!")*, and expressed his views freely and frankly. During the initial stages of the World War I, he opposed Italy's entry into the War. However, he changed his opinion soon and started writing articles in favour of Italy's intervention in the war. He had to resign from Avanti!, and was also expelled from the Socialist Party.

Mussolini

As a bold editor of another newspaper, *Il Popolo d'Italia* ("The People of Italy"), he strongly urged the Italian government to join the war on the side of the Allies. Subsequently, he served the cause of his country as a private during the war and was wounded. He was honourably discharged. After the war Mussolini denounced the socialists and communists as traitors and founded his own party called the National Fascist Party (PNF) in 1921. His party had strong leanings towards nationalism and totally rejected communism. Mussolini criticised the role of the Italian government at the Paris Peace Conference for not projecting the aspirations of the people of Italy. It was surprising for him that Italy could not secure the control of the eastern Adriatic Sea coast. He supported the extreme nationalists when they seized Fiume, and organised a large demonstration as a protest when the government decided to interfere. He made virulent attacks on the communists through the columns of his newspaper and gained a large number of supporters. When the "Red Threat" declined, the Fascist Party gained immense popularity. Factory owners and landlords gave large donations to the party. Unemployed veterans and youths became its active members and wore blackshirt uniforms and carried clubs everywhere. Mussolini gave orders to them to disturb the meetings of his enemies and wreck their newspaper offices. Their trade unions were smashed and the Italian officials remained as silent spectators to what was going on because they secretly admired Mussolini. Mussolini was later to claim that he saved Italy from the jaws of communism.

Mussolini tried to refurbish the image of his party by adopting a populistic programme with a view to securing popular support during elections. If his party assumed power, he declared, it would provide jobs to the unemployed, improve conditions of workers, offer lands to the landless peasants and protect private property and enterprise. He would work sincerely for establishing a strong and stable government in his country and also ensure her 'rightful place' among the great powers of the world. The election results of 1921 caused disappointment to Mussolini since the Fascist party could secure only a small number of seats in the Chamber of Deputies. As impatient as ever, he warned the government in September 1921 about the impending revolution if it does not mend its ways. When his demand for a fresh election went unheeded, he said, "either the government will be given to us or we shall seize it by marching on Rome". The Italian government hardly bothered to pay attention to his threat and therefore was taken aback when thousands of Blackshirts converged on Rome ("March on Rome", October 1922). The Italian cabinet thought of employing armed forces to meet the threat but King Victor Emmanuel III did not agree. He dismissed the government and invited Mussolini to form his ministry.

Mussolini's Dictatorship

Mussolini foisted his dictatorship on Italy gradually. He spread the doctrines of Fascism such as the deification of the State and the Ruler, absolute sovereignty of the State, denial of fundamental rights, insistence on the duties of the citizens, and unflinching loyalty of citizens to the State and the ruler. He asked the King to grant him emergency power for restoring law and order in Italy. He appointed his henchmen to the key-posts of the government and eliminated all opposition to his rule by means of terror and violence. He used the Blackshirts to influence voters. He gagged the press and subdued all his opponents. As a result of these Fascist methods, he won a majority of seats for his party in the parliament (1924 election). After assuming power, he made the Fascist party the only political party to function in Italy. He was popularly known as *Il Duce* (The Leader). During the 1929 election, he ensured that almost all the votes were cast in favour of his party. He took drastic steps to see that all opposition to him was eliminated.

The Lateran Treaty (1929) with the Pope

Mussolini realised that his government needed the support of the common people, a majority of whom were staunch Catholics. Therefore, in order to please them his government negotiated a settlement with the Pope. It may be remembered that the Church and the State were not on good terms ever since the liberation of Rome (1870) from the control of the Pope. The Government at that time tried to compensate for his loss, but the Pope had rejected the same as unsatisfactory. Mussolini's government arrived at a settlement by which the Pope was recognised as the ruler of the Vatican city, and a large amount was paid to him as compensation for the lost territories. Catholicism was recognised as the official religion of the state and religious instructions were made compulsory in all schools. In return for these favours, the Pope recognised Mussolini's government as legitimate and agreed to appoint bishops after consulting the Italian government.

Measures to Improve Italian Economy

Italy's economic problems were turning from bad to worse, and they required drastic measures. The government controlled inflation by deeply slashing its expenditure. Thousands of officials in the bureaucracy were found to be redundant and therefore they were dismissed. The government also imposed heavy taxes on the rich. Strikes and lock-outs in the factories were outlawed. Mussolini created a climate of trust and confidence among the workers and proprietors of factories. He set up councils or corporations for each industry with the representatives of workers, employers and nominees of the Fascist party to improve production. He also fixed 8 hours-a-day as working time in factories, and compelled the factory-owners to contribute towards the life insurance of their employees. Hundreds of unemployed men were provided with jobs in the newly sponsored government undertakings or public works. The public works included the construction of rail-roads, merchant-marines, reforestation and reclamation works. Another campaign he launched was the "Battle of the Wheat", a programme to grow more food by adopting scientific methods of agriculture. Farmers who produced abundant food by adopting scientific methods were awarded prizes by the State. He introduced high tariff on imports to discourage traders from spending the State's meagre foreign earnings. However, to augment Italy's precious foreign currency reserves, he encouraged exports. In the course of a few years, Italy earned a lot from the tourist industry, thanks to the measures taken by Mussolini to make Italy attractive to the foreign tourists. So Mussolini's multi-pronged efforts to bring about the economic development of the country met with considerable success. Whatever success he achieved in improving the economy of his country was nullified by the advent of the 'Great Depression' of 1929. When his efforts to fight the depression failed miserably, he sought to achieve Italy's glory by means of war.

Mussolini's Foreign Policy and Its Failure

Mussolini sought his panacea for the ills of Italy from the two important doctrines of Fascism-nationalism and militarism. He whipped up enough propaganda to rouse his countrymen to reach great heights of glory through wars. It may be noted that ever since the Fascists came to power a compulsory military service had been introduced to all the youth in the country. Mussolini dreamt of building a great empire for Italy, similar to the one the Romans had built in ancient times, and thought of converting the Mediterranean Sea into *Mare nostrum* ('our sea'). He succeeded in acquiring the Dodecanese islands and the city of Fiume by signing the necessary treaties. He attacked Ethiopia, a backward country in Africa, for the reason that she had invaded the Italian colony of Somaliland. After a few months of fighting there, this country was conquered. The conquest of this African country added to his troubles since the League of Nations imposed economic sanctions against Italy. Furthermore, the conquest proved very expensive to a poor country like Italy. Despite these handicaps, the *Il Duce* carried forward his vigorous foreign policy to its logical end. In 1936, he sent Italian army to help Gen. Franco who was making strenuous efforts to gain control over Spain. It took three years for Gen. Franco to succeed, but Italy's help to him proved very costly. About 1936, Mussolini concluded a treaty of friendship with Germany which was later converted into a military alliance in 1939. During the same year (April 1939) Mussolini conquered Albania, a small country in the Balkans. In 1940, Italy entered the World War II on the side of Germany and Japan with the hope of sharing the spoils of war soon after its successful conclusion. However, the war did not go well for Italy. Her attempts to conquer Egypt and Greece during the war were foiled by the Allies. Italian armies failed to win a single battle and her defeat seemed imminent. She lost all her African colonies, and in 1943, the Allies launched their attack on Sicily and later the peninsula. Unable to resist the Allied invasions, the Fascists turned their wrath on their leader and deposed him. Mussolini escaped from southern Italy, and with the help of the Germans, set up a puppet government in the north. But when Germany was defeated, Mussolini tried to escape. He was caught and executed by Italian partisans at Giulino di Mezzegra (Como province of Italy) in April 1945. It may be noted that the Italian government led by the King ceased hostilities with the Allies and signed an armistice agreement in September 1943. But the German forces in northern Italy continued their fight.

Spanish Civil War (1936–39)

The Spanish monarchy was in trouble before the outbreak of the World War II. King Alphonso XIII was forced to flee in 1931 following a rebellion. A republican government was set up which too failed to control the political situation in the country. The rebels formed a "popular front" and fought the 1936 elections. Since no party gained a clear majority, the country was again plunged into a civil war. In the meantime, a number of military generals were dismissed by the ad hoc president for their undesirable activities. One of those generals was Francisco Franco who participated actively in the civil war. He went into exile, and subsequently became the leader of Spanish Morocco. He established a rebel government after forming Falangist Party.

General Franco obtained the support of Fascist Italy and Nazi Germany (both anti-communist), and moved on to Spain to crush his enemies in 1939. He became *El Caudillo* (the undisputed leader) before the outbreak of World War II. He sympathised with axis powers, but remained neutral during the war. Russia suffered a setback in Spain because the communists did not gain control. Britain and France did not like General Franco because they considered him a pariah. However, after the war his government was given due recognition by the allied powers. Franco gained legitimacy as the leader of Spain because he was anti-communist. During the Cold War he always supported the west. In the 1950s and 1960s, Spain made great economic progress. In 1969, Franco appointed Prince Juan Carlos as his would-be successor. He restored monarchy eventually, but became a permanent regent of the Spanish Crown till his death in 1975.

Lesson Review

1. Describe the causes for the rise of Fascism in Italy. What were its early achievements?
2. Trace the causes for the downfall of Mussolini.

46
GERMANY AND WORLD WAR II

The World War II was the direct outcome of the Nazi leader Adolf Hitler's ambition to dominate the whole world. With surprising rapidity Germany rose from the ashes to defy the world in 1939.

Weimar Republic
After signing the Treaty of Versailles, the Allies permitted Germany to have a Republic. It was called the Weimar Republic which lasted fourteen years. But the new Republic had no strength left to tackle effectively some of the serious economic problems the country was facing. Those problems included inflation, unemployment and food shortage; to this was added the burden of reparation debts to the allies. More than all, the nation was forced to submit to the most humiliating treaty in world history. The Germans never forgave their government for signing this most disgraceful treaty. There followed mutual recriminations and the Republic had to face the threat of enemies from all sides. In 1923 Germany suffered the effects of worst inflation. It caused a huge loss of value to the German currency.

Difficulties of Germany and the Rise of Adolf Hitler
Despite the early difficulties, Germany was able to make a rapid economic recovery due to the efforts of the statesman, Gustav Stresemann, who was the Chancellor (1923) and Foreign Minister (1923-1929) of the Weimar Republic. But this recovery proved to be short-lived, as Europe was overtaken by the Great Depression (1929). Foreign investors and German businessmen lost all hopes of recovery and closed their companies. So millions of Germans were thrown out of jobs. The Germans suffered untold miseries during the early years of 1930s. It was under these circumstances that the Germans turned towards Communism. It appeared as though Communism would be able to avert a national catastrophe. But the National Socialists (Nazis) succeeded in weaning away millions of Germans from the path leading towards Communism. The Nazis held out a promise to the

Germany and World War II

Germans of a bright future. The leader of the Nazis at that time was young Adolf Hitler. Hitler was an Austrian by birth. He was a customs inspector's son. Hitler's childhood was not happy. His early career was full of struggles. He became a house decorator and was not very successful. In the meanwhile, World War I broke out. He enlisted himself in the German Army and fought. He received a decoration for outstanding bravery and got promotion as a corporal. He was wounded and was hospitalised. The defeat of Germany caused great disappointment to Hitler. He was unemployed for sometime and suffered great hardships. He organised a band of German youth in Munich and secretly worked for the overthrow of the Weimar Republic.

Nazi Party

Subsequently, Hitler's organisation came to be known as the National Socialist German Workers' Party (in short known as Nazi) which stood for extreme, nationalism combined with socialist philosophy. Hitler believed that the Germans were pure Aryans by blood and therefore fit to rule the whole world. In 1919 the Nazi Party was founded. Hitler condemned the Treaty of Versailles and demanded the rearming of Germany and the restoration of her colonies. He attacked the Jews in Germany saying that they were intruders and aliens. He called for a bold economic programme for the rapid recovery of German economy. Encouraged by Mussolini's success in Italy, Hitler attempted a *coup d'etat*. The *coup* failed and it resulted in his imprisonment in 1923. It was in prison that Hitler wrote *Mein Kampf* ("My Struggle") wherein he explained his plans and ideas to make Germany strong if he came to power. After his release he found that his party had not made much progress due to a short spell of economic recovery. But when Germany suffered from the effects of the Great Depression, the picture changed from one of ridicule to open admiration of the Nazi party by the Germans. The middle class and the wealthy, were afraid of the communists coming to power. Therefore, they supported the Nazi party. Thus the Nazi party which had a humble origin eventually became a most popular political party in Germany. Hitler got funds from the wealthy classes which enabled his party to become strong. He employed thousands of storm troopers for the Nazi propaganda. He held huge rallies where his "brownshirts" marched to the tunes of martial music followed by his

Hitler

thunderous speeches. Hitler stirred up the emotions of the Germans by condemning the Treaty of Versailles, heaped abuses on the allies for imposing it, and pledged that he would abrogate it if he came to power. He attacked the Jews in Germany as undesirable aliens in whose hands the wealth of Germany was concentrated. He promised to distribute lands to the landless peasants and employment to the unemployed. In the 1932 elections, the Nazis and the Communists increased their strength in the Reichstag. Unfortunately, these parties refused to cooperate with one another. Therefore, no stable government could be established. Chancellor after chancellor came to be appointed to cope with the deteriorating situation and all of them proved to be unequal to the task. So in a desperate mood, the German President Paul von Hindenburg appointed Adolf Hitler as the new chancellor of Germany in January 1933. Hitler ordered for the re-election (March 1933) to the Reichstag with the hope of making the communists unpopular in Germany. At the time of the election, he secretly ordered his henchmen to burn down the building housing the Reichstag and blamed the communists for this incident. He said that the communists do not have faith in German democracy. He declared a National Emergency and suspended the freedom of speech and press. All his efforts proved fruitless because the election results gave his party only a slender majority. However, the new Reichstag gave him dictatorial powers. After the death of President von Hindenburg in 1934, Hitler became the president as well as the chancellor. He eliminated his opponents with the help of his secret police, the *Gestapo*. Thousands of suspects were arrested, tortured and killed. Many others were sent to the concentration camps. He cancelled the civil liberties, abolished the free press and radio, and controlled all the educational institutions. He appointed Dr Goebbels as the minister of propaganda to propagate the achievements of the Third Reich (Nazi regime in Germany, 1933-1945). One of the most gruesome tragedies of the Nazi regime was the persecution, torture and slaughter of millions of Jews in Germany.

Foreign Policy of Nazi Germany

Hitler banned the trade unions and established State control over industry and labour. German economy made rapid recovery particularly after his decision to rearm Germany. The Disarmament Conference in 1933 failed to satisfy the German demand. Germany had demanded that the other powers should disarm as per the promise given to her at the time of the signing of the Treaty of Versailles. So Hitler denounced the Versailles treaty as one-sided and partial. Germany left the League of Nations. Hitler began to treat the Treaty of Versailles as a scrap of paper. He began to violate clause after clause of the treaty of Versailles. Italy and Japan also joined Germany with the hope of extending the borders of their respective empires. Their alliance came to be known as Berlin-Rome-Tokyo Axis. Germany got rearmed in 1935. She reoccupied the Rhineland in 1936. He increasingly carried on the propaganda that the Germans residing in the neighbouring countries were not treated well. It became an excuse for him to demand the territories of other countries where Germans lived. He set up his propaganda machine in Austria to make the Germans demand union with Germany. At the orders of Hitler, the Austrian Chancellor Engelbert Dollfuss was murdered in cold blood (July 25, 1934). In March 1938 Hitler ordered the German army to march across the borders and capture Vienna. He declared that Austria always wanted a merger with Germany. Britain and France protested at Hilter's aggression. In September 1938, Hitler turned his attention to the conquest of Sudetenland in Czechoslovakia which was a predominantly German-populated territory. The British and French prime ministers became nervous and met Hitler to dissuade him from conquering the Sudetenland. But Hitler was adamant and both the prime ministers agreed for its annexation with Germany. Before they agreed with Hitler they got a promise from him that he would not demand the territories of others. Hitler gave his consent no doubt but he had no wish to fulfil the promise. But Stalin, the prime minister of Russia, was angry at this betrayal. So he concluded a separate treaty with Hitler (non-aggression pact). In March 1939, German forces occupied the rest of Czechoslovakia. European statesmen kept their fingers crossed and spent restless nights. It appeared that Hitler wanted to conquer the whole world. Britain and France realised that Poland was in imminent danger and therefore, gave a guarantee to protect her from German aggression. But Hitler was not afraid of Britain and France and so German forces attacked Poland on September 1st 1939. Britain and France declared war on Germany on 3rd September 1939 in order to protect Poland. Thus World War II began in September 1939.

The Course of the World War II

Hitler adopted a new method called Blitzkrieg to defeat his enemies. The German troops and tanks attacked Poland. Poland surrendered to the Germans in September 1939. Russia annexed the eastern part of Poland according to the terms of the non-aggression pact with Germany. In the meanwhile, Russia also took a part of Finland. Hitler conquered Norway and Sweden in 1940. Holland and Belgium fell next after offering stiff resistance to the Germans. In June 1940, Hitler achieved his greatest victory—the surrender of France. Between August 1941 and April 1942, Hitler concentrated his attention on war with Britain (the Battle of Britain). However, he did not make much progress. As the concerted effort of Italian invasion of Greece and North Africa failed, Hitler diverted his attention to the conquest of the same by the German forces. Rumania, Bulgaria, Yugoslavia and Greece surrendered to the German forces one after the other. Hitler succeeded on the North African front due to a series of victories won by his ablest tank-commander, Gen. Rommel.

The German conquest of the Balkan countries was not liked by Stalin. He broke non-aggression pact with Germany and joined the allies. Hitler attacked Russia in June 1941 but failed to achieve his objective. He met the same fate as Napoleon had in 1812. Like his Battle of Britain, his Russian campaign also ended in miserable failure.

America's Entry into World War II

America maintained a strict neutrality which hurt Britain and France. The indifference of United States of America towards the war gradually changed. The Americans began to sympathise with Britain for waging a lone war against the brute force of the Germans. American Congress passed the Lend-Lease Act (March 1941) to give President F.D. Roosevelt the authority to supply weapons on a loan basis to Britain and her allies fighting the axis powers. The U.S.A. tried to restrain Japan from her military adventures in the Pacific by taking several measures such as the cancellation of the trade treaty and the freezing of Japanese assets in the U.S.A. Japan, under the premiership of General Tojo, ordered a surprise aerial attack on the Pearl Harbour where U.S. Pacific fleet had its base. The Pearl Harbour attack (December 7, 1941) was sudden and the U.S.A. was shocked. The U.S. government made up its mind to throw in her lot with Britain to defeat the axis powers. A formal declaration of war was made on the axis powers and a large number of South American states also joined the U.S.A. and Britain. In all, there were 49 nations waging a war with the axis powers. The axis partners got the support of Rumania, Hungary and Bulgaria.

Japanese and German Offensives (1942)

Japan took advantage of her initial thrust and quickly conquered countries of Southeast Asia like Thailand, Malaya, Burma and the Philippines. Germany attacked Russia again in the summer but faced disastrous defeat.

The late 1942 turned the tide in favour of the allies. Britain gained victories in Egypt and the U.S.A. landed its forces in North Africa to compel the Germans to retreat. Finally the Germans and the Italians surrendered in North Africa. The patriotic Russians fought heroically to defend their city,

Stalingrad, from falling into the hands of Germans. The Russians surrounded the Germans and compelled them to surrender. The Red Army marched forward for nearly two thousand miles to push back the Germans from their borders. During the summer of 1943, Russia began her offensives to liberate Poland, Baltic Republic and the Balkans from the German control. The allies of Germany, namely, Rumania, Bulgaria, Finland and Hungary were defeated one by one by the Russians. Inspired by their victories the Russians made rapid advance to conquer Germany. Meanwhile, Italy surrendered to the Allies in September 1943. In June 1944, the Allied army under the command of Gen. Eisenhower, landed on the beaches of Normandy and pushed forward to liberate France. From there it moved slowly but steadily to liberate Belgium and Netherlands from German control.

Germany Surrenders

The Germans fought the Battle of the Bulge along the frontier in a fresh bid to drive back the invaders. The British made their advance from Belgium to Germany from the north-western side. The Americans moved along the river Rhine into the very heartland of Germany. The Russians reached the outskirts of Berlin in 1945. Hitler committed suicide and Germany surrendered to the Allies in May 1945.

Pacific Theatre and Dropping of Atom Bombs on Japan

Gen. Douglas MacArthur checked the Japanese advance which commenced in May-June 1942 by heavy naval and aerial operations. The Americans started their offensive against Japan from August 1942 to liberate the islands in the south-west Pacific from Japanese control. But the Japanese resistance was strong. However, the American navy and air force destroyed the Japanese fleet. Japan was surrounded in February 1945 by the American forces but the Japanese refused to surrender. An ultimatum was given to Japan to surrender but the Japanese Government led by the military leaders refused to do so. On August 6, 1945, the city of Hiroshima was destroyed by the Americans after the dropping of an atom bomb. On August 9, the American forces dropped another atom bomb on Nagasaki. The Japanese forces surrendered to the Americans on September 2, 1945. It may by remembered that the Russian offensive on Japan began in Manchuria on 8th August 1945. The atom bomb dropped on Hiroshima killed about 80,000 Japanese instantaneously and destroyed the whole city.

The World War II (1939-1945) was more deadly than the earlier one. The use of nuclear weapons for the first time by a great power changed the very nature of war. The war ended in the overthrow of German, Italian, and Japanese dictatorships and imperialism. Millions of people were killed and millions wounded. The world was confronted with the dangers of a nuclear war. The U.S.A. and Russia emerged as great powers in the world. The war caused unimaginable hardships to the people of the world. The world economy was in doldrums. From the ashes of the war, the United Nations Organisation (U.N.O.) was born which gave a fresh hope of peace to the ailing mankind.

Lesson Review

1. Trace the factors responsible for the rise of Nazism in Germany.
2. Describe the events which led to the outbreak of World War II.
3. Write short notes on: (a) Russo-German Non-aggression Pact; (b) Surrender of Japan.

47
THE UNITED NATIONS

"That men do not learn very much from the lessons of History is the most important of all the lessons that history has to teach" was the comment of famous novelist Aldous Huxley on the two world wars fought in the 20th century. Even before the termination of the Second World War, Prime Minister Winston Churchill of Britain and President Roosevelt of the US agreed on certain principles on the basis of which an international institution would be built for maintaining peace and security for the post war period. Known as the "Atlantic Charter", this document was signed by 26 nations (fighting Axis powers)–their support for constituting "United Nations" (1942). As a followup, leaders of the US, UK, USSR and Nationalist China met in Moscow and Tehran with the intention of setting up of the United Nations. In the Dumbarton-Oaks Conference (1944), the leaders of the said countries prepared the actual plan which included the objectives, structure and manner of functioning of the supposed UN. On February 11, 1945, Roosevelt, Churchill and Stalin met at Yalta to establish the U.N. without further delay. Delegates from fifty nations met in San Francisco at the United Nations Conference on International Organization (April 25, 1945 - June 26, 1945) and drafted the United Nations Charter (containing 111 Articles) which was signed by them on June 26, 1945. The United Nations (UN) was born on October 24, 1945, after the Charter was ratified by the five permanent members—the United States, the United Kingdom, France, the Soviet Union and China—of the Security Council and most of the other signatories. Poland, which did not participate at the San Francisco Conference, was admitted as the fifty-first member on the day the UN came into existence. The headquarters of the U.N. was located in Paris, but later on shifted to New York. Today 193 nations have become members, attend the sessions of the General Assembly (mostly held in September of the year) and participate on issues concerning the general welfare of mankind. It is just like a World Parliament with community of nations accepting the principles of the U.N. Charter, the Universal Declaration of

Human Rights, and the Geneva Conventions. All the three influence the nations to follow international laws so as to make the world a better place to live in.

The principal organs of the United Nations are six, and they are the General Assembly, the Security Council, Trusteeship Council, the Economic Council, the International Court of Justice and the Secretariat.

The General Assembly
One hundred ninety three nations send their representatives to the General Assembly which meets once in a year (September), and each nation has one vote to exercise at the time of electing non-permanent members of the Security Council, or electing members to the Economic and Social Council or for that matter electing judges of the International Court (along with members of the Security Council). The General Assembly appoints the Secretary General (for a five year term), the High Commissioner of Refugees, and the Managing Director of the IMF. It passes the annual budget, considers the reports submitted by various agencies or committees, and passes resolutions with simple majority (on minor issues), or by two-thirds majority (in the case of important issues). The General Assembly elects its own President and vice-presidents every year. The Secretary - General may convene a special-session, if so desired by the Security Council. The General Assembly adopted the plan to bring about the states of Israel and Palestine (1947), took up the question of Apartheid in South Africa (1952), approved the internationally agreed principles on sea-bed and ocean-floor zones (1970,1982), and declared economic crisis in Africa (1984). It held special session at the time of Suez-canal crisis (1956) despite the veto in the Security Council.

The Security Council
It meets often. It is the most important organ of the UN and consists of five permanent members (the U.S., the U.K., Russia, France, and People's Republic of China), and ten non-permanent members with a two-year term. It hears complaints of member-states regarding threats of war and violations of peace-treaties, and takes immediate steps to resolve the issues. It tries to settle disputes among nations by arranging negotiations. It employs sanctions and economic military interventions to deter the aggressor. The five permanent members enjoy the power of exercising the veto, and all resolutions need their *concurrence* for passing. Concerned member-state or states may be invited when the issues are discussed (of course without voting rights). The council elects its president on rotation and whose term is only one month. In recent years, India, Germany, Japan and Brazil have

staked their claims to a permanent seat in the Council. Since the Gulf War I, the Security Council has not only restricted to peace-keeping role but also as a *peace-enforcer.*

Trusteeship Council

The UN Charter provided for Trusteeship system for the people of those territories who were unable to govern themselves. So they were entrusted to nations like France, U.K., USSR, China and the U.S. for temporary governance till such time they could be recognised as independent states or willing to join other independent states. The original trust territories held by these powers have become independent.

The Economic and Social Council

The UN was established not only for maintaining international peace and security in the world but also to undertake work for uplifting the common masses of developing countries. In fact the world is better off now because of the efforts of this Council. The Council consists of representatives of 54 nations whose main job is to promote better standard of living for the people. Matters like economic conditions, education, culture and health come under its purview. This Council has set up Regional Commissions such as the ECE (Economic Commission for Europe), ESCAP (Economic and Social Commission for Asia and the Pacific), ECA (Economic Commission for Africa), ECLAC (Economic Commission for Latin America), and ECWA (Economic Commission for West Asia), for the purpose of better governance and focus.

The International Court

It consists of 15 eminent judges drawn from different nations to hear appeals on disputes brought before it. Its headquarters is at Hague. All member-states who have signed the UN Charter have automatically become parties to the statutes of the court. The decisions of the court are binding on the parties to the dispute. For example, the International court settled the dispute between India and Pakistan over the Rann of Kutch. The General Assembly and the Security Council occasionally seek the opinion of the Court on legal matters. Two languages (the French and the English) out of the six official languages are used in the Court.

The Secretariat

The Secretariat happens to be the backbone of the UN. The offices of the UN are located in the same premises. The secretary general (Kofi Annan, a Ghanian) is elected by the General Assembly for a term of five years (tenure may be extended). Being the chief-executive officer, he is busy throughout the year. He conducts meetings of all the important bodies, maintains records, and publishes reports. He convenes the meetings of the Security Council to deal with important problems affecting world peace and security. He is ably assisted by his staff drawn from several countries, notably by deputy secretary-general, under secretary generals and assistant secretary-generals. The expenses for running the U.N. are shared by member-nations —bulk of the money coming from the U.S. Several agencies of the U.N. maintain their offices located in the capital cities across the world.

The United Nations renders assistance to the people of developed and developing countries in various ways. It is running 14 major programmes and fundings, especially for the people of developing countries. To name a few, there are the United Nations Development Programme (UNDP), the UN Fund For Population Activities (UNFPA), the United Nations Environment Programme (UNEP), and the United Nations International Children's Emergency Fund (UNICEF). This is not all. The UN provides relief to the refugees and disaster victims through its agencies like the United Nations High Commissioner for Refugees (UNHCR), the UN Disaster Relief Coordinator (UNDRO), and the UN Relief and Works Agency (UNRWA). The last one has provided assistance to Palestinian refugees. In 1993, the UN appointed a high commissioner for human rights.

Specialised Agencies

There are at present eighteen independent and specialised agencies working under the auspices of the UN Each has its own role cut out as can be made out from its nomenclature. Food and Agricultural Organization (FAO) at Rome sponsors world food programme to the needy developing countries its financial assistance. The International Bank for Reconstruction and Development (IBRD i.e. World Bank) offers financial assistance to developing countries. United Nations Educational Scientific and Cultural Organisation (UNESCO at Paris) offers assistance for the preservation of great monuments etc. The International Labour Organization (ILO at Geneva) brings about labour welfare. The World Health Organization WHO at Geneva) promotes health standards and engages in research for incurable diseases. Small pox was eradicated. The other agencies are the International Civil Aviation Organisation (ICAO), Universal Postal Union (UPU), the International Atomic Energy Agency (IAEA), the International Telecommunication Union (ITU), the World Meteorological Organisation (WMO), the United Nations Industrial Organisation (UNIDO), the International Development Association (IDA.. administered by the World

Bank), the International Finance Corporation (IFC, affiliated to the World Bank), the International Maritime Organisation (IMO), World Intellectual Property Organisation (WIPO), the International Fund for Agricultural Development (IFAD), and the World Trade Organisation (WTO). The last named has replaced the General Agreement on Tariffs and Trade (GATT) in 1995 which frames rules for member states engaging in international trade. With the backing of the Western countries, it is promoting globalisation. Its rules have favoured rich countries and multi-national or Transnational companies. Developing nations have joined the WTO for reaping certain 'comparative advantages'.

Achievements of the UN

Despite complex situations created by the Cold War, the UN could still maintain international peace and security. It was able to avert world war like situations at least on two occasions. The Suez canal crisis in 1956 would have blown into a full-fledged world war (France and U.K. pitted against Egypt) but for the intervention of the UN. The U.S. at that time supported the UN efforts for maintaining peace, and France and the U.K. had to make humiliating retreat. In 1962, the United nations played an important role in averting a nuclear war between the two super-powers over what is known as 'Cuban Missile Crisis'. The U.S.S.R. had to remove its missiles from Communist Cuba buckling under the U.S. threat of waging a nuclear war.

The efforts of United Nations met with varying degree of success on many issues relating to maintaining international peace and security. In the early years, the UN supported the end of the mandate system as well as colonial rule in many parts of the world. Syria and Lebanon which were semi-independent appealed to the UN in 1946 and achieved their independence. With the prodding of the UN the USSR had to withdraw its troops from Iran. The UN intervened in the dispute between India and Pakistan and arranged for ceasefire. The Dutch aggression against Indonesia compelled the non-aligned countries to appeal to the UN to intervene, and the latter brought about a ceasefire (1947). Eventually Indonesia became free from Dutch colonial rule.

After the birth of the state of Israel (1948), the Arab nations took up the cause of displaced Palestinians which resulted in an armed conflict. Israel won, but the UN had to intervene and arrange armistice agreement. For the first time in its history, the UN had to *militarily intervene* in vacating the aggression of North Korea (Communist) against the South (1950-53). The United Nations Emergency Force (UNEF) was sent to Egypt (following the Suez canal crisis) to act as a buffer between Israeli and Egyptian forces along the demarcated line. The UN cleared the Suez canal of all obstacles and paved way for shipping. In 1960, the newly independent state of Congo sought the help of the UN in averting a civil strife, and the U.N. had to send peace-keeping force. The armed conflict between the Greek Cypriots and the Turkish Cypriots in Cyprus in 1964 came to an end when the UN peace-keeping force intervened and arranged ceasefire. In 1971 Bahrain became independent nation after the UN settled the dispute between Iran and the U.K. The UN intervened in the Arab-Israeli war (known as Yom Kippur war) and arranged a ceasefire. Its peace-keeping force was stationed at Sinai and Golan Heights. Israeli army invaded southern Lebanon in 1978, and the UN had to move in with its Interim-Force for keeping peace. In 1988 the Iran-Iraq ended at the instance of the secretary general's appeal. Soon after the Gulf War I (1991), the Security Council of the UN applied economic sanctions on Iraq (the latter had failed to agree on vacating her forces from Kuwait). In October 1991, all the factions involved in the conflict of Kampuchea agreed for implementing peace plan of the UN. The UN sent observers to supervise a general election there in 1993.

While the efforts of the UN to maintain international peace appear to be sketchy, its contributions to other fields should not be ignored. It has taken upon itself the responsibility of making the world a better place to live in. Ever since its birth, the UN has been trying to find solutions to many global problems, problems which transcends the boundaries of sovereign nations.

The UN has been able to muster the support of its 14 major programmes and funds and 18 independent specialised agencies for achieving its various objectives. It was at the forefront in bringing about decolonisation, the ending of apartheid and other discriminations, rendering help to millions of refugees (Palestinians, Bangladeshis and so on), insisting on peaceful uses of atomic energy, highlighting the problem of population explosion, and championing human rights by asking members to sign the Human Rights convention. In the field of disarmament, it has made many member-states to sign the Non-Proliferation Treaty (1970). It has urged the nations not to damage the environment and set standards laid down in the Stockholm Conference in 1972. The Earth-Summit in Rio-de janeiro was held to highlight issues which endanger planet and how to solve them.

The economic institutions like the IMF, the World Bank and the WTO have helped developing nations to overcome major crises in their economies like the debt burdens etc., and persuaded the rich countries to remove trade restrictions imposed on the poor. The UNESCO has been doing good work in the preservation of culture and promotion of educational and scientific activities. The WHO has been doing splendid work in the eradication of common diseases affecting people. Smallpox was eradicated but Malaria still continues in some parts of the world. Research work in famous laboratories are undertaken to contain HIV-AIDS and SARS. Millions of neglected and malnourished children all over the world receive help from agencies run by the UNICEF. The UNDP and UNIDO have helped many developing nations in their ongoing projects for economic development. The UN specialised agencies are thus service-oriented. The UNCHR received Nobel Peace Prize twice in 1955 and 1981 for its excellent work, and the ILO the same in 1969.

The UN Failures

During the past decade, there has been an intense debate on the efficacy of the UN as an instrument for bringing peace and development. Critics point out that the UN has become a 'pawn' in the hands of the U.S., especially after the Gulf War. The Gulf War II has affirmed that the UN has become redundant, and it will meet the same fate like the League. A major failure of the UN has been in the field of disarmament. It has failed to force the nuclear-haves to destroy their nuclear stockpiles, and thereby rid the world of nuclear wars. Another major failure of the UN has been its inability to resolve the west Asian crisis. Israel had defied the UN Security resolutions number of times. The UN had been unable to prevent aggression against many countries by the big powers: Russia's aggression on Hungary (1956), on Czechoslovakia (1968), and Afghanistan (1978-79). It has not been able to settle disputes concerning Kashmir and the Palestine. It could not intervene in Vietnam and prevent U.S. bombings on civilians. It was marginalised during the Gulf Wars in recent years. It was unable to prevent genocides, particularly in Kampuchea. It could do little in Sri Lanka when there was civil war. Also in Afghanistan, after the exit of the Russian troops (1988). On the issue of human rights, it could do nothing in China, Myanmar and some countries in Africa and Latin America. Discriminations continue in the island of Fiji where democracy was laid to rest.

With big powers wielding their veto in the Security Council, we can hardly expect the UN to be effective. Unfortunately the UN Charter provides for the Veto power in the Security Council to be exercised by the Big Five Powers (Founders of the UN). There is a serious erosion in the decision-making powers of the UN in recent years, and the U.S. is mainly responsible. President Bush has rejected the Kyoto Protocol on climate change, defied the authority of International Criminal Court, violated WTO rules, and is going ahead with his pet project, i.e. the National Missile Defense System (NMD) in violation of the Anti-Ballistic Missile Treaty signed with Russia in 1972.

COLD WAR

Even before the people could heave a sigh of relief at the end of the World War II, there emerged what is called as the "cold war". It was not an armed conflict but an "armed truce". During the next four decades, the world was to witness an ideological and power conflict between the two super-powers—the United States and the U.S.S.R. The latter led by its dictator Joseph Stalin decided to dominate the world by spreading communism to Eastern Europe, Asia, Africa and Latin America. Eastern Europe and Mainland China witnessed the triumph of Communism. The U.S. under President Truman retaliated with measures to protect the "Free World". The Cold War dominated many aspects of international relations. It embittered the world peace with its characteristic features, such as mutual suspicion, propaganda, subversive activities, espionage, threats of war and forming of military alliances. Britain and the U.S. built up their network of espionage systems (the C.I.A. and M.I.5) while Russia had its secret service (KGB).

Russia violated the Yalta and Potsdam agreements by retaining her control over East Germany and setting up the "Berlin blockade". This provoked the Western allies and forced them to establish the North Atlantic Treaty Organisation (NATO) in 1949 with 12 Western nations.

The year 1949 was significant to Russia for it was in that year that the Chinese communists gained control over the mainland China (the Chinese Revolution of 1949) against the U.S. backed Nationalist government led by Chian-kai-shek. Secondly, Russia manufactured the atom bomb and thus broke the American nuclear monopoly. The next few years witnessed the Cold War reaching its peak, with armed conflict breaking out in Korea (1950-53), the enunciation "Dulles Doctrine", the establishment of Warsaw Pact (1955), the production of hydrogen bombs and their explosions by both the U.S. and Russia in 1952 and 1953 respectively. The United States Government formed another military alliance called SEATO in 1954 to defend free countries against the two communist giants — Russia and China. Eventually it got involved in the Vietnam War (1954-1973). After Stalin's death, the cold war did not stop, and Kruschev took tough stand in respect to the revolt of Hungarians and also the Anglo-French invasion of Egypt (the Suez canal crisis) in 1956. The nuclear arms race between the two super-powers continued when both of them produced Inter Continental Ballistic Missiles (ICBM). Russia launched its man-made satellite, 'Sputnik' to outer space and the U.S. became jealous. Their rivalry in space began.

America's misadventure called 'Bay of Pigs' attempted to overthrow communist rule of Cuban dictator Fidel Castro tarnished its image. Russia provided financial assistance and supplied missiles to Cuba. President Kennedy came to know that the missiles could easily strike U.S. territory and therefore threatened Russia with nuclear strikes if she did not withdraw them. Krushchev agreed and the world heaved a sigh of relief.

Nikita Krushchev believed in healthy competition between the communist and capitalist countries and rejected nuclear war as an option. His soft approach towards the west enraged Mao's China. Communism began to lose its strong hold in the wake of popular unrest in Eastern Europe. To avoid nuclear strikes, Russia and the U.S. signed the Antiballistic Missiles Treaty in 1972. It was followed by the Helsinki agreement in 1975. Incidentally, the Vietnam War also came to an end. Since the era of Krushchev, the 'Iron curtain' (Churchill's description of Communist Russia) began to lift. Russian invasion of Afghanistan (1979) and U.S. support to the Taliban intensified the Cold War. However, when the Russian troops withdrew from Afghanistan in 1989, the Cold War came to an end. It was the year when the Berlin wall was demolished thereby symbolising the end of Cold War. Some Nations which were caught in cross fires of the raging cold war decided to remain neutral and formed what is known as the Non-Aligned movement in 1961 (with 25 nations participating).

Lesson Review

1. Trace the events leading to the birth of the U.N. What are its aims?
2. Trace the achievements of the UN?
3. Write short notes on: (a) Atlantic Charter; (b) San Francisco Conference (c) Security Council.
4. Write any essay on the achievements and failures of the U.N.

48

TURKISH AND ARAB NATIONALISM

After World War I, the Paris Peace Conference stripped the Ottoman Empire of its Balkan and other territories with the result she became a small nation. However, the peacemakers failed to notice the rise of nationalism in Turkey. The Turkish National movement began during the early decades of the twentieth century. It was spearheaded by the 'Young Turks'. The Young Turks were alarmed at the growing weakness of their state and the subsequent loss of territories. They staged a bloodless revolt against their Sultan and compelled him to grant liberal constitution. After the war, the Turkish empire was reduced to a small size. When the Allies stripped her of her territory to create new nations, they hurt the feelings of the young Turks. Some of the territories of the Ottoman Empire were ceded to Greece on the Turkish mainland. However, when the Greeks decided to occupy the same land, the Turkish nationalist forces led by a young officer, Mustapha Kemal Pasha, drove them out. This young officer persuaded the Sultan to get the Treaty of Sèvres (August 10, 1920) revised in favour of Turkey. Mustapha Kemal Pasha subsequently deposed the Sultan and declared himself as the president of the Turkish Republic (1923–1938). He worked hard to modernise his nation by introducing a number of reforms. These reforms extended to the fields of educational system, religion, Turkish language, customs and manners. He gave the Turkish women equal rights and opportunities for their advancement. He did much to remove poverty, ignorance, feudal customs and illiteracy. He reorganised the Turkish armed forces and helped the nation to industrialise herself.

Nationalism in Egypt
After World War I, Egyptian nationalism rose to a high pitch. The nationalists demanded independence and withdrawal of British troops from their country. They frequently staged revolts against the British domination which sometimes resulted in bloodshed. Subsequently, Britain recognised the independence and sovereignty of Egypt and withdrew all her troops

from Egypt except in the Suez Canal zone. This was done as per the treaty signed in London in 1936. During World War II, Egypt remained neutral although her territory was occupied by the Allied army. After World War II, the Egyptian nationalists demanded the withdrawal of the British troops from their country. Britain withdrew from Egypt in 1954. Egypt's relations with Britain came under a heavy strain over the question of joint control of Sudan. Britain wanted to grant independence to Sudan much against the will of Egypt. Egypt desired to annex the territory of Sudan into her kingdom. A plebiscite was held in Sudan in 1955 and the Sudanese chose to remain independent. So Sudan was given independence in 1955 and her government was led by Abdulla Khalil.

President Nasser (1956–70)

Meanwhile, a few Egyptian Army officers led by Gen. Naguib overthrew the Egyptian King, Farouk, after a military *coup* in 1953. A republic was proclaimed and Gen. Naguib became the president. His regime was a short one for he was deposed by his clever rival, Gamal Abdel Nasser in 1954. President Nasser of Egypt became extremely popular since he symbolised the aspirations of all the Arabs in the Middle East. He forced the British troops to withdraw from guarding the Suez Canal zone in 1954. Under the leadership of President Nasser, Egypt remained a strictly neutral country. She did not join the side of Russia or America. Nasser improved the economy of Egypt by introducing several reforms. He was a socialist by his political leaning and desired to nationalise several key industries. One of his ambitions was to build the Aswan dam across the river Nile. U.S. refused to grant his request for a loan because Nasser decided to remain neutral in foreign relations. The American decision regarding the refusal to grant loan made Nasser angry. It led him to nationalise the British-French owned Suez Canal company. France and Britain launched a war against Egypt but failed to succeed since U.S. did not support them. As a first step towards uniting the Arab world, Nasser permitted Syria to join Egypt. The merger of these two countries took place on February 1, 1958. The new state was called as the United Arab Republic with Cairo as its capital. Unfortunately, the merger of Egypt and Syria did not survive. Syria got herself separated in 1961.

Syria and Lebanon

After the World War I the Turkish possessions in the Middle East mostly came under the control of Great Britain and France. They were governed as mandated territories by these two powers. Syrian nationalism met with a stiff resistance from France. The French government adopted repressive methods to suppress Syrian nationalism. The French also lost the sympathy of the Arabs by establishing an Arab-Christian state called Lebanon. The Syrian nationalists launched a long struggle for attaining independence. Finally, the French government was forced to grant liberal political concessions to Syria and they included a free election and the choosing of a Cabinet Government. After the fall of France in 1941, Syria and Lebanon gained independence. The French garrisons withdrew from both these countries in 1946. The people of Lebanon chose to form a republic and joined the Arab League in 1945. In 1958, President Nasser of Egypt launched a new national movement called the Pan-Arab-National movement for the maintenance of Arab unity against Israel. The Lebanese rose against their pro-western government and established a government of their own. The new Lebanese government sought economic assistance from the U.S. to save itself from chaos.

Iraq

Iraq is an oil-rich country in the Middle East. She was ruled by Britain as a mandated territory. The Iraqi nationalists staged a revolt against the British to gain independence. The British had established a monarchical form of government for sometime. The British ultimately granted independence to Iraq in 1932 but kept a military garrison there. Britain also retained the right to control Iraq's oil companies. But after several protests by the nationalists, Britain withdrew her troops from Iraq in 1935. In 1958, the regime of Nurias-Said became unpopular and the revolt led by Abdul Karim Kassem resulted in the overthrow and murder of the former. After that, Iraq was disturbed by revolts, murders and military *coups* in 1963.

Trans-Jordan

Britain ruled Trans-Jordan with an Arab population as a mandate. In 1928, Britain allowed self-government to the Jordanians due to heavy pressure. After World War II, Britain withdrew herself from this area. The Hashemite family came to power there and Jordan joined Iraq to form the Arab Federation. This was done to fight the union of Syria and Egypt (UAR) in 1958.

Saudi Arabia

King Hussein ruled over the small state of Hejaz. Unfortunately, he was not popular due to his servility to Britain. An Arab Chieftain, Abdul Aziz Ibn Saud (the leader of the Wahabis), extended his small kingdom and attacked Hejaz in 1925. King Hussein abdicated his throne in favour of his son but the latter was defeated and forced to go into exile. Abdul Aziz continued his conquest and in the course of time conquered all the tribal kingdoms of Arabia. He brought about the political unity of his enlarged kingdom and renamed it as Saudi Arabia in 1932. He became the richest ruler in the world due to the discovery of oil deposits in the country. After Ibn Saud's death, his son Saud, ascended the throne. Britain maintained friendly relations with Saudi Arabia and also with the small neighbouring kingdoms of Kuwait, Bahrain, UAE and Oman because they supplied oil.

Lesson Review

1. Write a short note on: (a) Turkish nationalism; (b) Independence of Egypt; (c) National movements in Syria, Lebanon, Iraq, Jordan and Saudi Arabia.

49

DECOLONISATION OF AFRICA (1956-62)

By decolonisation of Africa we mean the abandonment by the Western powers of their former colonies in Africa—a long process preceded by the nationalist struggles during the recent decades. The decolonisation of Africa may be said to be one of the most important post-war changes the world had witnessed. Colony after colony gained self-government as a first step from its respective master followed by complete independence. It may be remembered that each colony received complete independence only after a protracted struggle for freedom.

North Africa

Sudan

Its early history goes back to the days of ancient Egyptians of 4000 BC. In those days Sudan was known as Nubia, with the river Nile flowing from South to North. Off and on, the Egyptians were ruling over this country. Around 6th century AD, the Christian missionaries converted the blacks of this country. For the next six or seven centuries, a few black Christian kingdoms existed in the neighbourhood of the Muslim kingdoms of Egypt.

The Muslims of Egypt were migrating towards northern part of Sudan. Muhammad Ali Pasha, the Egyptian governor (*Wali*), conquered Northern Sudan in 1820. By 1874, Egypt conquered the whole of Sudan and supported the British in their attempt to exploit this country. Muhammad Ahmad al-Mahdi led a Muslim revolt against the British and captured Khartoum in 1885. He established an Islamic theocratic state of Sudan. The British defeated Al Mahdi in 1898 and ruled Egypt as well as Sudan simultaneously. The British adopted a 'Divide and Rule' policy (1924-1956) and governed Sudan as two separate territories— the Muslim North and the Christian South. The governments of Britain and Egypt signed a treaty in 1954 that paved the way for the Sudanese independence on 1st January 1956 (after 136 years of union with Egypt, and 55 years of direct British rule).

Ever since its independence the Muslim north and the Christian south had been at loggerheads. The country had experienced two civil wars (1955-1972 and 1983-2005). The Sudanese People's Liberation Army representing the three Christian districts of the south fought against the 12 northern Arab districts of Sudan. In 2005, the Comprehensive Peace Agreement (CPA) also known as Naivasha agreement, was signed between the Sudanese government and the Sudan People's Liberation Movement (SPLM). As a result of this long conflict and frequent famines, nearly 1.5 million people died. This conflict resulted in the displacement of nearly 4 million people. In January 2011, a referendum for south Sudanese independence was held, and an overwhelming majority (98.83%) voted in favour of independence. On 9th July, 2011 Republic of South Sudan gained independence, with Juba as its capital.

The peoples of Republic of Sudan (North Sudan) and Republic of South Sudan are extremely poor, and they suffer from severe famines and food shortages almost every year. The UN is doing its best to assist them. Currently, South Sudan is falling into a trap as a failed state, and is in frequent conflict with the north over the possession of the oil fields at the border. Its oil exports are also affected.

Independence of Tunisia

It may be noted that France had established her protectorate over Tunisia in 1881 after defeating its Sultan. In 1922 the people of Tunisia gained a political concession in the form of a Consultative Assembly. However, this assembly had been constituted in such a way that 50 per cent of the seats were occupied by the French nationals. When the French members dominated the assembly, the Nationalists protested and carried on their agitation under the leadership of Habib Bourguiba. As the nationalists became impatient and violent, the French government forced the Sultan and Habib Bourguiba into exile. The Neo-Destour party led by Bourguiba was proscribed. The struggle for freedom continued after World War II and it would have succeeded but for the opposition to it by the French colonists. In December 1952 the issue came up before the United Nations and it recommended bilateral negotiations between the disputed parties. In 1954 negotiations were started between the nationalists and the French Premier, Pierre-Mendes-France, which ended in the granting of self-government to this colony (1955). France granted independence to Tunisia in 1956 but retained the naval base of Bizarte. Habib Bourguiba became the president, and he negotiated for the acquisition of Bizarte without any success. Angered by the French attitude he forced the issue by recourse to armed action. In the end (1963), the French agreed to withdraw their forces from there if compensation was given. Accordingly, this territory was liberated in 1963.

Morocco

France had established a protectorate over Morocco in 1912 after a bitter rivalry with Germany and Britain. Spain also had established its control over the northern tip of Morocco. After the World War II, the tide of nationalism had swept through the whole of Northern Africa. The Sultan gave his unstinted support to the nationalist Istiqlal party. The French authorities let loose their engine of oppression following a political strike in 1952 which resulted in the killing of hundreds of persons. The Sultan who had given his support to the nationalists was forced to go into exile. The French appointed his meek uncle as the new ruler. But the nationalists made it almost impossible for the French to govern their country effectively. Therefore, the French government was forced to invite the exiled Sultan, Mohammed Ben Yousef, in 1955 on account of the international pressure brought through the UN. In 1956 the French granted independence to Morocco. After an agreement with the Spanish Dictator, Gen. Franco, the Spanish held Morocco became a part of the Independent State of Morocco.

Algeria

Between 1870 and 1914 thousands of French citizens came to Algeria and settled there. Northern Algeria developed very rapidly and the French citizens sent their representatives to the French Parliament. The native Muslims were given a measure of self-government. But they were not happy and so they rose in rebellion against the French in 1954. Their frequent rebellions made it impossible for the French to rule that colony effectively. Many of the French settlers were opposed to the idea of giving freedom to the natives. At one time (1956) France maintained four hundred thousand troops to suppress the frequent rebellions of the natives. The nationalists demanded total independence. A section of the French army and the French settlers also rose in rebellion against the French government fearing that it would grant independence to the colony. It was for these reasons that Algeria's independence could not be achieved early. The result was chaos. The fourth French Republic fell in 1958. The French president appointed Charles de Gaulle as the premier and the latter promised the Algerians a status of equality with the French settlers and also self-rule. He tactfully dealt with the mutineers in the French Army. The Algerian independence issue was brought before the U.N. in 1957. An armed rebellion of the Algerians failed to achieve its objectives. However, the French premier granted independence to Algeria in July 1962. The Algerians decided to form a Republic. After the establishment of the Republic they chose Ben Bella as their first president.

West Africa

During the nineteenth century West Africa was partitioned by the British French, and Germans. After the World War I, the Germans lost two of their West African colonies—Togo and Cameroon. The British and the French ruled over them as mandates and they became independent during the 1960s.

Ghana

The Gold Coast (now known as Ghana) received her independence from Britain in March 1957. It was all due to the efforts of a great leader, Kwame Nkrumah. It may be remembered that this British colony received a measure of self-government in 1951. However, the nationalists led by Kwame Nkrumah were not happy. So Britain had to yield to pressure in 1957. Ghana became a member of the UN in 1975 and also joined the Commonwealth of Nations.

Nigeria and Other Colonies

Nigeria received her independence in October 1960. She could have achieved her independence even before this date but for the prevailing internal feuds. A number of smaller British colonies also received their independence during the 1960s. They were Sierra-Leone and Gambia. They became independent in 1961 and 1975 respectively.

French West Africa

France established a federation for her colonies in West Africa. These colonies included Senegal, French Sudan, Ivory Coast, Upper Volta, Dahomey, Niger with Mauritania. This federation continued even after World War II. Thereafter, each one of them gained its independence. Before that each colony had sent its representatives to sit in the French Parliament. After De Gaulle came to power, the French president governing each colony was replaced by a local leader (1958). Each colony was given a choice either to become independent or become a part of France. All except Guinea voted to become a part of the French community. Gradually, each colony began to have second thoughts. Subsequently, they demanded full independence. So all these colonies were granted independence by about 1960.

French (Central) Equatorial Africa

During the 1960s, the four French colonies of equatorial Africa, namely, Chad, Gabon, Ubhangi Shari and the middle Congo, received their independence. Ubhangi Shari became the Central African Republic and the middle Congo, the Republic of Congo (Brazzaville).

Central Africa

The British formed a federation comprising the three territories in Central Africa, namely, southern Rhodesia (a self-governing colony), and the protectorates of north Rhodesia and Nyasaland in 1953. But the African natives, who did not get their share in the political life of their country, raised objections. They did not want to be ruled by the whites. In 1959 they rose in revolt against the British under the leadership of Dr. Hastings Banda. Subsequently the British were forced to grant self-government. In 1964, Nyasaland received its independence and took the name of Malawi. Regarding northern Rhodesia, the white settlers in that mineral-rich colony came in the way of her receiving independence. However, the nationalists led by Kenneth Kaunda, carried on their agitation vigorously. In the end northern Rhodesia received her independence in October 1964. She was renamed as Zambia. Thus, the federation was broken up leaving southern Rhodesia in isolation. The British gave a measure of self-government to this colony. But the Black majority could not gain control over the government. The British government was ready to grant independence but the white minority there led by Prime Minister Ian Smith opposed this move. He unilaterally declared the independence of southern Rhodesia with white minority government in power in November 1965. Britain and other members of the UN protested and later on applied economic sanctions against this country.

Belgian Congo

In 1908 King Leopold of Belgium transferred his control over Congo to the Belgian Parliament. The Belgian Parliament introduced reforms in her colony. However, she was not prepared to grant self-rule to the native Congolese. But after the 1959 elections, the Belgian government changed its mind. She became more lenient towards her colony. Finally, she granted independence to Congo in 1960 with the hope of securing major economic concessions. She was very much disappointed when the native government refused to accede to her demands. The Belgians became angry and her troops returned to Congo. The Congolese Prime Minister Patrice Lumumba appealed to the UN for help. The UN sent its peace-keeping force to Congo to bring about a settlement. Meanwhile, Katanaga, a province of Congo, revolted against the centre and accepted Belgian assistance. Patrice Lumumba was assassinated in Katanga. After that the UN played its role in bringing about the expulsion of Moise Tshombe, the leader of the secessionist movement, and in reuniting that unfortunate country. After months of exile, Moise Tshombe returned to become the Prime Minister and led a coalition government at Leopoldville in 1964. In 1965, Moise Tshombe was deposed by President Kasavubu. Kasavubu was also deposed by Gen. Joseph Mobutu who became the new President. The Belgian Trust territory, Ruanda-Urundi, took more time to achieve independence since each had its own King. Ruanda became independent in July 1962. A little later Urundi also received her independence and chose constitutional monarchy.

Southern Africa

The Republic of South Africa

It is one of the richest states in the continent of Africa, accounting for forty per cent of gold and over thirty per cent of diamond production in the world. The Republic of South Africa was earlier known as the Union of South Africa. The latter came into being when the British annexed colonies like Cape Colony, Transvaal, Natal and Orange River in 1910. The Orange Free State and Transvaal belonged to the Dutch earlier. The Union of South Africa became an independent Republic on May 31, 1961, following a referendum (October 5, 1960). It left the British Commonwealth after the international community condemned it for its Apartheid policy. The word 'Apartheid' means racial discrimination. One should note that fifteen per cent of the white-settlers ruled over eighty per cent of the natives in the Union of South Africa. The white-minority government treated the natives very badly by denying them their fundamental rights. When Apartheid was made the official policy in 1948, the whole world condemned it. The UN later imposed economic sanctions.

The black majority in the country became politically conscious after the formation of the African National Congress (ANC) as a political party. The ANC carried on a long struggle for the natives against the white minority government for nearly four decades. One of its greatest leaders was Nelson Mandela. Nelson Mandela was born on July 18, 1918 near Cape of Good Hope. He studied law, and joined ANC in 1944. On March 21, 1960, the Sharpeville Massacre took place which resulted in the death of 69 native protestors due to police firing. This incident enraged Nelson Mandela to such an extent that he gave up his non-violent struggle against the white minority government. He founded *Spear of the Nation* as a military wing of the ANC, and carried on a violent struggle against the whites. President Verwoerd was assassinated, but the struggle continued till 1990. Mandela was arrested in 1962 for his unlawful activities and sentenced to life imprisonment. His long struggle and imprisonment attracted the attention of the whole world, and public opinion was built against the continuance of the white minority government in South Africa. It was in 1990 that President F.W. de Klerk released Mandela from prison and both of them made sincere efforts to end Apartheid policy and establish a transitional government. Mandela became president of the ANC in 1991, and in 1994, he was elected President of South Africa by a popular vote. A new nonracial constitution was introduced in May 1996. The Apartheid policy came to an end following the adoption of the new constitution. Nelson Mandela and President de Klerk jointly received the Nobel Peace Prize in 1993 for ending Apartheid. Mandela also received the highest civilian honour from India, the *Bharat Ratna*. South Africa's most flourishing cities are Pretoria, Cape Town, Johannesburg and Durban. The first two are administrative and legislative capitals.

East Africa

East Africa now consists of the former British colonies of Kenya, Uganda, Tanganyika, Zanzibar, Somaliland, Italian Somaliland, French Somaliland and the French island of Madagascar.

Kenya

Kenya was occupied by the white settlers since 1885. They grabbed all the fertile lands for themselves. These lands were claimed by the native African Tribe, Kikuyu. The British were not prepared to grant independence to the natives of Kenya because of the opposition of the white settlers. Therefore, the black natives of Kenya, formed a secret society called Mau Mau. It was led by a great leader called Jomo Kenyatta. Jomo Kenyatta carried on his secret activities. He was accused of Mau Mau terrorism and sentenced to a long imprisonment. In early 1960 the British were forced to grant self-government. Kenya's independence came little earlier than expected due to the struggle carried on by the Kenya African National Union. The KANU won almost all the seats in the elections and thereby indicated its desire for independence. The British granted independence to Kenya in 1963. Jomo Kenyatta was released from prison. He became Kenya's first prime minister.

Uganda

Uganda's freedom was not achieved till 1962 on account of the non-cooperation of a very small native kingdom, Buganda. It was ruled by Kabaka. The issue of Buganda's self-government within the sovereignty of Uganda was settled. Kabaka became the Head of the sovereign state of Uganda in 1962 and Milton Obote became his prime minister.

Tanganyika (Tanzania)

Tanganyika was a Trust territory administered by Britain. Julius Nyerere, the nationalist leader, organised the Tanganyika African National Union. He won all the seats in the elections and Britain granted independence to this territory in 1961. Zanzibar (with majority of Negroes) was ruled by the Arabs till the late nineteenth century. However, they lost this colony to Britain. Zanzibar gained her independence from Britain in 1963. Unfortunately, the Arab minority government ruled over the African majority. So the Africans staged a *coup* and expelled the Sultan. A revolutionary council was set up which was headed by Obeid Karume. He reached an agreement with President Nyerere of Tanganyika. This agreement led to the Union of Tanganyika and Zanzibar in 1964. The new state was called as Tanzania.

Somalia

After World War II, British, who had conquered Italian Somaliland (during the War), returned it to Italy. Italy held it as a Trust territory. The Italian Somaliland became independent on July 1, 1960. The British Somaliland was governed by Britain as a protectorate. A nationalist party in the British Somaliland desired merger with the former Somaliland. In the ensuing election, this issue came up. After the election, the British agreed for the union of the two Somalilands. The two Somalilands came to be merged and known as Somalia.

Madagascar

During World War II, Madagascar's strategic importance was realised by Britain. She took over the territory from the Vichy French. She turned it over to the free French. France suppressed frequent revolts here which were organised by the extreme nationalists who desired independence. In the meanwhile, a moderate nationalist Philibert Tsiranana, organised a moderate party and won a large number of seats in the subsequent election. France granted independence to Madagascar in June 1960. Madagascar became Malagasy Republic with Tsiranana as its elected president in 1960.

Lesson Review

1. Write a note on Tunisian independence or Algerian independence.
2. Write short notes on: (a) Moroccan independence, (b) Kwame Nkrumah, (c) Belgian Independence, (d) Jamo Kenyatta.

50
SCIENCE AND TECHNOLOGY IN THE MODERN WORLD

It may not be an exaggeration to say that the Industrial Revolution in England gave a tremendous fillip to the growth of science and technology. The textile industry which needed large-scale bleaching and dyeing gave stimulus to practical chemistry and machine-technology. The transport of materials and finished products by sea necessitated navigational innovations and it was not long before the sextant and chronometer were invented. So during the next few centuries a chain of scientific discoveries and technological innovations continued to take place in the world. The people who marvelled at these things thought of establishing Academies of Science, and the industrialists who got immense benefits out of this felt the need for founding Industrial Research Laboratories.

Terms of Science and Technology Defined
By science we mean a "cumulative body of systematised knowledge gained by observation, experimentation, and reasoning". The word "technology" is defined as "the fundamental application of scientific knowledge to the practical arts, resulting in improved industrial and commercial products of greater value to the people". These two things became hand-maids of modern civilisation. They marched hand in hand and rendered great services to the growth of human civilisation. Scientific discoveries and inventions changed the very approach to life. There was the scientific temper pervading or developing in the Western societies. We call this as the intellectual revolution. Every aspect of nature came to be thoroughly studied and formed a separate subject-matter. Let us examine the achievements of each subject of natural sciences.

Geology

The credit for laying the foundation for the subject of geology goes to Nicolaus Steno, a Dane, who found curious fossils of marine life on the mountains. Abraham Werner (1750-1817) was a German scientist who contributed much to the study of crystallography and different forms of rocks. Gievanni Ardunio (1713-95), an Italian scholar, worked on the geological chronology and correctly estimated the successive ages of the earth's crust. His work was followed by an Englishman, James Hutton, in 1795. Louis Agassiz contributed much to marine life and the glacial geology by publishing his works on the *Fresh Water Fishes, Research relating to Fossil Fishes,* and *Study relating to Glaciers* during the 1840s. William Nichol (1810-70), a professor in Edinburgh rendered valuable contribution to the development of petrography, the microscopic study of rocks and fossils. His research methods later came to be applied by Henry Sorby for his study of crystals (1858). Charles Lyell (1797-1875) studied at Oxford and published his *Principles of Geology*. He was the first to "conceive the idea of classifying the tertiary formations of the Cenozoic Age into four divisions, Eocene, Oligocene, Micocence and Pliocene". All these terms are in common use by the geologists. Thus, the development of Geology as a scientific subject for study extended its scope and widened the horizon of human knowledge of the earth we live in.

Astronomy—Halley's Discoveries

In the field of astronomy, Edmund Halley, an English astronomer, studied the comet which appeared in 1682 and discovered that the same comet had appeared in 1607, i.e., 76 years earlier. After studying its orbit he predicted that it would be seen again in the year 1758. Some of his achievements include the discovery of the "Periodicity" of comets and a method to measure the distance between the Sun and the Earth. Balthaskar Bekkar, a Netherlander, made a deep study on comets and published his findings in the *Inquiry into the Meaning of Comets* in 1683. A year earlier, Pierre Bayle had published his book *Various Thoughts on Comets* in which he exploded the myth that the appearance of comets portend disasters. In 1796, Pierre Simon de Laplace published a book, *System of Universe,* wherein he declared that all the planets and stars had taken birth from the same source—a rotating nebula of incandescent gas. One of the most remarkable astronomers of the 18th century was William Herschel (1738-1822). Besides producing telescopes and discovering the planet Uranus and the sixth satellite of Saturn, he drew up a picture of the shape of the galaxy. It resembled "the form of a double convex lens with the Sun near the middle". Astronomy made some more progress with the findings of John Couch Adams, Urbain Leverreir, Gustaf Kirchoff and Robert Bunsen. The last two contributed to astrophysics since they tried to determine the physical nature of stars. One of the greatest astronomers of the 19th century was Giovanni Schiaparelli (1835-1900) who said that comets stop shining and become meteors. He made special study of the three planets, Mars, Venus and Mercury. He observed "canals" and climate resembling that found on the earth on the planet Mars.

Development of the Science of Physics

Physics studies different forms of energy and matter. It made rapid strides of progress due to the impetus provided by the Industrial Revolution in England. Some physicists were interested in understanding how the steam engine converted heat into motion. They applied the results of their researches while inventing gasoline engine and the like. Other physicists studied metals and produced new metals like steel, etc. During the 19th century, James Clerk Maxwell and Heinrich Hertz did research work in electromagnetic waves and energy. It may be remembered that Michael Faraday experimented with magnetism and later on invented the dynamo which produced electricity. A little later a group of physicists were interested in electricity and magnetism, and a major breakthrough took place when Heinrich Hertz established the existence of electromagnetic waves. The contributions of Hertz paved the way for the invention of the Wireless. It also led to substantial developments in the fields of electronics and telecommunications. Ernest Rutherford played a stellar role in the field of nuclear physics, and was awarded the Nobel Prize for Chemistry in the year 1908.

Modern Physics

Modern physics is of recent origin and it was nurtured by John Dalton and Max Planck. The latter came forward with a new theory on light as well as the quantum theory. He explained the properties of atom. With the advent of the 20th century, the world witnessed the birth of Nuclear Physics. It began with Roentgen who discovered the X-rays and subsequently a French couple, Pierre and Marie Curie found out that radium also gives off radiation. It was not long before the scientists discovered marvellous things about the atom. Later, Albert Einstein predicted that by splitting the atom tremendous energy can be released. His theory paved the way for the production of atom bomb, and the Americans dropped it on the Japanese cities of Hiroshima and Nagasaki with catastrophic results. The Age of the Atom bomb began since the middle of the twentieth century. Einstein's theories on relativity and gravitation represented a profound advance over Newtonian Physics and revolutionised scientific and philosophical inquiry.

Development in Chemistry

Chemistry had its humble beginning and it took time to grow as an independent science because it had been shackled by alchemy. The names of George Stahl, Henry Cavendish and Antoine Lavoisier helped to develop this subject. Henry Cavendish obtained the hydrogen gas after experiments and discovered that water is not an element but a compound of hydrogen and oxygen. Antonie Lavoisier is described as "the Newton of Chemistry". He burnt different substances in his closed chamber and discovered that their basic elements remained the same though they had altered in appearance. An English chemist, John Dalton, tried to explain this new phenomenon through his atomic theory. According to Dalton's theory, all matter is made of minute atoms or "building blocks", and the atoms of different elements differ in sizes and traits. Although the elements mix to form a new substance, their atoms always remain intact. Extending this line of thinking, a Russian scientist, Dmitri Mendeleev prepared a table of all the identified elements according to their atomic weights (Mendeleev's periodic table). Research in chemistry led to its being utilised for the material prosperity of man. Chemistry has enabled us to create synthetic materials, fertilisers, plastics, pesticides, and has also played useful role in refining petroleum. The chemists also helped man by creating life-saving drugs.

Progress in Biology

Biology is a study of all living things. Several distinguished scientists are associated with its development. Carl Linnaeus, a Swedish scientist, divided all natural objects into stone, animals and vegetables. He also invented the system of giving biological nomenclature to all plants and animals. Rene de Reaumur made a special study of insect life. He is also credited with inventing a thermometer and an unpublished manuscript, *Natural History of Ants*. John Hunter was interested in studying comparative anatomy of animals and birds. Georges Cuvier studied not only the animal world but also the past life of the earth (Paleontology). Some biologists studied the "living jelly" or protoplasm. There were others who took interest in nutrition. One of the most revolutionary figures in modern biology was an English naturalist, Charles Darwin. His *Magnum opus* was the *On the Origin of Species* which was published in 1859. Darwin said that living organisms had been evolved from a common ancestor which was the first to take birth on the earth hundreds of millions of years ago. The living species—including man—which exist today are the result of a long process of evolution. This long process was painful and slow since many died in between. In other words, Nature did not allow all species to multiply, and selected only those which could best adapt themselves to the existing environment. So the long and painful process of evolution was characterised by a struggle for existence. That was how the numbers in each kind of species were kept more or less constant.

The long process of evolution of living species and the change in their forms led to the development of the new science called genetics. Francis Galton (1822-1911), a cousin of Darwin, studied the hereditary characteristics of geniuses and published work on it. While Galton's contribution may be strictly assigned to the science of Eugenics, the foundation for the science of genetics was laid by an Austrian monk, Gregor Mendel (1822-1884), who crossed varieties of garden pea. He finally discovered that hereditary characteristics of each are passed on in a definite form or pattern. Mendel's law propounds that "when two or more contrasted characters are crossed, the characters separate out in the later generations independently of each other". The science of genetics has been of immense benefit for it enables breeding superior varieties of plants and animals.

Progress in Medical Field

Medical science has made enormous strides of progress during the last 200 years and thereby extending the average life-expectancy of mankind. It may be remembered that before 1796 there were no vaccines against smallpox, plague and other types of fever. The victims were left helpless and many crude native remedies were adopted. An English doctor, Edward Jenner, found out that those who had cowpox (a mild disease) earlier appeared to be free from the attack of smallpox. He experimented with a young boy by inoculating him with cowpox serum. Jenner's experiment against the deadly disease, smallpox, proved highly successful. That was how vaccination (1796) against certain diseases became popular. Nobody knew how these diseases were caused. However, it was not until 1865 that a French Professor, Louis Pasteur (1822-95), showed that these infectious diseases were caused by germs. He explained how fermentation takes place i.e., souring of milk and putrefaction of meat. He correctly guessed that the silk industry in France had been destroyed by plague. He also discovered the cause for the cattle-disease. But his outstanding achievement was his discovery of successful treatment of persons suffering from hydrophobia (disease caused by the bite of a mad dog). For a couple of years the 'germ theory' of Louis Pasteur was ridiculed but it assumed credibility under a German scientist, Robert Koch (1843-1910).

With the aid of microscope, Koch discovered the germs which caused diseases known to us as cholera and tuberculosis. When the 'germ theory' was accepted as a fact, doctors started discovering vaccines or serums to protect the people from such diseases like diphtheria and the like. Emil von Behring protected children from diphtheria by vaccination. His success led to the discovery of several vaccines on such diseases like typhoid fever, tetanus and others. Walter Reed, an American doctor, found that yellow fever was spread by mosquitoes. Over a span of half a century, scientists discovered powerful drugs such as penicillin and sulfa to combat these deadly germs. Today we have the most powerful antibiotic drugs used against diseases ranging from infantile paralysis to diseases like cancer and heart-trouble. In the field of surgery, the discovery of anaesthetics happened to be a milestone. It is used to deaden the pain of a patient during the time of surgery. Another important factor in the field of surgery was the discovery of X-rays. It enabled surgeons to see the affected part or organ of the body. Since the advent of the 20th century, scientists discovered the energy producing and health-giving properties of various kinds of food. Their deficiencies led to the deteriorating physical conditions of a person. It was in 1906 that scientists discovered vitamins as essential for maintaining good physical condition. Meanwhile, the dangers from surgical operations on patients were minimised by sterilising the tools used by the doctor before the operation. In the bygone days Lord Lister, an English doctor, used carbolic acid to prevent festering of wounds.

Technological Innovations

The use of iron and steel marked the beginning of the modern world. As mentioned in an earlier chapter (see Industrial Revolution), it was Sir Henry Bessemer who invented a method for "removing the impurities from iron and making it harder". This refined iron was called as steel. Iron and steel were used for making machines and tools. Mechanical sewing was introduced by an American, Isac Singer, with the help of a sewing machine operated by a treadle (1851). The steam-driven printing press was introduced in 1813 by two Germans, Friedrick Koening and Andrew Bauer. Ottmar Mergenthaler invented the linotype printing technique. Toblert Lanston invented the monotype printing method. The manufacture of paper with the help of a machine was made possible by Henry Foundrinier. In 1867, an American, Christopher Sholes, invented the typewriter and the Remington factory bought Shole's rights for manufacture of typewriters. The development of photography began with the efforts of Thomas Wedgwood who produced contact prints. The next important milestone in the science of photography was achieved when Joseph Niepce discovered the method of making permanent photographic images. The next important person who greatly contributed to the modern photography was an American, George Eastman. He invented the "Kodak" camera.

Motion Picture

With the invention of photography it was not long before the motion pictures came into vogue. This was made possible by Charles F. Jenkins who produced a motion picture projector in 1894. Gabriel Lippman introduced colour motion pictures. The earliest movies were silent movies and were soon replaced by talkies. Cartoon movies were produced by Windsor Mckay.

Technological Innovations in the Means of Transport

Technological innovations in the methods of transport began in the early years of the 19th century in England. The first railway locomotive was built by Richard Trevithick and its first journey took place in 1804. In 1807 an American, Robert Fulton, built a steamboat which commenced its regular service on the river Hudson. Refrigerators and cars were introduced in 1875. In 1830, the Liverpool and Manchester Railway opened its modern railroad service to the public. The first steamship to cross the Atlantic in 1833 was a Canadian vessel, *The Royal William*.

Motor Vehicles

Karl Benz, a German engineer, introduced motor transport by inventing his motor-car in 1885. During the same year another German engineer, Gottlieb Daimler, introduced a gasoline engine for running a motorcycle.

The modern air transport began in the early twentieth century. The Wright Brothers flew a motor-driven plane successfully in 1903. In 1908, they travelled nearly 100 miles on their motor-driven plane. In 1919, Alcock and Brown flew in a plane across the Atlantic. The first flight around the world was in 1924. The next adventure was made by Charles Lindbergh who flew alone from Long Island in New York to Paris in 1927. During World War I planes were used for reconnaissance and bombing. The Germans used "Zeppelins", a large floating air-ship filled with nitrogen gas. It carried some adventurous passengers across the Atlantic. The first commercial jet service started with the flight from New York to Miami. In recent years, an average of 350 passengers are carried by the Jumbojet (747) passenger aircrafts. Military jets fly at a faster rate and at very high altitudes. After the development of rockets, man has been able to fly in space and reach the moon.

Revolution in Communication System

The system of communication was also revolutionised with the new technological inventions such as telegraphy, wireless telegraphy and the telephones. Transmitting messages by means of electric wires was called telegraph. The first telegraphic instrument for commercial purpose was introduced by Samuel Morse. In 1844, he used a hand-operated telegraphic key and transmitted a message in Morse code, and telegraph system came to be used for commercial purpose from that year. Thirty-two years later, Alexander Graham Bell invented the telephone to transmit the human voice through wires. In 1899, the problem of carrying messages to long distances was solved by Guglielmo Marconi. He had earlier invented the Wireless Telegraph in 1896. He was the first to send radio-signal across the Atlantic in 1901. Based on Marconi's invention, radio-broadcasting and television were developed during later years. His method of sending messages by wireless (electro-magnetic waves) came to be adopted by navigators of ships and planes. In the course of time undersea cables were laid for sending telegraphic messages across the Atlantic. Another wonderful invention was the television. Charles Jenkins developed a mechanical television system called radiovision and in 1925, he successfully demonstrated synchronized television transmission of both pictures and sound. John Logie Baird, a British engineer, is credited with the first demonstration of both "colour and stereoscopic television." His company, Baird Television Development Company (BTDC), "achieved the first transatlantic television transmission between London and New York." By 1933 regular television programme came to be broadcast from a New York Station. The first television programme started in Britain in 1936. The invention of the radar after 1935 was another notable event. The radar was used to detect the approaching enemy planes by ships and planes. Through science man has been able to unlock the secrets of nature.

Lesson Review

1. Describe scientific discoveries and inventions of the Modern Age.
2. Define the term "technology". How does technology enable man to improve commercial and industrial production?

51
TOWARDS THE NEW MILLENNIUM

During the last quarter the 20th century, the world has changed a lot. The Cold War continued despite several agreements reached between the two superpowers namely, the Anti-Ballistic/Missile Treaty of 1972, and the conclusion of the Helsinki agreement in 1975. There was a short period of *detente* (understanding) which was followed by the invasion of Afghanistan by the Soviet troops in 1979, and its occupation in 1980. The U.S. President/Reagan described the Soviet union as "focus of evil" and determined to check its might with the announcement of the "Star Wars". However, he kept the door open for negotiations with the Soviet Union which was in tune with the spirit of understanding i.e. *detente*. Fortunately for the U.S. president, the election of Gorbachev as liberal leader in the Soviet Union in 1985 augured well for the cessation of the Cold War. Gorbachev rejected the "Brezhnev doctrine" (communist countries should unite and fight when one of them go astray — i.e. deviate from the path of communism), and repeated that Soviet Union has no intention of spreading communism to other countries. The four summit meetings held between the two leaders in Geneva, Reykjavik, Washington and Moscow until 1989 resulted in the cessation of Cold War and great progress on the disarmament front. In the meantime, the Soviet Union withdrew its troops from Afghanistan in 1989. The INF (Intermediate-Range Nuclear Force) treaty (signed in 1937 by the US and Russia) was historic because it banned the use of specific nuclear weapons by the two superpowers. The confrontation between the NATO countries and the Warsaw-Pact countries too ended since Gorbachev was interested in building" a common European home". In 1989, the Berlin Wall separating the East and West (a symbol confrontation between East-Germany (Communist) and West Germany (capitalism) was demolished.

The Fall of the Soviet Empire

When Gorbachev took over the reins of the government the Soviet economy was really in bad shape. He was convinced that the nation could retain its superpower status, but only at an enormous cost. It would cause great sufferings to the people. It was time that the nation came to terms with bitter realities such as food shortages, rising unemployment, inflation, foreign debt, and federal deficits. His country needed a new ideological framework to inspire people to work for their better future.

His ideas for a better fututre based on *Glasnost* (openness), *Perestroika* (transformation of society), and democracy offered hope to the people who had been groaning under the oppressive rule since the Stalinist era. Carried away by his own vision of changing a stagnant society, Gorbachev failed in his efforts to transform it. The die-hard conservatives in his party opposed his plans, and he had to rely on the support of the people. In a fiercely contested election (1989), Gorbachev won the presidency, besides retaining his post as general secretary. Armed with wide powers, he got decrees, laws and ordinances passed for transforming the society and economy, but unfortunately they could not be implemented. The pace of reforms slowed down, and the workers were angry and struck work. Before Gorbachev left the scene, he allowed the eastern Europe (all communist countries) to go its own way. The Soviet troops were withdrawn from those countries. People saw the demise of Communism. Movements for independence within the Soviet Union started due to Gorbachev's policy of glasnost, and there was a coup. Boris Yeltsin, an upcoming leader, opposed the coup after rallying the support of the people of Moscow and got Gorbachev released from confinement. The whole world was watching the situation in the Soviet Union with bated breath. Gorbachev and Yeltsin agreed for changes and the Communist party lost its importance. The leaders agreed for the reunification of Germany. Soon the USSR disintegrated but the republics (in all eleven in number) joined what is known as Commonwealth of independent states. Russia came to be known as Russian Federation in course of time and it embraced market economy after rejecting the planned-economy model. Boris Yeltsin became president and ruled Russia for eight years. Thereafter, he chose Vladimir Putin as his successor in 1999. The U.S. assured Russia of its financial assistance, and the latter joined the NATO as partner country.

Rise of Communist China

After the overthrow of Chiang Kai-shek's Nationalist government, the Communists under the leadership of Mao-Dze-Dong took over the reins of government. The Marxist-Leninst principles influenced the leader, and China launched Five Year Plans for economic and social development; and tried successfully to check the growth of population. The 'commune system' was introduced for rural development after the individuals landholdings were abolished. The educational system was revamped. Mao urged the Chinese to practice the virtue of self-reliance and did not seek foreign aid. Unfortunately, his 'Great Leap Forward' (his strategy of Economic development) undertaken during 1957-59 failed miserably, and it is said that nearly 27 million people perished due to frequent famines and floods. Mao had to step down for a while, but he regained his position. He launched the 'Cultural Revolution' (1966-69) after appealing to the people to follow his thoughts and participate in the economic development of the country. Before he died (1976), Communist China acquired nuclear weapons— a great step in achieving Big-power status in the world. In 1971, Communist China replaced Chiang's Formosa (Taiwan) as a permanent member in the Security Council of the UN. After overcoming the challenge from Madam Mao and her 'Gang of Four', Deng Xiaoping wore the mantle of leadership. He rejected Mao's ideas and persuaded the party's third plenum to approve his agenda of 'economic construction'. During the last years of his life, he advocated building socialism through the medium of 'socialist market economy'. His reforms came to be known as the "four modernizations", namely, modernization of agriculture, industry, science and technology and defence. Special economic zones were created in the coastal regions of China to implement his theory of economic construction. He gave a new Constitution to the people in 1982. Unfortunately, China under Deng did not give attention to democratic aspirations of the people and showed disrespect for 'human rights' with the result that Tiananmen tragedy took place (1989)— peaceful demonstration demanding political reforms was crushed leaving nearly five thousand killed and another ten thousand injured. Leaders of the demonstration mostly students were arrested. The western world was shocked and China was condemned for violating human rights.

China's Foreign Relations

During the early years of the Cold War, China supported the Soviet Union, backed Communist North Korea against South Korea, took Tibet after suppressing a rebellion, and invaded India (1962). India felt betrayed since China had earlier signed a treaty of Peaceful-Coexistence (Panchsheel). India was at the fore-front in recommending China's entry into the U.N. China quarreled with the Soviet Union (her ally) pertaining to their common border.

China had remained isolated for a long time, and the rest of the world knew very little about what was happening there. The antagonism between Mao's People's Republic of China and the West had resulted in the latter barring the former's entry into the UN for more than two decades. China helped communist North Vietnam against US supported South Vietnam in the Vietnam War. The defeat of South Vietnam was indeed a victory for the Communists (1975). The U.S. and her allies were finding it difficult to stem the spread of Communism. China's relations with the West improved a little after 1976. Her nuclear status and market reforms definitely impressed the West. Britain handed over her colony of Hongkong to China in 1997. The U.S. adopted the policy of one-China, although she had some reservations. China signed the Nuclear Non-Proliferation Treaty (NPT) in 1992. Portugal handed over the territory of Macau to China in 1999 after ruling it for nearly 442 years. Currently China's attitude towards the U.S. hinges on Taiwan's merger with the mainland (the U.S has been supporting the Nationalist government in Taiwan). With the market economy flourishing in the special economic zones, China has been welcoming foreign investments since the early nineties. In 2013, it attracted US $117.6 billion in foreign direct investment according to Reuters. It has enjoyed an average GDP annual growth rate of more than nine percent in the last two decades. Having the second largest economy in the world, it hopes to become an economic superpower. China had earlier gained entry into the World Trade Organisation (WTO) in December 2001.

The Role of the UN

The UN celebrated its golden jubilee in 1995. Its role and achievements have been remarkable, given the limitations or constraints. Ever since its birth it supported decolonisation, championed human rights, opposed racial discrimination (apartheid in South Africa), helped millions of refugees all over the world, promoted non-nuclear war agreements and the Non-Proliferation treaty (1970) and assisted solving disputes so as prevent wars. It experienced innumerable difficulties due to the raging cold war, and quite often been blamed for coming under the influence of the U.S. It successfully intervened in many war-situations such as Korea, Vietnam, Arab-Israeli wars, Cambodia, Kashmir, Congo, Cyprus, Iran-Iraq war, Iraq-Kuwait (Gulf War I), Somalia, Bosnia, Afghanistan. The UN always condemned military interventions in the early years but in recent times advocated the use of force on grounds of humanitarian issues involved, or violation of human rights (the UN Charter). It made countries aware of the dangers of enormous growth in world population and also about the dangers of global-warming (meetings held in Stockholm and Rio-de-

Janeiro). Through its agencies, the UN has rendered yeoman's service to humanity in combating poverty, malnutrition and AIDs. However, the danger of nuclear war has not receded despite many treaties, with the U.S. revoking the anti-Ballistic missile treaty and planning for what is known as Nuclear Missile Defence (NMD) system to protect the country from the rogue-states (North Korea and Iran).

After the Gulf War I and the fall of the Soviet Union, the UN appears to have changed its role from one of peace-keeping to peace enforcement, that is from non-intervention to humanitarian intervention, thanks to the prodding of the U.S. Some say that the U.S. is using the UN to carry out its wishes, or sometimes bypassing the UN itself as in the case of Gulf War II (2003).

The U.S. after 9/11 (2001)

The Arab-Israeli conflicts in the Middle East, and the support of the U.S. to Israel, despite long negotiations, have angered the Muslims all over the world. Fundamentalist Islamic organisations became active, and the *Jihadi* elements gave vent to their anger by means of terror. Osama bin Laden (exiled from Saudi Arabia) sheltered in Taliban's Afghanistan conspired to strike at the U.S. interest. The twin towers of the World Trade Centre were brought down by the suicide-bombers who hijacked two passenger-planes to carry out the task. The Pentagon was attacked and partly destroyed. There was shock and disbelief, and President Bush (Jr.) immediately declared war on terror and appealed to all countries to help him. The world watched on TV the U.S. war on Taliban's Afghanistan. The U.S. failed to capture the world's most dreaded man, Osama bin Laden, though Afghanistan fell after heavy U.S. bombings. After setting up a new government there, under the leadership of Hamid Karzai, the U.S. under President Bush called upon Saddam Hussein's Iraq to dismantle Weapons of Mass Destruction (WMD). The Iraqi dictator denied having weapons of mass destruction, and allowed the weapons-inspectors to search. The U.S. was not convinced about the report of the weapons inspectors who said they could not find these, and launched war against Iraq (March 20, 2003), despite protests from Russia, Germany and France. The coalition forces led by the US toppled Saddam's regime in March 2003. Saddam Hussein was captured in his hometown, Tikrit, on December 13, 2003, and finally executed in December 2006 for crimes against humanity. Being the sole superpower (or Hyper-power), the U.S. with the support of Britain's prime minister Tony Blair continued to have some kind of paranoia. Syria or North Korea may become the next target. While Syria is accused of helping Iraq, North Korea is blamed for violating the Nuclear Non-Proliferation treaty, by engaging itself in making nuclear bombs.

Regional Groups

During and after the Cold War, many regional groupings were formed for achieving certain objectives — NATO, CENTO, SEATO for the sake of protecting countries around the world from Communist insurgencies; the EU, ASEAN, the G8, for achieving growth and prosperity, and the NAM for the purpose of keeping away from the superpower rivalry. While the SEATO and CENTO became extinct, the NATO remains very much alive today in partnership with Russian Federation. As of January 2014, Twenty-eight countries of Europe have joined the European Union (EU), and eighteen of them have chosen the Euro as their common currency. The ASEAN was founded in 1967 by the Southeast Asian Nations, namely, Indonesia, Malaysia, Philippines, Singapore and Thailand, and in recent years joined by Myanmar, Cambodia, Laos, Vietnam and Brunei. The G8 consists of seven rich countries and later joined by Russia. SAARC was founded in 1985 by the nations of South Asia, namely, India, Pakistan, Bangladesh, Nepal, Bhutan, Maldives and Sri Lanka. Its main aim is to achieve economic cooperation.

There are many other organisations which are promoting peace and economic prosperity, like the Commonwealth (53 nations), The Arab League (22 Arab-nations), the Commonwealth of Independent States (12 states of the former USSR), the Organisation of American States, Organisation of African Union (53 member-states), Organisation of Petroleum Exporting Countries and so on.

The largest non-regional organisation is the Non-Aligned Movement (NAM), which was started way back in 1955 (Bandung Conference) and today it is represented by 120 member nations and 17 observer countries. Its purpose is to keep away from superpower rivalry and work for achieving peace, disarmament, development, and eradication of poverty and illiteracy. The NAM consists mainly of developing nations which became free from the West's colonial rule (Asia, Africa and Latin-America).

GLOBALISATION

The domination of the U.S. extended to economic aspects, such as trade and commerce of the countries all over the world. After the demise of communism (fall of the Soviet Union), it became obvious that the capitalist system had triumphed. The U.S. and its financial institutions like the I.M.F., the World Bank, and the World Trade Organisation have been extolling the virtues of capitalism and advocating globalisation as the *mantra* for eradicating all the economic ills of the Third World countries (i.e. poor countries). Globalisation intends to integrate the economy of poor countries with those of other countries by means of encouraging economic reforms such as liberalisation and privatisation. Those Third World countries which sought loans from these financial institutions, particularly the I.M.F. and the World Bank have been asked to fulfil certain conditions. Those countries which joined the World Trade Organization (WTO), including Communist China (which joined in 2001), have to adhere to certain rules— rules which have been found to be unjust and unfair especially to the Third World countries. In the W.T.O. conference held in Seattle in December, 1999, the Third World countries exposed the double-standard adopted by the West. It is no exaggeration to say that Globalisation is making rich countries richer and the poor poorer. Prof. Stiglitz (Nobel-Laureate and former World Bank's chief-expert) has proved that the economies of the Third World countries has been damaged by globalisation programme. Then what are the benefits accrued to countries embracing globalization? Economists point out that free trade (core of globalisation) improves efficiency (due to competition), finances (attracts foreign investments), factor-incomes and gains from the migration of skilled workers. But all of these have not taken place; instead Multinational corporations (of western countries) became the real beneficiaries of the globalisation programme. It is said that poorest countries lost 3% to 5% of their export earnings because of globalisation, and in fact paying more for their food-imports. The Human Development Report (1999) published by the UN Development Programme (UNDP) states: "The top fifth of the world's people in the richest countries enjoy 82 percent of the expanding export trade and 68 percent of foreign direct investment—the bottom fifth, barely more than 1 percent." According to the World Bank's estimate of 2008, about 1.3 billion people in the developing countries lived on less than $1.25 a day.

Therefore the prescriptions of the IMF, the World Bank, and the WTO for the ailing economies of the Third World have not gone down well, and the people are protesting everywhere. Their protest marches are led by social activists, labour-union leaders and leading intellectuals like Joseph Stiglitz, Arundhati Roy and so on. The Ministerial Conference held in Seattle in December 1999 was disturbed by wave of protests. Even humanising globalisation has not found much support. The Asian Social Forum held in Hyderabad (2003) tried to organise rally to protest against imperial globalisation.

Human Sufferings
Wars, civil strifes, terrorism, and natural disasters have caused immense sufferings. The Bengal Famine (1943), and the cultural revolution of Mao-

Tse-Tung took heavy toll of lives. The Civil wars such as in some southern African and South American countries as also in Congo, Sri Lanka, and Kampuchea (Cambodia) caused deaths to millions. Millions of people became refugees after the creation of Israel and in the recent war in Afghanistan. The Vietnam War cost nearly $ 150 billion and 27,000 American lives. The U.N. is looking after 28 million refugees under its UNHCR.

A new dimension has been added to human sufferings, i.e. the spread of HIV AIDS all over the world. There is no vaccine produced as yet to check this scourge. It has caused 16.3 million deaths so far since its appearance some years ago. Then there was this phenomenon of 2002-03 called the Severe Acute Respiratory Syndrome (SARS) which originated in China. It spread to Hong Kong, Singapore, Canada, India and so on. It is a new kind of pneumonia for which there is no remedy or preventive vaccine discovered as yet.

TERRORISM

In our world, terrorism has caused immense sufferings and terrorist outfits exist in many parts of the world to avenge the wrongs perpetrated by some states. These outfits demand separate state, like the Basque in Spain, the Irish Republican Army in northern Ireland, the Intifada in West Asia, the LeT in the state of Jammu and Kashmir in India, the LTTE in Sri Lanka, Hamas in Jordan, the Abu Sayaf in the Philippines, and of course, the Al Qaeda (hiding in Pakistan and Afghanistan). They indulge in kidnapping, torture and killings, of their supposed enemies, and many innocent people have been their victims. Osama Bin Laden (Al-Qaeda) wanted Muslims to wage *Jihad* (holy war) against the U.S. His organisation has established links with many terrorist outfits across the world. The suicide squads of his organisation carried out the bombings of the twin-towers of the World-Trade Centre and the Pentagon on September 11, 2001. The U.S. President George. W. Bush did not lose much time in declaring America's war on terrorism. He called on all countries to wage this relentless war—to eradicate this evil from the face of the earth, no matter how much time it takes, or sacrifices to be made. Taliban's Afghanistan which gave shelter to Osama Bin Laden and his followers faced the U.S. airstrikes. Mullah Omar and Osama Bin Laden fled, leaving Afghanistan to be occupied by coalition forces. The U.S. and its allies, set up an interim government, led by Hamid Karzai. The Pakistani Government, which had been a staunch supporter of Taliban Government in Afghanistan, was forced to co-operate with the U.S. forces —amidst protests from the members of the extremist-Islamic organisations. India has always accused Pakistan of sponsoring cross-border terrorism, and the U.S. is quite aware of it. The U.S. government is worried about some Pakistani scientists having colluded with the Al Qaeda in attempting to make atom bomb.

Violation of Human Rights

The declaration of human rights is enshrined in the U.N. Charter and nations joining the U.N. had to abide by it. During the period the Cold War, the U.S. alleged that the communist countries always violated human rights—i.e. the right to freedom of speech, freedom of faith etc. Communist China had to wait for a long time for getting admission to the U.N. (she was admitted in 1971). Again she had to wait for long to get admitted to the World Trade Organisation. Human rights record of each nation came under scrutiny by the U.S. and the Amnesty International. Taliban's regime in Afghanistan, and its atrocities against women was highlighted. China's suppression of the Tibetans, student activists (remember the Tiananmen Square incident), and the members of Falung gong (a new cult) showed her in poor light in regard to respect for human rights. Burma's military-junta too is in the dock, with respect to the dissident leader, Aung Saan Suu Kyi, who started a non-violent movement called National League for Democracy (NLD). The second Gulf War (2003) is described as 'Operation Iraqi Freedom' which means liberating the people of Iraq from the tyrannical regime of Saddam Hussein. The gulf-states under the Sheikhs are worried, lest they be dubbed as tyrannical regimes by the U.S., and receive the same treatment from the U.S. as on Iraq. The Gulf States of Oman, the U.A.E., and Bahrain have become liberal in outlook—the last named has given voting rights to its women. The UN General Assembly Resolution in 1993 created the Office of the High Commissioner for Human Rights (OHCHR) which consists of 53 members.

Human rights, in all its aspects, constitute the very essence of democracy, and people of more than forty countries during the last three decades switched to this political system. Democratisation with economic liberalisation may evolve a state into a truly welfare state. Singapore, Taiwan, South Korea and Hong Kong are shining examples of such a system.

Expanding Frontiers of Knowledge

According to the Management *Guru*, Peter F Drucker, the future belongs to the 'Knowledge society'. Therefore, it is necessary to keep track of the ever-expanding frontiers of knowledge. To begin with, right down from Nicolaus Copernicus, astronomy attracted a large number of scientists.

There is the 'Big Bang' theory that tells us about the origin of the universe, which many say is thirteen billion years old, and the earth anywhere about 4.5 billion years old. Many space exploration missions were undertaken to study the universe and the solar system and the first breakthrough came when *Sputnik* was launched by Russia (October 4, 1957). Another important landmark was the lunar mission, *Apollo 11*, which landed the first humans, American astronauts Neil Armstrong and Edwin Aldrin, on the moon on July 20, 1969. The Russians and the Americans complimented each other with their space missions, and the former established an orbiting space-station, *Mir*, in 1986, which was another important milestone in the history of space exploration. In February 2003, the space shuttle *Columbia* exploded while re-entering the Earth's atmosphere, killing all the astronauts, including the brave Kalpana Chawla, an American of Indian origin.

Scientists found out that the emission of green house gases (GHG) during last few decades have depleted the ozone layers to such an extent that the earth is experiencing a rise of 0.5 degree in temperature every year. This will have catastrophic consequences in the years to come, like more people suffering from skin-cancer, change in weather conditions (remember El Nino), rise in sea-levels, and increase in the number of acid rains, droughts, famines and floods around the world. The Earth-Summit in Rio and the recently held conference in Delhi tried to address these issues and every one agreed to ratify the Kyoto Protocol (the U.S. and some western nations have not ratified the same).

Today we are living in the midst of unparalleled changes, and science and technology has made tremendous progress. Some of the established theories (which remained valid for centuries) are getting outdated. Thomas Kuhn, a famous science historian (author of *Structure of Scientific Revolution*), talked about what is known as 'paradigm shift', which many see as 'Key to innovation' or 'pathway to progress'. Scientists and business leaders have been so much influenced by his theory, that they are getting more in-depth analysis about their study or operations.

Medical Science

Thanks to technological revolution, the field of medical science has made great progress. Today we have better health-care system. Multi-Speciality hospitals with highly qualified surgeons carry out by-pass surgeries, organ transplantation, CAT scan, ultra-sound tests, key-hole surgery and so on. Telemedicine makes it possible for distant patients to receive guidance from specialists. Experiments are taking place using robots to undertake surgeries.

The Human Genome Project, which was launched in 1990 as a combined enterprise (18 countries and 250 laboratories participating in it), was successfully completed in 2003. Indeed, it is one of the most outstanding contributions ever made. It succeeded in identifying and mapping the set of genes present in the human cell.

Vaccines have helped in preventing children and adults from succumbing to many deadly diseases such as smallpox (which has been eradicated), polio, whooping cough and so on. Curative-medicines are available for treating T.B., cancer, snake-bites, rabies, cholera, malaria, typhoid and so on. Computer application has enabled doctors to diagnose the diseases at an early stage and prescribe remedies.

Information Technology

Information technology has been aptly described as the second industrial revolution of the twentieth century. It is rated as the best and fastest-growing industry in the world. Acquisition and dissemination of knowledge and the application of that knowledge in different fields, like business, has brought about cascading effects. In fact, the world has become a global village, thanks to this I.T. industry. The Internet has played a vital role. Information acts as an important source of knowledge and application of that knowledge in different spheres of life enables many countries to boost their overall growth (education, economy, health-care, literacy and so on). Fortunately, India has been a front-ranking leader of this industry and hoping to reap rich rewards. Software professionals of India have made a mark by their technical skill and zeal all over the world. In 2012, a couple of Indian IT companies (Infosys and TCS) made it to the Forbes list of top 100 innovative organizations in the world. Knowledge as a resource and utility "is now fast becoming the *one* factor of production, sidelining both capital and labour." (Peter F. Drucker)

Along with the information technology, the telecommunication technology too has made rapid advances. For these there exist no time and place barriers. Through satellite communication, the transnational and multinational corporations around the world have been able to increase their business four-fold. Business executives around the globe need not necessarily have to travel, thanks to the improvements in optical fibre technology, which has brought the videophone and teleconferencing facilities to their offices. The quality of life of many middle-class people across the globe has greatly improved, thanks to the research in superconductivity, bio-technology and ceramics. Electrical and Electronic gadgets (based on fuzzy logic) like the automatic washing machine, microwave ovens, cameras, camcorder, air conditioners and refrigerators are available in the super-markets, and all these consumer items adorn the houses of the middle class and the rich.

Computers, fax machines, telephones, intercom, cine-projectors, electronic type-writers and so on have helped the office-personnel to do their work intelligently and efficiently. Super-computers and artificial intelligence have added a new dimension to our ways of acquiring information and intelligence. Super-computers deal with very very complicated problems while artificial intelligence enable machines to think for us. India has produced super-computers after the U.S. refused to supply them. In the 1990s, the US prevented Russia from transferring to India the cryogenic propellant technology that is used to develop rocket engines.

New technology (based on electronics) has enabled advanced nations to produce supersonic-jet planes and super-fast trains. Many motor-vehicles in future may use solar-energy or batteries.

New technology enabled the U.S. and its allies to defeat the enemies without difficulty and the recent wars in the Gulf and in Afghanistan provide classic examples. The U.S. used satellite surveillance system to trace the desired targets for bombing. It used laser-guided missiles to hit the targets with pin-point accuracy.

Electronic mail (E-mail) and Electronic commerce (E-Commerce) have established links within the country and the outside world, and the cell-phone has gone a step further in creating a communication revolution. Our parliament has passed what is known as the Cyber-laws (as urged by the U.N. resolution) to provide for a regulatory regime.

52

FROM THE AFGHAN CIVIL WAR TO ARAB SPRING

The Soviet occupation of Afghanistan, and its support to the Communist Government was galling to many Afghan rebel groups. The Afghan Mujahideen (holy warriors) started resisting the Soviet occupation, but were unable to make much progress. Najibullah became the President of Afghanistan in 1989. With several countries, prominent among them being the US and Pakistan, supporting several groups of Mujahideens to fight against the Soviet-controlled regime he could not make headway. In the meantime, the UN proposed a peace plan that intended to end the Soviet support to the Najibullah government in Afghanistan, and invited the old Afghan King Zahir Shah to take charge. The Soviet leader, Mikhail Gorbachev, and the US President gave their consent. However, the Mujahideen groups were not happy. As the Soviet troops in Afghanistan found it difficult to control the rebel Mujahideen groups, the Soviet leader decided to withdraw in 1989. President Najibullah announced the formation of a military council in order to rule the country, but the rebel Mujahideen groups set up an interim government in exile led by Sighbatullah Majaddidi. He transferred his power to a Mujahideen leadership council. After launching major offensives against the Soviet-backed regime of Najibullah, the Mujahideen factions reached the outskirts of the Afghan capital, Kabul. Najibullah's regime was overthrown in 1992, and he took shelter in the UN office in April.

The Civil War

After ousting Najibullah's government in Kabul, the warlords of the rebel Mujahideen groups started fighting among themselves over power sharing. Hekmatyar's forces which controlled the outskirts of Kabul and the town of Jalalabad, fought forces of the new President, Burhanuddin Rabbani. The latter had the support of General Abdul Rashid Dostum. After some time, General Dostum deserted the president and supported Hekmatyar.

The fighting reduced the capital, Kabul, into a rubble. The civil war took nearly 10,000 lives, mostly civilians. Half the population of the city fled. The control of the capital became a very important issue between the rival guerilla warlords.

The Rise of Taliban

Taliban is a fanatical Islamic movement, which originated in the Kandahar district of Afghanistan. The founder was Mullah Mohammed Omar who lost an eye while fighting the Soviet troops which had occupied Afghanistan. After the Soviet troops left the country in 1989, he found that the warlords had turned the country into rubble with their internecine fights, and innocent people were put to severe hardships like looting, bribery and rape of women. He started a school with about 30 members —mostly young students (Taliban means 'Students of religion'). This movement showballed into a big organisation with moral, material and financial support of countries like Pakistan and Saudi Arabia. In the course of time, the Afghan refugee students who had fled the country due to civil war joined hundreds of madrasas (started by Pakistan on its side of the border), run by Jamiat-e-Ulema Islami, a traditionalist Sunni party. By 1994-95 the Taliban had established its military outfits in order to unite the country under its banner.

Talibanisation of Afghanistan

Gulbuddin Hekmatyar who had 'parted ways' with President Rabbani in 1994 returned to the fold, and the former was made the prime minister in June 1996. However, Rabbani's government was suddenly overthrown by the Taliban militia in September 1996 after they captured Kabul. The Taliban militia took Najibullah, the former Communist President, captive and hanged him in the heart of the city. In the meanwhile, both Rabbani and Hekmatyar fled the city. The Taliban militia took complete control of Kabul and set up a six-member interim government. The government employees and the people were ordered to strictly follow Islamic customs, manners and dress. The Afghan women were put to severe hardship. The ousted government which was dominated by the Tajiks like Rabbani and Ahmad Shah Masood retreated to the Tajik traditional strongholds in the north. The theatre of the Afghan civil war shifted to the north after 1996, with Pakistan fully backing the Taliban militia. Countries neighbouring Afghanistan, mainly Iran, Russia and India, took serious note of the spillovers of the civil war, especially with outside interference. The Theeran Conference took up this matter. The year 1997 did not go well with the Taliban as the northern-based opposition coalition made some headway in its effort to push back the Taliban militia towards Kabul.

Role of the UN

The civil war in Afghanistan left thousands of Afghan families homeless, with more than 20,000 civilians dead, and 100,000 wounded. The UN was deeply concerned about the situation and offered its mediation in 1998 to end this conflict.

Although both the parties to the civil war agreed to work for peace, exchange prisoners, and restore normalcy, they violated the UN-brokered deal. Fighting between the two erupted on May 2, 1998. In addition to the tragedy caused by the civil war, Afghanistan was rocked by two earthquakes, the first one in February, and the second in April, with 4,000 and 5,000 dead respectively. In August the Taliban captured Mazar-e-sharif and other towns in the north, and claimed to be in control of ninety per cent of Afghanistan.

Support to Militants

The Taliban, which received moral and material support from Pakistan and Saudi Arabia, unleashed terror by organising and training terrorists. The Al Badr recruited Pakistani militants who were let loose in Kashmir to foment trouble. Then, there was the Harkat-ul-Ansar which also operated in Kashmir with the support of Al Badr. The Al Badr also recruited foreigners (Arabs and Sudanese) to lend support to the rebels operating in Chechnya, Bosnia and Dagestan. The Taliban gave shelter to the exiled Saudi millionaire, Osama bin Laden, who was running terrorist camps in Afghanistan. The US believed that he masterminded the bombing of her embassies in Africa. The UN did not recognise the Taliban Government, but its representative was allowed in the UN. It is said that there are ten million landmines still scattered around in Afghanistan posing serious dangers to its citizens. Nearly two million Afghans took shelter in Pakistan and Iran. Afghanistan is the least developed country in the world.

UN Sanctions

The UN Security Council imposed sanctions on the Taliban's tyrannical regime in December 2000 for its human rights abuses, giving refuge to Osama bin Laden (the Al-Qaeda leader) and other atrocities (not forgetting the destruction of the monolithic statue of the Buddha at Bamian). Taking shelter in Afghanistan, the Al-Qaeda was involved in the bombings of the US embassies in Kenya, Tanzania and fomenting rebellion in Russian controlled Chechnya. India welcomed the move because the Taliban in December 1999 had supported the Pakistani hijackers of Indian Airlines Flight 814 who had held the passengers as hostages. Moreover, Pakistan was in the dock for having patronised the Taliban regime along with Saudi Arabia.

US Strikes

The Taliban's support to Al-Qaeda's terrorist activities even after the 9/11 attacks on the WTC in New York and Pentagon (the US Defence Establishment) in 2001 forced the US administration to act swiftly. When the Taliban regime refused to handover the leader of Al-Qaeda and his gang to the US, the US forces started aerial strikes and bombardments to dislodge the Taliban regime. Ground support to the US came from the Northern Alliance led by Ahmed Shah Masood and Rabbani (all Tajiks). The high-tech war (missiles from warships and precision guided bomb attacks) carried on by the US and allied forces flattened Kabul and other strongholds of the Taliban. The Taliban forces led by Mullah Omar fled to the mountains bordering Pakistan, and hoped to retrieve their position with the help of the Pushtun warlords. It must be remembered that it was the US which had supported the Taliban in its efforts to oust the Soviet forces in Afghanistan years earlier. In the meantime, the US and its allies put pressure on Pakistan to force the Taliban to surrender. In spite of its best efforts, Pakistan failed to achieve this goal. Unfortunately, Pakistan was caught in the web of its own making, that is, supporting and recognising the Taliban Government.

Afghan War

During the months of October and November the US started its intensive bombings while the ground troops of Northern Alliance (which received military hardware from the US) made headway towards Kabul. The civilian population of Afghanistan suffered heavy casualties when bombs missed the military targets. Finally, the Taliban militia fled to the mountains leaving Kabul to be occupied by the forces of Northern Alliance. The common people rejoiced at the defeat of the Taliban. Except for a few pockets of resistance, Afghanistan, by and large, remained peaceful. This situation enabled the leaders to form an interim government with the blessings of the exiled king. Hamid Karzai became the president, and many of the Afghan warlords agreed to recognise the new government and promised to support it. The NATO troops are stationed in Kabul and other cities as a protection force to help the government. The new government immediately restored civil rights to the people and promised to give a democratic constitution. On January 2, 2004, the new constitution was approved (after protracted negotiations with the warlords) by the *Loya Jirga* (Grand Council). The new constitution provides for a democratic setup under a presidential system. Amidst tight security, never seen before, the presidential election took place on October 9, 2004. Mr Hamid Karzai won, after defeating 15 rivals; most notably his greatest rival Mr Yunus Qanooni. The Taliban made many efforts to trigger violence during the election period, but none of them succeeded. Mr Karzai received 41,05,122 votes, that is more than the fity per cent of the votes cast and he was officially declared the winner on November 3, 2004.

The new president has an arduous task ahead of him. He has to maintain law and order in the country in the face of several threats coming from the Taliban which is regrouping its forces in the mountainous areas. He has to win over all the warlords to his side. He needs financial and military supports from the Western allies and India. He has to secure the support of the common people Pushtuns, Tajiks, Hazaras, Bahichis and Ugbeks owing allegiance to their respective warlords to carry out several development projects. It is hoped that this war-torn country would have a bright future under the leadership of the new president. It is also hoped that the Taliban and the Al Qaeda would be brought to justice in the new democratic framework of Afghanistan.

Iran-Iraq War (1980-88)

Navigation on the Shatt al-Arab (a river in southwest Asia) had remained a bone of contention between Iraq and Iran which defied solution. Furthermore, Iran had occupied the islands of Abu Musa, Greater Tunb and Lesser Tunb in 1971—islands also claimed by the United Arab Emirates (UAE). In July 1979, Al-Bakr (fourth president of Iraq) resigned and paved the way for Saddam Hussein to succeed him. There was a peaceful transfer of power. President Saddam Hussein who considered himself 'the defender of the Arab world' faced two important problems on assuming power – the rebellious Kurds in the north and a hostile Iran in the east.

Iran and Iraq traded charges; Iraq blamed Iran for training and arming the Kurds in her territory, and also annexing the three islands (Arabistan). Iran accused Iraq of suppressing the Shia population in her territory. Iraq was also afraid that Iran under Ayatollah Khomeini (spiritual leader of the Shia community) may export the Islamic revolution to her territory.

Border clashes between the two countries brought about the war which was officially declared in September 1980. The immediate cause of the war was that Iraq charged Iran with attacking a number of Iraqi villages. The Iraqi army made strategic moves to capture the Abadan oil fields in Iran. When the war began, Syria supported Iran. She accused Iraq of supporting religious fundamentalists in her country. The Security Council of the United Nations then called upon both the countries to observe truce. The long war between Iraq and Iran brought about exhaustion, and finally they agreed to observe the truce in 1988.

The Gulf War (1991)

Hardly had the war ended between Iraq and Iran, there came another war – the Gulf War – between Iraq and the US led coalition. The main cause of the war was Iraq's invasion of Kuwait in August 1990. Kuwait was a British protectorate in 1914. Iraq considered Kuwait as a part of its kingdom. Soon after the independence of Kuwait (1961), Iraq claimed it as its own. But she did not pursue the matter. However, in 1990 Iraq and Kuwait had a dispute over pricing of oil. This matter precipitated Iraq's invasion and occupation of Kuwait. The Arab nations were taken by surprise, and all of them condemned this action. When Saddam Hussein refused to vacate his troops from Kuwait, the UN had to intervene. When the efforts of the UN also failed to get Iraq to vacate by January 15, 1991, the US and her allies (34 nations in all) started their military attacks on Iraq—condenamed: Operation Desert Storm. Saddam Hussein urged his compatriots to fight this powerful coalition, and called it 'mother of all battles'. This high-tech war carried on by the US and her allies (with laser-guided missiles and stealth bombers) destroyed Iraq's main installations. The oil wells of Kuwait were set ablaze which caused ecological damage to the Gulf region. Unable to fight, the Iraqi soldiers surrendered without a fight on the ground. Saddam's forces suffered massive defeats, and Iraq agreed for peace after withdrawing from Kuwait.

Cease-fire Agreement (1991)

Saddam survived this humiliating defeat, and his representative to the UN, agreed to obey the UN terms of peace. The UN imposed economic sanctions, and this was to continue till Iraq's armaments and chemical weapons were totally destroyed. For achieving these objectives, the UN sent its inspectors to Iraq's factories and laboratories. The economic embargo on Iraq by the UN caused great hardships to the people, but they still adore their hero, Saddam. Iraq's oil-revenues from exports came to a dead-halt and she was not allowed to purchase anything from other countries.

Plight of Iraq

The US and its allies tried to eliminate Saddam Hussein but they did not succeed, for the Iraqis admire him. Thereafter the US and the allies made serious efforts to cause severe hardships to the Iraqis by imposing economic sanctions.

Oil for Food Programme

Following repeated appeals from Iraq to the UN to lift the sanctions and the co-operation extended by her to the UN inspectors, the Security Council agreed finally to start what is known as "the Oil-for-Food" programme in 1996. Iraq was allowed to import basic necessities such as food and medicines for her 22 million subjects. The UN set up what is known as the Weapons Inspection team (UNSCOM) for enforcing Iraq's compliance with the Security Council's resolution to destroy its lethal and chemical weapons.

The Threat of War

Iraq took on a collision course when Saddam Hussein called on his compatriots to wage a holy war against his oppressors in January 1998. In February, the US threatened to strike when the weapons inspection team reported non-cooperation from Iraq. However, the war was averted when Kofi Annan, the UN Secretary-General, brokered a peace deal between the two. In July 1998, Saddam declared he would take action if the UN embargo was not lifted. Pictures of innocent and ailing children suffering due to various maladies and malnutrition had no effect on the oppressors. The US and her allies had been maintaining a large military presence in the Gulf, and in December 1998 the US and UK began air strikes on Iraq (December 28, 1998 – January 4, 1999). This was done in retaliation to Iraq's alleged non-co-operation to the inspection team. Iraq suffered heavy damage as in the 1991 war. (In 1995, Saddam was re-elected president indicating his popularity.)

The Second Gulf War

Exercising its sovereign right, Iraq forced the UN weapons inspectors (who were investigating Iraq for Weapons of Mass Destruction) to quit the country in 1998. Since then the US and its allies were waiting for an opportunity to strike at Iraq for they desired a 'regime change'. After the defeat of the Taliban in Afghanistan, President George W Bush and Tony Blair put intense pressure on the UN Security Council for approval to strike at Iraq. The Iraqi Government finally yielded to the UN Security Council's desire that the weapons inspectors be permitted once again to investigate Iraq's WMD. Before the inspection was over, the US and its allies decided on a pre-emptive strike on Iraq. But France, Germany and Russia opposed this move in the UN Security Council. These three powers wanted a report from the chairman of the weapons inspection commission (Hans Blix) who had inspected Iraqi weapons establishments.

Despite the disagreement in the Security Council, the US-led coalition attacked Iraq. The reason for the war being that Saddam was developing weapons of mass destruction, had used chemical weapons against Iran and his own people (at Halabja) and had violated human rights of his subjects. Moreover, the US-led coalition led by President Bush presumed that Saddam Hussein of Iraq was in touch with Al-Qaeda terrorists. But many members of the UN including the Gulf States believed that the US-led coalition was more interested in acquiring the vast oil resources of Iraq after the removal of the Iraqi president. Iraq's oil resources are vast, next only to Saudi Arabia.

The UN became a mute spectator when the US-led coalition served a 48 hours ultimatum to President Saddam Hussein and his sons to leave the country. When there was no response, the war began on March 20, 2003, despite warnings from Iraqi president that he would take the war anywhere in the world. He appealed to his people to 'draw your sword' against the invaders. The world watched the high-tech war (through TV channels) conducted against Iraqi political and military establishments, and the large scale destructions of cities and towns including the capital, Baghdad. It was in Baghdad that the coalition faced fierce attack by Iraqi ground forces. By May 1, the war officially ended in the defeat of Saddam Hussein, and on December 13, he was captured after months of search. His sons were killed earlier in his home town Tikrit. Iraq was occupied by the coalition forces, and Mr Paul Bremer was appointed administrator of Iraq. The Iraqi resistance against occupation forces after the capture of Saddam Hussein continued unabated. This happened even after the transfer of sovereignty by the occupation forces to the new Iraqi Government on June 28, 2004 (two days ahead of the supposed transfer). The US troops that numbered 135,000 protected the interim government. The interim Prime Minister of Iraq, Mr Iyad Allawi, had declared amnesty to resistance fighters involved in minor crimes. On 31 January, 2005, a transitional government was elected by the Iraqis. In April 2005, Jalal Talabani, a Kurdish politician, was elected the sixth president of Iraq; and in the following month, Ibrahim al-Jaafari assumed the office of the prime minister. The transistional government was replaced by a permanent government which was formed in May 2006 following the general elections of December 2005.

Financial Aspects of the War

During the war, the US president appealed to the Congress to sanction $75 billion for waging the war. Among the coalition partners, the most important were Britain, Spain, Italy, Australia and subsequently Japan. Most of the Iraqi towns, including the capital, were subjected to large-scale bombing which caused heavy civilian casualties besides immense damage to buildings, bridges, civilian and military installations. The defeated army set fire to oil installations during the period of resistance. With the advent of the war, Russia, India, and several other countries suffered heavy financial losses (due to Iraq's inability to meet its contractual obligations). India suffered because Iraq could not supply oil under 'food-for-oil' programme. Russia lost $3 billion. The Iraqis are suffering the most today as their lives are seriously disrupted. Hospitals, schools, colleges and other establishments have been closed. Tens and thousands of Iraqis have lost their jobs.

Iraq Today

A radical Shia cleric, Muqtada al-Sadr, with a large number of his supporters carried on violent resistance against the government. Before the parliamentary elections of March 2010, he had called upon the people of Iraq to vote for those politicians who advocated the expulsion of foreign coalition forces from Iraq. The new parliament started functioning from June 14, 2010, and they re-elected Jalal Talabani (of Patriotic Union of Kurdistan) as president on November 11, 2010. Nouri al-Maliki of the Islamic Dawa Party too continued as the prime minister. The withdrawal of the coalition forces from Iraq began in 2004 and was completed by the end of the year 2011. The last to withdraw were the UK forces in May 2011 and the US forces in December 2011. Between March 2003 and December 2011, an estimated 4,802 coalition military personnel died. On the Iraqi side, more than 160,000 civilians and combatants lost their lives, with about 1.6 million people internally displaced. The financial cost of the war to the US was about $802 billion according to the Congressional Research Service and that for the UK was about £9.24 billion according to the British government.

Illegality of the Iraq War

An enquiry commission in the US reported in March 2005 that Iraq did not possess any weapons of mass destruction (the main reason for launching the war by the US president); also a CIA report in the same year mentioned that Saddam Hussein had no formal links with the Al Qaeda before 2003. The legality of pursuing the war without any specific resolution of the UNSC was questioned by the international community. The US Government also came under fire for abusing human rights of the Iraqi prisoners held at Abu Ghraib prison in Iraq.

Iraq's Economy

The mainstay of Iraq's economy is oil. Nearly one-third of the population depends upon agriculture. The value of the Iraqi dinar has depreciated since the Second Gulf War. The war caused total chaos. Oil exports came to a standstill since the pipelines were destroyed by insurgents. Unemployment and inflation rates rose. At a donor conference held in

Madrid in October 2003, the donors pledged billions of dollars of aid money to Iraq for its reconstruction. In 2004, the Paris Club (group of 19 wealthy economies in the world) agreed to waive 80% of Iraq's $40 billion debt to them.

Dawn of The Twenty-first Century

People of the world fervently hoped that the 21 st century would augur well for peace and prosperity. However, they were in for a big shock. The new century began with a big bang... the Al Qaeda terrorists struck at the very heart of the US financial centre, ramming two planes into the twin towers of the World Trade Centre in New York City on September 11, 2001. The twin towers collapsed within two hours of the attack. The terrorists also crashed another flight into the Pentagon (US defence Headquarters) in Arlington, Virginia. More than three thousand people were killed in these attacks. The US President George Bush Jr. declared war on terror and promised the Americans that he would punish the perpetrators, no matter how long it might take. The US President urged all leaders of the world to join him in this Global War on Terror. The mastermind of the 9/11 attacks was Al Qaeda's founder, Osama Bin Laden, who got protection from the Taliban regime in Afghanistan.

The US lent support to the Northern Alliance led by Ahmad Shah Massoud which was fighting to dislodge the regime of Taliban in Afghanistan. The Northern Alliance was made up of non-Pashtum groups like the Tajiks, Uzbeks etc. With the US ground support the northern alliance defeated the Taliban, and a new government was set up in Kabul under the leadership of Hamid Karzai. Thereafter, American troops and fighter jets started bombing the strong holds of the Taliban along the border with Pakistan. It took nearly ten years for the Americans to avenge the tragedy of 2001.... Bin Laden was shot and killed by US Navy Seals at Abbottabad, Pakistan (2nd May 2011) on the orders fo the US President Barack Obama.

Sri Lanka

The long ethnic conflict in Sri Lanka ended in May 2009 with the surrender of the LTTE forces (Tamil Tigers) to the Sri Lankan government. The conflict began in 1949 when the Tamil workers in nothern Sri Lanka were denied citizenship rights. The Tamils in Sri Lanka felt that they were treated as second class citizens. In 1972, the Sri Lankan government recognised Buddhism as its official religion and changed the name of Ceylon to Sri Lanka. The Tamils are concentrated in the north and north-east of Sri Lanka. In 1976, Velupillai Prabhakaran became frontline leader of the

Liberation Tigers of Tamil Eelam (LTTE) which carried on a violent struggle against the Sri Lankan government. The goal of the LTTE was to create an independent state for the Tamils (Eelam) in the north and north-eastern parts of Sri Lanka. The Sri Lankan government failed to bring the LTTE to the negotiating table to solve the ethnic conflict. The Sri Lankan government sought the help of India in negotiating peace with Tamil Tigers in 1987. The Indian government dispatched the Indian Peace Keeping Force (IPKF) to Sri Lanka for the purpose of arranging truce between the two warring parties. However, the efforts of IPKF failed and it left Sri Lanka in March 1990 upon President Premadasa's request. Subsequently, the Tamil Tigers carried out the assassinations of Rajiv Gandhi (former Indian PM) in 1991 and Sri Lankan President Premadasa in 1993.

President Chandrika Kumaratunga failed to engage the Tamil Tigers in ending the ethnic strife. So began the third Eelam war by LTTE in 1995. After losing Jafna to the Sri Lankan forces, the LTTE put up a fierce resistance and the Norwegians intervened to mediate in 2002. The peace efforts of the Norwegian mission failed and the war continued. After repudiating the ceasefire agreement with the LTTE, the Sri Lankan forces went on the offensive and captured Kilinochchi (LTTE's capital) in 2009. Mahinda Rajapakse, who was elected as the Sri Lankan President in 2005, vowed to end the conflict at the earliest with his slogan "fight to finish". All the important strongholds of the LTTE, including Mullaittivu, were captured by General Fonseka in April 2009. The LTTE accepted defeat, and on May 18th 2009 its supremo, Prabhakaran, and his seven commanders were killed. The downfall of the LTTE may be traced to the over-confidence of its leader. The LTTE leadership ignored the determination of the new Sri Lankan President Rajapakse to carry on the war to its logical conclusion. The LTTE leader did not bother about the concerns of the Government of India about the repercussions of continuing the conflict. The arms supply to the LTTE began to dwindle and the war came to an end abruptly. The Tamil Tigers took the civilians as hostages during the last phase of the war.

The Sri Lankan government brought to an end the emergency which was declared by President Kumaratunga in 1995. During the course of the ethnic conflict more than 80,000 people lost their lives. It is difficult to estimate the collateral damage caused by this conflict. The Sri Lankan government is arraigned by the United Nations Human Rights Council (UNHRC) for the excesses committed on the Tamil civilians by the Sri Lankan forces.

Japan

On March 11th, 2011, Japan was hit with triple disasters—the earthquake of magnitude 9, the tsunami, and also the damage to nuclear reactor at Fukushima Daiichi. The meltdown of the nuclear reactor released great amount of radiation which has caused wide-spread damage to the ecology. People had to be evacuated to safer places, i.e. beyond the 20-kilometre exclusion zone. Japan had never experienced such a disaster since the dropping of atom bombs on Hiroshima and Nagasaki in August 1945. Thousands of foreigners were stranded and many Chinese students had to leave Japan. Due to the tsunami, nearly 16000 lives were lost and many towns along the Japanese coastline were devastated. It is estimated that the triple disaster caused loss of tens of billions of US dollars. Fortunately, the civil society groups rendered great help to those affected by the disaster. The national mood in Japan became sullen and the Prime Minister Naoto Kan had to resign. Japan lost its place as the second largest economy in the world. Its place has been filled by China. On 30th August 2011, the democratic party of Japan elected Yoshihiko Noda as the new Prime Minister. Noda introduced austerity measures to combat the growing economic crisis in the country. He also indicated that he would increase the rate of the consumption tax for the reconstruction of the areas destroyed by the tsunami.

The Chinese Dragon

China's economy grew at the rate of 10 per cent before the global economic recession (2008-10). The Chinese government had undertaken several infrastructure projects in countries like Bangladesh, Myanmar, Sri Lanka, Pakistan and several countries in Africa and Latin America. It has so far held two trillion dollars of US government bonds and enjoyed favourable balance of trade by manipulating its currency, Yuan. China has replaced Japan as the world's second largest economy. China's exports account for 40 per cent of its GDP. It holds more than 3 trillion US dollars in foreign exchange reserves. In view of its declining domestic petroleum production and its rapidly expanding economy, import of oil and gas has assumed great importance. It is investing money and material in oil and gas fields abroad to ensure its long-term energy security. It is also investing money in exploring alternative sources of energy.

China today is flexing its muscles against the neighbouring countries in order to expand its territory. Earlier it had taken control of Tibet in 1950. In 1962, China invaded India and occupied large tracts of territory in the Jammu and Kashmir state of India (Aksai Chin). It has not recognised the Mac Mahon line as its border with India. Today it is putting forward its claim to Arunachal Pradesh, an integral part of India. Similarly it has border disputes with neighbouring countries by claiming a few islands in the South China Sea as its own. It considers Taiwan as a renegade province, and hopes to unify this island in course of time. It is constantly reminding the US government to follow "One China Policy", thereby recognising China's legitimate claim over Taiwan.

In recent years, China has been supporting Pakistan with financial and military assistance. It had clandestinely assisted Pakistan in building its nuclear arsenal. It has undertaken construction projects in the Pakistan Occupied Kashmir (POK) which is also claimed by India as its own. China has widened and repaired the Karakoram Highway which runs from Kashgar (Xinjiang region) to Pakistan via POK. It also wants to develop rail link from Kashgar to Pakistan through POK. China has taken over the Gwadar deep water port in Balochistan (Pakistan) which it wants to convert into an energy hub. In the future it wants to build an oil pipeline between Gwadar and Xinjiang region. The idea behind the above mentioned projects is to receive oil and other goods from the Gulf countries through Gwadar port. These will also serve as alternative routes for Chinese imports from West Asia.

Thailand

In a bloodless coup by the Thai army and supported by the People's Alliance for Democracy (PAD), Thaksin Shinawatra, the Thai Premier was overthrown in September 2006. The Thai Premier had gone to New York to participate in the assembly of the United Nations. The Thai army took control over this monarchical state after forcing the Thai Premier to go into exile. However, the army could not appease the protesting crowd who were demanding the restoration of democracy. Therefore, the army introduced a constitution and held elections in December 2007. The People's Power Party comprising of Shinawatra's allies won the elections and formed a coalition government in February 2008. The new Premier could not continue for long; he was unseated. Another Prime Minister was elected, but he too had to go because the court annulled his election. In September 2008, there was a massive protest organized by the Yellow Shirts which took over the Bangkok airport and other government buildings. The Yellow Shirts were protesting against the demand for the restoration of democracy by pro-Thanksin Red Shirts. It was in these circumstances that the army had to intervene. With the support of the army, Abhisit Vejjajiva of the Democrat Party was elected the new Prime Minister on December 17, 2008.

Thaksin Shinawatra, who had been ousted from power, was accused of subverting the state system to promote his own business according to the judgement of the Thai courts. The Red Shirts who supported Shinawatra stormed the ASEAN summit in 2009 which resulted in violence. Some of the delegates were evacuated from the summit so as to facilitate their return to their respective countries.

Prime Minister Vejjajiva declared a state of emergency in the capital, Bangkok. Despite the emergency, the Red Shirts launched their protests to bring down the government which had been supported by the army. The core demand of the protesters was that the constitution should be so amended as to restore real democracy in the country. They considered Vejjajiva's government as illegal. The Prime Minister held several negotiations with the Red Shirts so as to bring peace. However, the latter stood firm, and the House of Representatives had to be dissolved so as to facilitate fresh elections. The Thai army also supported this move in order to end the political chaos in the country. The general election was held on July 3, 2011, which resulted in a victory of the Pheu Thai Party. Its leader Yingluck Shinawatra became the country's first female Prime Minister. The 44 year old Prime Minister happens to be the sister of the former Prime Minister Thaksin Shinawatra. The election results indicated three things. Firstly, the people of the country have warned the military elite not to interfere in democratic politics. Secondly, the people wanted a genuine democracy. And thirdly, they desired a unified nation which would work for the welfare of poor people. The new Prime Minister will be facing many challenges which include bringing about an integration of the Muslim community into the mainstream of Thai society. Thailand is Buddhist-majority country. She has promised to grant some form of autonomy to Muslim areas in southern Thailand.

Nepal
During the medieval period, many small kingdoms existed in Nepal. These kingdoms got united in the Kathmandu valley due to the efforts of King Prithvi Narayan Shah in 1790. Nepal became the only country where Hindu monarchy existed. However, in 1846 Ranas wrested power from the king and became virtual rulers. They ruled Nepal for nearly 104 years. It was during this time that the Ranas introduced a regal code which divided the Nepali society into five castes. The members of the ruling family as well as the Taghadaris (Brahmins) constituted the upper class. The rest belonged to the impure class, the lowest being the untouchables. A large majority of people groaned under the tyrannical rule of the Ranas, and thereafter under the kings. It was in 1951 that King Tribhuvan wrested power from

the Ranas. His successor, Mahendra, banned all political parties in 1960 in order to maintain law and order. King Mahendra died in 1972 and was succeeded by his son Birendra. King Birendra came under heavy pressure to lift the ban on political parties due to pro-democracy movement. A new constitution was drafted which provided for the representation of the people and a constitutional monarchy. It was during his time that a multi-party democracy was ushered in.

In 1996, the Maoists, who represented the poor by and large, launched a rebellion and tried to topple the constitutional monarchy. In 2001, King Birendra and his family members were killed by crown prince Dipendra. He committed sucide and thereafter Gyanendra assumed power. In the meantime, the Maoists gained great influence in large parts of Nepal and demanded the abolition of monarchy. Gyanendra abused his power and tried to crush the Maoist rebels in 2005. In spite of his serious efforts, he failed. Large scale rebellion by the Maoists took place all over Nepal in April 2006 which forced the king to give up his absolute powers. He appointed G.P. Koirala, the leader of the Nepali Congress Party to form the government. Prime Minister Koirala formed the CPN-UML coalition and tried to bring the Maoists into the mainstream politics. It was he who tried to convince the Maoists that a new constitution would bring about an end to the monarchy. A constituent assembly had to be elected so as to draft a new constitution. On May 28, 2008, the Hindu monarchy of Nepal came to an end and the king became an ordinary citizen. A republic was proclaimed and the king had to vacate the Narayanhiti palace. On April 10, 2008, the Maoists won a clear majority in the constituent assembly. A coalition government was formed by Prachanda, the Maoist leader. But his government failed to draft a new constitution because of raging controversies in the constituent assembly. In the meantime, food prices had shot up, cooking oil became scarce, and agricultural output remained stagnant. Rural poverty and illiteracy continued since there was anarchy. Successive Prime Ministers could not maintain law and order. It was in these circumstances that Baburam Bhattarai became Prime Minister (2011). Political analysts believe that his coalition government would hopefully bring peace and prosperity to the country.

North and South Korea
Following the Russo-Japanese war of 1905, Korea was annexed by Japan. At the end of the Second World War, the Japanese occupation of Korea ended, but unfortunately, it was again occupied by Soviet troops in the North and the American forces in the South. The line dividing the two parts of Korea runs along the 38th parallel. The United Nations peace

keeping forces conducted elections in the South, but the Communist North did not participate. In 1950, communist troops of North Korea crossed the 38th parallel and invaded South Korea. The Korean War continued for three long years. Finally, an armistice agreement was signed between the two. Unfortunately, this agreement could not be converted into a full-fledged peace treaty since both the parties claimed entire Korea as their own. In other words, North and South Korea till today remain technically at war. North Korea had the full support of two major powers, namely, Communist China and the Soviet Union. Kim Jong-il converted North Korea into a military state with himself as the dictator. The South embraced democracy with the support of the west.

Constant tensions between the two Koreas became the order of the day. From January 1968 to March 2010, there were frequent clashes between the two. In the meantime, North Korea became a nuclear state, thanks to the clandestine support of Communist China and Pakistan. Along with other countries, North Korea had signed the nuclear Non-Proliferation Treaty (NPT). However, in 2003 it renounced the treaty. On 9th October 2006, the North Korean government announced that it had successfully tested a nuclear device.

Nuclear North Korea sent a submarine on a spy mission to South Korea which ended in failure. More than 30 North Korean sailors were killed by South Korean security forces in September 1996. In June 2002, there was a bloody skirmish in the Yellow Sea betweeen the North and the South, resulting in the death of 6 South Korean and 13 North Korean sailors. In March 2010, a South Korean corvette *Cheonan* sank under mysterious circumstances killing 46 South Korean sailors. An investigation later revealed that it was torpedoed by a North Korean submarine. In November 2010, a South Korean island, Yeonpyeong, was subjected to constant artillery shelling by the North Koreans, resulting in the death of two South Korean marines and injuries to five others. South Korea responded to these attacks by retaliatory firings.

All these incidents have caused lot of anxiety among the international community. It must be remembered that South Korea has the backing of the US government which has stationed more than 28,500 troops there. The US has committed to help South Korea under all circumstances. It has appealed to China and other interested parties in restraining North Korea from plunging this region into a nuclear conflict zone. North Korea, might appears to have become aggressive with respect to the South in order to gain attention of the US so as to secure economic aid. It has remained as a pariah state for too long, and the US with the help of China would like it to join the international community at the earliest. North Korea with all its nuclear might has remained a poor country due to agricultural stagnation and crippling economic sanctions imposed on it by the international community.

In contrast to its northern neighbour, South Korea has become an economic powerhouse. It has become highly industrialised, specializing in consumer electronics and automobiles. It has developed a highly export-oriented economy, and remains as one of the four Asian Tigers.

The Arab Spring: Revival of Pan-Arabism

The winds of change are sweeping over Middle East since January 2011 in the form of full-blown pro-democracy movements against the authoritarian rule. It should be remembered that the domination of the US over the Arab nations is slowly receding in the wake of what is known as the Arab Spring. The revival of pan-Arabism has been due to the maladministration of the Arab countries by their despotic rulers (some of them had the backing of the US), and also due to the unstinted support Israel receives from the US. The economic conditions of the Arabs and their yearning for democracy have been ignored by these Arab rulers. Their administration reeked in coruption, bad governance, and great deal of repression. Arab Spring got its name from the spontaneous overflow of powerful feeling of Arab hatred towards their despotic rulers as manifested in their recent revolts. The pro-democracy movements came as its sequel.

Tunisia

The first indication of the Arab Spring appeared in Tunisia where an unemployed graduate, Mohamed Bouazizi, committed self-immolation on 17th December, 2010. This trivial episode triggered a chain reaction all over the Middle East. There was groundswell of sympathy for this dead graduate which finally resulted in the overthrow of the Tunisian dictator, Ben Ali. However, the members of the old regime are still controlling the destiny of this country with the support of the US government. But agitations are still continuing.

Egypt

The uprising in Tunisia has spread like a wildfire. The next country to be affected was Egypt where President Hosni Bubarak had been ruling like a dictator for nearly three decades. The uprising began on 25th January, 2011, in Egypt at Tahrir square, Cairo, following the youth movement led by Egyptian activist, Asmaa Mahfouz. It continued for 18 days and brought the country to a standstill, with the Egyptian army remaining as a mute spectator. The most important cities affected were Cairo and Alexandria where people gathered in tens of thousands shouting slogans against Hosni Mubarak. This agitation was led mostly by the tech-savvy and liberal youth who used social media internet sites like Facebook and Twitter to communicate with each other. The Islamists of the Muslim Brotherhood and the liberals of the Wafd party joined the protests. This upsurge of Egyptian nationalism culminated in the resignation of Hosni Mubarak on February 11th, 2011. The US government advised him to resign and pave the way for a smooth transition to democracy. At the time of writing, the ex-president has been accused of unleashing terror on the protesters and is standing trial. The army intervened and suspended the constitution and the parliament and promised the people a new constitution and elections within six months.

Algeria

The next country to be affected by the pro-democracy movement is Algeria. The Algerians gathered in large numbers in their capital, Algiers, and started shouting slogans against their dictator Bouteflika. They carried posters reading "Give back our Algeria", "Bouteflika Out" etc. on February 12th, 2011. The agitation resulted in lifting of the 19-year old state emergency in the country on February 22nd, 2011.

Yemen

In Yemen, thousands of people gathered in the capital Sana'a on February 3rd, 2011, and demanded that their long ruling President Ali Abdullah Saleh to leave the country. The ruler, a strong ally of the United States, promised that he would not run for the presidency during the next term. The blast in the presidential compound's mosque on June 4th, 2011, resulted in his injury, and he had to leave for Saudi Arabia for treatment. After his medical treatment, he returned to his capital Sana'a on September 23rd, 2011, and began to face street protests. Yemen has become a sanctuary for the Al Qaeda terrorists. It is a very poor country facing a civil war and with 40 per cent unemployment. It is said that 20 million people get a daily wage of less than two dollars.

Bahrain

The protests in Bahrain (Shia-dominated gulf country, having the headquarters of the US fifth fleet) that began on February 14th, 2011, were largely peaceful. But on the night of 17th February the police conducted raids on the protestors who were sleeping at Pearl Roundabout, Manama, which resulted in the death of three protesters. The government forces again opened fire on protesters, mourners and journalists on 18th February. This incident prompted the protesters to demand the end of monarchy. On

22nd February nearly one hundred thousand people marched to protest against the atrocities committed by the security forces. The Bahraini monarch, a Sunni, requested the assistance of GCC countries like Saudi Arabia and UAE to quell the revolt. On 14th March Saudi troops entered Bahrain and opened fire on the protesters killing many. Finally, these protests resulted in the dismissal of some ministers, release of political prisoners and granting of economic concessions.

Libya
On 15th February, 2011, the pro-democracy movement gathered momentum in Benghazi after the arrest of human rights activist, Fethi Tarbel. The protesters here clashed with the police and 14 of them were injured. The people were fed up with the oppressive rule of Muammar Gaddafi who had been in power for more than four decades. A group of people, whose relatives were killed in 1996 firing, started demanding the end of Gaddafi's dictatorship. Human rights organisations and prominent Libyans also joined the pro-democracy movement. They were supported by the governments of the west, most notably, France, UK and the United States. The protest movement enraged the Libyan dictator, and his forces began suppressing it. In the course of time, the struggle between the protesters and Gaddafi's supporters turned into a civil war. The United States along with France and UK championed the cause of democracy in Libya by supporting the pro-democracy movement. The NATO warplanes started bombing the port of Tripoli in May 2011. The west invoked the UN's doctrine of "responsibility to protect" the civilians in the ongoing civil war. The NATO forces started bombing all the strongholds of Gaddafi which resulted in the death of Gaddafi's youngest son and three grandchildren. The International Criminal Court (ICC) had issued an arrest warrant against the Libyan leader, his son and the intelligence chief for war crimes.

Russia, China and India (non-members of the ICC) had been critical about the sharp escalation of NATO military strikes. Gaddafi was dragged out of a drain in his hometown, Sirte, and killed by the rebel forces on 20th October, 2011.

Jordan
Inspired by the ongoing pro-democracy movements in the neighbouring countries, protesters in Jordan, led by trade union members and the leftist parties, demanded the dismissal of the government of Prime Minister Samir Rifai on 14th January, 2011. The demonstrations against the government gathered momentum with the participation of 5000 people who denounced

the government's economic policies a few days later. On 1st February, King Abdullah dismissed the government of PM Rifai and asked a former army general to form a new cabinet. He also ordered him to introduce reforms in order to strengthen democracy. The protesters were not happy and they carried on their agitations.

Syria

The pro-democracy movement in Syria started on 26th January, 2011. The protesters called for political reforms and restoration of civil rights. They also demanded an end to the state of emergency which had commenced in 1963. The movement was intensified on 15th March with thousands of protesters marching in major cities of Syria. The regime of President Bashar al-Assad has come in for severe criticism by western powers for suppressing the people's legitimate aspirations. The west has imposed economic sanctions since long, for they did not like the President's hostile attitude towards Israel, and friendly attitude towards Iran. He has been accused of instigating the murder of former leader of Lebanon, Rafik al-Hariri. Syria has always been supporting the Hamas, a militant organisation, that now governs the Gaza Strip.

The street protests in Syrian capital, Damascus, and other towns resulted in great violence, with 14000 people dead and nearly 10000 people fleeing to neighbouring countries. President Assad saw foreign conspiracy in these rising protests as attempts to dethrone him. He revoked the emergency laws and also agreed to introduce political reforms. The US and its allies are bent upon bringing about 'regime change' in Syria. The president is still popular among certain sections of the society. On 17th July, 2011, his supporters held a rally on the occasion of the seventeenth anniversary of his swearing-in ceremony. The president got full support from his army, the Ba'ath party and the militant organisation, Hezbollah. Russia has also supported the Syrian President since it has been providing defence equipments and port facilities to Syria. Syrian army tanks entered several Syrian cities on 31st July to suppress the revolt which has resulted in bloody clashes–the bloodiest since the movement started.

Similar pro-democracy movements began in countries like Morocco, Oman and Sudan. To some extent Saudi Arabia was also affected, where the king announced economic concessions, women's participation in the next Shura council, and holding of municipal elections.

BIBLIOGRAPHY

Encylopaedia Section
I. *Encyclopaedia Brittanica* (rel. vols.), *Encyclopaedia of Social Sciences* (rel. vols.). *New International Encyclopaedia* (rel. vols.), *The Columbia Encyclopaedia, Langer's Encyclopaedia of World History, The New Collegiate Encyclopaedia,* James Mitchell's *History and Culture* (2 Vols.), *The Reader's Digest Great Encyclopaedic Dictionary* (Vol. 3), *American Educator Encyclopaedia* (rel. vols.).

General Section
UNESCO Published *History of Mankind: Cultural and Scientific Development.* (rel. vols.)
1. Weech, W.N., *History of the World.*
2. Zebel Sidney and Sidney Schwartz, *Past to Present.*
3. Nehru, Jawaharlal, *Glimpses of World History.*
4. Lucas, H.S., *A Short History of Civilisation.*
5. Brinton, Crane *et al., Modern Civilisation : A History of the Last Five Centuries.*
6. Nevins, Allen, *A Gateway to History.*
7. Wells, H.G., *An Outline History of the World.*
8. Wells, H.G., *A Short History of the World.*
9. Collingwood, R.G., *The Idea of History.*
10. Shapiro, Irwin (Ed.), *Universal History of the World.*
11. Hayes *et al., World History*
12. Savelle, Max (Ed), *A History of World Civilization* (2 Vols.)
13. Breasted, J.H., *The Conquest of Civilization.*
14. Durant, Will, *Lessons of History.*
15. Durant, Will, *Story of Civilisation* (rel. Vols).
16. Davies, *World History.*
17. Ketelby, C.D.M., *A History of Modern Times.*
18. Palmer, R.R. and J. Colton, *A History of the Modern World.*

Select Bibliography

19. Scott F.D. & A. Rockefeller Jr., *The 20th Century World, a reading guide.*
20. Easton, Stewart C., *World since 1918.*
21. Langsam, W.C., *The World since 1919.*
22. Webster, *World History.*
23. Brinton, C., *et al., A History of Civilization.*
24. Grant and Temperley, *Europe in the Nineteenth and Twentieth Century.*
25. Fisher, H.A.L., *A History of Europe.*
26. Hays, C.J.H., *Contemporary Europe since 1870.*
27. Thomson, David, *Europe since Napoleon.*
28. Benns, F.L., *European History since 1870.*
29. Ergang, R.R., *Europe in Our Time, 1914 to the present.*
30. Buss Claud, *History of Asia.*
31. Panikkar, K.M., *Asia and the Western Dominance.*
32. Clyde and Beer, *History of the Far East.*
33. Latouratte, K.S., *A Short History of the Far East.*
34. Vinacke, H.M., *A History of the Far East in Modern Times.*
35. Williams, T.H. *et al., A History of the United States* (to 1877)
36. Bailey, T.A., *A Diplomatic History of the American People.*
37. Hitti, P.K., *History of the Arabs.*
38. Lenczowski, George, *Middle East in World Affairs.*
39. Carr, E.H., *The Bolshevik Revolution* (Vol. I).
40. Pares, Bernard, *A History of Russia.*
41. Munshi, K.M. (Ed.), *History & Culture of Indian People* (rel. Vols.).
42. Majumdar, R.C., *et al., An Advanced History of India.*
43. Chopra, Pran *et al., A Social, Cultural and Economic History of India* (3 vols.).
44. Hoskins, H.L., *European Imperialism in Africa.*
45. Paton, Alan, *The Land and People of South Africa.*

INDEX

AIDS, 347, 371, 375 (see also HIV)
ASEAN, 378, 395
Aachen, 142
Abbottabad, 391
Abelard, Peter, 152
Abhidamma Pitaka, 90
Abhiras, 101
Aboukir Bay, 225
Abraham, Hebrew prophet, 28, 38
Abu Musa, 386
Abu Simbel temple, 20
Abyssinia, 324
Achaeans, 70
Acropolis, 76
Actium, battle of, 114
Adams, Joh Couch, 361-62
Adil Shah, Sultan, 163
Adrianople, 267
Aegean Civilisation, 70, 74
   palace of King Minos, 70
Aegean Sea, 70, 84
Aegospotami, battle of, 78
Aeschylus, 77
Aetolians, 70
Afghanistan (Afghans), 74, 100, 161, 163, 287-88, 347, 371, 375, 379
   Afghan wars, 272, 385
   Amanullah Khan, 288
   Kabul, 51, 164
   Karzai, Hamid, 372, 375, 385
   Mulla Omar, 375
   NWFP, 287
   Nadir Shah, Mohammed, 288
   Russian invasion of, 349, 368
   Taliban's regime in, 372, 375-76
   U S and its allies set up interim government in, 375-76
   Zahir Shah, 288
Africa, 7, 41, 112, 114, 130, 133, 183, 184, 186, 242, 263, 269, 310, 311, 332, 347, 348, 354-59, 373
   British East Africa (Kenya), 278

Banda, Hastings, 357
   Smith, Ian, 357
coasts, 168
decolonisation of, 354-59
ECA, 343
East, 129-30, 358-59
economic crisis in, 342
French (Central), Equatorial Africa, 357
French West Africa, 356
German East Africa, 279
German South West Africa, 279
Negroes in, 186
North, 14, 17, 41, 112, 129, 131, 140, 144, 145, 160, 338, 354-56
North-east, 17, 126
Organisation of African Union, 373
partition of, 277-79
South Africa, 278, 342, 359, 371, 375
   apartheid in, 342
   Union of South Africa, 278
West, 14, 41, 183, 279, 356
   Economic Commission for West Africa, 343
Western imperialism in, 277-79
Agade (Akkad), 29, 42
Agadir crisis, 311
Agassiz, Louis, 361
Ahimsa, 85, 90
Aix-la-Chapelle, treaty of, 203
Akkad, 29, 42
Al Badr, 384
Al Firdausi, 132
Al Hambra, 133
Al Hasan of Basra, 132
Al Hawi, 132
Al Idrisi, 133
Al Qaeda, 375, 376, 384, 385, 389
Al Tabari, 132
Aland island, 324

Index

Alara, 88
Alaska, 308
Albania, 324, 332
Alberuni, 133
Alcazar, 133
Alcmaeonidae, 73
Alcock, 366
Acuin, 142
Aldrin, Edwin, 377
Alexandria, 146, 186
Alexander the Great (see Greece)
Alexius I Comnenus, 135
Algebra, 66, 138, 278
Algeria, 355-56, 399
    Ben Bella, 356
    North, 355
Allies, 227, 281, 308, 312, 321, 328, 332, 333, 338, 326, 350, 351, 371, 375, 379
Alpine passes, 109
Alps, 109, 112, 177
America (United States of America) (USA), 7, 14, 139, 183, 184, 186, 192, 203, 204, 209, 220, 228, 237, 238, 273, 280, 285, 286, 289, 291, 306, 316, 312, 321, 324, 326, 327, 341, 342, 343, 344, 348, 349, 351, 352, 369, 371, 372, 373, 375-76, 377, 379
American War of Independence, 209-16
    British mercantilist policy, 210-12
        Stamp Act and its repeal, 212
        Sugar Act, 211
    Boston Tea Party, 213
    Continental Congress, first, 213-16
    declaration of independence, 214
    results of war, 216
        skirmishes at Lexington and Concord, 213-14
    development in 13 English colonies, 209-10
    Townshend Act, 121-13
Antiballistic Missiles Treaty (1972), 349
atom bombs on Japan, dropping of, 326-27
Bay of Pigs, 349
Bush, George W, 347, 372, 375, 388, 389, 391
C I A, 348
    entry into World War II, 338
    Foreign policy, 306

Hamilton, Alexander, 305
Harding, 39
Hay, John, 274
I N F treaty (1937), 368
Indians, 14, 67, 68-69, 241-42
Jackson, Andrew, 306
Jacksonian Democracy, 306
Jay Treaty, 305
Jefferson, Thomas, 305
Johnson, President, 292
Kennedy, John F, 3, 349
Lend-Lease Act, 338
Lincoln, Abraham, 215
    Civil War (1861-65) and, 307-08
    further expansion of USA, 308
MacArthur, Douglas, 289, 326
Mickinley, 308
Monroe, 243, 306
Nixon, 292
nuclear strikes, 349
Open Door Policy with regard to China, 274
Organisation of American States, 373
Pearl harbour, attack on by Japan, 338
Pentagon, terrorist attack on, 372, 375
Perry, Commodore, 275
Pilgrim Fathers came to, 209
Reagan, 368
Roosevelt, F D, 338, 341
satellite surveillance system, 379
September 9/11 (2001), after, 374
Social Science Research Council, 5
Truman, 348
Washington, George: early years of new republic and, 305-07
    controversial issues which divided nation, 306-07
    expansion of US territory, 305-06
    Monroe doctrine, 243, 306
    North-South differences, 307
War of 1812 and its results, 306
Washington Conference (1921-22), 285, 326-27
Wilson, Woodrow, 312, 322
world power, emergence of as, 305-08
World Trade Centre, terrorist attack on, 372, 375

America, Central
   Mayan civilisation (Mayas), 67-68
      art and architecture, 68
      intellectual pursuits, 68
      ceremonial centres, 67-68
      economic conditions, 68
      political conditions, 68
      religion, 67-68
      social conditions, 68
America, Latin, 244, 347, 348, 373
American Indians, 241-42
   ECLAC, 343
   revolutions in, 241-43
      causes of revolts in, 241-42
      course of revolutions, 242
      Martin, Jose De San, 242-43
      Monroe doctrine, 243, 306
America, North, 13, 67, 185, 209, 226, 228
   Northern American Arctic, 14
America, South, 183, 184, 241, 242, 243, 310, 375
   Incas (red Indian tribe), 14, 68-69, 210
      civilisation, features of, 69
   Quechua, 69
      strings which talk, 69
      Machu Picchu, remains of, 69
Amnesty International, 378
Anatonlia, 135
Andes mountains, 69
Anglicanism, 199
Anglo-Burmese War (1824), 272, 288
Anglo-French invasion of Egypt, 349
Anglo-French rivalry, 269-70
Anglo-Iranian Oil Company, 286, 287
Anglo-Japanese Treaty (1902), 276, 284
Anglo-Mysore war, 271
Anglo-Russian Convention of 1907, 287
Anglo-Saxons, 139, 160, 197
Anglo-Sikh war, 272
Angola, 279
Anthropology, 6
Antioch, 146
Antwerp, 186
Apennine mountains, 109
Arab World (Arabs, Countries, Empire, Nations) (*see also* Islamic empire), 126-27,129, 130, 131, 132, 133, 134, 135, 140, 141, 142, 144, 145, 266, 351, 352, 359, 373
   Abbasids, 131
   Arab Federation, 352
   Arab-Israeli wars, 346, 371, 372
   Arab League, 352, 373
   Arabic numerals, 138
   contributions to literature, 132
   contributions to science and medicine, 132
   Fatimid of Cairo, 131
   geographers, 133
   Ibn Saud, Abdul Aziz, 352-53
   Moors, 154
   nationalism, 350-53
   Omayyad of Cordova, 131
   scholars, 131, 132
   Wahabis, 352
Arabia, 14, 108, 127
Arabian peninsula, 126
Arabian sea, 79
Arab Spring, 398
Aranyakas, 82
Archaeology
   archaeologists, 5, 8, 13
   history and, 5
Archimedes, 80
Architecture, 23-24, 35
Arctic cap, 185
Ardunio, Gievanni, 361
Argentina, 242
Aristotle, 77, 79, 132, 138, 146
Arithmetic, 66
Arjunayanas, 101
Arkwright, Richard, 235
Armament race, 311
Armstrong, Neil, 379
Aryanisation, process of, 50
Aryans (*see also* Vedic Civilisation), 4, 14, 36, 42, 50-53, 335
   area of occupation, 51-52
   Aryan wars and settlements, 50
   Aryan Gods, 50
   Indo-Aryans, 50
   Indo-Europeans (Aryans), 50
   invasion of India, 50
   political organisation, 52-53
      government, forms of, 53
   Sabha and Samiti, 52-53
Asia (Asian Countries), 7, 12, 19, 40, 67, 80, 130, 183, 186, 238, 264, 269, 272, 284, 285, 314, 310, 348, 373
   Asian Social Forum, Hyderabad, 374
   Asiatic cultures, 79
   Central, 61, 205

ESCAP, 343
nationalism in South and South-East, 286-304
South, 63, 131, 373
South-East, 107, 289, 302, 338, 373
West, 14, 47, 126, 136
Asian crisis, 347
ECWA, 343
Intifada in, 375
Asia Minor, 27, 30, 36, 50, 63, 70, 74, 75, 111, 124, 135, 136, 140
Hittites of, 20, 30
West, 113
Assyria, 36 (*see also* Mesopotamia)
Assyrians, 20, 30-31, 39, 40
Astronomy, 66, 32, 66, 146
Astronauts, 377
Astrology, 32, 107, 119, 376-77
Astronomers, 66, 68
Halley's discoveries, 361-62
Athens (*see* Greece)
Atlantic, 185, 186, 216, 237, 308, 366, 367
Atlantic Charter, 341
Atom bomb (*see* Nuclear)
Atoms, theory of
Democritus set forth his, 78
Attila, 159
Augsburg, Peace of, 192
Augustenburg, Duke of, 256, 257
Australia, 14
Austria, 203, 204-06, 207, 217, 223, 225, 226, 231, 245, 246, 248, 249, 250, 251, 253, 254, 256, 257, 259-62, 263, 265, 267, 315, 309, 310, 311, 324, 325, 335, 337
agitations and redressal of grievances, 261
Austro-Prussian War (1866), 251-52, 256, 257
Charles V, 204
compromise (1867) between Hungary and, 260
Congress of Vienna, 226, 230-32, 242, 244, 246, 253, 263, 289, 337
Dollfuss, 337
Easter Rising and Division of Ireland, 261-62
Ferdinand, Archduke, 204
murder of, 311-12
Habsburgs, 201, 204-05

Home Rule Bill, 261
Irish Free State (Eire) under Eamon De Valera, 262
land reforms, 261
Metternich, role of, 230-32
alliance systems, 231-32
Metternich system supported reactionary rulers, 232
principle of compensation, 231
principle of legitimacy, 230-31
spirit of nationalism suppressed, 232
nationalism in, 259-62
protest revolt, 204
quarrel between Hungary and, 259-60
Rudolph, 204
Theresa, Maria, 203
Thirty Years War, 201, 204
Westphalia, treaty of, 204
Austria-Hungary, 260, 266, 268, 311, 321
Avars, 144
Averrhoes, 132
Averroists, 132
Avicenna, 132
Avignon, 188
Ayatollah Khomeini, 386
Axis powers, 341
Berlin-Rome-Tokyo Axix, 337
Aztec Civilisation, 241
Aztecs, 184

Babylonia, 19, 33-37, 39
architecture and art, 35
Babylonians, 33-35
cities, 34-35
civilisation, 33, 36
Code of Hammurabi, 33, 34
economic life, 33-34
Hammurabi, 33
learning and literature, 35
religion, 34-35
sciences, 35-36
slaves, 34
society, 34
temples, 34-35
Bacon, Francis, 180
Bacon, Roger, 179
Baghdad, 131, 133
Bahamas, 183
Bahrain, 346, 353, 376, 399
Balboa, Vasco Nunez de, 184

Balkans, 231, 265, 332, 326
  Balkan affairs, 260
  Balkan countries (nations) (region), 265, 266, 338
  Balkan League, 267
  Balkan nationalism
    on rise, 264-68
    break up, 266-67
  Crimean War (1854-56) and Treaty of Paris (1856), 264-65
  Eastern question and, 263-68
  first Balkan War (1912), 267
  Indo-Turkish War (1911-12), 267
  Pan-Slavism and Russo-Turkish War (1877-78), 265-66
  political turmoil, 266
  Second Balkan War (1913), 267
  Yung Turk Revolution (1908), 266
Balkan peninsula, 260, 263
Balkan territories, 350
Baltic Republic, 326
Baltic Seas, 148, 149, 151, 206
Bamian, 384
Banditry, 117
Banbung Conference, 373
Bangladesh, 346, 373
  refugees, 4
Barcelona, 131
Bardinia, 112
Bashar al-Assad,   401
Bauer, Andrew, 365
Bay of Bengal, 102
Bayle, Pierre, 361
Behring, Emil von, 365
Bekkar, Balthaskar, 361
Belgian Congo, 357-58
  Kasavubu, 358
  Lumumba, Patrice, 357-58
  Mobutu, Joseph, 358
  Tshombe, Moise, 358
Belgium, 114, 226, 231, 232, 277-78, 321, 337, 326, 326, 327
  independence, 245
  Leopold, King, 357
  Leopold II, 277-78
Bell, Alexander Graham, 237, 367
Benz, Karl, 366
Berents, 185
Bering Straits, 67
Berlin-Rome-Tokyo Axis, 337
Bessemer, Henry, 235
Bethlehem, 116, 122

Bhutan, 373
Bible, Holy, 38, 39, 123, 160, 178, 190, 193, 194
Big Powers, 327
Big Five Powers, 347
Biology
  human biology
    Genome Project (1990), 378
    progress in, 363-64
Birendra, 396
Black Death, 157
Black Sea, 265, 314
Bodhisattvas, 90
Boers
  Boer War (1899), 278
Bolingbroke, 4
Bolivar, Simon, 242, 243
Bolivia, 243
Bombs (*see also* Nuclear)
  Age of Bomb, 362
  atom bomb, 376
Bosnia, 260, 265, 266, 267, 311, 371
Bouazizi, Mohamed, 398
Bourbon, 230
Bouteflika,   399
Brazil, 183, 241, 243, 342
Brihaspati, 103
Bretons, 142
Britain (England, Great Britain, UK), 114, 117, 139, 148, 151, 157, 161, 166, 169, 186, 189, 192, 196-200, 203, 209, 210, 225, 226, 231, 234, 238, 245, 249, 250, 257, 261-62, 264, 271, 278, 284, 286, 287, 289, 290, 292, 293-94, 306, 310, 311, 312, 337, 338, 326, 327, 342, 343, 345, 346, 348, 350, 351, 353, 355, 357, 359, 366, 371
  Adams, Samuel, 212, 213
  Alfred the Great, 197
  Anglican Church, 193, 199
  Anglicanism, 199
  Anglo-Saxons, 139, 160, 197
  Attlee, 304
  Bentinck, William, 271
  Blair, Tony, 372
  Boston massacre, 212
  British East India Company, 213, 269-71, 273, 288, 293
  British Honduras, 67
  Burgoyne, 214-15
  Burke, Edmund, 213

Index

Burma, conquest of, 288-89
Catholic Emancipation Act, (1829), 261
Charles I, 199
Charles II, 199, 200
Charles V, 193
Chatham, Lord, 213
Chelmsford, Lord, 196
Churches of Puritans in, 192
Churchill, Winston, 301, 341, 349
Clive, Robert, 204, 270
Continental Congress
 second, 214
Cornwall, 41
Cornwallis, 215
Cripps, Stafford, 301-02
Cromwell, Oliver, 199
Curzon, Lord, 287, 295
Dalhousie, Lord, 238, 272, 288, 293
Disraeli, 278
Edward I, 198
Edward VI, 193, 199
Elizabeth I, Queen, 193, 199
Factory system in, 236
Gage, Thomas, 214
George III, 211, 213, 215, 216
George, Lloyd, 262
Gladstone, 261
Glorious Revolution, 200
Great Council, 198
Grenville, George, 212
Hastings, Warren, 270
Henry II, 197
Henry III, 198
Henry VII, 198
Henry VIII, 192-93, 199
Home Rule Bill, 261
Humanist movement, 177
Irwin, Lord, 300
James I, 199
James II, 200
Jamestown settlement, 209
Jay Treaty, 305
John, King, 198
Labour Party, 304
London, 186
Lytton, Lord, 294
Mary, Queen, 193, 199, 202
mercantilist policy, 210-12
Minto, Lord, 296
Model Parliament, 198
Montagu, 296

Munro, 270
Mutiny Act of 1765, 212
North, Lord, 212, 213
Pilgrim Fathers, 209
Pitt, William, 204, 226
Protestants, 193
Quebec Act, 213
Reformation Movement in, 192-93
Regulating Act of 1773, 270
renaissance in, 177
Richard, King, 136, 137
Richard I, 197
Ripon, Lord, 295
Sino-British relations, 273
Stamp Act (1765), 212
Stuart rulers, 199-200
Sugar Act (1764), 211
Tudor rulers, 198-99
Victoria, Queen, 293, 294
War of 1812, 306
wars in South India, 271
Washington, 214-15
Wolfe, James, 204
Wycliffe, John, 189-90
Bronze Age, 8
Brown, 366
Brubei, 290, 373
Bruno, Giordano, 179
Buddha, Gautama, 82, 83
 ashtanga marga, 89
 Buddhist (*Sangha*) order of monks established, 89
 early life of, 87-89
 great renunciation, 88
 statues of, 66
 teachings of, 88
Buddhism, 61, 62, 64, 65-66, 82, 87-91, 92, 96, 98
 Ahimsa, 85, 90
 art and architecture, 91
 Buddhist Council, 90
 Buddhist monks, 65-66, 91
 Buddhist schools, 66
 contributions to Indian culture, 90-91
 Dharmaraksha, monk, 66
 first sermon at Deer Park near Benares, 88
 four Noble Truths (*Arya Satya*), 88
 Kasyapa Matanga, monk,
  in China, 61, 62, 64, 65-66
 Mahayana Buddhism, 65, 90
 middle path (*Madhyama Marga*), 89

monastries, 91
sacred text, 90
stupas of Sanchi and Bharhut, 91
Buganda, 358
Bulgaria, 265, 267, 312, 324, 338, 326
    Bulgars, 146
    Treaty of Neuilly (1919), 313
Bunsen, Robert, 362
Burma, 272, 347, 373
    Anglo-Burmese war, 272, 288
    Aung Sang, 288-89
    British conquest of, 288-89
    National League for Democracy (NLD), 376
    nationalism, 288-89
    Ne Win, 289
    NU, U, 289
    Suu Kyi, Aung Saan, 376
    Treaty of Yandoboo (1826), 288
Byzantine empire, 129, 137, 139, 143-47 (*see also* Europe, middle ages)

CENTO, 373
Cabot, John, 185
Caesar, Julius, 114-15, 119
Cairo, 131
Calderon, 177
Calendars
    Lunar, 25
    Solar, 25
Calicut, 183
Calvin, John, 177, 192
Cambodia, 168, 290, 291, 371, 373, 375
Cameroon, 356
Canada, 12, 204, 209, 211, 216, 226, 241, 366, 375
Cape Breton island, 185
Cape of Good Hope, 183, 231
Cape Route, 186
Capitalism, 368, 373
Cardiz, 186
Caribbean islands, 241
Caribbean Sea, 183, 243
Carlyle, Thomas, 1, 4
    French Revolution by, 2
Carr, E H, 1
Cartier, Jacques, 185
Cartwright, Edmund, 235
Cavendish, Henry, 363
Cavour, 3
Cease-fire Agreement (1991), 387
Ceylon (*see also* Sri Lanka), 14, 133, 231, 289

Sinhalese, 289
Tamilians, 289
Chad, 357
Chalcolithic Age, 8
Chaldeans, 31
Champollion, Jean, 24
Chile, 69, 242
China, 5, 9, 99 107, 115, 133, 168-69, 181, 185, 205, 269, 272-74, 275, 285, 290, 291, 292, 293, 324, 326, 327, 341, 342, 343, 347, 348, 374, 375, 376
ancient
    astrology, 66-67
    Chang-Heng, 67
    civilisation, 58
    culture and civilisation, features of, 59, 62-67
    art and architecture, 66
    economic conditions, 63-64: trade and commerce, 63-64
    literature, 66
    political organisation, 62-63
    religion and philosophy, 64-66: Buddhism, 61, 62, 64, 65-66; Confucianism, 64-65; Mencius, 65
    Taoism, 65
    science, 66-67
    society, early, 64
geographical factors, 58
Great Wall of China, 60, 66
Han dynasty (Golden Age), 61-62, 66, 67
    Civil Service examinations, 61
    diplomatic relations, 62
    educational progress, 61
    State patronage to arts and literature, 61-62
    trade and commerce, 61
I-Hsing, 67
industries, 63
inventions, 67
Lao Tze, 60, 65, 66
literature, destruction of old, 60
mathematics, 66
medicine, 67
Meng Tzu (Mencius), 65

Index

Peking Man, 59
political history, 59-60
Chou dynasty, 59-60, 66, 67
Shang rule, 59, 66
slavery, 64
Ssu-m Chien, 66
Tai Li PO, 66
Tai Sung, 62
Tang dynasty, 62, 66
Tu Fu, 66
Qin dynasty, 60
Qin Shihuangdi, 60, 62
WU-Ti, 61, 62
Chiang Kai-shek, 282, 283, 348
Communist China, 369-70
Chinese Dragon, 393
Chinese Revolution (1949), 283, 348
Cultural Revolution (1966-69), 370, 374-75
Dowager Express, 280
Europeans, advent of, 168
Fahien, 102
Five Year Plans, 370
foreign relations, 370-71
four modernisations (reforms), 370
Gang of Four, 370
Great Leap Forward, 370
Hieun Tsang, 99
Kublai Khan, 138, 181
Manchu emperors, 168-69
Manchu government, 281, 284
Mao-Dze-Dong, 369-70
Mao, Madam, 370
Mao Tse-Tung, 282, 283, 349, 376
Mings, contribution of, 168
mutiny (1911), 281
Nine-Power treaty, 285
Opium Wars (1839-42), 169, 273
Peaceful-Coexistence (*Panchsheel*) treaty with India, 370
Peace Conference, 285
Peking, 11
Sino-British relations, 273
Sino-Japanese war (1894-95), 274, 276
Sun Yat Sen, 281-82
Tiananmen Square incident (tragedy), 370, 376
USA advocates Open Door policy with regard to, 274
undeclared war between Japan and, 282-83
West, 130
Western imperialism in, 280-83
Xiaoping, Deng, 370
Yuan Shihkai, 285
Christ, Jesus, 8, 10, 90, 120, 146, 135, 188
birth of, 116, 122
crucifixation of, 123
father: Joseph of Nazareth, 122
life of, 122-25
mother: Virgin Mary, 122, 125, 143
teachings of, 123-24, 159
Christianity, 62, 120, 124, 139, 140, 141, 143, 145, 147, 160, 161, 184, 194
Carolingian Church, 160
Catholicism, 199
Catholic Church, 140, 159
Catholic Emancipation Act (1829), 261
Catholics, 201, 209, 261, 331
Christian Church, 124, 125, 181, 188-94, 218
Christian disunity, 136
Christian merchants, 148
Christian missionaries, 169, 187, 272, 275, 280
Christian monks, 159-60
orders of monks: Carthusian and Cistercian, 160
Christian nations of Europe, 245
Christian pilgrims, 135, 137
Christian subjects, 263, 265, 266
Christian virtues, 124
Christians, 4, 8, 116, 118, 123, 124, 125, 127, 136, 142, 148, 188, 190, 265
European Christians, 135, 148
Holy Land of, 135, 136, 137
Greek Orthodox Church, 206
Lutheran Churches, 191
rise and spread of, 124-25
Roman Catholics, 262
Russian Orthodox Church, 206
Civil wars, 238, 375
Cochin, 168
Cold War, 345, 348-49, 368, 370, 373, 376
Collingwood, R G, 2
Columbia, 69, 242

Columbus, Christopher, 4, 183-84
Commonwealth, 289, 356, 373
Communication system
 revolution in, 237, 366-67, 379
 satellite communication, 378
Communism, 334, 348, 349, 368, 369, 371, 373
Communists, 283, 336, 369
Computers, 378, 379
 super-computers, 379
Confucius, 60, 64-65, 66
Confucian classics, 61
Confucianism, 64-65
Congo, 277-78, 345, 357, 371, 375
Constantinople, 129, 135, 137, 146-47, 181, 263
 Queen of cities, 143
Copernicus, Nicolaus, 179, 376
Cordova, 131
Corsica, 112
Cortez, Hernando, 184
Crete island, 47, 70
Crimean War (1854-56), 264-65, 315
Crompton, Samuel, 235
Crusades (holy wars waged by European Christians), 135-38
 advantages spirit, 138
 caused growth of towns, 148
 children's and other Crusades, 137
 Conrad III, 136
 Constantinople, 137
  feudalism, decline of, 138
  first Crusade, 135-36
  fourth crusade, 137
  Godfrey of Bouillon, 136
  Holy Land of Christians, 135, 136, 137
 knowledge and scientific discoveries, 138
 Peter the Hermit, 136
 Pope Eugenius III, 136
 Pope Innocent III, 137
 results, encouraging and positive, 137-38
 second Crusade, 136
 third Crusade, 136-37
 trade relations, 138
 Walter the Penniless, 136
 Zara, 137
Cuba, 183, 308, 345
Castro, Fidel, 349
Cuban Missile Crisis, 345
Culture and
 civilisation 8-9
 culture grows with knowledge and ideas, 10
 factors for rise and development of, 9-10
 economic well-being and leisure, 9
 geographical, 9
 healthy political and social climate, 10
 trade, 10
 urban bias of culture, 10
Curie, Marie, 362
Cuvier, 363
Cyber-laws, 379
Cyprus, 265, 346, 371
Cyril, 147
Czechoslovakia, 321, 337, 327, 347

Dahomey, 356
Daimler, Gottlieb, 366
Dalton, John, 362, 363
Damascus, 129, 130, 131
Darwin, Charles, 11, 363-64
De Vega, Lope, 177
Decolonisation
 of Africa, 354-59
Denmark, 151, 206, 255-56, 321
 Canute, King, 197
 war with Germany, 255-57
Descartes, Rene, 179-80
Devdasi system, 3
Dharmasastras, 107
Diaz, Bartholomew, 183
Dickens, Charles, 239
Diderot, 220
Diogenes, 81
Disarmament, 326, 327, 346, 373
Disarmament Conference (1933), 336
 Non-Proliferation Treaty, 346, 371, 372
Discoveries, 80, 361-62, 364-65, 365
 geographical, 181-87 (*see also* Geographical)
Dodecanese islands, 332
Dominicans, 160
Dorians, 70
Dostum, 382
Drake, 185
Dravidians, 14, 42-43, 50
Drucker, Peter F, 376, 378
Dubois, 11
Dulles Doctrine, 348

Index

Dumbarton-Oaks Conference (1944), 341
Durant, Will, 1
Dürer, Albrecht, 178
Dutch, 185 (see also Netherlands)

E-commerce (Electronic Commerce), 379
E-mail (Electronic mail), 379
Earth
    origin and life of, 11-12
    earliest man, 11-12
Earth-Summit
    in Delhi, 377
    in Rio, 3469, 377
East (Eastern World)
    Sea-borne trade between West and, 186
Eastman, George, 365
Economy (Economic)
ECA (Economic Commission for Africa), 343
ESCAP (Economic and Social Commission for Asia and the Pacific), 343
ECE (Economic Commission for Europe), 343
ECLAC (Economic Commission for Latin America), 343
EU (Economic Union), 373
Economic institutions, 346
Economic Commission for West Africa, 343
Ecquador, 242
Egypt, 1, 5, 9, 28, 30, 31, 36, 38, 40, 42, 47, 79, 80, 114, 115, 129, 225, 228, 278, 332, 338, 345, 352, 398
    Age of Feudalism, 19
    Age of Pyramids, 18-19
    agriculture and other developments, 17-18
    Ahmos, 19
    Akhenaten, 20, 21
    Amenhotep-I, 19
    ancient, 60, 154
    Anglo-French invasion of, 348
    art and architecture, 23-24
        Pyramids, 23-24
    Breasted, J H, 24
    civilisation, contribution to, 24-25
    Cleopatra, 20
    Colossi, 20
    economic life, 21-22
    Edwin Papyrus, 25
    Farouk, 351
    Flinders Petrie, W M, 24
    geographical factors, 17
    Hatshepsut, Queen, 20
    Hawass, Zahi, 24
    history, classification of early, 18-19
        early dynastic period, 18
        middle kingdom, 19
        Imperial Age (New Kingdom), 19-20
    Khafra, 19
    Khufu (Cheops), 19
    literature, 24
    medicine, advance in, 25-26
    Memphis, 18, 19
    Men Kau-re, 19
    Menes, King, 18
    middle class, rise of, 21
    Moses, 20
    Naguib, 351
    Nasser, Gamal Abdel, 351, 352
    nationalism in, 350-51
    new kingdom, 18
    Nubia, 19, 20
    old kingdom, 18
    Osiris (Egyptian God), 19, 22
    Pan-Arab-National movement, 352
    Pharaoh Akhnaton (Amenhotep IV), 22
    Pharaohs, 18-19, 20, 22, 38
        new Pharaohs, 38
    Ptolemies, 80
    Pyramids, 23-24
    Ramses I, 22
    Ramses II, 20, 22
    reforms, 351
    religion,
        monotheism, 22
    Rosetta Stone, 24
    Saladin emperor, 136, 137
    science, advance in, 25-26
    sculptors, 23
    slaves, conditions of, 21
    Sneferu, 19
    society, early, 20-21
    temples, 20, 22, 23
    temple Abu Simbel, 20
    temple of Amon at Karnak, 20
    temple of Osiris, 20

Thebes, 19
Thutmose-I, 19
Thutmose-II, 20
Thutmose-III, 20, 22
tombs, 23
   at Abydos and Saqqara, 18
Tutankhamen, tomb of, 21
women, position of, 21
writings, 24
Zoser, King, 18, 25
Einstein, Albert, 362
El Greco, 177
El Nino, 377
Engels, Frederick, 240
Earth-Summit in Rio-de Janeiro, 346
Epicureanism, 120
Epirus, 112
   Pyrrhus king of, 112
Erasmus, Desiderius, 178
Eratosthenes, 80
Eritrea, 279
Eskimos, 14
Ethiopia, 279, 332
Euphrates, 27
Euripides, 77
Euro (common currency), 373
Europe, 14, 50, 67, 68, 70, 132, 133, 134, 135, 138, 181, 183, 185, 186, 187, 188, 189, 201, 202, 203, 204, 217, 222, 223, 224, 226, 229, 230, 234, 238, 242, 248, 259, 263, 264, 272, 295, 306, 314, 309, 321, 337
   advent Europeans in Japan, 171
   between two World Wars, 328-31
   Central, 154
   Christian nations of, 245
   civilisation, 70
   ECE (Economic Commission for Europe), 343
   EU (Economic Union), 373
   East, 348, 349, 369, 373
   European powers, 225, 267, 269, 279, 281, 306
   famines and plague (Black Death), 140
   feudalism in, 154-58 (*see also* Feudalism)
   Hundred Years' War, 140
   imperialism, 269
   imperialists, 269
   liberalism in, 232
   medieval
      Christian church in, 159-61
      church vs state, 161
      medieval Church and Papacy, 160-61
      monasticism, 159-60
      merchants, 138
   middle ages in, 139-52, 154
      Byzantine empire, 143-47
         architecture and art, 145
         civilisation of, contributions of, 145-47
         Christianity, spread of, 146
         Constantine, 143-44
         decline of, 145
         Diocletian, 143-44
         estimate, 147
         Justinian, era of, 144-45
         Justinian Code, 144, 145-46
         law and literature, 145-46
         learning, centres of, 146
         theocratic state, 145
         trade and commerce, 146-47
      Capitularies, 142
      Charlamagne, 141, 142
      definition of middle ages, 139-40
      early middle age, 139-40
      later middle age, 140
      Holy Roman empire, 140-43
      Carolingian dynasty, 141-43: administration, 142; Charlamagne and his conquests, 141; laws, 142-43; learning, 142
   Martel, Charles, 140, 141
   medieval cities and guides, 147-51
      conditions in Europe after fall of Roman empire, 147-51
      craft guilds, 150
      Crusades caused growth of towns, 148
      European cities, role of, 148-49
      guilds and crafts, 150
      guilds, decline of, 151
      guilds formed by towns, 150-51
      Hanseatic League, 149
      new middle-class in towns and cities, rise of, 149-50
      political role of cities, 149
      universities, medieval, 151-52
      early universities of Europe, 151-52
      earning in middle ages, 151
      Otto the Great, 142-43

Index

nation-states in, rise of, 196-207
  Austria, 205-06
    Habsburgs of, 205-06
  England: first nation-State, 196-200
    limitations on royal power, 197-98
    model parliament, 198
    royal absolutism, 197
    Stuart rulers, 199
  France, 200-02
    Bourbon monarchy in, 201-02
  Prussia, 203-04
    enlightened despotism, 204
    rise of under Hohenzollerns, 203-04
  Russia, 205-07
    Catherine II (Catherine the Great), 207: foreign policy, 207; war with Turks, 207
    foreign policy, 206
    geographical factors, 205
    Peter the Great, 206
    under Czars, 205-06
    Westernisation of under Peter, 206
  Spain, 202
  Switzerland, 202
North, 12, 148
  renaissance in, 177-78
Ottoman invasions, 140
peace movement in (1919-39), 326-27
post-first World War, 322-25
renaissance in, 173-80 (*see also* Renaissance)
revolutions in, 245-46
Seven Years' War, 203, 210, 211
trading companies, 278
West, 138, 142, 147, 173, 206
Eustachi, Bartolomeo, 180

Fahien, 102
Falung gong, 376
Far East, 290, 317
  nationalism in, 280-85
Fascism
  in Italy, 328-31
Ferdinand, King, 183
Fertile Crescent, 20

Feudalism, 138, 148, 222
  Age of feudalism, 19
  in Europe, 154-58 (*see also* Europe)
  Chivalry, age of, 155-56
  decline of, 157
  definition, 154
  evolution of, 154-57
  feudal life, 156-57
  homage ceremony, 155
  land tenure, system of, 155
  manor, 156
Field, Cyrus W, 237
Finland, 206, 231, 321, 324, 337, 326
Five Power Naval Limitation Treaty, 326, 327
Florida, 184, 216
Foundrinier, Henry, 365
Fonseka, 392
Formosa, 274, 283, 284, 372
Four Power Pact, 326
France, 12, 13, 112, 114, 129, 135, 136, 141, 142, 148, 154, 160, 161, 185, 188, 189, 192, 200-02, 203, 204, 209, 210, 211, 215, 216, 217-29, 230, 231, 237, 238, 245, 246, 249, 250, 257-59, 278, 279, 291, 292, 306, 314, 309, 310, 311, 321, 337, 338, 326, 339, 327, 342, 343, 345, 351, 352, 354-55, 356, 359, 364, 372
  Albigensians, 189
  Anglo-French invasion of Egypt, 348
  Anglo-French rivalry, 269-70
  Antoinette, Marie, 218, 222
  Augustus, Philip II, 136, 200
  Bank of France, 227-28
  Barry, Madame due, 222
  Bismarck
    plan to keep France isolated: World War I, 309-12
  Bourbon monarchy of, 201-02, 218
  Capet, Hugh, 200
  Charlamagne emperor, 154
  Charlemagne, 200
  Charles VII, 201
  Charles X, 245
  Christian kingdoms, 202
  Colbert, 218
  de Gaulle, Charles, 355, 356
  defeat at Metz and Sedan, 258
  defeat in Waterloo battle, 238
  Diderot, 220

explorations, 185
Fayette, La, 216
federation of her colonies in West Africa, 356
Ferdinand of Aragon, 202
Fourth French Republic, 355
Franco-Prussian relations, 257-59
Franco-Prussian war (1870), 253
French East India Company, 269
French Indo-China, 290
French Revolution, 1, 157, 201, 216, 217-23, 242, 244, 245
   constitution of, 1795, 222-23
   course of, 221-22
   economic causes, 219
   intellectual awakening, 219-20
   King, role of, 220-22
      course of revolution, 221-22
   political causes, 217-18
   results of, 222-23
   social causes, 218-19
      First Estate (Church), 218
      Second Estate (Nobles), 218-19
      Third Estate (Common people), 219
French Revolution of (1848), 254
Henry IV of Navarre, 201
Huguenot Church in, 192
Huguenots, 201, 202
Hundred Years' War, 200
intellectual awakening, 219-20
Louis VII, 136
Louis IX, 200
Louis XI, 200
Louis XIII, 201, 218
Louis XIV, 185, 201-02, 217
Louis XV, 217
Louis XVI, 217, 222
Louis XVII, 245
Louis XVIII, 227, 230
Metternich, 244, 246, 248
Najibullah, 382, 383
Napoleon Bonaparte, 3, 4, 24, 144, 217, 222, 224-29, 230, 231, 236, 238, 244, 246, 253
   achievements, lasting, 227-29
   administration, centralisation of French, 229
   Bank of France, 227-28
   Child of the Revolution, 229
   Code Napoléon, 227
   Concorbat, 227
   death of, 227
   divorced Josephine and married Marie Louise, 226
   educational system, new, 228
   Legion of Honour, 228
Napoleonic era, importance of, 229
   Napoleonic wars, 226-27, 238, 242
   defeat in final battle of Waterloo, 227, 230
   overseas empire of France, 228
   public works, 229
Napoleon III, 250, 253, 256, 257, 290
Paris commune, 221
Pierre-Mendes-France, 354
Philip IV, 200
Philippe, Louis, 245
renaissance in, 177
Richelieu, Cardinal, 201, 218
Rousseau, Jean Jacques, 220
scholars, 178
St. Bernard: Abbot of Clairvaux in France, 160
Talleyrand, 231
Thirty Years' War, 201
Treaty of Frankfurt (1871), 258-59
Treaty of Paris, 203-04, 308
Treaty of Paris (1783), 216
Treaty of Paris (1856), 264-65
Treaty of Tilsit, 226
Versailles, 201-02
Voltaire, 203, 204, 219
Waldenses, 189
William, Duke of Normandy, 197
Franciscans, 160
Free World, 348
French Sudan, 356
Fukushima, 393
Fulton, Robert, 237, 366

G 8, 373
G H G (Green Houses Gases), 377
Gabon, 357
Gaddafi, Muammar 400
Galen, 180
Galileo, 179
Galton, Francis, 368
Gambia, 356
Gandhi, Mahatma, 3, 10, 85, 90 (see also India)

Index

Garibaldi, 3
Garrelt, 165
Gaul, 114, 139
Geneva, 323
Geneva Conference (1954), 291
Geneva Conventions, 341
Geneva summits, 368
Genoa, 186
Geography, 80
  geographical factors, 9
  history and, 5
Geographical discoveries
  Balboa discovered Pacific Ocean, 184
  Columbus discovers New Continent, 183-84
  discoveries of English explorers, 185
  explorations of Portuguese navigators, 183
  factors aiding, 181-87
  Ferdinand Magellan: his voyage round world, 184
  French explorations, 185
  Hernando Cortez conquers Mexico, 184
  Henry Hudson and Dutch claims, 185
  results of, 186-87
Geology, 360
Geometry, 66, 80, 146, 180
Germanic tribes, 116, 139
Germany, 4, 136, 142, 149, 160, 161, 203, 207, 223, 226, 229, 231, 232, 238, 245, 246, 261, 265, 273, 278, 279, 285, 288, 317, 319, 309, 310, 311, 312, 322, 324, 332, 333, 342, 355, 356, 369, 372
  Barbarosa, Frederick, 136
  Berlin, 303
  Berlin blockade, 348
  Berlin Wall, 349, 368
  Bismarck, Otto von, 254-59
    diplomacy of, 258
  Congress of Berlin (1878), 260, 265, 309
  East, 368
  economic imperialism of, 310-11
  foreign policy, 336-37
  German Confederation, 256, 257
  Goebbels, 336
  Hanseatic League, 149, 150-51
  Hindenburg, 336
  Hitler, Adolf, 4, 334-35, 336, 337, 338, 326

Humanist movement, 178
liberals, 254
nationalism in, rise of, 253-57
Nazi Germany, 4, 325
Nazi Party (Nazis), 334-35
  foreign policy of, 336-37
Nazis (National Socialists), 334-35
Neanderthal valley, 12
North German Confederation, 257-58
offensives (1942): World War II, 338-39
Protestant Reformation in, 190-92
renaissance in, 178
Rommel, 338
scholars, 178
Stresmann, Gustav, 327
Treaty of Sèvres (1920), 313, 350
unification of, 253-59
  Austro-Prussian War (1866) and results, 257
  blood and iron policy, 256
  Franco-Prussian relations, 257-59
    Bismarck's diplomacy, 258
    events leading to Franco-Prussian war, 258
    French defeat at Metz and Sedan, 258
    Treaty of Frankfurt (1871), 258
  French Revolution 1848, 254
  friction over spoils of war, 256-57
  nationalism, rise of, 253-57
  war with Denmark, 255-56
  William I King and his Iron Chancellor, Bismarck, 254-55
  Zollverein (Customs Union), 254
War with Denmark, 255-57
West, 238, 368
William II, Kaiser, 312
William I King, 259
World War II and, 334-38
  American's entry into World War II, 338
  course of World War II, 337-38
  Germany surrenders, 326
  Hitler, Adolf: difficulties of Germany and, 334-35

Japan and German offences (1942), 338-39
Pacific theatre and dropping of atom bombs on Japan, 326-27
Weimar Republic, 334-35
Ghana (Gold Coast), 356
Nkrumah, Kwane, 356
Gilbert, 185
Globolisation, 373-75
Golconda, 133
Gonçalves, Lopo, 183
Goths, 144
Graeco-Persian wars, 1
Great Britain (see Britain), 351
Great Depression of 1929, 332
Great Schism, 188
Greater Tunb, 386
Greco-Roman civilisation, 147
Greco-Roman spirit, 173
Greco-Roman classics, 173
Greece, 10, 40, 109, 113, 267, 324, 332, 338, 350
    Alexander the Great, 20, 37, 40, 79, 80, 81, 92-93, 96
    Anaxagoras, 78
    Archimedes, 80
    Athens (Athenians), 10, 72, 73-74, 75, 76-77, 78, 119, 146
    Corfu crisis, 324
    Delean League, 75, 78
    Democritus, 78
        theory of atom by, 78
    Diogenes, 81
    education, 77
    Eratosthenes, 80
    geographical influence, 71-72
        City-states, development of, 71-72
    government, forms of, 72-77
        Athenian democracy, 73
        Athens rebuilt as most beautiful city, 76-77
        Cleisthenes, 73-74
    Golden Age, 76
        Ionian Greeks, revolt of, 74
        Persian threat, 74
        Persian wars, 75
        Thermopylae and others, battle of, 75
Greek City-States, decline of, 78-79
Greek literature, 77-78
Greek philosophers, 77
Greek-speaking tribes, 70
Greek tribes, 70, 71
Gregor, 364
Hellenistic civilisation, 80-81
    art and architecture, 81
    decline, 81
    Greek language, 80
    philosophers, 81
    scientific discoveries and inventions, 80
Herodotus, 77
Hipparchuss, 80
Hippocrates, 78
historical background, 70-71
Lycurgus, 73
Ottoman emperor, 244
Periclean Age, 77, 78
Philip of Macedonia, King, 79
Plato, 77
Rhodes, 119
science, 78
slavery, 81
Sparta, 72-73
Zeno, 81
Greeks, 1, 5, 20, 26, 27, 37, 40, 70-81, 98, 109, 111, 112, 117, 119, 175, 176, 244-45
    ancient, 117
    classics, 134, 147, 150
    culture, 116
Greek Orthodox Church, 206
    rule in India, 98
Greek War of Independence (1827), 244-45
Grünewald, Matthias, 178
Guam, 308
Guatemala, 67
Guinea, 356
Gulf States, 376, 379
Gulf War I (1991), 342, 346, 347, 371, 372, 387
Gulf War II (2003), 347, 372, 376
    Operation Iraqi Freedom, 376
    Western countries, 107
Gwadar, 394

HIV-AIDS, 347, 375
Haiti, 183
Halley, Edmund,
    discoveries of, 361-62
Hals, Frans, 178
Harijans
    ill-treatment of, 3

Index

Harkat-ul-Ansar, 384
Harvey, William, 180
Hawaii islands, 308
Hebrews, 26, 38-39
    Amos, Hebrew prophet, 38
    David, King, 38
    Hosea, Amos, 39
    Isaiah, 39
    Micah, 39
    Nebuchadnezzar, King, 39
    Samuel, 39
    Saul, King, 38
Heidelberg, 11
Hekmatyar, 382, 383
Helsinki agreement (1975), 349, 370
Henry, 181-83
Herder, 5
Herodotus (Father of History), 1, 5,17, 19, 41, 77
Herschel, William, 361
Hertz, Heinrich, 362
Herzegovina, 260, 266, 267, 268, 311
Hidalgo, Father, 243
Hieun Tsang, 99
Hildebrand, 160
Hindukush mountains, 36
Hinduism, 82, 85, 87, 92, 96, 132, 165, 167, 296, 298
    karma, Hindu doctrine of, 89
Hipparchuss, 80
Hiroshima, bomb on, 326, 362 (*see also* Japan)
History
    archaeology and, 5
    definition of, 1
    geography and, 5
    historical knowledge, 3-4, 6
    laboratory social sciences, 3
    lessons of, 4
    manifest destiny, 3-4
    science or art, 2
    social sciences and, 5-6
    values of, 2-4
    world history
    chronology of, 8
    need for its study, 7-8
    periodisation of, 8: historic, prehistoric, 8
    purpose of, 7
Holbein, Hans, 178
Holland, 192, 200, 226, 231, 245, 277, 310, 312, 337
    Dutch Reformed Church in, 192

Flemish School, 178
    renaissance in, 178
    scholars, 178
Homeric Age, 154
Hong Kong, 371, 375, 376
Howe, Elias, 235
Hoysalas, 85
Hudson, Henry, 185
Hudson river, 366
Human race, 12-13
Human rights
Human Right Convention, 346
    Universal Declaration of Human rights, 341
    violation of, 376
Human sufferings, 376-77
Humanist movement, 177-78, 180
Hungary, 192, 315, 321, 324, 338, 326, 348
    compromise (1867) between Austria and, 260
    quarrel between Austria and, 259-60
    Treaty of St. Germaine, 321
    Treaty of Trianon (1920), 321
Huns, 116
Hunter, John, 363
Huntington, Ellsworth, 5, 9
Huss, John, 190
Hutton, James, 361
Huxley, Aldous, 341
Hwango Ho (Yellow) river, 58
Hyksos, 19

IMF, 342, 373, 374
Ibn Batuta, 133
Ibn Hakaul, 133
Ibn Khaldun, 132
Ibn Rushid (Averrhoes), 132
Ice Ages, 11, 12
Ice land, 185
Imperialism
    economic imperialism, Britain and Germany, 310-11
    in Japan, 284-85
    modern, 269-76
    Western imperialism
    in Africa, 277-79
    in China, 280-836
Incas, 184
India (*see also* Britain), 5, 9, 42, 50, 61, 79, 85, 90-91, 115, 130, 133, 183, 184, 185, 186, 203, 204, 238, 269, 288, 342, 343, 370, 373, 375, 376, 379

Agra, 162, 163
Ahmednagar, 165, 166
Ahoms, 168
Ajatasatru, 89
Ajmer, 164
Akbar, 163, 164-65
  administration, 165
    estimate, 165
    Mughal paramounting in India, establishment of, 164-65
    religious policy, 165
All-Party Conference, Delhi, 299
Allahabad, 101, 270
Alwar, 101
Amber, 164
American Red Indian tribe, 68-69
Amritsar, 297
Anglo-Mysore war, 271
Anglo-Sikh war, 272
archaeologists, 5
Arjundev, Guru, 166
Arthasastra of Kautilya, 96
Arya Samaj, 294
Aryan invasion of, 50
Aryabhatta, 103
Asirgarh, 165
Assam, 301
Aurangzeb, 167
Babur, 162-63
Bairam Khan, 163, 164
Baluchistan, 42, 164, 301
Bannerjee, W C, 295
Benaras, 92, 100
Bengal, 162, 164, 165, 270, 297, 301
  famine (1993), 302, 374
  partition of, 296
Berar, 164
Besant, Annie, 296
Bihar, 96, 101, 270, 300
Bijapur, 165, 167
Black Hole tragedy, 270
Bombay, 271, 300
Bose, Subhas Chandra and INA, 302-03
Brahmans, 81, 97
Brahminical religion, 82
Brahmo Samaj, 294
Brihaspati, 103
British East India Company's wars, 269-71
British empire, expansion of, 271

British rule, legacy of, 293-94
British wars in South, 271
Buddhism to Indian culture, contributions of, 90-91
Bundelas, 166
Burhanpur, 165
Buxar, 270
Cabinet Mission, 303-04
Champa, 92
Chauri Chaura (UP), 298
Chawla, Kalpana, 377
China invaded (1962), 370
Chitor, 86
Civil Disobedience Movement, 299, 300
Communal Award, 300
Constituent Assembly, 303, 304
Cripps Mission, 301-02
cross-border terrorism by Pakistan, 376
Curzon's regime, 295
Dandi March, 299, 300
Das, C R, 298
Daultabad, 165
Dayanand Saraswati, Swami, 294
Deccan, 104, 164, 166, 167
Delhi, 162, 163, 164, 299
Dominion status, 299
Durgawati, Rani, 164
Dyer, General, 297
Ellora, 86
extremism, rise of, 296
extremists, 296
Forward Bloc, 303
freedom struggle, 3, 299
Gandhara, 100
Gandhi, Mahatma (Gandhian era), 297-304
Gandhi-Irwin Pact (1931) and Communal Award, 300-02
Gazni, 163
Gokhale, G K, 296, 297
Golconda, 166, 167
Gondwana, 164
Government of India Act of 1858, 293
Government of India Act of 1909, 296
Government of India Act of 1919, 297, 298, 299
Government of India Act of 1935, 300-01

Index

Great Uprising of 1857, 293
Greek rule in India, 98
Gujarat, 162, 164, 298
Gwalior, 86, 164
Haldighat battle, 164
Hindu empires (Hindu imperialism)
  Post-Buddhist period, 92-96
    Alexander's invasion, 92-93
    Ashoka emperor and Kalinga war, 89, 90
    economic conditions, 95-96
    learning and literature, 96
    Mauryan administration, 94-95
    Mauryan art and architecture, 96
    religious conditions, 96
    social conditions, 95
    Bimbisara, 85, 89, 92
    Bindusara, 92, 93-94
    Chandragupta Maurya, 85
    joint family system, 95
    Nanda rule over Magadha, 92
    Rajgir, excavations at, 92
    Rome, relations with, 92
    Trade and commerce, 92
  Post-Maurya period, 97-108
    Chalukyas of Badami, early, 85, 104
    Chandragupta II, 101-03
    religion, 103
      Gupta Age, the Gilded age, 103
    Chashtana and Rudradaman, 99
    Cholas, 105-07
    Gupta Age, 100-01, 103
    Kanishka (founder of Saka Era), 89, 90, 99-100
    Kanva rule, 97
    Kushanas, 99
    Pallavas of Kanchi, 104-07
    Parthians, 98
    Rajaraja the Great, 105-06
    Rajendra Chola, 106
    Sakas or Seythians, 98-99
    Satavahanas of Deccan, 97-98

Sungas, 97
Vardhana dynasty, 103-04
Harshavardhana, 89
Vijayanagara empire, 107-08
  Ashtadiggajas (eight famous poets), 108
Hindu-Muslim unity, 165, 298
Home Rule movement, 296
Hughli, 166
Humayun, 163-64
Hume, Allen Octavian, 295
INA, 302-03
Indian Councils Act of 1892, 295
Indian National Congress (Congress), 295, 296, 298, 299, 300, 301, 302, 303, 304
  Meerut session, 303
Interim Government, 303
Iqbal, Mohammed, 301
Jaipur, 101
Jalandhar, 163
Jallianwala Bagh Tragedy, 297
Jammu and Kashmir, 100, 164, 301, 347, 371, 375
Jaunpur, 164
Jehangir, 165-66
Jeziya, 165, 167
Jinnah, Mohammed Ali, 301, 302, 304
Kabul, 51, 164
Kalidasa, 103
Kangra, 165
Karnataka, 85
Kashgar, 100
Kashmir, dispute concerning, 347 (*see also* Jammu and Kashmir), 384, 393, 394
Kathiawar, 42, 102
Kausambi, 92
Kautilyas, 82, 87
Khandesh, 164
Khanua battle (1527), 163
Khilafat movement, 298
Khotan, 100
Kora, 270
Kshatriyas, 82, 87
Lahore, 163, 301
Lal-Qila (Red Fort), 166
Lodi, Alam Khan, 162
Lodi, Ibrahim, 162
Lodis, 162-63

Lucknow Pact, 296
Madras, 271, 300
Maharana Pratap, 164
Maharashtra, 296
Malabar, 298
Malwa, 101, 102, 162, 164
Malwa-Kathiawar, 99
Marathas, 167
Mathura, 86, 99
Mehta, Pherozeshah, 296
Mewar, 163, 164, 165
Mir Jafar, 270
Moderates, 296
Montagu Chelmsford Report, 297
Mount Abu, 85, 86
Mountbatten, Lord, 304
Muddiman Committee, 298
Mughal empire, fall of, 269-70
Mughal emperors, under, 162-67
Muslim League, 296, 301, 302, 303, 304
NWEP, 301
Narada, 103
Nationalism, 293-97
   developments, 296-97
   factors responsible for rise of, 294-96
Nehru, Jawaharlal, 3, 299, 303, 304
Nehru, Motilal, 298, 299
   Nehru Committee, 299
   Nehru Report, 299
Non-cooperation movement, 298
Nurjehan, 165, 166
Orissa, 86, 164, 270, 300
   Hathigumpa caves, 86
Oudh, 100, 270
Pakistan, demand for, 302, 303-04
Pakistan movement, origin of, 300-01
Panipat battle, (1526), 162
Panipat battle (1556), 164
partition of (division) (free) (independence), 304
Peaceful Co-existence (*Panchsheel*) treaty with China, 370
Peshawar, 100, 163
Peshwas, 272
political reforms, 296-97
poorna swarajya, 299
Porus, King, 79
Prathana Samaj, 294

Punjab, 42, 50, 100, 163, 297, 298, 301
Quit India Movement, 302
Rajagopalachari C, 302
Rajagriha, 92
Rajasthan, 101
Rajputs, 164
Ram Mohon Roy, Raja, 294
Rama krishna Mission, 294
Rama krishna Paramaham, Swami, 294
Rana Sangrama Singh, 162
Rana Sanga, 163
Rann of Kutch, 343
Rani Laxmibai of Jhansi, 272
Round Table Conference, first, 300
Round Table Conference second, 300
Round Table Conference third, 300
Rowlatt Act, 297
Rowlatt Report, 298
Saketa, 92
Sambhal, 163
Sarhind battle, 163
sati, abolition of, 294
satyagraha, 298
Sepoy Mutiny, 293
Shah Alam, 270
Shah Jahan, 166
Shivaji, 167
Sikander Shah, 163
Sikh Gurus, 166, 167
Sikhs, 166, 167
Simla Conference (1945), 302, 303
Simon Commission, 299
Sind, 42, 100, 129, 164, 301
Siraj-ud-daula, 270
Sisodiyas, 164
Software professionals, 378
South, 14, 107
Sovereign Democratic Republic, 304
Sravanabelagola, colossal statue of Gomateswar in, 86
Sravasti, 92
Subahdars, 166
Swadeshi movement, 296, 298
Swarajya Party, 298
Tagore, Rabindranath, 297
Taj Mahal, 166
Takshashila, 99
Tegh Bahadur, Guru, 167
Theosophical Society, 294

Index

Tilak, Lokamanya Bal Gangadhar, 296
Treaty of Allahabad, 270
Udaigiri, 86
Vaishali, 92
Varahamihira, 103
Vivekananda, Swami, 294
Wavell Plan, 302
Western, 96
Indian Ocean, 279
Indo-China, 14, 273, 290, 291
    Ferry, Jules, 290
Indo-Europeans (Aryans), 25, 50, 70, 109
Indo-Iranians, 50
Indonesia, 130, 292, 373
    Java, 11, 168
    Sukarno, 292
Indus river, 79
Indus Valley Civilisation, 42-49
    amusement, 46
    contributions, 48
    decline of, 48-49
    defence, 48
    drainage system, 43
    economy, urban, 46
    economy, rural, 46
    founders, 42-43
    funeral customs, 48
    Great Bath, 44
    Harappa, 46, 47, 48
        culture, date of, 42
        religion, 43
        Tata Institute of Harappan Culture, 42
    Mohenjodaro, 43, 46, 47, 48
    religion, 47
    seals, 47
    secular outlook, 48
    socio-economic life, 44-46
    trade and commerce, 46-47
    women, freedom and position (status) of, 44-46
Industry
Industrial Research Laboratories, 360
Industrial Revolution, 7, 151, 186, 234-40, 360, 362, 365
    effects of, 238-40
    features of, 234-37
    coal-mining industry, 236
    factory system in Britain, 236
    iron and steel industry, 235-36
    invention of steam engine by Newcomen and James Watt, 236
    Mc Adam improved road construction, 237
    revolution in communication system, 237
    revolution in transport, 237
    inventions, 234-35, 236, 237
    origin of, 234
    significance of, 237-38
    spread of, 238
    Japan and, 238
    iron and steel industry, 235-36
    steel, 238
Industrialisation, 316
Information technology (IT), 380, 381
    as second industrial revolution, 378
Intelligentsia, 9
International Boundaries Commission, 323
International Court, 343
International Criminal Court, 347
Internet, 378
Inventions, 80, 234-35, 236, 237, 366-67
    clermont, 237
    cotton gin, 235
    flying shuttle, 234
    gasoline engine, 366
    kodak camera, 365
    motion picture, 366
    motor car, 366
    photography, 365, 366
    powerloom, 235
    radio-broadcasting, 367
    rocket, 237
    sewing machine, 235
    spinning jenny, 235
    spinning mule, 235
    steam engine, 236
    telegraphy, 369
    telephones, 367
    television, 367
    water-frame, 235
    wireless, 367
    wireless telegraphy, 369
Ionians, 70
Iran (*see also* Persia), 50, 126, 286-87, 372, 383, 384, 386, 387, 388, 401
Indo-Iranians, 50
IPKF, 392
Iran-Iraq war (1980-88), 371, 386

Shah of, 286; 287
Tehran, 341
Iron Age, 8
Iraq, 126, 346, 352, 386, 387, 388, 389, 390
Iran-Iraq war, 371
Iran-Kuwait (Gulf War I), 371
   Kassem, Abdul Karim, 352
   military coups (1963), 352
   nationalists, 352
   Nurias-Said, 352
   Operation Iraqi Freedom, 376
   Saddam Hussein, 372, 376
   Weapons of Mass Destruction (WMD), 372
Ireland, 160, 261-62
   Easter Rising and division of, 261-62
Irish Free State (Eire) under Eamon De Valera, 262
Irish Home League, 261
Irish Republican Army in northern Ireland, 375
   nationalists, 261
   peasants, 261
   Sinn Fein, 261
Isabella, Queen, 183
Islam, 135, 140, 314, (*see also* Mohammed the Prophet)
   birth of, 126, 128-31
   Caliphs Othman and Ali, 130
   Hussain (son of Ali), murder at Karbala of, 130
   legacy of, 131-34
   architecture, 133-34
   art, 133-34
   autocracy, enlightened, 131
   history, 132
   learning, 131-34
   centres of, 131-32
   literature, 132
   manufactures, 133
   medicine-rhazes, 132
   sciences, exact, 132
   spread of, 129-30
   trade, 133
   travel, 133
Islamic empire (*see also* Arabs)
   Abba, 131
   Abbasides, 130-31
   Abdur Rahman, 131
   Abu Bekr, 128, 129, 130
   Ali, 130
   Calphs Othman, 130
   Mamun, 131
   Muawiyah, 130
   Omar, 130
   Omayyads, 130-31
   Shias, 130
   Sunnis, 130
   Tarik, General, 130-31
   Yezid, 130
Israel, 30, 38, 39, 342, 345, 347, 352, 375
   Arab-Israeli conflicts (wars), 346, 371, 372
   Samaria, 30
Isthmus of Panama, 184
Italy, 3, 10, 13, 75, 109, 111, 112, 113, 129, 138, 148, 176, 178, 185, 223, 225, 226, 231, 232, 245, 256-57, 272, 279, 310, 312, 324, 332, 333, 336, 326, 326, 327
   Albert, Charles, 248
   Cavour, Count, 247, 249-50
   Corfu crisis, 324
   economy, measures to improve, 331-32
   Emmanuel II, Victor, 248, 249, 251
   fascism in, 328-31
   Franco, General, 332
   Garibaldi, 247, 250-53
   Great Depression of 1929, 332
   Italics, 109
   Italo-Turkish War (1911-12), 267
   Lateran Treaty (1929) with Pope, 331
   Mazzini, Joseph, 3, 247-48, 249, 250, 251, 253
   merchants, 181
   Mussolini, Benito, 329-31, 335
   dictatorship of, 330-31
   foreign policy and its failure, 332-33
   rise of fascism and, 329-30
   nationalism in, rise of, 246-50
   Ostrogoths, 139
   Palestrina, 176
   post-war conditions in, 328-29
   Rome liberated, 253
   Satellite republics in, 226
   unification of, 246-53
   1848 revolution, 248-49
   Venice united with Italy, 251-52

Young Italy movement, 248
Young Italy, 248, 250
Ivory Coast, 356

Jainism, 92, 96
   Ahimsa, 85
   art and architecture, 85-86
   Bhadrabahu, 84
   caste-system, 85
   contributions of, 85-86
   Digambara Jains, 84-85
   equality principle of, 85
   facets of, 84
   Hari Bhadra, 85
   Hemachandra, 85, 86
   Jaina monasteries, 85
   Jaina stupas, statues and carved pillars, 86
   Mahavira, 82-85, 86 (see also Mahavira)
   Nagachandra, 85
   Parsvanatha, 82-83
   Pujyapad, 85
   religious literature, 84
   scholars, 85
   Sidha Sena, 85
   spread of, 85
   Svetambara Jains, 84-85
   Syadvada, philosophy, 85
   temples, 85-86
   Tirthankaras, 82
   women, freedom of, 85
Japan, 10, 14, 273, 275-76, 281, 283-85, 286, 288, 290, 324, 332, 336, 326, 327, 342, 389, 393, 396
   Anglo-Japanese Treaty, 276, 284
   atom bombs on, dropping of, 326-27
   Chinese influence on, early, 169-70
   economic reforms, 283-84
   educational system, 284
   Europeans, advent of, 171
   forces, reorganisation of, 284
   Heian period, 170-71
      Hojo's administration, 170-71
      Yoritomo becomes Shogun, 170
   Hiroshima, bomb on, 326, 362
   imperialism, 284-85
   industrial revolution and, 238
   Lansing-Ishii agreement, 285
   Meiji revolution, 275-76, 283

Mutsuhito, 275
Nagasaki, bomb on, 326, 362
offensives (1942): World War II, 338-39
Pearl Harbour, attack on, 338
Russo-Japanese war (1904-1905), 276, 281, 317
Sino-Japanese war (1894-95), 274, 276
Tojo, 338
Tokugawa Shogunate, 171
Twenty-one Demands, 285
undeclared war between China and, 282-83
Jayagondar
Jiwaka Chintamami by, 107
Jefferson, Thomas, 176, 214, 228
Jenkins, Charles F, 366, 367
Jenner, Edward, 364
Jerusalem, 30, 31, 36, 38, 39, 116, 122, 123, 136, 137
Jesuits, 194
Jews, 4, 20, 36, 38-39, 124, 127, 148
Joad, C E M, 9
   What is Civilisation?, 9
Joan of Arc, 10, 200-01
Joilet, 185
Jordan, 400
   Hamas, 375, 401
   Trans-Jordan, 352
Judah, 30, 39
Judaism, 314
Julius Caesar, 4, 197

Kalinga
King Kharavela of, 85
Kamban
   Ramayana by, 107
Kampuchea (Cambodia), 346, 347, 375
Kant, 5
Kapila, 82
Kay, John, 234
Kenya, 278, 358
Kenya African National Union (KANU), 358
Kenyatta, Jomo, 358
   Mau Mau, secret society, 358
   Mau Mau terrorism, 358
Kepler, 179
Khayyam, Omar, 132
Khokand, 61
Kiel Canal, 311

King Abdullah, 401
Kirchoff, Gustaf, 362
Knowledge, 378
    expanding frontiers of, 376-77
    knowledge society, 376
Knox, John, 192
Koch, Robert, 364
Koening, Friedrich, 365
Korea, 61, 274, 284, 348, 371
    North, 273, 345, 370, 372
    South, 345, 370
Krober, Alfred L,
    Configurations of Culture, 9
Kuchuk Kainarji, treaty of, 207
Kuhn, Thomas, 377
Kurds, 386
Kuwait, 346, 353, 387
Kyoto Protocol, 347, 377

La Sale, 185
Labour
    ILO, 323, 344
Laden, Osama bin (*see* Osama), 384, 391
Lal-Qila (Red Fort) (*see* India)
Lambard League, 149
Land
    land reforms, 261
    land tenure, system of, 155
Lanston, Toblert, 365
Laos, 291, 373
Laplace, Pierre Simon de, 361
Latium, 109
Lavoisier, Antoine, 363
League of Armed Neutrals (Russia, Denmark and Sweden), 215
League of Nations, 322-25, 332, 336, 326-27
    achievements of, 324
    aims of, 322
    efforts of, 327
    International Boundaries Commission, 323
    International Labour Organisation (ILO), 323
    failure, causes of its, 324-25
    organs of, 322-23
    WHO, 323
Lebanon, 22, 345, 346, 351-52
Leeuwenhoek, Anton Van, 180
Leon, Ponce de, 184
Leonardo Da Vinci, 4
Lesser Tunb, 386
Leverreir, Urbain, 362

Liberalism, 232, 245, 315
Liberia, 279
Libya, 279, 400
Lindbergh, Charles, 366
Linnaeus, Carl, 363
Lippman, Gabriel, 366
Lisbon, 186
Lister, Lord, 365
Livingstone, David, 277
Lothal, 42, 47, 48
Louisiana, 209
Loya Jirga, 385
Loyola, Ignatius, 194
Lunar calendar, 25, 66, 67
Luther, Martin, 190-92
Lydia
    Croesus, King of, 74
Lyell, Charles, 361

Macau, 371
Macaulay, 219
Macedonia, 113
Machiavelli, 246
MacIver, 9
Madagascar, 279, 360, 361
    Tsiranana, Philibert, 359
Madrakas, 101
Magellan, Ferdinand, 4, 184
Malawi, 357
Malaya, 14, 107, 130, 272, 290, 338
    Abdul Rahman, Tunku, 290
    Yew, Lee Kuan, 290
Malaysia, 373
Maldives, 373
Malta, 231
Manchuria, 61, 324, 326
Mankind
    Cro-Magnon man, 12, 13
    earliest man, 11-12
    Homo Sapiens, 12
    human race, 12-13, 14-15
    Caucausoid (Caucasian), 13, 14, 18
    types of 14: Alpines, East Baltics Mediterraneans Nordic, 14
    Mongoloid, 13, 14
    Negroid, 13, 14
    Java man, 11
    Neanderthal man, 12, 13
Maoists, 396
Marco Polo, 138, 181, 272
Marconi, Guglielmo, 237, 367
Samuel de Champlain, 185
Marshall, John, 42

Index

Martin, Jose De San, 242-43
Marx, Karl, 240, 317
Marxist-Leninst principles, 370
Mathematics, 66, 68,119, 133, 180
  zero in, concept of, 68
Mauritania, 356
Mauritius, 231
Maxwell, James Clerk, 362
Maya Civilisation, 241
McAdam, 237
Mckay, Windsor, 366
Mecca, 129
  Shrine of Kaaba at, 127
Medical science, 377-78
  progress in, 364-65
Medicine
  advance of, 25-26
Medina, 127, 128, 130
Mediterranean Sea (region), 17, 40, 63, 71, 80, 109, 112, 113, 115, 117, 129, 147, 148, 186, 332
  Eastern, 81
  trade, 10
Megasthenes, 95
Mencius, 60
Mendel, Gregor, 364
Mendeleev, Dmitri, 363
Mergenthaler, Ottmar, 365
Mesolithic Age, 8
Mesopotamia, 5, 9, 38, 42, 50, 117, 129, 205
  Assyrians
    conquest, 30-31
      Assyrian contributions, 31
      fall of Assyrian, 31
      military glory, 30-31
    culture, 31
    kings
      Assurbanipal, 31
      Sargon II, 30
      Sennacherib, 30
      Tiglethpileser III, 30
      Romans of Asia, 31
  Babylonian empire under Hammurabi, 29-30
  Code of Hammurabi, 29-30
  geographical factors, 27
  Hittiti conquest, 30
  Mesopatamians, 14
  new Babylonian empire, 31-32
    Babylon, revolt of, 31
    Babylonians, 31
    Chaldeans, 31, 32
    Nebuchadnezzar, 31, 32
    Nobopolassar, 31
    Persian invasion, 32
  sites, 42
  Sumerians, 27-29
    decline and fall of Sumerian kingdoms, 29
  Sumerian city-states, 28-29
Metals
  Age of metals, 14
Methodius, 147
Metternich, 253, 259
Mexico, 184, 186, 241, 242, 243, 256, 308, 312
  Yucatan peninsula, 67
Middle Ages, 10, 11, 186, 188, 196, 203
Middle East, 131, 351, 352, 372
Milton, John, 177
Mississippi river, 185, 216, 306
Missiles (*see also* Nuclear)
  Anti-Ballistic Missile Treaty (1972), 348, 349, 368, 372
  Anti-Ballistic Missile Treaty (1972), 368
  Anti-Ballistic Missile treaty, 372
  Continental Ballistic Missile (ICBM), 349
  laser-guided missiles, 379
  National Missile Defence System (NMD), 348
  Nuclear Missile Defence (NMD), 372
Modern Age, 8
Mohammed the Prophet (*see also* Islam), 130, 140
  birth of, 126, 127
  life of, 127-28
  teachings of, 128-29
Mohammedans (*see* Muslims)
Mohawk Indians, 213
Mohenjodaro, 42
Monasticism (monastic movement), 159-60
Mongols
  Chenghis Khan, 205
Monogamy, 53
Monoloid race, 59
Monotheism, 37
  ethical, 39
Montaigne, 177

Montenegro, 267
Moon
  astronauts stepped on (1969), 377
Moors, 154
Morocco, 279, 311, 355
  Yousef, Mohammed Ben, 355
Morse, Samuel, 237, 367
Morse code, 367
Moses, 38
Motion picture, 366
Motor vehicles, 366
Mozambique, 279
Mubarak, Hosni, 399
Mujahideen, 382
Murillo, 177, 178
Muslim Brotherhood, 399
Muslims (Mohammedans), 108, 135, 136, 137, 140, 145, 147, 149, 165, 202, 296, 298, 301, 355, 375
  craftsmen, 133
  Fundamentalist Islamic Organisations, 372
  missionaries, 130
  Shias, 130
  Sunnis, 130
  traders, 130
Myanmar, 347, 373 (*see also* Burma)

Nagasaki, bomb on, 326, 362 (*see also* Japan)
Nationalism, 4, 229, 246-50, 309, 321
  Arab nationalism, 350-53
  in Austria, 259-62
  in Burma, 288-89
  in Egypt, 350-51
  in Far East, 280-85
  in Germany, 253-57
  in Italy, 246-50
  in Persia, 286-87
  in South and South East-Asia, 286-304
  nationalists, 283, 354, 355
  rise of, 253-57
  spirit of, 232
  Syrian, 352
  Turkish, 350-53
Near East, 14, 114, 136
Negroes, 14, 359
Neolithic Age, 8, 12
Neolithic society, 13
Nepal, 14, 293, 373
  Mahendra, King, 293

Netherlands, 192, 193, 209, 215, 245, 326, 326
Nevins, Allen, 3-4
New France (Canada), 209
New Guinea, 292
New Testament, 122, 123
New Zealand, 14
Newcomen, Thomas, 236
Newton, Issac, 179
Nichol, William, 361
Niepce, Joseph, 365
Nigeria, 356
Nile, 5
Nile river valley, 5, 17, 18, 19, 21, 79
Nine Power Treaty, 327
Nineveh, 31
Non-aggression Pact, 337
Non-Aligned Movement (NAM), 349, 373
  Bandung Conference, 373
Non-Proliferation Treaty (1970), 346
Normans, 142
North Borneo, 290
North Korea, 397, 398
Norway, 337
Notation system, 119
Nubia, 19, 20, 21
Nuclear (*see also* Missiles)
  Age of Atom, 362
  American nuclear monopoly, 348
  atom bomb, 376
    manufactured by Russia, 348
  bombs, 372
  bombs on Hiroshima and Nagasaki, 362
  Continental Ballistic Missiles (ICBM), 349
  Helsinki agreement (1975), 349
  INF (International-Range Nuclear Force) Treaty (1937), 368
  nuclear arms race, 348-49
  Nuclear Missile Defence (NMD), 372
  Nuclear Non-Proliferation Treaty, 371, 372
  nuclear physics, birth of, 362
  nuclear strikes, 349
Nyasaland, 357

Obama, Barak, 391
Old Testament, 38, 123
Olympics, modern, 75
Oman, 353, 376
Open Door Policy, 274

Index

Operation Desert Storm, 387
Opium Wars (1839-42), 169, 273
Osama bin Laden, 374, 377, 384, 391
Ottoman empire, 207, 264, 266, 278, 350
Ottoman Turks, 137, 146, 181, 263
Oxus Valley, 99

Pacific, 308, 338, 326
  coast, 3
  ESCAP, 343
  islands, 14
  ocean, 58, 184, 314
Paganism, 125
Pakistan (see also India), 343, 373, 375, 376
  cross border terrorism, 376
Paleolithic Age, 8, 12, 59
Palestinian, 4, 20, 40, 129, 144, 342, 345, 346, 347
Palestine refugees, 344
Pamirs, 61
Panama, 242, 308
Pan-Arabism, 398
Paris Peace Conference, 328, 329, 350
Parivrajakas, 82
Pasteur, Louis, 364
Peace
  movement in Europe, 326-27
Peaceful-Coexistence, 7
Peaceful-Coexistence (*Panchsheel*) treaty, 370
Pearl Roundabout, 399
Peasants, 21, 63, 156-57, 207, 217, 261
Pentagon, 385, 391
Perry, Commodore, 10, 238
Persia (Iran) (Persians) (see also Iran), 1, 20, 31, 32, 36, 40, 61, 75, 78, 79, 80, 129, 144, 145, 186, 205, 286-87, 288
  Ahura Mazda, God, 37
  Anglo-Iranian Oil Company, 286, 287
  Cambyses II, 36
  Cyaxares, 31, 36
  Cyrus the Great, 36, 40, 74
  Darius the Great, 36-37, 74, 75
  Darius II, 37
  Darius III, 37
  invasion, 32
  Khosru I, Emperor, 144
  Medes, 31, 36
  nationalism in, 286-87
  reforms, 286
  Reza Pehlavi, 286
  Shah of, 286, 287
  Tehran conference, 286
  Xerxes, 37, 75
  Zarathustra and Zoroastrianism in, 37
Persian Gulf, 27, 31
Peru, 69, 184, 186, 241, 242, 243
Peter's pence, 188
Petroleum
  Organisation of Petroleum Exporting Countries, 373
Philippines, 14, 289-90, 308, 338, 373
  Abu Sayaf, 375
  Filipinos, 289, 290
  Magsaysay, Ramon, 290
Philippines Independence Act (1934), 289
  Quezon, Manuel, 289
Phoenicia (Phoenicians), 22, 26, 40-41, 129
  alphabet, 40
  cities paid tributes, 40
  colonies, 41
  Hanno, 41
  voyages, great, 41
Pierre, 362
Piracy, 117
Pisa, 186
Pizarro, Francisco, 184, 241
Planck, Max, 362
Plato, 77, 146
Pliny, 92
Poland, 204, 206, 207, 245, 263, 315, 321, 324, 337, 326, 327
Poles, 314, 315
Polygamy, 53
Pope (Adrian I), 141
Pope Clement V, 188
Pope Gregory II, 160
Pope Gregory VII, 140, 160, 161
Pope Innocent III, 137, 161, 198
Pope Leo I, 159
Pope Leo III, 141
Pope Leo X, 190
Pope Urban II, 135
Portugal (Portuguese), 108, 166, 181, 183, 184, 185, 226, 241, 242, 243, 272-73, 279, 314, 310, 326, 371
  navigators, 182-83

Pedro, Dom, 243
Potsdam agreement, 348
Prabhakaran, Velupillai, 391, 392
Prachanda, 396
Promised Land, 38
Prussia, 203-04, 206, 207, 226, 231, 245, 255-57, 315
    Austro-Prussian war (1866), 251-52, 256, 257
    Bismarck, 229, 251, 265, 266
    Agreement of Olmütz (1850), 254
    Customs Union (Zollverein), 254
    enlightened despotism, 204
    Franco-Prussian relations, 257-59
    Franco-Prussian War (1870), 253
    Frederick the Great, 204-05
    free trade area, 254
    (The) Great Elector, 203
    Hohenzollern dynasty, 203-04
    junkers, 255
    Moltke, 255, 257
    tariff reforms, 254
    Von Roon, 255
    William, Frederick, 203
    William IV, Frederick, 254
Ptolemy, 179
Puerto Rico, 308
Puranas, 97, 103, 107
Pushtuns, 385, 386

Quadruple Alliance, 231
Quakers, 209
Quran (Koran), Holy, 127, 128, 129, 130, 132, 133
Quebec, 185

Rabbani, 382, 383, 385
Rabelais, Francois, 177
Rafik al-Hariri, 401
Rajapakse, Mahinda, 392
Rajiv Gandhi, 392
Raleigh, 185
Ramayana by Kamban, 107
Rao, S R, 48
Rashtrakutas, 85
Reaumur, Rene de, 363
Red Indians, 14, 68-69, 210
Red Sea, 17, 127, 279
Reed, Walter, 365
Reformation movement, 178
    anti-Church movements 189-90
    Calvin, John, 192
    counter-reformation, 193-94
    Council of Trent, 194
    Society of Jesus founded Ignatius Loyola, 194
    Xavier, St Francis, 194
    humanist scholars, attack on, 190
    in England, 192-93
    indulgences, sale of, 190
    nation-states, rise of, 189
    Papacy, decline of, 188-94
    Predestination, doctrine of, 192
    Protestant reformation in Germany, 190-92
    secular attitude, rise of, 189
    State vs Church, 189
    Zwingli, Ulrich, 192
Refugees, 375
    UNHCR, 375
Regional groups, 373
Religion
religious orders, 82
Remrandt, 178
Renaissance, 173-80, 246
    age of, 147
    architecture, 176
    art, 174-75
    birth of, 199
    de Medici, Lorenzo, 175, 176
    growth of, factors for, 173-76
    humanism, 192
    in northern Europe: England, France, Germany, Holland, Spain, 177-78
    music, 176
    Palestrina, 176
    Robbia, Luca della, 176
    Sanzio, Raphael, 175
    scholars, 174
    sculpture, 176-77
    scientific progress and, 179-80
    scientific thought and scientists, 179-80
    term, 173
    Venetian School: Titian, 176
Renier, Prof, 1
Reuchlin, 190
Reykjavik summit, 368
Rhazes, 132
Rhineland, 324
Rhodes, Cecil, 120, 278
Rhodesia, 278, 357
Rifai, Samir, 400

Index

Rio
  Earth-Summit in, 377
Rio-de-Janerio summit, 371
Road construction
  McAdam improved, 237
Roentgen, 362
Rome (Roman empire) (Romans), 4, 20, 40, 61, 81, 109, 112, 113, 122, 124-25, 139, 160, 161, 176, 183, 197, 202, 246, 253
  Aequians, 111
  Age of Antonines, 116
  Antony, Mark, 114
  Apennines, Central, 112
  architecture, 118
  aristocratic in character, 111
  aristocratic Romans, 118
  Augustan age, 115
  Augustus, 115-16, 119, 120
  successors of, 116
  Aurelius, Marcus, 116, 119, 120
  Brutus, 114
  Byzantium, 116
  Caesar, Julius, 114-15, 119
  Carthage, 112-16
  Cassius, 114
  Cato, 113
  Christianity, 120, 124
  Cicero, 119
  classics, 147, 150
  Cleopatra, Queen, 114-15
  coin age system, 114
  conditions in Europe after fall of Roman empire, 147-51
  Constantine, 116, 124
  Crassus, 114
  dictatorship in, rise of, 113-14
  Diocletian, 116, 120
  Eastern Roman empire (Bryzantine), 125
  engineering, 118
  Epicureanism, 120
  Etruscans, 111, 112
  expansion of, 111-13
  clash with carthage, 112-13
  fall of, 116
  Galen, 119
  Gauls, 111, 112
  Generals, famous, 114
  geographical factors, 109
  Golden age of Augustus marked by reforms, 115
  Heraclius, 129
  Horace, 115, 119
  Julian calendar, 114, 119
  Justinian, 118, 120
  Justinian Code, 118
  Juvenal, 115, 119
  Latin literature, 119
  Latin and others, 109-111, 112
  learning, 119
  legacy of, 116-120
  liberated in 1870, 253
  Livy, 115, 119
  Lucretius, 120
  mistress of Italy, 112
  mistress of Mediterranean world, 113
  Nero emperor, 124
  notation system, 119
  Octavian, 114
  Ovid, 115, 119
  Panaetius, 120
  Pax Romana (Roman peace), 117-120
  personal cleanliness, 119
  philosophy, 120
  Pilate, Pontius, 123
  Pliny the Elder, 115, 119
  Plutarch, 119
  Pompey, 114
  Ptolemy, 119
  Punic wars, 112-13
  religion, 119-20, 122
  revolts, 113
Roman Catholic Church, 159, 160, 188-94, 314
Roman laws, 117-18
Romanus, 135
  Samnites, 112
  science, 119
  Seneca, 119, 120
  Sosigenes, 119
  stoicism, 120
  Strabo, 119
  Tacitus, 115, 119
  Theodosius emperor, 125
  Tiber, river, 109, 111
  twelve tables, 117
  Virgil, 115, 119
  Volscians, 112
  Western Roman empire, 125
  writers, famous, 115
Rousseau, Jean Jacques, 220
Roy, Arundhati, 374

Ruanda-Urundi, 358
Rumania, 267, 321, 338, 326
Russia, 13, 146, 151, 205-06, 225, 226, 231, 245, 250, 256, 258, 260, 264, 265, 266, 272, 273, 276, 284, 286, 287, 308, 309, 310, 321, 322, 328, 337, 338, 326, 342, 348, 349, 351, 372, 373, 377
Afghanistan's invasion by, 349
Augustus III, 207
Bolshevik Revolution, 318-20, 312
Bolsheviks, 318-20, 328
Brezhnev doctrine, 368
Catherine, Queen, 314
Catherine II or Catherine the Great, 207
Czar Alexander I, 315
Czar Alexander II, 315-16
reactionary rule of, 316
Czar Alexander III, 316
Czar Nicholas I, 232, 315
Czar Nicholas II, 316-17
Czar Nicholas, 263, 264
downfall of and provincial government, 318
Czarist autocrats, 314-15
Czars, under, 205-06
Eisenhower, 326
Five Year Plans, 320
foreign policy, 206, 207
geographical factors, 205
Gorbachev, 368
help to Sun Yet Sen (China), 282
Hungary, aggression on, 347
IMF treaty (1937), 368
industrialisation of, 316
Ivan the Terrible, 205-06
KGB, 348
Karensky, Alexander, 318, 319
Karensky's Menshevik government, 318
Kotzebue, 253
Krushchev, 348, 349
Lenin, Vladimir and Bolshevik Revolution, 318-20
Lenin, 240, 318-20, 312, 328
early measures, 319-20
new economic policy, 320
Menshevik government, 318
Mongols, 205
Moscow summit, 341, 368

New Economic Policy, 320
nuclear strikes, 349
October Revolution, 240
Pan-Slavism movement, 316
peasants, 207
Peter I (Peter the Great), 206, 207, 263, 314
Peter III, 207
Putin, Vladimir, 369
Reinsurance Treaty (1887), 310
Romonov, Michael: Ivan the Terrible, 206
Romonovs, 206
Russian Federation, 369, 373
Russian Orthodox Church, 206
Russian Revolution (1905), 317-18
Russian Revolution (1917), 286, 314-19, 313
Russo-German Non-aggression Pact, 337
Russo-Japanese War (1904-05), 276, 281, 317
Russo-Turkish War (1877-78), 265-66
Sputnik satellite, 349, 377
Stalin, Joseph, 319, 320, 337, 338, 341, 348
Stalinist era, 369
Triple Alliance, 310
Trotsky, Leon, 319
Turks, war with, 207
Westernisation of under Peter, 206
Yeltsin, Boris, 369
Rutherford, Ernest, 362

SAARC, 373
SARS (Severe Acute Respiratory Syndrome), 347, 375
SEATO, 292, 348, 373
Saadi, 132
Second Gulf War, 388, 390
Saddam Hussein, 386, 387, 388, 389, 390
Sahara region, 17
Saivism, 107
Samkhya school, 82
Samprati, 85
Sarawak, 290
Sargon of Agade (Akkad), King, 42
Sastras, 107
Satavahanas, 85
Satellite
Satellite communication, 378

Index

Satellite surveillance system, 379
Sputnik, 349
Saudi Arabia, 352-53, 372
   Hussain, King, 352-53
Saville, 186
Savonarola, 190
Schiaparelli, Giovanni, 362
Schism, 90
Science and Technology in modern world, 362-69
   academies of science, 360
   advance of science, 25-26
   biology, progress in, 363-64
   Chemistry, development of, 362-63
   communication system, revolution in, 366-67
   geology, 360
   medical field, progress in, 364-65
   motion picture, 366
   motor vehicles, 366
   physics, development of science of, 362
   physics, modern, 362
   scientists, 376-77
   technological innovations, 365
   terms of, 360
   transport, technological innovation in means of, 366
Scotland,
   Presbyterian Church in, 13, 192, 198
Sea of Azov, 206
Seattle
   Ministerial Conference in (1999), 374
Secretes, 10
Seleucus, 79
Seljuk Turks, 135
Semple, Allen, 5
Senegal, 279, 356
Serbs, 146, 260, 266, 267, 268, 311
Seville, 131
Shakespeare, William, 177
Shatt al-Arab, 386
Shinawatra, Thaksin, 394, 395
Shiva, Lord, 107
Sholes, Christopher, 365
Shramanas, 82
Siam, 168, 290
Sicily, 75, 111, 112, 114, 129, 251, 332
Sierra-Leone, 356
Silesia, 203, 204, 205, 324
Singapore, 272, 290, 373, 375, 376

Singer, Isac, 365
Sinkiang river, 58
Slaves (Slavery), 4, 21, 34, 64, 81, 95, 116, 222
Slavs, 145, 146, 147, 259
Social sciences
   history and, 5-6
Socialism, 370
   scientific, 240
socialists, 329
Socrates, 77
Software, 378
Solar system, 377
Somaliland (Somalia), 278, 279, 358, 359, 371
   Eastern: Punt, 20
   French Somaliland, 358
   Italian Somaliland, 358
Sophocles, 77
Sorby, Henry, 361
South Korea, 396, 397, 398
Soviet occupation of Afghanistan, 382
Spain, 12, 69, 112, 113, 114, 129, 131, 132, 139, 140, 141, 142, 145, 148, 154, 183, 184, 185, 189, 202, 209, 215, 226, 228, 230, 241-42, 243, 246, 258, 277, 279, 289, 306, 308, 310, 332, 355
   Basque, demand for, 375
   Carthaginians, 202
   Charles V, 202
   Cortes, Hernando, 241
   Ferdinand VII, 242, 244
   Franco, General, 355
   Iberians, 202
   Inquisition (Church Court), 193
   Isabella, Queen, 202
   Mohammedans, 202
   Moors, 202
   painters, famous, 177
   Philip, King, 199
   Philip II, 202, 204
   renaissance in, 177-78
   revolution in (1820), 244
   scholars, 177-78
   South, 144
Spaniards, 68, 184, 186
Spanish American War (1898), 289
Spanish Civil War (1936), 324, 333
Visgoths, 139, 202
Spitsberger, 185
Sri Lanka (*see also* Ceylon), 347, 373, 375, 391, 392, 393

LTTE, 375, 391, 392
St. Augustine, 160
St. Benedict, 160
St. Boniface, 160
St. Dominic, 160
St. Francis of Assisi, 160
St. Lawrence river, 185
St. Patrick, 160
St. Peter, 160
St. Peter's Church, 175, 176
St. Thomas Aquinas, 179
Stahl, George, 363
Stanley, Henry M, 277
Star wars, 368
Steno, Nicolaus, 361
Stephenson, George, 237
Stiglitz, Joseph, 374
Stockholm Conference (1972) (summit), 346, 371
Stoicism, 120
Stone Age
   New Stone Age, 13
   barter system, 13
   neolithic crafts, 13
   Old Stone Age, 12-13
   migration and human race, 12-13
Sudan, 351, 354, 355
   Abdullah Khalil, 351
Suez Canal, 186, 278
   crisis (1956), 342, 348
   Suez Canal Company, 351
   Suez Canal Zone, 351
Sumatra, 168
Sumerian
   city-states, 28-29
   decline and fall of kingdoms, 29
Sumerians, 34, 35, 47
Super-powers, 348, 349, 368
Sweden, 151, 209, 231, 324
Switzerland,
   Protestant movement in, 13, 192, 202, 204, 323
Swiss Cantons, 202
Swiss Reformation Movement, 192
Syria, 20, 21, 30, 31, 61, 114, 127, 129, 130, 144, 345, 351-52, 372, 401
   Damascus, 30
   Hyksos, 19
   nationalism, 352

Taiwan, 370, 371, 376
Tajiks, 383, 385, 386, 391

Taj Mahal (*see* India)
Tarbel, Fethi, 400
Taliban, 349, 372,375, 383, 384, 385, 386, 388, 391
   Mullah Mohammed Omar, 375, 383, 385
   Osama bin Laden, 372, 375
   regime (government) in Afghanistan, 375-76
Talmud, 39
Tanzania (Tanganyika), 358, 359
   Karume, Obeid, 359
   Nyerere, Julius, 359
Tanganyika African National Union, 359
Taoism, 64, 65
Tata, Jamshedji, 238
Technology (*see also* Science and Technology)
   new technology, 379
Telecommunication technology, 364, 380 (*see also* Communication)
Telegraphy, 366
   wireless telegraphy, 366
Ten Commandments, 38, 39
Terrorism, 375-79
   cross-border, 376
   September 9/11 (2001) attacks, 372, 375
   terrorist attack on Pentagon, 371, 375
   terrorist attack on World Trade Centre, 371, 375
   terrorist outfits, 375
Tetzel, John, 190-91
Thailand (Siam), 292, 293, 338, 373
Third World, 374
Thomas, 24
Thucydides
   Pelopenesian Wars by, 1
Tiber river, 109, 111
Tibet (Tibetans), 14, 59, 370, 376
   Tiananmen Square incident, 376
Tigris, 27
Tikrit, 372
Togo, 356
Toltecs, 68
Toynbee, Arnold J,
   World and the West by, 9
Transport
   revolution in, 237
   technological innovations in means of, 366

Index

Treaties (Agreements, Alliances, Charters, Pacts, Treaties)
Anglo-Japanese Treaty, 276, 284
Anti-Ballistic Missile Treaty (972), 348, 349, , 368, 372
Atlantic Charter, 341
Five Power Naval Limitation Treaty, 326, 327
Four Power Pact, 326
Helsinki Agreement (1975), 349, 368
INF (Intermediate-Range Nuclear Force) Treaty (1937), 368
Jay Treaty, 305
Lansing-Asia Agreement, 285
Lateran treaty (1929), 331
Locarno Pact, 327
Nine Power Treaty, 285, 327
Non-aggression Pact, 337
Nuclear Non-Proliferation Treaty, 346, 371, 372
Peaceful-Coexistence (Panchsheel) Treaty, 370
Potsdam Agreement, 348
Quadruple Alliance, 231
Reinsurance Treaty (1887), 310
SEATO (military alliance), 348
Treaty of Aixe-la-Chapelle, 203
Treaty of Allahabad, 270
Treaty of Frankfurt (1871), 258-59
Treaty of Kuchuk Kainarji, 208
Treaty of Lausanne (1912), 267
Treaty of London (1913), 267
Treaty of Mutual Assistances 91923), 327
Treaty of Neuilly (1919), 313
Treaty of Paris, 203-04, 308
Treaty of Paris (1783), 216
Treaty of Paris (1856), 264-65
Treaty of Prague, 260
Treaty of Sevres (1920), 313, 350
Treaty of St. Germaine, 313
Treaty of Tilsit, 226
Treaty of Trianon (1920), 313
Treaty of Versailles (1919), 313, 322, 324, 334, 335-36
Treaty of West-phalia, 204
Treaty of Yandaboo (1826), 288
Treaty of Zurich, 250
Triple Alliance, 310, 312
Triple *entente*, 310
Warsaw Pact, 348, 368

Yalta Agrement, 348
Trevithick, Richard, 366
Trigonometry, 80
Trinidad Heligoland, 231
Tunisia, 279, 310
Bourguiba, Habib, 354
independence of, 354-55
Turkistan, 205
Turkey, 207, 244, 245, 249, 263-64, 266-67, 279, 287, 288, 312, 313, 324
Italo-Turkish War (1911-12), 267
nationalism, 350-53
Pasha, Mustapha Kemal, 350
Russo-Turkish War (1877-78), 265-66
Treaty of Laussane, 267
Treaty of London, 267
Tunisia, 398
Turkish National movement, 350
Turks, 59, 136, 144, 147, 181, 206, 245, 265
Ottoman, 137, 146
Sejuk Turks, 135
Young Turk Revolution (1908), 266
Young Turks, 266, 350
war with Russians, 207
women, equal rights to, 350

UAE, 353, 376
UAR, 352
UNO (United Nations Organisation), 7, 283, 287, 288, 292, 327, 341-49, 354, 357, 358, 370, 371, 375, 376, 379
achievements of, 345-47
Annan, Kofi, 343, 388
Charter, 341, 371, 376
Economic and Social Council, 342, 343
FAO (Food and Agricultural Organisation), 344
failures, 347-48
General Assembly, 341, 342
IAEA (International Atomic Energy Agency), 344
ICAO (International Civil Aviation Organisation), 344
IDA (International Development Association), 344
IFAD (International Fund for Agricultural Development), 344-45

IFC (International Finance Corporation), 344
ILO (International Labour Organisation), 344, 347
IMF, 346
IMO (International Maritime Organisation), 344
ITU (International Communication Union), 344
Interim-Force for keeping peace, 346
International Bank for Reconstruction and Development (World Bank), 344
International Court, 343
Regional Commissions, 343
role of, 371-72
Secretariat, 343-44
Security Council, 341, 342
specialised agencies, 344-45
Trusteeship Council, 343
UN C H R, 347
UNDP (United Nations Development Programme), 344, 347, 374
UN Disaster Relief Coordination, 344
UNEF (United Nations Emergency Force), 345
UNEP (United Nations Environment Programme), 344
UNESCO (United Nations Educational Scientific and Cultural Organisation), 343, 344
UNFPA (UN Fund for Population Activities), 344
UNHCR (United Nations High Commissioner for Refugees), 344, 375
UNICEF (United Nations International Children's Emergency Fun), 344, 347
UNIDO (United Nations Industrial Organisation), 344, 347
UNRWA (UN Relief and Works Agency), 344
UPUC (Universal Postal union), 344
WHO (World Health Organisation), 323, 344, 347

WIPO (World International Property Organisation), 344
WMO (World Meteorological Organisation), 344
WTO (World Trade Organisation), 345, 346
World Bank (IBRD), 344
USA (United States of America) (see America)
USSR (see also Russia; Soviet Union), 341, 343, 345, 348, 369
Commonwealth of Independent States, 373
disintegrated, 369
Ubhangi Shari, 357
Udraka, 88
Uganda, 278, 358
Kabaka, 358
Obote, Milton, 358
Untouchability, removal of, 3, 298
Upanishads, 51, 82
Upper Volta, 356
Urundi, 358
US Strikes, 385
Uzbeks, 391

Vaccines, 378
Vaishnavism, 107
Varahamihira, 103
Vasco da Gama, 4, 183, 184
Vedic Civilisation (see also Aryans)
  Aryan area of occupation, 51-52
  Aryan wars and settlements, 50
  economic conditions, 55-57
  industries, 56
  occupations, 55
  professionals, 56
  religion, 56
  Rigvedic Pantheon, 56-57
  trade and transport, 56
  education, 53, 57
  founders of, 50
  literature, 50-51
  marriage, 53
  political organisation, 52-53
  Sabha and *Samiti*, 52-53
  government, forms of, 53
  society, 53-55
  amusements, 55
  class distinctions, beginnings of, 54
  dress and ornaments, 54-55
  food and drinks, 54

Index

marriage, 53
morality, standards of, 55
Vedic literature
   Brahmanas, 51, 81, 97
   Sutras, 51
   Vedangas, 51
   Vedas, 50, 51, 57, 89, 107
      Rig Veda, 50, 51, 52, 53, 54, 56
      Yajur Veda, 51
Vejjajiva, 394, 395
Velazquez, 177
Venezuela, 242
Venice, 137, 138, 186, 251-53
Venus de Milo, 81
Vermeer, Jan, 178
Verne, Jules, 4
Vesalius, Andreas, 180
Vespucci, Amerigo, 184
Vietnam, 291-92, 347, 371, 373
   Bao Dai, 291
   HO Chi Minhi, 291
   NLF, 291-92
   Ngo Dinh Diem, 291
   North, 291, 292, 371
   South, 291, 292, 371
Viet Cong (soldiers of NLF), 291-92
Vietminh forces, 291, 292
Vietnam War (1954-73), 348, 349, 371, 375
   World War II and liberation movements, 291-92
Vikings, 142, 183
Vishnu, Lord, 107
Voltaire, 203, 204, 219

Wahabis,
   Abdul Aziz Ibn Saud, leader of, 352
Wales, 198
Warsaw, 231
Warsaw Pact (1955), 348, 368
Washington summit, 368
Waterloo, battle of, 227, 230, 238
Watt, James, 236
Weapons of Mass Destruction, 388
Wells, H G, 4
Werner, Abraham, 361
West (Western countries) (Western powers), 10, 138, 187, 210, 238-39, 280, 281, 348, 371, 373, 374
   Sea-borne trade between East and, 186
Western imperialism in Africa, 277-79

Westernisation, process of, 10
Weston, Stephen, 24
West-phalia, treaty of, 204
Wheelers, Dr, 42
Whitney, Eli, 235
Women
   atrocities against, 376
   equal rights and opportunities, 350
   freedom and position (status) of, 21, 44-46, 85, 95
   honour of, 156
World Bank (IBRD), 344, 373, 374
World Court, 323
World Trade Centre, 391
World Trade Organisation (WTO), 345, 347-48, 371, 373, 374, 376
   terrorist attack on, 372, 375
World War I, 238, 260, 267-68, 278, 281, 282, 285, 287, 289, 296, 308, 317, 309-13, 328, 350, 351, 356, 366
   armament race, 311
   Balkan wars created tension, 311
   beneficial results of, 313
   Bismarck's plan to keep France isolated, 309-12
   colonial rivalry heightens jealousies, 310
   course of war, 312-14
   economic imperialism of Britain and Germany, 310-11
   international crisis, 311
   murder of crown prince of Austria, 311-12
   results, 312-13
World War II, 279, 283, 286, 288, 289, 291-92, 301, 325, 332, 341, 348, 351, 352, 355, 356, 359
   America's entry into, 338
   course of, 337-38
   Germany and, 334-38 (see also Germany)
   liberation movements: Vietnam and, 291-92
World War III, 7
Wright Brothers, 366
Wycliffe, John, 189-90, 192

Xavier, Francis, 168, 194
Xinjiang, 394

Yalta, 341
　　Yalta agreement, 348
Yangtze river, 58
Yaudheyas, 101
Yellow river, 58
Yemen, 399
Yugoslavia, 313, 324, 338

Zahir Shah, 382
Zambia, 357
Zanzibar, 358, 359,
Zeno, 81
Zeppelins, 366
Zero, 133 (*see also* **Mathematics**)
　　concept of, 68
Zoroastrianism, 37, 62
Zurich, 192
　　Treaty of Zurich, 250
Zwingli, Ulrich, 192